*Witching Culture*

CONTEMPORARY ETHNOGRAPHY

Kirin Narayan and Paul Stoller, Series Editors

A complete list of books in the series is available from the publisher.

# *Witching Culture*

## Folklore and Neo-Paganism in America

SABINA MAGLIOCCO

**PENN**

University of Pennsylvania Press

Philadelphia

Printed in the United States of America on acid-free paper

10 9 8 7 6 5 4 3 2 1

Published by
University of Pennsylvania Press
Philadelphia, Pennsylvania 19104-4011

Library of Congress Cataloging-in-Publication Data
Magliocco, Sabina, 1959–
Witching culture : folklore and neo-paganism in America / Sabina Magliocco.
p. cm. — (Contemporary ethnography)
Includes bibliographical references and index.
ISBN 0-8122-3803-6 (cloth : alk. paper) — ISBN 0-8122-1879-5 (paper : alk. paper)
1. Neopaganism—United States. 2. Folklore—United States. I. Title. II. Series.

BF1573.M34 2004
299'.94'0973—dc22 2004040712

*In memory of Andrew Vázsonyi*
*1906–1986*

# Contents

*Introduction*

# The Ethnography of Magic and the Magic of Ethnography

In February of 1995, at the first Pantheacon, a conference of Pagans and academics in San Jose, California, I attended my first Reclaiming ritual and had my first powerfully affecting ritual experience in a Neo-Pagan context. Pantheacon 1995 became a turning point in my field research; the ritual was for me the beginning of a new understanding of the movement I was studying. In my field notes, I attempted to capture the intensity of the experience I had.

**Field notes, February 17, 1995**

The ritual starts late, like most Pagan events. About a hundred people are gathered in a large conference ballroom in a San Jose hotel; chairs are arranged all around the walls and people sit, some uneasily, some talking in groups, some laughing or gossiping. Starhawk, a plump, middle-aged woman in a loose print dress, leggings, and incongruous red ankle socks, stands near the room's center, where a pile of scarves has been placed. She tests the sound system, confers with others, finally begins to call the rag-tag assembly to order and explain the purpose of the ritual: to find what is most sacred to us, what we most deeply value.

She begins by asking us to imagine that we are trees rooted in the soil, our roots reaching deep into the earth's molten core, our branches drawing down the moon's shining light, cool silvery energy meeting hot, fiery energy in our beings. When we are all grounded and centered, the quarters are called,[1] and then she calls the goddess as Brigid[2] and the God as the greening god, the Green Man, "the force that through the green fuse drives the flower" (Thomas, 1957:10), calling him through redwood, oak, artichoke, zucchini, and garlic into our midst—"Greening god, redwood god; / Greening god, artichoke god . . ."—while she drums and we sway and dance. Some take up scarves from the center and dance around us, waving them. One smiling young man comes toward me waving a scarf and we dance awhile, twirling and twisting to the drumming and chants. Finally our voices reach a crescendo and then fall silent.

Now Starhawk is taking us on a guided meditation to find the sacred. She asks us to form small, intimate groups where we can talk about our experiences. A small group of us sitting on the floor join hands to form a ring.

I follow Starhawk's words and find myself walking along a path to a dark wood, and I think of the words from Dante's *Inferno* that my father used to recite to me—"Nel mezzo del cammin di nostra vita / Mi ritrovai per una selva oscura / Che la diritta via era smarrita"[3]—and I think of how in the last year I, too, have seemingly lost my way unexpectedly in the middle of my life's journey. I feel as though I have jumped off the edge of a precipice; I'm hanging in midair, waiting to see whether I fall or am held aloft.

Starhawk asks us to contact the holy of holies, what we consider sacred. Several notions flash before me in response to her words: my connection with nature, my love for animals, some inner core of strength and integrity I grope for—only to be discarded as the real center of my life unfolds: my work, my teaching, my writing, and my efforts to convey to my students not only other peoples' and cultures' basic humanity but their own as well. As Starhawk speaks of the difficulties, the obstacles to achieving one's goal, I feel as though she has already thought my thoughts. She asks if Brigid has us on her anvil and is tempering us in her fire, making us sharper, beating us with her hammer as she clamps us in her tongs, and I think of my struggles during the past several years: my frustrated search for a tenure-track position, my troubled relationship with my Sardinian field site, and my failed marriage. Tears run down my face and drip onto my chest, and in my thin dress I shiver with grief and cold.

Now we are supposed to share our idea of the sacred with the group. I open my eyes and realize I am not the only one crying. One by one, the members of my circle speak of their families, their children; as my turn approaches, I begin to feel selfish and egotistical for considering my work sacred. But somehow I manage to blurt it out and somehow, blessedly, the others don't get up and leave in disgust, or chastise my arrogance, but gather around me and support me.

Another guided meditation takes us to the forge where Brigid tempers us on her anvil, shaping us. Another forest path, another clearing: this time I recognize the road that goes down to the valley below Monteruju, the town in Sardinia where I did fieldwork, and a clearing under a live oak tree where a woman is working at a forge. Her hair forms a fiery red halo around her; her white raiment is embroidered with living leaves and tendrils; her golden eyes burn into mine. I bring her a gift: it is my heart, broken in pieces, swollen and bloody like meat from a butcher shop. She takes that heart and puts it into her forge, heating it till it's white-hot; then she beats it with her hammer. The blows resound through my whole body, and with each stroke I shudder in pain.

"This is your heart, and fire will make it whole," she says as her eyes burn through me once again. She takes that red-hot heart and slips it into my chest, where its heat spreads through my reptile-cold body.

Then, using her tools again, she makes a sharp pocketknife and a pen, which she cools in her sacred well and hands to me. And now she directs me to drink from that well, and I do, and I find myself at the spring of Funari,[4] and E.T.,[5] my blood sister from St. John's Eve, is drinking with me and walking up the path beside with me back to the real world.

In the conference room we dance the spiral dance as we chant in harmony, "We will never lose our way to the well of her memory / And the power of the living flame it will rise, it will rise again!" Our voices, spiraling in unison, grow ever more intense; the dance, as always, pulls us along, dragging the whole community in front of us, so that we all see one another, as at Santa Maria.[6] For the first time I really feel the "cone of power" Pagans are always talking about, rising from us all, from our own combined voices and tears; it rises through the ceiling of the hall and onward, upward to the heavens. The energy is grounded,[7] and at last the circle is uncast and opened.

## The Ethnography of Magic

This book is about how North American Neo-Pagans use folklore, or traditional expressive culture, to establish identity and create a new religious culture. As a folklorist and an anthropologist, I am interested in how these groups use folklore culled from ethnographic and popular sources, as well as in folklore that arises out of the shared contemporary Pagan experience at festivals, conferences, summer camps, and small worship groups. While Neo-Paganism is a global movement with branches on all the continents, I am concentrating here on North American Neo-Paganism, especially as practiced in the United States. North American Neo-Paganism has developed its own particular culture and concerns due to the specific historical, social, and political circumstances under which it took root during the 1950s and 1960s and spread during the 1970s and 1980s, and it differs in important respects from Neo-Paganism in Europe and elsewhere in the world. One thing unique to North American Neo-Paganism is its distinctive tendency to reflect and refract the cultural politics characteristic of the American experience. American Neo-Paganism developed in a context wherein nationalism and ethnicity are linked differently from their linkages in other Western nations. North America is multiethnic, a culture of ubiquitous borders where customs come into contact and sometimes conflict. Many of America's greatest cultural contributions, including jazz, bluegrass, rock and roll, and the blues, to name just a few musical examples, grew out of this climate of interethnic and intercultural contact. The globalization of the late twentieth and early twenty-first centuries has brought even more cultures into contact on the North American continent, resulting in new kinds of hybridity and cultural mixing. I will explore these issues with respect to Neo-Pagan magic and spirituality in Chapter 7.

*Neo-Paganism,* a term coined in Britain in the 1890s (Hutton, 1999:28–29), and rediscovered and popularized in the United States by Tim "Oberon" Zell in 1971, designates a movement of new religions that attempt to revive, revitalize, and experiment with aspects of pre-Christian polytheism (Adler, 1986:10). Their goal is a deeper connection with the sacred, with nature, and with community. Neo-Pagans consider nature sacred, and divinity immanent in every natural thing and living being. While they do not reject technology and science, they perceive modernity as a force that has alienated humans from a way of life that followed the rhythms of seasonal cycles and regularly brought them into contact with the divine in nature. Pagans believe that as humans became more detached from nature, they ceased to see it as sacred. It is this sense of the numinous, the magical, the sacred in nature and in the human form that their religions attempt to recapture. Pagans are interested in folklore because they see the folk traditions of European peasants and indigenous peoples as repositories of an ancient nature-based spirituality that venerated the immanent divine and celebrated the natural world and its cycles. For Pagans, folklore becomes an important tool to discover the past and bring authenticity to contemporary spiritual practice.

The historical roots of Neo-Paganism are deeply intertwined with those of folkloristics, the academic study of folklore. Both emerged from late eighteenth-century European movements whose aim was to critique the Enlightenment, yet both are undeniably products of the Enlightenment as well. The Enlightenment and the scientific revolution brought about a sea change in European understandings of folk traditions. As Europeans became aware that their own traditions could be compared to those of peoples from their colonies, they created a new discourse of rationality aimed at banishing traditional ways of knowing from educated perspectives (Motz, 1998:341). Many folklorists from this period collected and compiled lore in order to debunk it, with the certainty that traditional practices were destined to disappear as more rational views prevailed. Some compared European folklore to material from travelers' reports of the colonies, in order to demonstrate its primitive and superstitious character. At the same time, Enlightenment philosophers gained inspiration from the works of Classical authors, despite the fact that these authors themselves had been part of pagan cultures considered "barbaric" by Enlightenment standards.

Yet the same impulse that led to the growth of rationalism also gave rise to a reaction against it. As industrialization and urbanization transformed the European countryside and irrevocably changed society and economy, the Romantic revival emerged as a critique of the Enlightenment. Romantic philosophers such as Jean Jacques Rousseau and Johann Gottfried von Herder expressed a yearning for a lost sense of connectedness and authenticity, which they located in the changing countryside and in the lives and customs of European peasants. This "search for authenticity" was at the root of the birth of folkloristics as a discipline (Bendix, 1997). During the nineteenth century, as folklorists increasingly sought to structure and codify their discipline by making it more scientific, thus moving further away from folklore as lived experience (Bendix, 2000), other groups were bent on recapturing the experience of the numinous by recreating traditional practices (or their impressions of them) in art, literature, and folk practice. These groups were profoundly influenced by the new science of folkloristics and its early theories, sometimes creating or changing practices based on fashionable interpretations of the time. These included the "doctrine of survivals," an idea championed by Edward B. Tylor, the father of cultural anthropology, and his disciple Sir James Frazer, author of the venerable *Golden Bough*. Inspired by Charles Darwin's theory of biological evolution, the idea that life on earth developed in an unbroken line from the simple to the more complex, unilinear cultural evolutionists posited that human cultures developed in a similar progression, from the "savage" or "primitive" to the intermediate "barbarian" stage (a level often identified with ancient Classical paganism as well as with European peasant traditions), until they reached the apex, "civilization," identified, of course, with the types of complex societies that produced the scholars themselves.[8] According to the doctrine of survivals, folklore was believed to preserve the essence of earlier stages of human development, which were assumed to be identical for all cultures. According to the survivalist paradigm, ancient peoples everywhere must have been obsessed with the fertility of their herds and crops, and developed year-cycle rites to ensure it. Survivalists used the comparative method to draw analogies between apparently similar customs of culturally and historically diverse peoples, assuming that similarities in customs meant either direct transmission of knowledge or the parallel development of customs by peoples in the same stage of unilinear cultural evolution.

By the 1920s, folklorists and cultural anthropologists had largely abandoned the notion of survivals, as Franz Boas's theory of cultural relativism replaced earlier racist and ethnocentric ideas and as fieldwork increasingly became a component of research methodology. Yet survivalist paradigms had left their mark on the arts, literature, and popular consciousness, influencing the ideologies of new metaphysical and occult societies. Revival Witchcraft, the largest component of Neo-Paganism, emerged from this confluence of ideas. English historian Ronald Hutton has traced its development to the unique mix of English Romanticism, nationalism, and literary and anthropological theory that was the crucible of a number of occult societies in the late nineteenth century (Hutton, 1999).

Neo-Paganism and revival Witchcraft have been studied from a number of different perspectives. There is a large and growing literature on the movement. Among the most important works to date are Margot Adler's sweeping survey of Neo-Paganism and Witchcraft in the United States, *Drawing Down the Moon* (1986); Tanya M. Luhrmann's *Persuasions of the Witches' Craft* (1989), a study of a London coven; Loretta Orion's *Never Again the Burning Times* (1995), a wide-ranging work using qualitative and quantitative methods with a specific focus on East Coast and Midwestern American Neo-Pagan communities; and Helen Berger's *A Community of Witches* (1999), a sociological study of an East Coast Neo-Pagan community. Two recent, substantial studies are Sarah Pike's *Earthly Bodies, Magical Selves* (2001), an in-depth examination of Neo-Pagan festivals and their role in the creation of both individual and group identities; and Jone Salomonsen's *Enchanted Feminism* (2002), an ethnographic and theological analysis of Reclaiming Witchcraft, an eco-feminist tradition based on the writings of Starhawk, one of the best-known Witches in the United States.

With the exception of Salomonsen's work, all of these studies have focused primarily on Neo-Pagan groups on the East Coast and in the Midwest. While I also observed groups in the Midwest and upper South, my primary study site was in northern California, the seat of one of the largest, oldest, most influential, and most active Neo-Pagan communities in North America. Within North American Neo-Paganism, California occupies a special position because of its status as the source of much of the 1960s counterculture, a movement that helped popularize Neo-Paganism (as well as other New Religious movements) throughout North America and the rest of the world. California has been at the vanguard of cultural production on a number of fronts, from the film industry to the manufacture and distribution of electronic and technological components; historian Ronald Hutton argues that its importance in the early twenty-first-century global cultural scene can be compared to that of Athens in the fifth century B.C.E., Rome in the first century C.E., and Florence in the fifteenth.[9] Many Neo-Pagans who began their careers in other parts of North America either passed through or wound up in California, in the San Francisco Bay Area. Currently, San Francisco is the headquarters of Reclaiming Witchcraft and its most famous spokesperson, Starhawk.

Catherine Albanese has examined Neo-Paganism within the context of "nature religions," a designation that has been embraced by many in the movement. According to this paradigm, nature religions share a cluster of characteristics, including a celebration of the "natural" and "folk" as pure and simple, a liberal political bent, millenarian beliefs, an attraction to "natural" (e.g., homeopathic or herbal) healing, and an affinity for techniques and practices that induce alternate states of consciousness (Albanese, 1990:6). Albanese argues that in these movements, nature becomes a metaphor for social, environmental, and theological harmony, while it allows groups to pursue an agenda of control. The trouble is that while Neo-Paganism and Witchcraft share some of these points, others (for example, millenarian beliefs and an agenda of social control) are alien to them. Furthermore, Neo-Paganism's embrace of the environmental movement is a relatively recent phenomenon that can be traced to the influence of the 1960s counterculture in North America.

Other scholars of the movement have noted its revitalizing qualities: Loretta Orion (1994:25–27) compares it to Anthony Wallace's "nativistic cult," a type of revitalization movement that attempts to revalue what is native, homegrown, and free from foreign influence (Wallace, 1970:188–99), while Margot Adler describes it as a Euro-American movement to discover lost roots through folklore (Adler, 1986:253). Most recently, Ronald Hutton has called it "revived religion," drawing parallels between Neo-Paganism and other kinds of revival movements (Hutton, 1999:415–16).

I believe these assessments can be verified more substantively. The evidence shows that Neo-Paganism represents the most important folk revival movement since the folk music revival of the 1950s and 1960s.[10] Like the earlier folk music revivalists, Neo-Pagans in North America are predominantly white, middle-class, well-educated urbanites who find artistic inspiration in folk and indigenous spiritual traditions. Their use of vernacular magic ranges from attempted reenactments to the borrowing of narrative motifs, songs, rhymes, and elements from calendar customs and festivals. Yet far from being copies of the originals, Neo-Pagan forms are of necessity novel and hybridized: "The transvaluation of the obsolete . . . , dead and defunct produces something new" (Kirschenblatt-Gimblett, 1996:4). They draw from many different cultural and historical traditions, from European folk customs to the religions of Classical antiquity, ancient Egypt, the Celts, and the Norse, occasionally mixing in material appropriated from Native American or Afro-Caribbean traditions. Material from these sources is used for a variety of purposes: to create a link to the historical past, imagined as a more spiritually authentic time; as a symbol of Euro-American ethnic identity and affiliation; to help bring about altered states of consciousness and activate the autonomous imagination; and to create a satisfying oppositional culture where such experiences and aesthetics are valued.

Neo-Pagan cultural borrowing takes place in the context of larger globalizing forces that daily give us new aesthetics and choices in the realm of popular culture: "world" music, fashion, body ornamentation, and ethnic cuisines mix liberally in modern urban, suburban, and virtual landscapes. While a great deal of attention has been paid to the effects of globalization and hybridization on the more sensually accessible genres—food, music, festival, material culture—it has been harder to document cultural mixing in the realm of spirituality and belief. Here I examine hybridization in a spiritual framework, exploring how the human desire for connection and transcendence can go beyond conventional cultural and social boundaries.

The use of folklore in this context is neither new nor unexpected. A variety of regional and national groups have used traditional folklore and created new folkloric forms to construct identities (Hobsbawm and Ranger, 1983; Handler and Linnekin, 1984; Kirschenblatt-Gimblett, 1996; Bendix, 1997); this has been most thoroughly documented in the cases of emerging nation-states or regional movements that consolidate the "naturalness" of what Anderson has called "imagined communities" (Anderson, 1983). In the case of nation building, however, the sacred component is often lost once the nation transmutes into a state and the decidedly sober democratic process takes over. The loss of sacredness in the national paradigm—or its intentional absence, in the case of the United States—makes the appeal of tradition as a measure of spirituality especially strong. Ultimately, though, I argue that spirituality allows American Neo-Pagans to transcend traditional concepts of identity linked with nation, region, and ethnicity: as Pagan composer and performer Ruth Barrett sings, "The heart is the only nation."

In the context of examining a form of folk revival, I am also exploring the concept of "folklore reclamation," a term I developed to address a particular kind of folk revival that I first encountered in minor form in my study of religious festivals and globalization in Sardinia (Magliocco, 1993, 2001). Reclamation involves the rediscovery and revaluation of traditions previously abandoned because they were considered markers of backwardness or low status, especially by a colonizing culture. Like other forms of revival, folklore reclamation usually indicates a break with tradition and signals a deeply felt need to heal that rift or at least explain it. Reclamation differs from other forms of cultural revival in that it presupposes a relationship of power imbalance between a dominant culture (sometimes, but not always, a colonizing culture) and a marginalized, silenced, or subdominant folk group. Reclamation focuses on exactly those traditions, elements, even words that the dominant culture considers emblematic of the subdominant group's inferiority. By reclaiming them, groups give these elements a new and illustrious context in which they function as important symbols of pride and identity—a reconstructed identity consciously opposed to the one portrayed by the dominant culture.

While postcolonial cultures are common settings for instances of reclamation, most North American Neo-Pagans do not live in a situation of colonization or domination in the margins of a larger polity. Yet they are engaged in the reclamation of a marginalized and silenced tradition: the magico-religious practices, beliefs, calendrical rites, techniques for religious ecstasy, and assorted other folklore genres that were once part of a European tradition of vernacular magic. This tradition was maintained historically through oral transmission and magical texts that were thought to contain mystical knowledge. The European magical tradition never fully disappeared, but it became increasingly marginalized as industrialization and urbanization brought an end to the socio-cultural context in which it flourished: rural subsistence farming, small, face-to-face communities, and intense social relations that characterized much of Europe before the industrial revolution. The rise and codification of science as a method of inquiry also brought tremendous changes in the way reality was socially understood: numinous phenomena that were not testable and reproducible in a scientific context came to be considered "supernatural," or beyond the laws of nature, and therefore essentially incomprehensible. These "alternate ways of knowing," as Motz calls them (Motz, 1998) were marginalized as the province of the ignorant and superstitious and were sometimes actively suppressed by religious and state authorities.

Folk discourses conserved elements of a pre-Enlightenment magico-religious worldview and practice; it is from them that Neo-Pagans often derive material that they reinterpret and reassemble for their own purposes. This is in part because, as David Hufford has argued, folk beliefs and discourses often preserve the numinous quality of spiritual experience in a way that scholars' accounts do not (Hufford, 1995). But the reclamation of these discourses may also represent a means of gleaning oppositional power—secret, magical knowledge that conveys understandings more "authentic" than those proffered by the dominant culture.

## The Magic of Ethnography

Nearly all the major studies of Neo-Paganism have remarked upon the extraordinary creativity and imaginativeness of its adherents. In this work, I look expressly and in detail at the cultural productions of this subculture. My contention is that by examining a group's expressive culture and aesthetics, we glean more clues about its appeal than through statistical or psychological analyses. At the core of my argument is an examination of the Neo-Pagan experience of religious ecstasy—what many informants call the *juice* in ritual—as the key to understanding the movement as a form of creative resistance. I base my assertion on David Hufford's experience-centered approach (Hufford, 1995): the assumption that somatic experiences are at the root of some beliefs. I argue that some Neo-Pagan beliefs arise from what they experience during religious ecstasy and that the marginalization of such experiences in mainstream American culture lies behind Neo-Pagans' need to create a context in which they are pivotal and valued.

As a scholar trained in both anthropology and folkloristics, I bring insights from both disciplines to this work. My methodology, participant observation, comes largely from anthropology, although today it is also used by the majority of folklorists. I draw heavily from anthropological approaches to religion and ritual, and I build upon the large body of anthropological literature on the construction of identities, whether at the level of state, polity, or locality. From folkloristics comes my concern with the performative, expressive, and creative aspects of religious culture, my focus on the experiential, phenomenological aspects of belief, and my insights into the impact of folklore and its study on emergent cultures. As a folklorist, I am also concerned with the role of expressive culture in tradition: that is, I see Neo-Paganism as part of a Western magical tradition with both vernacular and learned components stretching back at least to Classical times. Tradition, however, is not a static thing but an ongoing process. What some scholars have called "inventions," "folklorism," or "fakelore" I see as integral steps in the formation and elaboration of tradition, worthy of investigation in their own right. Ultimately, though, the disciplines of anthropology and folkloristics in the early twenty-first century are overlapping and complementary; my intent is not to draw sharp boundaries between them but to demonstrate how they illuminate and supplement each other in the analysis of culture. Because I perceive disciplinary boundaries as fluid and nonexclusive, I also draw from other fields of knowledge in my explication of Neo-Pagan culture, from history to recent neurological studies that help illuminate the phenomenological nature of some religious experiences.

I first became interested in Neo-Pagan rituals in the mid-1990s, as a means to explore the confluence of ritual, festival, gender, and politics—the subject of my earlier research in Italy—in a new context. I was initially interested in Neo-Paganism as a folk revival, in issues surrounding the use of folklore from academic sources, cultural appropriation, and the construction of authenticity in the invention of rituals. During the course of my research, I had an extraordinary experience while participating in a Pagan ritual, which led me to study in depth the role of religious ecstasy as the key experience uniting Neo-Pagans.

My original intention was to conduct a long-term study of a single Neo-Pagan group in order to better understand the dynamics of ritual creation. However, my life circumstances during the course of the study precluded this. Between 1994 and 1997, I held a series of temporary academic appointments in different parts of the country. This made sustained observation of one group unfeasible. As it turns out, because Neo-Pagans themselves often hold membership in several groups at once, concentration on a single group would not necessarily have exposed me to the kind of broad-based information I was seeking. I eventually found the best of both worlds in Berkeley, California, where I lived from 1995 to 1997.

The San Francisco Bay Area has one of the country's oldest and most active Neo-Pagan communities. Most Pagans in the area belong simultaneously to a number of different groups, whose members are connected by dense networks. In this area, I was able at last to observe a single coven over a period of time and participate in a larger web of Neo-Pagan activities and rituals. My entrée into the community was Holly Tannen, a fellow folklorist and performer of traditional ballads and satirical songs in the Northern California Neo-Pagan community. Because Holly is a much-admired community member, my performance with her at Pagan festivals and Berkeley coffeehouses accorded me instant recognition and trust. Through her, I made contact with the leaders of a local Gardnerian coven who were respected elders in the Bay Area community. I began to attend their open rituals and social events and eventually became acquainted with a range of individuals who belonged to a number of different Pagan traditions.

In 1996, I moved, quite by accident, into a small rental house in the Berkeley flats on what I soon learned was nicknamed Witch Row. My next-door neighbors were elders in the Fellowship of the Spiral Path; the next house over belonged to the late Judy Foster, a founding member of the New Reformed Orthodox Order of the Golden Dawn (NROOGD) who was also active in the Reclaiming tradition. Just a few streets away was the covenstead of Don Frew and Anna Korn, high priest and priestess of Coven Trismegiston, a Gardnerian group. Now my informants were also my neighbors, and my living situation began to approximate the immersion in a small community I had experienced in Sardinia.

Both Jeanne Favret-Saada, who studied witchcraft accusations in a small, face-to-face community in south-central France, and Paul Stoller, who studied sorcery in West Africa, have observed the impossibility of remaining a neutral observer when studying the practice of magic (Favret-Saada, 1980; Stoller, 1987). While, unlike Favret-Saada and Stoller, I was not studying magic in a traditional society, I, too, found it impossible to remain uninvolved with the traditions I was studying. There were several reasons for this. Some Neo-Pagan traditions still remain hidden from public view for fear of misrepresentation and persecution. This is understandable, because Neo-Pagans have often been sensationalized by the press and falsely accused of criminal activities. Their homes and businesses have been vandalized and their children removed from their custody by social-service workers who do not understand the nature of their religious practice. Even when Pagans are not feared by their neighbors, the tremendous stigma attached to practicing, in a secular society, a religion that purports to believe in magic can lead to ridicule and social ostracism. Establishing rapport with Pagans meant becoming a trusted member of the community by forming relationships in which favors, confidences, and information flowed in both directions; in the process, a number of my subjects became close friends. Another important factor driving participant observation is the mystical nature of some Neo-Pagan traditions. The deepest mysteries of the religions are closed to all except initiates; if one wishes to understand the mystery, one must become initiated. As Jone Salomonsen wrote, "there is no outside where the observer can literally put herself. In the practice of modern mystery religions, you are either in, or you are not there at all" (Salomonsen, 1999:9). Pagan rituals are not performance events that can be observed from the margins but demand active participation from everyone present. Had I observed without participating, I would have missed the principal experiences at the core of Neo-Pagan religious practice, in addition to making myself even more conspicuous.

I chose to actively participate in the religions I was studying, eventually undergoing initiation in Coven Trismegiston and beginning training in the Reclaiming tradition under the direction of several priestesses. My decision was not motivated only by expedience. I was aesthetically pleased and genuinely moved by some of the rituals I attended, and as a result of these experiences, I changed in significant ways. Because I decided to remain open and vulnerable during rituals, I gained access to imaginative experiences I had banished from my consciousness since reaching adulthood. These were crucial in helping me understand the essence of the culture I was studying; had I *not* had them, I would have failed to grasp the importance of religious ecstasy in the Neo-Pagan experience. I have been able to use the insights I have gained through these experiences to better understand those of other Neo-Pagans, and in some cases I have used my own experiences in rituals as a key to comprehension.

A number of factors from my personal background eased my immersion into Neo-Pagan culture. Like most of my Pagan consultants, I am a white Euro-American with a middle-class upbringing, and I share with them a liberal and rather critical worldview. This was particularly true in my Berkeley coven, where many members were academics, educated professionals, and, like me, transnational or bicultural. I had no strong religious upbringing to prejudice me against people calling themselves Witches and Pagans. Instead, like many Neo-Pagans, my childhood was steeped in Classical mythology and European folktales, a factor that influenced my choice of profession as well. My parents, Italian expatriates who left postwar Rome for better educational and economic opportunities in the United States, had raised me as a "halfie,"[11] maintaining Italian as our primary language and traveling to Italy most summers so my sister and I could spend time with our extended family. In Italy, the Classical past is never very far from consciousness. References to history and mythology are part of the everyday landscape of archeological ruins, public monuments, art, and literature. My interest in European and American folklore, my knowledge of folk narrative and mythology, made Neo-Paganism feel familiar and comfortable to me and contributed to my acceptance in the community. I share with many Neo-Pagans a childhood love of fantasy literature and imaginative games: as a small girl, I created elaborate cultures and folktalelike scripts for my troll dolls; as part of my high school Classics club, I acted in short skits based on Greek and Roman mythology. To me, Neo-Pagan rituals felt very similar to this kind of play.

No doubt, the fact that I undertook this study during a transitional period in my life precipitated my immersion into Neo-Pagan culture. A series of personal and professional setbacks had left me feeling vulnerable, and I began to question many of my assumptions. Since it seemed that my usual, rational way of approaching life had led only to failure and frustration, I figured I had nothing to lose by experimenting with new ways of looking at things, even if they differed considerably from my worldview. So in many ways, this field project became for me a spiritual as well as an academic quest.

Like many folklorists, my inquiry was in part driven by a quest for "authentic" experience as I had encountered it during my Sardinian fieldwork. In the earliest phases of my Pagan fieldwork, I was mourning the deterioration of my relationship with Monteruju, the village in Sardinia where I had done fieldwork in the 1980s. Neo-Pagan rituals, drawing inspiration from European folklore, followed a similar year cycle, and in them I found surprising connections to my earlier field experience. Through them, I sought to reexperience, albeit in a different context, some of the thrill of my Sardinian fieldwork and a sense of connection to the friends I still had in the village. After all, where else in North America could I dance the circle dance at the summer solstice and jump over the ashes of the bonfire, or leave offerings for my dead at All Souls, knowing that my friends half a world away in a tiny town on the island of Sardinia were doing the same thing?

During the course of my research, I had a number of "extraordinary" experiences: "experiences which fall outside of the range of what we tend to regard as 'normal,'" particularly "dreams and visions which carry an unusual degree of reality" (Young and Goulet, 1994:7). David Young and Jean-Guy Goulet postulate that spiritual experiences are much more widespread among anthropologists than previously suspected but that, for fear of ridicule and ostracism, they have remained unrevealed and undiscussed and therefore outside the realm of scientific investigation (8). However, they argue, the ethnological sciences stand to benefit from the open discussion and examination of such experiences, even though they may challenge our notions of reality. Rather than looking upon extraordinary experiences as "supernatural" or "paranormal," Young and Goulet propose that we "entertain the notion that what is seen at first as an 'extraordinary experience' is in fact the normal outcome of genuine participation in social and ritual performances through which social realities are generated" (9).

While in the past, few anthropologists or folklorists were willing to write about their own extraordinary or spiritual experiences in the field, recently a number of scholars who have had such experiences have begun to examine this issue. Anthropologist Bruce Grindal described how Sisala praise singers in Ghana raised a corpse from the dead: "Stretching from the amazingly delicate fingers and mouths of the *goka*, strands of fibrous light played upon the head, fingers and toes of the dead man. The corpse, shaken by spasms, then rose to its feet, spinning and dancing in a frenzy. As I watched, convulsions in the pit of my stomach tied not only my eyes but also my whole being into this vortex of power" (Grindal, 1983:68). Raymond Lee, working on Malay spirit possession, became involved with Islamic occultism and mysticism, culminating in a series of extraordinary experiences that left him shaken and afraid. His informant was able to calm him by giving him an amulet and a glass of *air jampi*, or blessed water (Lee, 1987). Lee concluded that the emotions stemming from his spiritual experiences were themselves important data: he postulated that emotions may be the link between the phenomenology and the sociology of magic (74). More recently, in a seminal essay Edith Turner recounts how while observing a Ndembu healing ritual, she saw a large gray blob, "something between solid and smoke," rise from the body of the afflicted person at the precise moment when the spiritual healer was drawing out the illness from her (E. Turner, 1994:83). Building on the work of her late husband, Victor Turner, she hypothesizes that symbols are not merely signs or referents to a known object, as we assume them to be in Western positivism, but that they embody the emotional force of all the activities, relationships, objects, and ideas to which they relate in the course of a ritual and within a broader cultural system (90). It is this "unitary power" that animates them, in addition to the context in which they are used: that is, the ritual with all of its cultural, social, and emotional charge. Symbols, in other words, are not just metaphors; they can cause changes not only in the emotions of participants but in physical reality as well. Accepting this hypothesis involves accepting that certain aspects of indigenous worldview, namely a belief in a nonmaterial reality, are not without foundation. "It is time to recognize that the ability to experience different levels of reality is one of the normal human abilities and place it where it belongs, central to the study of ritual," Turner concludes (94).

The work of these scholars emphasizes the socially constructed nature of reality: even when we are within our own culture, our experience of reality is context-dependent. Western culture is rife with experiences that blur the boundaries between the real and the imaginary: films, plays, concerts, and sporting events are all examples of "framed" experiences (Goffman, 1974) that cause us to momentarily leave one reality and become absorbed into an alternate one; yet few of us would look upon the "engrossment" we experience in these contexts as extraordinary or supernaturally induced. Young and Goulet maintain that the extraordinary experiences of anthropologists in the field are similarly the result of opening "one's self to aspects of experience that previously have been ignored or repressed" (Young and Goulet, 1994:9).

Like Edith Turner and the other anthropologists cited above, I take an experiential approach to the extraordinary experiences reported in this book. The essence of this approach is twofold: it involves, first of all, the conscious, willing, and full participation in ritual experiences intended to induce alternate states of consciousness, and the interpretation of visions and dreams as "alternate ways of processing insights, information about one's own life" (Young and Goulet, 1994:10). Second, this approach mandates that I consider informants' experiences seriously. In this, I follow the lead of David Hufford, Leonard Norman Primiano, Patrick Mullen, Marylin Motz, and Jone Salomonsen, among others, who have urged ethnographers to consider the possibility that informants who report numinous or "supernatural" experiences are relating actual somatic occurrences that may well have a basis in human physiology, but whose meanings in individuals' lives go well beyond physiological explanations. The wide cross-cultural distribution of "extraordinary" experiences points to their "core" nature: these are experiences fundamental to human existence that have cross-cultural phenomenological continuity and engender spiritual explanations (Hufford, 1995:29). In evaluating consultants' accounts, I have not attempted to explain away their perceptions, but have taken them seriously as experiences as well as expressions of religious belief.

My absorption into the Neo-Pagan community and my subjective spiritual experiences during fieldwork beg the question that always bedevils ethnologists: to what extent did my participation in the culture cause me to "go native," to adopt the beliefs, attitudes, and worldviews of the people I studied? Am I an insider or an outsider, and how can I be "objective" about a culture if I have adopted an emic, or insider's, perspective? The critique of anthropology during the late decades of the twentieth century has made questions of pure objectivity obsolete: there is now a greater understanding of the fact that research that depends on interpersonal relationships, as ethnographic research does, cannot produce completely objective results, because the biases of the researcher (as well as those of the subjects) influence the collection and interpretation of the data. But this does not eliminate the question of bias. While I have elucidated at length the reasons that led me to study Pagan culture, and the prejudices with which I entered the field, I have also admitted to being changed by my experiences, and one could legitimately ask whether I have adopted an insider's bias—the uncritical, enthusiastic embrace of the religious convert.

Discussions about insiders and outsiders, emic versus etic perspectives, are problematic in their own right, however, because they essentialize the very categories they attempt to elucidate. They remind me of the well-meaning people who would ask me, when I was a child, whether I was really more American or Italian. This question would always stump me, because it was perfectly obvious to me that I was both, and that being part of one culture did not exclude belonging to the other. By asking the question, my inquisitors seemed to be implying that I had to pick one. The trouble with categories such as "emic" and "etic," "insider" and "outsider" is that they presume identity to be fixed and essential, rather than the shifting, negotiated, contextual construction we now know it to be. My answer to readers who want to know whether I am "really" an insider or an outsider to the Pagan community is that I am neither and both—that how I look at things depends very much upon context, but contains both anthropological *and* Pagan perspectives at the same time. The ethnographic perspective is *not* about being an objective observer of a culture, but rather about containing within one body multiple, simultaneous frames of reference with which to interpret experience, and being able to shift easily from one to the other.

Feminist theologian and ethnographer Jone Salomonsen, who also studied Neo-Pagan Witchcraft in the San Francisco Bay Area, has called this the "method of compassion" (Salomonsen, 1999:4). "Compassion," she writes,

> does not refer to a wholesale positive embracement, nor to passionate criticisms and arguing, but to something in between. . . . It designates an attitude of *embodiment* in contrast to *disengagement*, and of "taking belief seriously," both existentially and emotionally. . . . Engagement is more than participation, and something other than pretending. To allow oneself to become engaged is to take the intent of ritual seriously. It is [being] willing to let the trance induction take you into trance, to be willing to be emotionally moved as is intended by certain ritual elements, and [to] go with what happens. (9, 11)

At the same time, the compassionate method also demands a constant shifting between engagement and distance, so symbols, lyrics, movements, artifacts, structures, and social interactions that are part of a ritual must be remembered and noted when the event is over. The compassionate method "demands that we enter [a] mystical path as apprentices, experiencing it as real *but without ever forgetting that we are scholars*" [emphasis in original] (Salomonsen, 1999:10). This self-reflexive methodology is similar to what anthropologist Ruth Behar calls the viewpoint of the "vulnerable observer." In her essay with this title, Behar writes of this kind of anthropological method: "because there is no clear and easy route by which to confront the self who observes, most professional observers develop defenses, namely "methods" that . . . drain anxiety from situations in which we feel complicitous with structures of power, or helpless to release another from suffering, or at a loss as to whether to act or observe" (Behar, 1996:6).

The understanding of how ethnographic experience affects and changes the observer is crucial to the ethnographic project. As early as 1967, George Devereaux, an ethnopsychiatrist, insisted that the emotions and reactions of the observer be made explicit in order to understand the nature of the ethnographic encounter (Devereaux, 1967:6, 84). Twenty years later, Renato Rosaldo made a parallel point in his essay "Grief and a Headhunter's Rage" (1989). Rosaldo uses his own enraged reaction to the death of his wife in the field to elucidate for readers the Ilongot's assertion that they hunt heads out of a rage born of grief. Though at first he had disbelieved his informants and searched for an economic or political motive for their actions, only when he experienced rage himself did he fully understand what they were trying to tell him. Rosaldo's article reminds us of the cultural force of emotions and of the necessity for anthropologists to pay attention to them—their own as well as those of their subjects. However, it also raises questions about the dangers of using (and *not* using) personal experience to understand emotion. On one hand, it is risky to assume that one's own experience is the same as that of one's subjects, especially when there are great differences in culture, age, gender, power, race, religion, or sexual orientation. On the other hand, assuming that cultural experiences create such vast gulfs between human beings that any mutual understanding is elusive at best creates a situation that erases shared aspects of humanity between subject and object, and ultimately reduces anthropology to a solipsistic endeavor. In using the compassionate method, in becoming a vulnerable observer, my intent is not to indulge my desire for autobiography, but to make Neo-Pagan experience more transparent to my readers. I have tried to tread a fine line between sharing too much of my experience, turning this into an autoethnography, and sharing too little, obscuring how my own subjectivity influenced my perspective and erasing the links between myself and my subjects. As Behar writes, "Vulnerability doesn't mean that anything personal goes. The exposure of the self who is also a spectator has to take us somewhere we couldn't otherwise get to" (1996:14).

When I have included some of my own spiritual experiences and reactions to rituals in this book, they have been set in a sans serif typeface to separate them from my more interpretive and analytic passages. By choosing this particular style, I emphasize the shifting, reflexive process inherent to ethnographic inquiry and make it available to the reader, at the same time clarifying which perspective I am taking at any given moment. The appearance of these texts on the page is the physical representation of the method of compassion, of the thought processes that accompany vulnerable observation.

The postcolonial critique of ethnography has illuminated how ethnographic writing is never just a presentation of facts, but a conscious act of construction, of narrative and evocation on the part of the ethnographer (Clifford and Marcus, 1986; Bruner, 1986). In presenting material in this book, rather than generalizing about Neo-Pagan beliefs and practices, I have attempted instead to evoke for readers the experiences of individual members of a community. In his essay "Post-Modern Ethnography," Stephen Tyler describes the ideal postmodern ethnography as an "occult document," an enigmatic combination of fantasy and reality that attempts to invoke or evoke a possible world (Tyler, 1986:134). He presents this document as a therapeutic, integrative work, like poetry, vision, or ritual, which has as its main aim *evocation*. While it is unclear what such an ethnography would actually look like, what is clear is that Tyler has essentially described an act of magical transformation.

One purpose of magic, according to modern Pagans and Witches, is to change consciousness at will, and the principal ways of doing so involve invoking (from Latin *in* + *vocare*, "to call into") or evoking (from Latin *ex* + *vocare*, "to call forth from") a particular entity, quality, or mood through a combination of words, actions, and material objects. This process of creative transformation is the nexus of ritual; in many Wiccan rituals, this is symbolized by the Great Rite, a metaphorical union of male and female principles in nature that Witches interpret as the fundamental creative act. For many Pagans, creativity is central to both spiritual development and the ability to contribute to society. Because creativity and artistry involve evocation and transformation, these acts become equivalent to magic. Thus the writing of ethnography becomes a magical act, no less than the creation of a ritual, the making of a spell, or the manufacture of a sacred object: the ethnographer is by definition a magician.

The magic of ethnography is precisely its capacity to evoke for readers the sensual, corporeal, emotional aspects of experience—those very aspects that first draw the researcher into the field and that attracted the attention of early, post-Romantic ethnographers during the eighteenth and nineteenth centuries. But as Regina Bendix outlines in her essay "The Pleasures of the Ear: Towards an Ethnography of Listening" (2000:36), the textualization of expressive culture and attempts to transform its study into a science led to a loss of its more sensual, descriptive elements—a trend that is particularly striking in the study of folk belief and religiosity, where the numinous has often been stripped from the text. Bendix invites ethnologists to develop ethnographic methods capable of grasping and conveying the kind of unspoken, profound moment that is characteristic of many field experiences but which is notoriously difficult to elucidate in writing. My attempt in this book, more than in any of my previous works, is to write in a way that evokes in the reader some of the sensual, experiential, numinous qualities of doing research among contemporary magical practitioners.

After the conference at which I experienced the ritual I described at the beginning of this chapter, I wrote in my journal:

There is a point at which fieldwork begins to suck you in; it draws you down like an undertow, and though you resist and resist it overpowers you, washes over you, crashes over you like surf until you yield, finally exhausted. You yield yourself up to it and it's like falling in love; it's a kind of falling in love. You are no longer sure of the boundary between observer and observed, between you and those you are studying. Their lives begin to dominate your thoughts and it's not just analysis, it's because you care what happens to them; your encounters cease to be about work and become your enjoyment. I don't remember exactly at what point Monteruju overtook me, but for Paganism this conference was the turning point. . . . What I know now is that fieldwork is made of those moments, of falling in love; this is how I learn about cultures, by getting inside other people's hearts, and letting them get into mine. Perhaps that is why the goddess put that searing red heart in my breast during my vision at Starhawk's ritual; perhaps that was what she meant by saying, "This is your heart, and fire will make it whole."

A few practical points: because this work deals with ritual magic, I have organized it according to the pattern of much Neo-Pagan ritual. Part I, "Roots and Branches," grounds the reader in the both the history and the contemporary reality of American Neo-Paganism. Part II, "Religions of Experience," is the core of the book: in these three chapters, I deal with the "energy" of the movement by examining the practice of magic, its expression through ritual, and the religious ecstasy at ritual's heart. In the final section, "Beyond Experience: Religion and Identity," I examine how Neo-Paganism fits into the larger structures of American society in the early twenty-first century, especially how it articulates with issues of cultural politics, hybridity, and multiculturalism. I have followed my field consultants' wishes as to the presentation of their names: most chose to have their real names appear in this book; some go by their ritual names; and a few selected pseudonyms, which I present in quotations the first time they appear in the text, but not thereafter. Throughout the text, I capitalize the words *Witch, Witchcraft,* and *Paganism* when they refer to contemporary religions, but use lowercase when they are used in an anthropological or historical context.

# Part I
# Roots and Branches

*Chapter 1*

# The Study of Folklore and the Reclamation of Paganism

**Field notes, October 12, 1996**

On a moonless night in October, five Witches walk silently along the quiet Berkeley streets until they come to a place where three roads come together to form a Y intersection: a trivia or crossroads, the traditional province of the goddess Hecate. Rather than hoods and cloaks, they wear fleece and barn jackets against the evening chill. One carries a paper plate with offerings to the goddess, as described in ancient Greek texts: cakes, sprat and mullet, a fertile egg, feta cheese, whole garlic cloves, and grape-must cookies. Another carries a container of household food scraps—the *katharmata,* or sacrificial rubbish, specified by the texts—and a third holds a clay burner with frankincense and myrrh, to stand for both the *katharsia,* or sacrificial leftovers, and the *oxuthumia,* or fumigation to protect the participants against any unfriendly spirits. When they reach the crossroads, the high priest recites one of the Orphic hymns to Hecate:

> I invoke you, beloved Hecate of the Crossroads and the three ways
> Saffron-cloaked goddess of the heavens, the underworld and the sea
> Tomb-frequenter, mystery-raving with the souls of the dead
> Daughter of Perses and Asteria,
> Haunter of deserted places who exults among the deer,
> Nightgoing one, protectress of dogs, unconquerable queen
> Beast-roarer, disheveled one of compelling countenance
> Tauropolos, keyholding mistress of the whole world
> Ruler, nymph, mountain-wandering nurturer of youth.
> Maiden, I beseech you to come to these holy rites
> Ever with joyous heart and ever favoring your priests and priestesses.

He carries the burning incense to the center of the crossroads and crushes it with his foot, leaving the plate of offerings on the curb as a decoy for the souls in the goddess's train. Then the small company turns and leaves silently without looking back. As they depart, it seems that all the dogs in the neighborhood begin to bark and howl—an excellent omen that the sacrifice has been well received by the goddess and her unearthly hounds.

Neo-Paganism and revival Witchcraft are esoteric, ecstatic magical traditions whose roots in Western culture can be traced to ancient times. While they have not existed as continuous, uninterrupted traditions since time immemorial, some of the most important constructs of contemporary magical practice have a venerable history. They are heirs to what anthropologist Loretta Orion called "an enduring—albeit submerged—aspect of Western culture" that she calls the "Western spiritual tradition" (Orion, 1995:79–80). This chapter traces the roots of many Neo-Pagan and Witchen concepts, practices, and terms through history, showing the links between contemporary praxis and ideas that have been part of a long-standing Western tradition. A much more complete history of Neo-Pagan Witchcraft has already been produced by historian Ronald Hutton, in *The Triumph of the Moon: A History of Modern Pagan Witchcraft* (1999). Rather than repeating his research, my aim here is to contextualize the practices I will be describing by framing them in time and space, revealing some of the sources of the many elements in this reclaimed tradition. A secondary goal of this chapter is to show how the study of folklore and its reclamation are part of the same strain of thought that arose from the Enlightenment and the earliest European contacts with non-Western peoples. These twin processes are so inextricably intertwined that to attempt to separate them means that half of the story remains hidden from view.

Much of the history of folkloristics in the nineteenth and twentieth centuries involves the construction of arguments authenticating folklore as a real, genuine artifact of a group of people, whether construed in terms of class or ethnicity (Bendix, 1997). "Pure" folklore, in this view, was an expression of the voice of the people, devoid of larger political, economic, or ideological goals. According to these arguments, the revival of folklore, or its popularization and diffusion by the mass media or elite culture, automatically inauthenticated the lore. American folklorist and historian Richard M. Dorson, for example, decried the emergence of "fakelore," the manufacture of folklorelike elements for commercial interests (Dorson, 1969); while in Europe, German folklorists coined the term *folklorismus* to describe folklore revived or altered for the purpose of attracting tourism or generating regional pride.[1] It was not until late in the twentieth century that folklorists began to understand revival and reclamation as part of the process of tradition, reflecting a larger shift in focus in the humanities and social sciences from studying texts and products to studying processes (Bendix, 1988; Handler and Linnekin, 1984). At the same time, historical research was illustrating how many traditions that appeared to be ancient were in fact of rather recent invention, and how claims of antiquity were themselves part of the process of authenticity construction (Wagner, 1981; Herzfeld, 1982; Hobsbawm and Ranger, 1983). Authenticity itself came to be viewed as a construct that depended entirely on the perspectives and interests of the constructors.

This shift in how scholars understand the process of tradition making has led to an interest in how traditions change in response to social transformation, and how new traditions take shape to meet emerging social needs. While earlier folklorists would have dismissed Neo-Paganism as an example of *folklorismus*, "invented tradition," or fakelore, folklorists today are more likely to understand it as part of the process through which traditions are shaped, selected, and reinterpreted by individuals and groups to serve larger social, political, and ideological ends.

But even by more conservative definitions of folklore as either "oral tradition" or the part-culture of oppressed groups, Neo-Paganism can be understood as a folk tradition on at least two levels. First, the Western spiritual tradition from which it draws has never been codified in a single text; rather, it has been preserved, like most folklore, through a combination of oral tradition and bits of writing, meaning that each successive generation has been free to change the tradition to better suit its purposes, and to interpret it according to the reigning ideologies of the time. Neo-Pagans are but the latest in a long line of tradition bearers who have adapted magical spiritual traditions to fit the surrounding cultural context. Second, this spiritual tradition has never been part of the dominant Western discourse; certainly since the Enlightenment, but I would argue even earlier, it has belonged to the occult subculture just below the radar of official institutions. Thus we can understand it as a form of resistance culture—an idea I will explore more fully in Chapter 6.

In laying out the history of the various elements that have come to be a part of this religious movement, I will show how the emergence of Neo-Paganism parallels the study of folklore and its construction of authenticity, and how academic concepts have had a broad and often unexpected influence on popular culture, beyond what their creators could imagine.

## Classical Roots

Neo-Paganism's earliest traceable roots go back to ancient Greece and Rome, with their polytheistic religions, mystery cults, and traditions of ecstatic knowledge and divination. While historians have usually chosen to emphasize the literary, philosophical, and scientific heritage the West owes to Classical civilization, they have often overlooked the mystical tradition to which Western culture is equally an heir. For alongside the Classical tradition of rationalism, there existed a tradition of ecstatic mystery religions that involved egalitarian societies with secret rituals where adherents directly experienced the sacred through altered states of consciousness, and shrines where seekers would consult priestesses who predicted the future, sometimes with the aid of hallucinogenic fumes. The mystery cults of Dionysus, of Attis and Cybele, the

Eleusinian mysteries, and the Delphic oracle are just as much a part of Western heritage as are the writings of the philosophers and critics who dismissed them.

In Classical pagan[2] cosmology, the universe was permeated by animated and divine forces that were immanent in nature, and could also become embodied in human or animal form. This worldview first emerged in writing in Egypt and Mesopotamia in the third millennium B.C.E., and continued to find expression in a variety of magical papyri and texts throughout the ancient Mediterranean and Near East until the period of late antiquity, the second and third centuries C.E., when many cults and religions combined in the Eastern Mediterranean to yield a rich and complex magico-religious culture. Greco-Roman Egypt in the third century C.E., like contemporary North America, was a meeting place for many cultures and religions—a fertile medium for religious syncretism and the emergence of hybrid forms. From this period and cultural context emerged an important set of magical documents often referred to as the Greek and Demotic magical papyri. This collection of hymns, rituals, and spells preserve much of what we know today about certain magical and religious practices in late antiquity. We can think of these texts as early grimoires, or compendia of magical knowledge and techniques—the precursors of contemporary Neo-Pagan Witches' Books of Shadows.

Two important sets of documents also preserved during this period are the Corpus Hermeticum and the Chaldean Oracles. Unlike the Greek and Demotic magical papyri, these texts preserve religious doctrine relating to the cults of Hermes and Hecate, deities associated with magic in late antiquity. The Hermetic texts were supposed to have been revealed by Hermes Trismegistos, himself a hybrid of the Greek Hermes, the god of communication and trade and the messenger of the otherworld, and the Egyptian Thoth, the ibis-headed god of wisdom and learning and the soul's guide to the underworld. Hermes Trismegistos's name means "thrice-greatest" in Greek, perhaps because he incorporated the greatness of more than one deity, or was believed by his followers to be three times as powerful as other deities. The Chaldean Oracles are said to be the prophetic utterances of a number of deities, including Hecate, a Greek goddess adopted by the Romans, who ruled over crossroads, magic, and the dead. Hecate, too, absorbed aspects of other goddesses in Classical antiquity: she was associated with Persephone, the daughter of Demeter, whose yearly migration to the underworld to be with her husband, Hades, was dramatized by the Eleusinian mysteries, one of the largest mystery cults in the ancient world, and with Artemis or Diana, the virgin goddess of the moon, ruler of the hunt and protectress of wild animals. Whatever we may think about cross-cultural borrowing today, it is clear that in late antiquity this kind of syncretism was the order of the day, and that material in these early texts is itself a collection of magical ideas adopted from other cultures and earlier epochs.

The following elements of Neo-Paganism can be traced to ideas and practices that come down to us from early Classical paganism:

the idea that the universe is composed of four elements: air, fire, water and earth;

the importance of the four points on the compass, or "cardinal points," in magic;

the existence of multiple deities, as well as spirits of other kinds;

the idea of correspondences in the natural world, such that each deity, for example, had its corresponding planet, number, plant, mineral, color, day of the week, and hour of the day;

the magical principles of sympathy, homeopathy, and contagion;

the use of amulets, invocations, spells, and special tools to control spirits and forces of the universe;

cults in which the faithful underwent initiations that involved the revelation of a sacred mystery, often in states of religious ecstasy.

## Neoplatonism

*Neoplatonism* is a modern term for the philosophical and religious principles of a group of late Classical authors who developed and refined the metaphysical ideas of the Greek philosopher Plato. Its founder was Plotinus, a Roman philosopher born in Egypt in the third century C.E.; other important Neoplatonists include Porphyry, Iamblicus, and Proclus. The doctrines of the Neoplatonists had a significant influence on the development of Western mysticism, from the early Christian founders, to the Renaissance magi, to the German and English Romantic revival. Gerald B. Gardner, the first to describe modern Neo-Pagan Witchcraft, believed that the spirit of Neoplatonic teachings lived on in the teachings of the Witches he was documenting (Gardner, 1959:188–89), and a number of my Wiccan consultants agree.

The central teaching of the Neoplatonists was the fundamental oneness of everything in the universe. "The One" was imagined as a divine unity that was infinite, perfect, and fundamentally unknowable by humans, given their limitations. From the One emanated a hierarchical set of realities that included the *nous*, or mind; the world soul; human souls; and the physical world of matter. Each emanation was thought to be a reflection of its predecessor in the hierarchy, so that all emanations existed as aspects of the One. Humans and the natural world were both believed to be manifestations of the One. "The Neoplatonists reasoned that if the One is immanent in all of the natural world, then (1) the natural world is fundamentally good and (2) all things in the natural world are paths to the One."[3] While it might seem counterintuitive to connect a modern movement reclaiming polytheism with the Neoplatonic monism, Neoplatonists did not deny the existence of multiple gods and goddesses but interpreted them, too, as manifestations of the One.

The Neoplatonists also taught that union with the One was achievable through a ritual process called "theurgy". In the Classical world, theurgy involved drawing down the power of the cosmos, either into the bodies of adepts or to animate statues of the deities. While few Neo-Pagans practice the making of animated statues, deity possession is a feature common to the majority of Neo-Pagan religions. Neoplatonists believed that when humans failed to perceive the essential interconnectedness of the universe, and thus their unity with the One, they could become arrogant and fall into depravity and sensuality. Yet human free will also allowed them to experience connection to the One through mystical ecstasy, the goal of theurgy.

Gerald Gardner saw several similarities between the teachings of the Neoplatonists and the coven he documented. One was their belief in the existence of a greater unity beyond the individual goddesses and gods. In *The Meaning of Witchcraft* (1959), he wrote: "[The Witches] . . . realize that there must be some great 'Prime Mover,' some Supreme Deity; but they think that if It gives them no means of knowing It, it is because It does not want to be known; also, possibly, at our present stage of evolution we are incapable of understanding It. So It has appointed what might be called various Under-Gods, who manifest as the tribal gods of different peoples; as the Elohim of the Jews, for instance. . . . and the Horned God of the witches" (26–27).

Gardnerian priest Don Frew likewise sees a reflection of Neoplatonic cosmology in the Dryghtyn prayer, which is recited at the end of every Gardnerian ritual meeting:

> In the name of Dryghtyn, the Ancient Providence,
> which was from the beginning, and is for eternity,
> male and female, the original source of all things;
> all-knowing, all-pervading, all-powerful, changeless, eternal.
> In the name of the Lady of the Moon,
> and the Horned Lord of Death and Resurrection;
> in the names of the Mighty Ones of the Four Quarters,
> the Kings of the Elements,
> Bless this place, and this time, and they who are here with us. (Crowther, 1974:39–40)

Don interprets the Dryghtyn as the Neoplatonic One: "eternal," "the original source of all things," "all-knowing, all-pervading, all-powerful," beyond human categories such as male and female. He equates deities (the Lady of the Moon, the Horned Lord of Death and Resurrection) with the *nous*, or mind aspect of the One; the Mighty Ones with the world soul; and the Kings of the

Elements with the natural world to which air, fire, water, and earth belong. He also explains the three initiatory degrees of Gardnerian Witchcraft as a process of theurgic ascent by which initiates achieve mystical union with the One in a series of stages, beginning with the world of matter and culminating in the level of mind, the third degree, at which time Gardnerian Witches learn the practice of theurgy, or surrendering the self to the deity during possession.

While there are a number of similarities between Neoplatonism and certain aspects of Gardnerian Witchcraft and, more broadly, Neo-Paganism, there are also many important differences between them. While American Neo-Pagans celebrate sensuality and the world of matter as fundamentally good, Neoplatonism was at its core an ascetic philosophy that drew strict distinctions between the spiritual and the material realms. Its adherents sought to free themselves from the slavery of the world of the senses by adhering to a life of austere discipline. Such a practice would not be embraced by the majority of American Neo-Pagans and Witches today.

Neoplatonism was rejected during the Middle Ages by some Christian dogmatists but reemerged during the Renaissance, when Italian magus and scholar Marsilio Ficino translated a number of Neoplatonic works, including the Corpus Hermeticum, attributed to Hermes Trismegistos, whom Renaissance magi erroneously believed to be a historical person living in ancient Egypt, around the time of Moses. Neoplatonism had a marked influence on the Romantic revival of the eighteenth and early nineteenth centuries. Whether or not Neo-Paganism is a direct descendant of Neoplatonism, each of these movements left is mark upon it. Among Neoplatonism's most important contributions to Neo-Paganism are:

the presence of a greater unity or harmony in the universe, fundamentally unknowable to humans but manifest through deities and in all aspects of the material and spiritual world;

the concept of the universe as an integrated whole, such that the macrocosm is a reflection of the microcosm, and vice versa;

the idea that geometry was a sacred science, and that many relationships could be summarized or symbolized in geometry;

a belief in human free will;

the practice of theurgy, a technique used to bring worshippers into mystical contact with the divine by drawing down the power of the One.[4]

## The Emergence of Renaissance Magic

The Western spiritual tradition embodied in Classical pagan and Neoplatonic principles has gone in and out of fashion during the past two thousand years.

Like a substratum underlying Western culture, at certain historical times it bursts forth into the larger popular consciousness, causing a flowering of interest in the occult, as well as in art, the imagination, and social reform. It is also preserved at an almost constant level in many folk magical traditions. During the early Middle Ages, the Corpus Hermeticum, Chaldean Oracles, and teachings of the Neoplatonists were preserved by the Byzantine and Islamic worlds, heirs of the Greco-Roman cultural legacy. They reentered Europe via the Crusades; some of these concepts helped fuel the Renaissance. However, the concept of an ordered, regulated, and magical universe was common to many worldviews at the time, including the one prevalent in Europe before the Crusades. Bits of earlier lore were preserved in folk magical practices and beliefs, which acquired a veneer of Christianity as the new religion gained cultural and political dominance. Many magical cures which had previously called upon pagan deities now called instead upon Christian saints: for example, in Italy, the goddess Diana's powers to heal epilepsy were gradually transferred during the Middle Ages to St. Valentine or St. Donato.

In the period between 1100 C.E. and 1400 C.E., pieces of the earlier Greco-Roman magical knowledge resurfaced in Europe, but were generally accessible only to the few who were literate. During this time, magical practitioners placed an emphasis on complex rituals designed to coerce spirits to do their will. Because of the influence of dualism, a philosophical notion adopted by Christianity that interpreted existence as a struggle between the powers of God, or absolute good, and those of the devil, representing absolute evil, these spirits were presumed to be demonic. Dealing with evil spirits was considered very dangerous, so medieval magicians' rituals were preoccupied with accuracy and precision; the least deviation from prescribed formulas could spell disaster by unleashing diabolical forces. It was during this period that the magic circle, borrowed from Hebrew magical texts, began to be used as a barrier to contain menacing spirits. Magicians carefully recorded their workings in books called grimoires, collections of spells to control spirits and get them to do the magician's will (Butler, 1998; Hutton, 1999:67; Kieckhefer, 1998). While only literate magicians kept grimoires, some amulets, talismans, and spells whose origins are almost certainly in grimoire material became part of the folk tradition, and could be transmitted by people with limited literacy because they consisted of diagrams and drawings. Likewise, material which almost certainly originated in the vernacular tradition found its way into grimoires—for example, love spells involving the use of blood, semen, and other bodily fluids (Kieckhefer, 1997:79). Thus, while it has been a scholarly convention to distinguish between "high" or ritual magic, concerned with spiritual matters, and "low" or "folk" magic, concerned with everyday matters, in practice these two categories existed as opposite ends of a continuum that contained a large body of magical knowledge and practice and was known to some individuals in all social classes.

It was during the Italian Renaissance that the Western spiritual tradition once again burst forth to flourish among the intellectual elite, fueled by Marsilio Ficino's translation of Hermetic and Neoplatonic texts for his patron, Cosimo de' Medici. His disciple Pico della Mirandola became fascinated by the Hebrew Kabbalah, a body of esoterism based on Hebrew scriptures that had been brought out of Spain by Jews fleeing the Inquisition. He combined these with the Hermetic texts in his own magical work, which was also influenced by a thirteenth-century Latin version of an Arabic grimoire known as the *Picatrix*. Ficino, Pico, and the sixteenth-century apostate monk and philosopher Giordano Bruno elevated magic to a high art form; their spells to invoke essences and deities brought together color, sound, visual images, and experiences in a kind of early performance art, the goal of which was to kindle in participants the spirit, form, and essence of the deity (Orion, 1995:87–88). Through the writings of Aristotle, Ficino reclaimed from Anaximenes, a fourth-century B.C.E. Greek philosopher, the concept of *pneuma* ("breath" or "spirit"), a substance which he envisioned as constantly in flux and animating everything in the universe. This notion is an early version of the modern Neo-Pagan idea of energy. Ficino also conceived of eros, or love, as the spiritual force that drove the universe (Orion, 1995:86–87). Again, this presages Neo-Pagan and especially Wiccan notions of the polarity between goddess and god, feminine and masculine energies in the universe, as the fundamental creative drive, and a central part of spirituality. In order to successfully channel and invoke these universal forces, Renaissance magicians cultivated both personal will and spiritual purity. Magic became a path to enlightenment, a way to develop human potential, a reflection of the emerging Renaissance emphasis on humanism (Hutton, 1999:67).

## The Protestant Reformation

The emergence of Protestantism on the European cultural scene, and the ensuing, often violent struggles between Protestants and Catholics, had a variety of effects on the Western spiritual tradition, some helpful and others ultimately deleterious. On the one hand, the cultural context in which the Reformation occurred included such developments as the mass diffusion of printed texts and the growing emphasis on the individual's relationship to the sacred. Protestantism spread quickly among the European learned classes, and the large-scale publication of the Bible in vernacular tongues spurred the spread of literacy among the growing bourgeoisie. The Reformation in fact saw an increase in the publication of magical works, many of which combined recently rediscovered knowledge of Neoplatonic and Hermetic philosophy with the Kabbalah. *De occulta philosophia* (1533), by the great magician Henry Cornelius Agrippa von Nettesheim, dates from this period; it was later rediscovered by the nineteenth-century French occultist Eliphas Levi, and played an important role in the occult revival. In England, the magician John Dee, who was also astrologer to the court of Queen Elizabeth I, published treatises on "natural philosophy," a combination of Hermeticism with mathematics, astrology, and kabbalistic magic that paved the way for new scientific understandings of the universe. It was also during this period that alchemy, the protoscience of transforming base metals into gold, flourished. Even after it became clear that the transformation of matter was a physical impossibility, alchemists continued to practice their arts in a spiritual vein, seeking to perfect and purify the human soul. These facts suggest that rather than being incompatible with emerging scientific, materialistic paradigms of the universe, the rediscovery of Hermetic magic actually accelerated and facilitated their development.

But even as magic became an object of study among the learned European classes, the Reformation dealt strong blows to vernacular magical traditions, which existed alongside learned magic and sometimes overlapped with it. Up until this time, the majority of European peasants had participated in a wide range of spiritual traditions, ranging from vernacular healing to the cult of saints, which included ecstatic practices. Trance was sometimes used by folk diviners and healers as part of the curative process. Religious ecstasy also characterized saints' cults, often involving participation in sacred sororities or fraternities whose activities during the saint's day celebrations could involve ecstatic dance, extreme physical exertions, and self-flagellation. The majority of liturgical feasts also included many secular aspects, such as plays, games, and popular amusements that invariably involved feasting and drinking to excess in a festive display of symbolic inversion.

All of this horrified Protestant reformers. For them, the core of Christianity was the individual's personal relationship with God, and they interpreted folk religiosity as pagan contamination. They sought to purge Christianity of these impure accretions, and focused specifically on manifestations they considered extraneous to that relationship: particularly, the cults of the Virgin Mary and the saints, and secular amusements associated with liturgical feasts. Their impropriety was attributed to their preservation of elements the Protestant reformers considered hallmarks of Classical paganism: idolatry, in the form of saint's cults, and godless debauchery, in the case of popular entertainments. When Oliver Cromwell and his followers railed against "the old religion" and forbade the performance of popular year-cycle customs, they were targeting the practice of Catholicism and customs associated with it, not the actual observance of pagan religions. Nevertheless, for the reformers they were practically one and the same. A connection, however ill-conceived, was formed in European, and especially British, thought between the practice of folk rituals and customs and "paganism."

But Protestantism was most successful among the emergent middle classes. While it sought to purify Christianity by reducing it to its most fundamental elements, its persecution of all forms of vernacular religion stripped the peasant classes of their spiritual connections, paradoxically severing them from the very ecstatic experiences that embodied their personal relationships with the sacred. This impact of Protestantism was most keenly felt in northern Europe and in the new colonies of North America, which were founded by particularly austere Protestant sects with the express purpose of creating a perfect society. In this brave new world, magic and ecstasy had no place.

## The Effects of the Enlightenment: The Emergence of Secret Societies

The Enlightenment saw a decline in interest in the practice of magic as a form of human edification, in part because the emerging scientific discourse excluded magic as irrational and superstitious. However, a great deal of what constituted the Western spiritual tradition became subsumed into new forms. Two of the most important of these to the development of Neo-Paganism were secret societies and the rediscovery of the Druids, which led to the foundation of the first modern Neo-Pagan order. I will deal with them in that order.

The late seventeenth and early eighteenth centuries saw the rise in Europe of a variety of "brotherhoods," or all-male secret societies, whose purpose was the cultivation of networks among members of the newly emergent urban middle class.[5] Brotherhoods were not a new concept; during the Middle Ages, Christian fraternities and sororities arose around the cults of saints and the practice of certain liturgical customs, such as those of Holy Week. While these voluntary associations persisted until the late twentieth century in some Catholic areas, they were abolished by the Reformation in much of Protestant Europe. Medieval trade guilds constituted similar voluntary associations that regulated trade and provided training and social support to their members, but by the mid-1600s they were no longer the powerful associations they had been in the Middle Ages. More than religious brotherhoods, trade guilds, or gentlemen's clubs, the new organizations of the seventeenth and eighteenth centuries incorporated elaborate initiation rites, complex hierarchies, and esoteric symbols borrowed from the Western spiritual tradition to create lasting and compelling social bonds among their members. In an urbanizing Europe where tradesmen, merchants, and professionals were separated from the networks of extended family that had characterized the rural landscape, these societies furnished a source of mutual support, as well as a locus for criticism of both church and state. As suited the emergent middle class, they were both hierarchical and egalitarian: the societies promised exclusivity, since admission was only through already existing members; within the organizations, complex grades of initiation were accessible to all, and members thought of themselves and each other as a brotherhood. It is no accident that many of the founding fathers of the United States were members of such societies; they fomented a spirit of democratic egalitarianism and provided a kind of secular spirituality independent of organized religion, where religious differences were erased by collapsing the distinctions between faiths into a reverence for a "Supreme Being" (Hutton, 1999:61). They also provided their members with glorious invented histories that created links to a purported ancient past with mystical symbols and elaborate, secret rituals.

Probably the earliest of these societies was the Masons, founded in Scotland in the late 1500s (Hutton, 1999:53). By the 1600s, an analogous society of Freemasons had arisen in England and from there spread throughout Europe. Along with the Freemasons, a number of similar secret societies flourished in Britain between 1700 and 1900, including the Oddfellows, the Order of the Buffaloes, the Foresters, Shepherds, Druids, and the Horsemen's Word (Hutton, 1999:56). Historian Ronald Hutton argues that much of the initiatory structure of British traditional Witchcraft owes a debt to Freemasonry. Some of the most striking elements of Freemasonry that are reproduced in Wicca include:

> elaborate, secret initiations with the bound, blindfolded initiate swearing an oath of loyalty at sword point;
>
> graded sets of incremental initiations, building up to the highest degree;
>
> formal speeches called "charges," through which initiates were taught their (invented) tradition and told of its illustrious founders;
>
> the name "the Craft," which originally referred to the practice of Masonry;
>
> the use of the term "Craft workings" for Masonic rituals;
>
> the ritual closing formula "Happy have we met, happy have we been, happy may we part, and happy meet again," which closely resembles the Wiccan "Merry meet, merry part, and merry meet again." (Hutton, 1999:56)

As a result of the diffusion of secret societies, the period between 1650 and 1850 saw a democratization of magic, as large numbers of European middle-class men became comfortable with a body of esoteric symbols through a secular religion of secret brotherhoods—societies which were both exclusive and egalitarian, as well as a nexus for social critique and in some cases revolutionary action. Several American founding fathers, including George Washington and Benjamin Franklin, were Freemasons as well as Deists; symbols from Freemasonry can still be found on the currency of the United States. The American ideals of an egalitarian society governed by *primi inter pares* and united through a secular, nationalist spirituality favoring no single religion above any other can be traced directly to the influence of secret societies on the worldview of the founding fathers.

## The Hellfire Club

*Hellfire club* was a generic term current in the seventeenth and eighteenth centuries for gentlemen's societies dedicated to dissipation and the pleasures of the flesh. Popular among the upper classes, these societies had some aspects of secret brotherhoods, but were more focused on debauchery than on spiritual matters. The exception was Sir Francis Dashwood's Brotherhood of the Friars of St. Francis of Wycombe and the Society of Dilettanti, both in the mid-1700s. Dashwood, a member of the British Parliament with an extensive magical library, including the works of Cornelius Agrippa, founded both societies (Towers, 1986). To all outward appearances, the Brotherhood of St. Francis was like other hellfire clubs: Dashwood threw wild parties and, it was rumored, orgies on his Wycombe estate; its motto was "Do what you will" (Ashe, 1974). However, there was also an inner circle of thirteen members who practiced magical rituals and initiations in subterranean tunnels beneath the estate. Because the club's papers were destroyed when the group dispersed, little is known about the group's actual practices. We do know, however, that members of this secret society referred to their practices as "British Eleusinian mysteries," a reference to the Classical mystery cult of Eleusis associated with Demeter and Persephone, in which initiates underwent a rite of rebirth. Members of the Brotherhood of St. Francis of Wycombe may have reenacted these rites; the presence of a stream bed inside the tunnels suggests that club members may have had to cross a "River Styx" as part of their initiation.

In *Witchcraft Today* (1954), Gerald Gardner hypothesized that Dashwood's group may have been an antecedent of the group he discovered. This view is shared by some American Gardnerian Witches, including Don Frew, who hears in "Wycombe" (pronounced "wickam") a possible source for the name of Gardner's group, the Brotherhood of the Wica [*sic*]. While the similarities between the Brotherhood and Gardner's Wica are tantalizing, at this point the links remain hypothetical. It is nevertheless possible that the roots of some modern Neo-Pagan, and especially Wiccan, practices can be found in the activities of Dashwood's so-called hellfire club.

## The Rediscovery of the Druids

The English secret society of the Ancient Order of Druids influenced the formation of the Welsh Gorsedd, or Assembly of Druids, an initiatory organization that had strong nationalistic as well as mystical aspirations and can be considered an early precursor of modern Neo-Paganism (Morgan, 1983:64). The Druids, the ancient priestly order of Gaul and Britain, came to the attention of upper- and middle-class Europeans through the works of Julius Caesar and Tacitus, whose *De bello gallico* and *De vita agricolae,* respectively, became a requisite part of a liberal education after the Renaissance. Caesar and Tacitus, writing from the perspective of sophisticated Roman citizens, portrayed the Druids as savage, superstitious practitioners of human sacrifice. But in eighteenth-century Wales, the Druids began to be reinterpreted as "sage[s] and intellectual[s] defending [their] people's faith and honor," the force "behind the resistance of the native peoples of Britain and Gaul to the Roman invaders" (Morgan, 1983:62–63). Early Welsh nationalists adopted the Druids as symbols of cultural resistance and continuity: Druids were said to have built Stonehenge and to have been the precursors of Welsh bards, medieval poets whose oral traditions included vaticination, a kind of prophetic verse recited in an ecstatic state (Morgan, 1983:62).

Probably the best-known Druid revivalist of the eighteenth century was Edward Williams, better known as "Iolo Morganwg." Iolo considered himself the last in a long succession of bards, and believed it was his duty to reveal the secrets of the Druids, preserved in bardic lore, to the Welsh people. To this end, he wrote *Cynfrinach y bairdd* (Secrets of the bards) and *Coelbren y bairdd* (Alphabet of the bards) (Morgan, 1983:66). In the latter, Iolo gave new interpretations of the Ogham-like script that survived in stone inscriptions from many parts of Britain, and probably dated from the third to fifth centuries C.E. Iolo's reinterpretation assigned each letter a mystical association and a corresponding tree. The influence of this reclaimed Druidic alphabet still lives in contemporary Paganism in the form of countless books, tarot card decks, and divination tools based on it. More than a secret society, Iolo's Druids had a spiritual component, largely based on his own Unitarian and Deist beliefs (Morgan, 1983:66–67). Like contemporary Pagans, Iolo's Druids took Druid names upon initiation. They dressed in colorful robes and performed elaborate rituals, often in the vicinity of megaliths that Iolo believed had served as sacrificial sites.

While Iolo's Druidism was not an attempt to create a new religion, it set the tone for the later Neo-Pagan movement. It portrayed Druids as wise and knowledgeable magicians and poets, keepers of an oral tradition that stretched uninterrupted into antiquity. Like other contemporary secret societies, Druidism incorporated initiatory grades and seasonal rites that were conducted, as far as possible, outdoors at sacred sites. Like contemporary American Paganism, it had a strong oppositional component: the Druids were depicted as leaders of a resistance against Rome's invasions and, by association, against Britain's first wave of colonial expansion into Wales. Moreover, the Druids, by dint of being Welsh, were understood to be "Celts"—a linguistic construction based on relationships between Welsh, Breton, and Cornish, which seventeenth-century French historian Paul Yves Perzon first traced to the "Keltoi" of ancient Greek writers (Morgan, 1983:67; Chapman, 1992).[6] *Celt* quickly came to refer to a people whose ancient territory had ranged from Scythia in Asia Minor to western Gaul (modern-day Brittany) and the British Isles.

Whether or not there had ever been any cultural connections between the Keltoi and the occupants of pre-Roman Gaul and Britain, the one thing that could be said about these cultures was that they were neither Mediterranean (i.e., Greek or Roman) nor Anglo-Saxon, yet they had been subjugated by both. Since relatively little else was known about them at the time, it was comparatively easy for eighteenth- and nineteenth-century nationalist poets and folklore collectors to project upon them whatever fantasies suited their political and social agendas. Thus was born the romance of the Celts, what folklorist and Reclaiming priestess Holly Tannen ironically calls "the Celtic Twilight zone": that blurry mixture of fact and fantasy that surrounds all things Celtic, within and outside of Neo-Paganism. As the early inhabitants of Gaul and Britain, and the first victims of British colonial expansion, the Celts became a powerful symbol of cultural survival and identity in Britain. It is no wonder that so many later practices, such as revival Witchcraft, were attributed to them.

## Folklore, Anthropology, and the Birth of Neo-Paganism

The Enlightenment and the Romantic revival that followed it went hand in hand with the emergence of the disciplines of folkloristics and anthropology. The same ideas that propelled authors, artists, and poets, as well as spiritual seekers, to look for authenticity of experience were giving birth to the modern humanistic and social sciences, through which Westerners constructed relationships of difference with the Other (Bendix, 1997). The presence of the Other, whether located historically, in the past, or geographically, in the colonies or closer to home among the European peasants, had a tremendous impact on the way westerners analyzed their spiritual experiences and imagined those of the Other.

The conception of a category of phenomena that encapsulated both Classical paganism and what we now call folklore, including popular rituals and calendar customs, was a product of the Protestant Reformation.[7] For Protestant reformers, ecstatic saints' cults, magical healing practices, and popular entertainments associated with holidays were not only irrational but represented the detritus of pagan religion that needed to be purged from Christianity. This link continued to find expression in the works of the eighteenth-century antiquarian folklorists, many of whom collected folklore in order to point out the error of its ways.[8] The study of rituals, calendar customs, and folk beliefs was part of a process of separating self from Other that characterized much of early ethnological scholarship. The Other was variously defined as either the (more or less noble) savage—the inhabitant of colonized territories—or the European peasant, whose political and economic relationship to the European urban elites paralleled that of Third World peoples at that time in history. Both were conceived of as having rites and rituals beyond which educated Europeans had progressed and which, in Protestant areas, were considered idolatrous. Authors frequently compared the customs of the people they studied to those of Classical pagans. One example is the work of the Jesuit missionary to Canada J. F. Lafitau. Lafitau published *Moeurs des sauvages amériquains, comparées aux moeurs des premiers temps* (n.d.) (Customs of American savages compared to the customs of the earliest times), an investigation of the religious life and customs of the Algonquin-speaking peoples of North America, in the early 1700s; his "mission was to explain classical civilization by drawing parallels with savages." (Cocchiara, 1981:103). As a Jesuit missionary whose education was steeped in the literature of the Classical authors, Lafitau was thrilled to discover possible analogies between Amerindians and the ancient Greeks and Romans. According to historian Giuseppe Cocchiara (1981:101), "These comparisons . . . are significant because they were used to demonstrate two theses, one about the classical world and the other about the primitive world. On the one hand, references to the classical world constituted a title of nobility for the savages; on the other hand, they established a presupposed community of origins for the savages and the ancient Greeks and Romans, one that demolished . . . the wall that had separated them."

Such comparisons therefore "othered" both colonized peoples and Europeans' own predecessors, lumping them into the same category—one that stood in contrast with the authors themselves. Pagans and Amerindians were, in this construction, symbolic and structural equivalents. At the same time, this comparison hinted at a kinship between self and other, European and "savage" pagan, which could be explained in developmental terms. This idea found its fullest elaboration a century and a half later, in the works of nineteenth-century survivalists.

Lafiteau's ideas were taken up and expanded by his countryman Jean Jacques Rousseau, whose 1768 *Discours sur l'origin et les fondements de l'inégalité parmi les hommes* (Discourse on the origin and basis of inequality among men) theorized a world before civilization in which savages had existed in a blessed, childlike state, in harmony with the natural world and enjoying complete individual freedom. According to Cocchiara, "Rousseau saw nature as the antidote for all evils. . . . an element of religion, nature is the measure of human simplicity, the source of man's moral energy, the faith that drives man to work well" (120–22). In *Emile*, Rousseau imagined a polytheistic religion based on nature which had existed in ancient times: "In the earliest times, . . . the stars, the winds, the mountains, the rivers, the trees, the villages, the dwellings themselves each had its soul, its god, its life. . . . all the works of nature and man were the first gods of mortals, and polytheism was their first religion" (cited in Cocchiara, 1981:122).

Rousseau idealized this state, and rued the fact that his contemporaries lived a very different kind of life, one that was marred by social artifice and inequality. But he believed that the savage spirit was still alive in humankind and that, given the right circumstances, it could be recaptured. He saw it at its most vibrant in the lives and customs of Swiss peasants, whom he had the opportunity to observe during his time in Geneva. Rousseau came to see "national traditions," as he called them, as reflecting the deepest desires and emotions of the people, a necessary part of living an authentic life. We see here the seeds of numerous Neo-Pagan ideals: the idealization of nature, the perception that primitive people and peasants live lives that are in harmony with natural forces, and the imagining of an early polytheistic religion where nature itself is sacred. Moreover, like many contemporary Pagans, Rousseau wrote out of a spirit of social activism. By recapturing some of the spirit of freedom that he imagined present in the noble savage, he believed he could bring about a better world of liberty and social equality for all. The practice of folk customs was a central part of this trajectory, for in contrast to both the Protestant reformers and the Enlightenment critics, Rousseau saw folklore as a path to nature, and therefore to the sacred (Cocchiara, 1981:124).

Rousseau's ideas influenced many Romantic philosophers, but perhaps none more than Johann Gottfried von Herder, who made it one of his main goals to fight against certain principles of the Enlightenment that regarded folklore and tradition as ignorance and superstition. Moreover, Herder's aim was also nationalistic: by reclaiming German folk traditions, he hoped to create an alternative to the French cultural hegemony that prevailed in his homeland (Cocchiara, 1981:168). Herder pioneered the concept of the *Volk*, which he conceived as a people united by common language and traditions. He saw traditions as the very soul of a people—its *Volksiele*, or popular soul. Yet while Herder argued for the fundamental equality of all human beings, savage or civilized, regardless of race or color, he also idealized the German people and argued for reclamation of German language and folk traditions in order to bring about a new nationalism (a word he coined): a German nation for the German people. Herder's contribution to the trends that led to the development of Neo-Paganism is captured in this paradoxical view: national traditions "belong" to a particular group united by language and culture and contain the essence of the soul of a people; all peoples have access to their own particular *Volksiele* through their own folk traditions, yet his own people's traditions were clearly the best, in his mind. Herder was, in a sense, the first multiculturalist.

Among Herder's most famous disciples were Jacob and Wilhelm Grimm, who, inspired by the philosopher, collected folktales, legends, and oral accounts from their neighbors and acquaintances. Both brothers made separate but equally significant contributions to the context in which Neo-Paganism developed. Jacob, the linguist and scholar, suggested in *Deutsche Mythologie* (1835) that German folktales were the detritus of Teutonic myths. The *Volk* thus came to be seen as keepers of the seeds of a great Germanic identity, expressed in narratives that belied their simple content. The idea of folktales as having mythic content grew to be widely accepted in late nineteenth- and early twentieth-century Europe and America, and influenced the ways contemporary Pagans perceive folk narrative. It is partly for this reason that folktales sometimes serve as templates for Neo-Pagan rituals: Pagans see folktales as preserving mythic patterns that were at the core of pre-Christian European cultures, and they attempt to re-create them through ritual.

Wilhelm Grimm possessed a completely different temperament and aesthetic from those of his brother. He gave the *Kinder- und Hausmärchen* (usually known as *Grimms' Fairy Tales*; 1812–14) their literary character, combining different versions of tales, changing endings he found too disturbing or not edifying enough, and in the process creating a unique folktale style, a voice that influenced, in one way or another, all future folktale collections. It was Wilhelm's vision of the *Märchen* world that became familiar to the European bourgeoisie through the fairy tales: a feudal world of enchanted nature and magical transformations, filled with lords and ladies, witches and wizards, and humble but often wise peasants. It was a world in which the lowly could eventually win out over the mighty, where the individual hero or heroine could gain access to magic by following the correct path. And it is this world that Neo-Pagan rituals strive to re-create in some measure. This is not by accident; most Neo-Pagans were exposed to the Grimms tales as children (if not in their original version, then as Disney adaptations), as well as to other collections of folk and popular narratives. Reclaiming priestess Macha NightMare writes: "When I was a little girl, my mother read stories of the Greek and Roman goddesses and gods to me. I spent many hours listening, entranced and dreaming of the possibilities. My mother also read the stories of the brothers Grimm to me, . . . as well as other fairy tales. . . . In my first year of college, I jumped at the chance to take a literature class in mythology and folklore. My interest in these genres continues. They stir my imagination and remind me there are other ways of seeing the world, other ways of knowing" (NightMare, 2001:48–49).

The "other ways of knowing" preserved in *Grimms' Fairy Tales* are just as much a product of Wilhelm Grimm's imagination, influenced by Herder, Rousseau, and the thinkers that preceded him, as they are of German peasant culture. Even for contemporary Pagans who are not familiar with European intellectual history and the birth of folklore as a discipline, these "other ways of knowing" live on through the tale world created by the brothers Grimm and the folktale collectors that followed in their footsteps.

## The Invention of Ritual

The study of ritual was as influential as the study of folklore in the creation of modern Neo-Paganism. As Catherine Bell aptly elucidates, the concept of ritual as a particular type of human behavior is rooted in the modernist project of delineating differences between the Western world and the Other: while Westerners had religion, the peoples they colonized had "rituals." The obverse of this enterprise has been a nostalgia for lost authenticity that was presumably present in the rituals of Classical pagans and "savages" (C. Bell, 1997:xi; Bendix, 1997). Ritual, the core of Neo-Pagan practice, must be understood as a part of this historical process: an attempt to reclaim structures and practices that rendered life more authentic and connected humans with both the natural world and the divine. Among the early anthropological theories of ritual that most influenced the emergence of modern Paganism are survivalism, with its emphasis on all rites as expressions of fertility and regeneration, and the myth-ritual school.

One of the earliest scholars to examine ritual was the German linguist Max Müller (1823–1900). Müller traced the roots of Greek mythology to a putative Indo-European past. He interpreted myths as poetic statements about the natural world, especially the movement of the sun, on which all agriculture was dependent, through the heavens. Müller believed the Indo-European's mythopoetic speech was later misinterpreted by the peoples they conquered, and that folktales, legends, and origin stories developed from these "broken-down," misunderstood myths. Müller's ideas generated a great deal of controversy, and were critiqued by the British folklorist Andrew Lang, who drew his inspiration from his compatriot Edward B. Tylor's "doctrine of survivals." Tylor's view of culture was not devolutionary, as Müller's had been, but evolutionary.[9] Applying Darwin's theory of biological evolution to human cultures, Tylor hypothesized that cultures, like biological organisms, evolve from the simple to the complex. According to his thesis, "survivals" were aspects of culture left over from an earlier stage in this unilinear evolutionary system. Included in this category were many types of calendar customs, folktales, legends, beliefs, and children's games, which had no obvious function as cultures evolved and replaced supernaturalism with pure reason. Tylor also hypothesized that primitive peoples saw animals, plants, and natural objects as possessing a soul, and capable of interacting meaningfully with humans. Three key ideas emerged from this debate and influenced the emergence of Neo-Paganism in Europe: the idea that myths were symbolic statements about the movement of heavenly bodies; the notion of folklore as a survival from a primitive, pre-Christian past; and the conception of this ancient world as animistic and suffused with sacredness.

Tylor's disciple Sir James Frazer (1854–1941) produced *The Golden Bough*, a work which was to deeply influence many founders of modern Paganism. In this work, Frazer attempted to develop a universal theory of ritual origins: all rituals, according to this scheme, were enactments of the death and resurrection of a divine king, whose life was linked to the fertility of the land and the prosperity of his subjects. For Frazer, the myth of the dying and reviving deity was the basis of all myth, and ritual was the root of all forms of expressive culture. Frazer's understanding of magic was also seminal to turn-of-the-century thought. He saw magic as a primitive form of science—not superstition, but a logical attempt by early humans to control the world around them through the principles of "sympathetic magic": homeopathy, or the idea that like causes like; and contagion, the principle that objects once in contact continue to influence one another, even when separated. Frazer's view of magic as a form of science helped to legitimize the study of magic in colonized societies, a trend which, much later, led to Neo-Pagans' experimentation with magical techniques borrowed from non-Western cultures.

What came to be called the "myth-ritual" school was inspired by the work of Frazer and Robertson Smith. Samuel Henry Hooke (1874–1968), a scholar of Near Eastern religion, argued that ancient Egyptian, Babylonian, and Canaanite religions centered on the ritual enactment of the death and resurrection of the divine king. Hooke and his followers "reconstructed a set of rites synchronized to the seasonal cycle of planting and harvesting," in which the king was killed, descended to the underworld, fought against the forces of darkness, then was resurrected to celebrate a divine marriage with the temple priestess / sacred concubine and rule peacefully over the land (C. Bell, 1997:6). Hooke's model became important in that it was applied to many other areas of culture, despite its critics. At Cambridge University in England, a group of scholars, Hooke's contemporaries, began to untangle the threads of ancient Greek religion. For the Cambridge school, as it came to be called, many forms of folklore could be traced to ancient ritual activities. These scholars scrutinized folktales, legends, myths, folk drama, and children's games for the ancient ritual practices underlying them: for example, Jane Ellen Harrison traced the roots of classical Greek drama and the Olympics to ancient rituals of death and resurrection. The Cambridge school had a tremendous influence on an entire generation of European and American scholars, as well as on the popular imagination. Fifty years after its emergence, Italian scholar Paolo Toschi still searched for the roots of the commedia dell'arte in the fertility rituals of Classical Greece and Rome as preserved by Italian peasants, while Theodore Gaster (1906–92) interpreted the motif of the dying and reviving god as underlying all seasonal rituals in *Thepsis* (1950). He saw calendar customs as involving cyclical rites of *kenosis* (emptying) and *plenosis* (filling) that symbolized death and resurrection. The myth-ritualists saw ritual as both the source and an enactment of myth—a universal monomyth that always involves death and rebirth. The study of folklore was thus central in constructing the idea that pagan rites were concerned with fertility—an idea that, while not necessarily completely wrong, ignored many other aspects of popular customs that may be much more important to tradition bearers. In any case, as a result of the diffusion of the theories of Frazer and the myth-ritualists, the idea of fertility as the main concern of ritual, especially calendrical ritual, became central to Neo-Pagan cosmology. And the practice of ritual as a form of cultural critique, an attempt to recapture what had been lost through the Reformation and industrialization, became the core of Neo-Pagans' search for authentic connections.

In part through the influence of Romanticism, and in part because of emerging new discourses about ritual, interest in the Western spiritual tradition reemerged into European popular consciousness in the middle of the nineteenth century, and took shape in a variety of movements, including Spiritualism and occultism.[10] Spiritualism revived, in a new guise, the ancient idea that the living could communicate with the dead, and imagined an otherworld, free from Christian constraints, that operated according to the laws of evolution. The new occultism, spearheaded by the French radical Eliphas Levi, blended Hermetic and kabbalistic materials with new ideas coming out of Asia. Levi's works successfully reclaimed many elements of the Western spiritual tradition and recast them in Romantic terms that had a tremendous appeal in nineteenth-century Europe, especially among intellectuals, nationalists, and revolutionaries. The blending of Spiritualism with the new European occultism in intellectual circles led to the emergence new spiritual movements, such as Theosophy, under the direction of Helena Blavatsky, and the Order of the Golden Dawn, an English society dedicated to the exploration of the new occultism; and to the introduction of the Eastern idea of reincarnation as an evolution of the soul. The incorporation of Eastern mysticism and ideas such as reincarnation into the spiritual bricolage of late nineteenth-century Europe and North America paralleled the expansion of Western political and cultural hegemony throughout the globe (Hutton, 1999:83). The result was a fusion of new ideas that contributed to the crucible in which Neo-Paganism was forged at the turn of the twentieth century. By the late ninteenth century, as Hutton asserts, "occultism became the language of the radical counter-culture. . . . It offered the thinkers of the age a middle way between a defensive Christian orthodoxy and a science which threatened to despiritualize the universe and question the special status of humanity" (72). Like parallel ideas in the developing fields of psychology and the human potential movement, late nineteenth-century occultism was "therapy designed to enable human beings to evolve further into deities" (82).

## Folklorist Cocreators: Leland, Murray, and Gardner

Modern Neo-Paganism would not have come to be were it not for the contributions of three amateur folklorists: Charles G. Leland, Margaret Murray, and Gerald B. Gardner. Significantly, while all three were members of folklore societies,[11] none of these authors had any formal training in folkloristics or anthropology. Yet they were conversant with some of the principal ideas from these disciplines, at least as they were embraced by well-educated middle-class Britons and Americans. It was in their popularized form that academic ideas entered the culture of the Neo-Pagan movement. This should not lead us to discount them; rather, it is a study in how influential academic theories can become outside of the Ivory Tower, even when they have been abandoned by academicians.[12]

## Charles G. Leland

Charles G. Leland (1824–1903) was born in Philadelphia to a well-to-do family.[13] From an early age, he was drawn to magic—some sources suggest because of the influence of his Pennsylvania German nanny (Mathiesen, 1998:26). As a young man, he became familiar with Cornelius Agrippa's *De occulta philosophia*, and at Princeton he read the works of the Neoplatonic philosophers and the Hermetic texts, as well as modern languages and literature. After college, he traveled to Europe, where he became familiar in Germany with the emergent discipline of *Volkskunde* (folkloristics) in all of its Romantic and survivalist glory. He also was exposed to radical nationalist ideologies that were swirling about in student circles. Swept up in the revolutionary fervor of 1848, he joined other students in Paris on February 24, 1848, and fought against the royalist troops of King Louis-Phillipe. His experiences with revolutionary zeal and the science of folkloristics were to leave a deep impression on Leland, which was reflected in many of his later writings.

After a period in the United States, during which Leland worked as a journalist for P. T. Barnum's sensationalistic *Illustrated News*, he and his wife returned to Europe, where he took up his avocation as collector of folklore. The Lelands frequented a sophisticated but eccentric crowd; many of their friends were Spiritualists and, later, Theosophists. In Britain, Leland developed an interest in Romany culture; he published extensively on the Gypsies between 1879 and 1891, and became the first president of the Gypsy Lore Society. In the 1880s, Leland visited Italy and became fascinated with collecting Italian folklore. His first work on the subject, *Etruscan Roman Remains in Popular Tradition* (1892), reflects many of the folkloristic ideas that he must have absorbed in his student days in Germany. Leland perceived Italian folklore, especially narratives and beliefs, as survivals of ancient Etruscan culture. His principal methodology seems to have been to travel through upper Tuscany and lower Emilia-Romagna, an area of Etruscan settlement, and to ask peasants whether they had heard of this or that Etruscan deity. At the time, Classical scholars still had a rather rudimentary understanding of the Etruscan language; much of their information was based on guesswork and on comparison of tomb inscriptions with information preserved by Roman authors. None of this deterred Leland from finding that Emilian and Tuscan peasant culture perfectly preserved cultural memories of Etruscan deities and customs. Still, *Etruscan Roman Remains* presents what is fairly typical Italian folklore, with analogues in numerous archival and scholarly collections: legends about witchcraft, the devil, and various types of local spirits, intermixed with a few folktales.

In 1888–89, Leland spent about a year in Florence. Shortly before this time he had made the acquaintance of a woman whom he called Maddalena, whose family lived near the Ponte Vecchio and who seems to have practiced fortune telling and charm making (Mathiesen, 1998:30). She became his principal informant for *Legends of Florence* and the source for all of the material in his most influential work, *Aradia; or The Gospel of the Witches* (1899). *Aradia* is a very different work from either *Etruscan Roman Remains* or *Legends of Florence*, although some material from *Legends* is repeated in *Aradia*. While the former present narratives, mostly legends mixed with folktales, that have clear analogues in European folklore, much of the material in *Aradia* is unique. In it, Leland purports to present the *vangelo*, or gospel, of Italian witches: women and men who follow *la vecchia religione* (the old religion) and worship Diana and her daughter Aradia, or Herodias, as a female messiah, sent to earth by Diana to teach peasants how to resist the oppression of the landed classes through sorcery. The witches meet naked when the moon is full to worship the goddess, and make a witches' supper consisting of crescent-shaped cakes of flour, salt, and honey. Leland gives instructions for conjuring the flour used in making cakes and for charming holy stones, for gathering rue and vervain for magical purposes and for compelling Diana to grant her worshippers' desires. To these, Leland adds material Maddalena told him separately from the gospel, as well as much of his own interpretation.

Mathiesen (1998:30) has carefully studied Leland's manuscripts, concluding that Maddalena was a real person, a woman named Margherita with whom Leland had a long correspondence even after he left Florence. Yet he also determines that Leland's editing, translation, and interpretation of Maddalena's material was strongly influenced by his own views of witchcraft, politics, and religion. Moreover, Maddalena represents only one voice on Italian occultism, and one that in all likelihood emerged as part of an intersubjective process between researcher and informant, in which she consciously or unconsciously shaped her answers to fit what Leland wanted or expected. "Maddalena to a certain extent invented herself in response to the interests and enthusiasms of her friend Leland, who . . . became her patron as well as her friend" (Mathiesen, 1998:49).

While Leland may not have manufactured the material in *Aradia* out of whole cloth, it is clear that he had a heavy hand in shaping it. Like many folklorists of his time, he may have seen this as essential to the process of "restoring" a tradition that was fragmentary or disappearing. Yet in the process, the original character of the material has been completely obscured. Instead, we are left with a pastiche of Italian folk rhymes and spells mixed with Leland's conjectures about witchcraft as a pagan survival, and with his political ideology grounded in the idealistic revolutionary climate of his youth. As Hutton illustrates, Leland's imaginative capacities were well known among contemporary members of the American Folklore Society and even his obituary writer makes reference to them (Hutton, 1999:147); and so his work was never taken seriously by either American or Italian folklorists. But it contributed greatly to the emergence of the Witchcraft revival, the central component of Neo-Paganism, including:

the concept of witchcraft as a religion of peasant resistance and a continuation of Classical paganism;

the idea that witches meet at the time of the full moon;

the name "Aradia" for one of the principal goddesses in revival Witchcraft;

part of the text of the "Charge of the Goddess," by which Diana instructs her followers, later rewritten by Gardner's high priestess Doreen Valiente;

the practice of naked worship, still maintained by Gardnerian and Alexandrian covens at private celebrations;

the equation of certain elements of peasant culture—legends, beliefs, divination, and folk medicine—with the practice of witchcraft, so that the presence of the former stood as proof of the existence of the latter.

This last concept is especially significant to the development of revival Witchcraft and Neo-Paganism. Combined with the contributions of Margaret Murray and Gerald B. Gardner by the early twentieth century it created a conflation of folklore with witchcraft in the popular imagination.

## Margaret Murray

Like Leland, Margaret Murray (1862–1963) was never a professional folklorist; her field was Egyptology.[14] She had even less training in folklore than him—Leland had, after all, attended lectures at German universities where current ideas about folklore were presented, but Murray could not pursue the study of folklore in Britain because at the time it was not offered as a subject in universities (Simpson, 1994:95). Yet, like Leland, she was profoundly influenced by the survivalism that permeated the study of popular traditions in her time, especially the works of Frazer; and, also like Leland, she possessed a fiery passion for a political cause: suffragism (Hutton, 1999:194). A student of the archeologist Sir Flinders Petrie, she was forced to halt her labors in Egypt by the outbreak of the First World War, turning her attention instead to the European witch trials of the sixteenth and seventeenth centuries. Murray's thesis, presented first as a series of papers and later as *The Witch Cult of Western Europe* (1921), was that witchcraft was the survival of an ancient pagan religion once practiced throughout most of Europe, which Inquisitors mistook for devil worship. A rationalist and skeptic at heart, Murray's goal was to give a rational interpretation to the European witch craze, a historical problem that continued to bedevil interpreters. Drawing on Frazer's theories, Murray presented this religion as a fertility cult centered on a horned god who symbolized the fecundity of herd animals and crops. In rituals, his part was played by a man wearing a horned mask, whom Christian Inquisitors misunderstood as the devil.

Murray's witches worshipped in groups of thirteen called covens, which met to celebrate esbats (full moons) and sabbats (the cross-quarter days between each solstice and equinox: that is, February 2, May 1, August 1, and November 1). Their rituals included circle dancing (a pan-European form of folk dance interpreted by nineteenth-century folklorists as a fertility rite), feasting, magic spells, the worship of their god in the person of the horned man, and sexual relations between participants and the god to encourage fertility. Murray initially added the less appealing practices of child and animal sacrifice, which she deemphasized considerably in her later book, *The God of the Witches* (1933). She adopted Leland's term for witchcraft, "the old religion," and gave it an ancient history stretching back to Paleolithic times (Hutton, 1999:197).

Murray's thesis was baseless, and was attacked as such by W. B. Halliday in a 1922 review in the British journal *Folklore* (Halliday, 1922:224–30, quoted in Simpson, 1994:90). In fact, Jacqueline Simpson argues that despite the publication of her book by Oxford University Press and her appearance in other contemporary folklore and anthropology journals, none of Murray's anthropological or folkloristic contemporaries took her very seriously. The greatest appeal of her theory was that it "broke the deadlock," as Simpson puts it, between specious witch-craze scholars such as Montague Summers, on one hand, who believed in the existence of actual devil worshippers with supernatural powers; and skeptics, on the other, who interpreted the witch crazes as "hysterical panics whipped up by the Churches for devious political or financial reasons," and witches as innocent victims whose fantastic tales were produced under torture (Simpson, 1994:90). Murray's greatest appeal was not among academically trained experts, but with popular readers. As Hutton explains, "It appealed to so many of the emotional impulses of the age: to the notion of the English countryside as a timeless place full of ancient secrets, to the literary cult of Pan as its deity, to the belief that until comparatively recently Christianity had represented only a veneer of elite religion covering a persistence of paganism among the masses, and to the characterization of modern folk customs as survivals from that paganism" (Hutton, 1999:199).

Murray's important contributions to the reclamation of witchcraft and paganism include:

the idea of witchcraft as an ancient pagan fertility cult that existed throughout Europe in much the same form, with roots in the Paleolithic;

the presence of the horned god in the person of the high priest, and his consort "the maiden";

the terms *coven, esbat,* and *sabbat*;

the circle dance as the witches' fertility dance;

sexual relations as a form of fertility magic at meetings;

the Christian misunderstanding and persecution of witchcraft;

a vague conception of the witchcraft religion as "Celtic," or of having survived longest in Celtic language areas such as Scotland, from which many of Murray's trial records came;

the persistence of this ancient religion in Europe until well into the seventeenth century.

As Simpson notes, however, Murray's idea of witchcraft is still very far from modern Neo-Pagan Witchcraft (Simpson, 1994:92). Nowhere in either of her books on witchcraft is any goddess mentioned. The maiden exists only as a consort for the horned god, not as a deity in her own right. For contemporary Witches and Pagans, in contrast, the goddess is the most important divine element; the god, her consort and son, is second in importance, and in some feminist versions of Witchcraft does not appear at all. It would take the genius of Gerald B. Gardner to transform popular notions about witchcraft as a folk survival into a new religion.

## Gerald B. Gardner

Gerald B. Gardner (1884–1964) is generally credited with the invention of modern Neo-Pagan Witchcraft. The story is more complicated than one of simple invention, for as we have seen, many of the elements of revival Witchcraft were already in place by the time Gardner was born into a middle-class family in Blundellsands, England, in 1884. Gardner had very little formal education. An asthmatic child, he did not attend school, and was tutored instead by governesses; one of them, Josephine McCombie, or "Com," as he called her, was to have a significant influence on his life (Bracelin, 1960:14). Because of his poor health, Gardner, accompanied by Com, traveled to the warm Mediterranean during the winters of his childhood, visiting the Canary Islands, Madeira, North Africa, and southern France. During these long voyages, the boy kept himself amused by reading adventure novels. Perhaps due to this early exposure to other cultures, and the romance of the novels that constituted his only form of instruction, he developed a passion for travel and an interest in anything that could be considered exotic. At the age of sixteen, he sailed with Com to Ceylon, where her husband had a tea plantation.

Gardner worked there for several years before continuing his colonial career as a manager of tea and rubber plantations in Borneo and a customs inspector in Malaysia.

While Gardner had been initiated as a Freemason in Ceylon (Bracelin, 1960:35), it was during his stay in Malaysia from 1908 to 1936 that he became interested in magic. He documented the spirit beliefs and practices of the Dayak peoples who lived deep in the rainforests of Borneo, attending what he called their "seances," borrowing the Spiritualist term to describe an indigenous Dayak divination practice (Bracelin, 1960:46–47).[15] As a result of his exposure to these practices, he developed a keen interest in anthropology and folklore. Always an autodidact, he began to read widely in those disciplines, amassed a large collection of indigenous artifacts, and even published several journal articles and monographs on Malay material culture. Gardner's voice in his early works is that of an amateur anthropologist or folklorist. His writings demonstrate keen observation skills and a pedantic tendency; his musings on origins and meanings from this stage in his career reflect the kinds of assumptions common in folklore and anthropology from that period—for example, the search for historical contacts between the Roman Empire and Asia through the study of material culture and numismatics.

In 1939, after retiring from his position as a customs inspector, Gardner and his wife, Donna, returned to Britain. The couple settled in Highcliffe, a suburb of Bournemouth, south of the New Forest region. After his exciting life abroad, Gardner must have found himself slightly bored with conventional suburban English society. He began to frequent esoteric circles: he joined the Rosicrucian Theater, an amateur dramaturgical society, in Christchurch, Hampshire, and through this group was drawn into a network of British occultists. In Bracelin's biography,[16] Gardner claims that it was through a small group of actors at the theater who called themselves the Crotona Fellowship that he met a local woman, whom he refers to as Old Dorothy, who headed a coven of Witches that practiced an ancient pre-Christian religion in the area of New Forest. This group he referred to as the New Forest Coven. He was initiated as a member, and became so fascinated with their practices that he devoted the rest of his life to publicizing his discoveries. In 1954, he published *Witchcraft Today*, an explanation of his findings.

Gardner portrays himself as an anthropologist presenting the facts about a group with which he has done fieldwork:

> Now I am an anthropologist, and it is agreed that an anthropologist's job is to investigate what people do and believe. . . . It is also his task to read as many writings as possible on the matter he is investigating, though not accepting such writings uncritically, especially when in conflict with the evidence as he finds it. Anthropologists may draw their own conclusions and advance any theories of their own, but they must make it clear that these are their own conclusions and their own theories and not proven facts; and this is the method I propose to adopt. In dealing with native races, one records their

folklore, the stories and religious rites on which they base their beliefs and actions. So why not do the same with English witches? (Gardner, 1954:18)

Yet it is clear that he freely mixes "fact" with interpretation throughout the book, making it difficult, at times, to separate what his Witches said and believed about themselves from what Gardner believed about them. Only a few paragraphs after the above passage, Gardner offers this analysis:

> Nearly all primitive people had initiation ceremonies and some of these were initiations into priesthoods, into magic powers, secret societies and mysteries. They were usually regarded as necessary for the welfare of the tribe as well as the individual. They usually included purification and some test of courage and fortitude—often severe and painful—terrorization, instruction in tribal lore, in sexual knowledge, in the making of charms, and in religious and magical matters generally, and often a ritual of death and resurrection. . . . I hold that witches, being the descendants of primitive people, do in fact do many of [these things]. . . . their practices are the remnants of a Stone Age religion and they keep to their old ways. (Gardner, 1954:19–20)

This passage clearly shows the survivalist assumptions, common to many early twentieth-century folklorists and anthropologists, with which Gardner was working.

Surprisingly little of *Witchcraft Today* actually describes the Witches' beliefs, rituals, and practices. The reader learns that Gardner's Witches worship a goddess and a horned god; that they believe that power resides within their bodies, and can be released by vigorous dancing in a circle; that they dance naked because they believe the wearing of clothes impedes the release of this power; that they conduct their ceremonies within a circle, which is "cast" by marking with chalk or by tracing with a black-hilted knife called an *athame*; that the circle is said to be "between the worlds" of the Witches and their gods, and is drawn to keep in the power that they raise; that they celebrate four sabbats, or major festivals, at May eve, August eve, November eve, and February eve, and that these correspond to the Gaelic "fire festivals" of Beltaine, Lughnassad, Samhain, and Brigid; and that they believe in reincarnation, after a period of rest and refreshment in a beautiful otherworld. Gardner presents snippets of their Yule ritual, performed around December 22, but omits that from the list of major festivals in the year cycle.[17] He also gives two crucial texts: the myth of the goddess's descent into the underworld, and the Charge of the Goddess (this was later reworked by Doreen Valiente).

The rest of the book is Gardner's attempt to contextualize the Witch religion based on survivalist theories and an anecdotal knowledge of history. Following Frazer and Murray, he calls the religion a fertility cult, and is particularly fond of linking it with the practices of "primitive" peoples throughout the world, with the religion of the Druids, and with the Greek, Roman, and Egyptian mystery cults. He suggests the origin of the religion in Britain might be attributable to the "little people," an early, small-statured race of inhabitants driven into the hills by later invaders and branded as "fairies." While these types of interpretations had long been rejected by the academic community in 1954, they are in keeping with the survivalist analyses that folklorists and anthropologists were making in Gardner's youth, fifty years earlier, and which remained prevalent in popular culture. These interpretations later became canonized as part of the sacred narrative of Witchcraft, along with Gardner's conjectural historical accounts, such as those linking the witch religion with the practices of the Knights Templar. Like many anthropologists and folklorists of the time, Gardner saw himself as doing "salvage anthropology": he considered Witchcraft to be a dying religion, and believed his duty was to preserve this material for posterity and to help keep it alive, if not altogether to restore it to its glorious original form.

But did Gardner in fact discover a coven of Witches practicing in the New Forest, or was the book an elaborate attempt to authenticate a religion he himself had concocted? Scholarly interpretations of the facts differ. Some critics (Rose, 1962; Kelly, 1991; Baker, 1996) have assumed that Gardner invented revival Witchcraft out of whole cloth—according to Kelly, for the purposes of his own sexual titillation (Kelly, 1991:27–29). Kelly's methodology and assumptions have been critiqued by Frew (1998) and Hutton (1999), and we have seen that much of the material in revival Witchcraft was already in place by the early twentieth century, so Gardner could not have completely invented it. But the question remains: how much, if any, of what Gardner presents actually existed before he formed his own coven in the late 1950s?

Hutton has argued that Gardner's story of "Old Dorothy," often identified as Dorothy Clutterbuck, a society matron in the New Forest area during the 1930s, is a red herring: Dorothy Clutterbuck seems to have had neither an interest in the occult nor a connection to Gerald Gardner and his social circle (Hutton, 1999:207–12).[18] But this does not prove that there was no coven—only that Dorothy Clutterbuck did not lead one. Gardner, in his impish way, may have used the name of a prominent socialite to distract attention from his real cocreator, a leading member of the Rosicrucian Theater and the Crotona Fellowship known only by her pseudonym "Dafo" (Hutton, 1999: 212–13). It is possible that by the late 1930s and early 1940s, members of the Crotona Fellowship were already performing rituals based on Co-Masonry (Dafo was a Co-Mason) and inspired by the writings of Margaret Murray, and that this was the group Gardner referred to as the New Forest Coven. The evidence for this is scanty, but may be provided by a document discovered behind a filing cabinet in Gardner's personal library. This notebook, entitled "Ye Bok of ye Art Magical," may be considered the earliest extant version of a Book of Shadows of modern Neo-Pagan Witchcraft.

While I have not seen the entire manuscript myself, I have seen portions of it in photographic reproduction. My analysis is based partially on what I have seen and partially on the interpretations of my consultants Don Frew, Anna Korn, and Allyn Wolfe, who have seen the entire manuscript, and the considerations of Ronald Hutton (1999:227–32). It appears that Gardner went to great pains to make this manuscript look like his idea of a medieval grimoire: he bound a number of sheets of paper into a leather cover taken from another book, the contents of which he had removed. The writing on the leather cover and in parts of the book itself is done in careful calligraphy. Some words are misspelled, perhaps intentionally, to make them appear archaic, or perhaps as a result of copier's errors. The book contains a collection of materials that appear to be copied from a variety of sources: S. Liddell MacGregor Mathers's nineteenth-century edition of the *Key of Solomon*, the Bible, the Kabbalah, and some works of Aleister Crowley. The book also contains several colored drawings. Gardner did not copy the texts sequentially; rather, he seems to have started copying various things at the same time in different parts of the notebook, leaving spaces in which he could fit more materials. In some cases, he appears to have written unrelated items onto sheets he had originally reserved for other material; the result is a jumble that is confusing and difficult to follow. Many of the pages show obvious copier's errors: words and sometimes entire lines are left out, then added later above the text; errors are inked over or crossed out as the copier is going along, with the effect that mistakes that appear in the originals are reproduced in "Ye Bok."

Mixed in with this copied material are rudimentary versions of the first- and second-degree Witchcraft initiations, along with another rite which eventually came to be part of the third-degree initiatory materials. The rituals differ from the rest of the texts: they are written in a much larger script, as if they were meant to be read from a distance. The Wiccan materials also utilize a kind of shorthand of symbols. In form and content, the initiations are similar to the Gardnerian initiations that appear in later Books of Shadows, and that continue to be used by Gardnerian Witches today. Occasionally Gardner has added marginal notes and stage directions to the rituals, such as "usually omitted nowadays." The insertion of marginalia suggests that he was commenting on an already existing practice; after all, if he had invented the rituals himself, there would have been no need to add commentary and stage directions.

The presence of these Witch texts in a book of material that Gardner clearly copied from preexisting sources has led some to hypothesize that Gardner may also have copied the Witch materials from an existing textual source—perhaps something in use by Dafo and other members of the Crotona Fellowship. Tantalizing new evidence to this effect comes from the Book of Shadows of the New Wiccan Church (NWC) in California's Central Valley. Allyn Wolfe, a high priest of the NWC, has compared his group's sacred texts with those of Gardner's notebook, and has deduced that the many similarities between them, as well as the differences between them and other early versions of the Gardnerian Book of Shadows, point to the existence of a prior work from which *both* "Ye Bok of ye Art Magical" and the NWC Book of Shadows were copied. This hypothetical prototext could have belonged to an early twentieth-century British occult group, a predecessor of the group that Gardner observed, one of whose members left Britain sometime between 1939 and 1951 to settle in California's Central Valley.

These data suggest that Gardner's claims of discovering a Witch coven may have some merit; only the society he discovered, far from being a survival from the Stone Age, was an early twentieth-century English occult group experimenting with rituals based on Masonic structures, overlaid with materials from MacGregor Mathers's *Key of Solomon* and from other contemporary magical texts. Proponents of this argument hold that Gardner himself was not a skilled ritualist, and in fact avoided inventing rituals even when he could have amply indulged his fantasy. In his novel *A Goddess Arrives*, he hints at rites but never actually describes them in detail, while in *High Magic's Aid*, what details he gives seem to be drawn from Mathers's rendition of Solomonic material. Doreen Valiente, who served as Gardner's high priestess from 1953 to 1957 and rewrote much of the material in the Book of Shadows, always asserted that Gardner's forte was not ritual creation, but that he encouraged his coveners to write and revise rituals.

It is also possible that Gardner may have quite deliberately set up "Ye Bok" to make it appear that material he invented was in fact copied, thus lending it a veneer of authenticity. Gardner was known to his associates for his playful qualities and mischievous sense of humor. Among his antics, he claimed to have had a doctorate—in reality a mail-order certificate—and was known to have produced additional "authentic" Witch material that fit specific circumstances a bit too suspiciously even for his followers.[19] This was the case of the "Craft Laws," a set of rules and regulations that did not appear in the early Books of Shadows (although elements of them are scattered in some of Gardner's earlier writings), but which Gardner was able to produce almost overnight to resolve a dispute among coven members in the 1950s. These incidents suggest that he possessed the type of personality that might have delighted in fooling people through an elaborate hoax. If Gardner set up "Ye Bok" as a hoax, however, his plan backfired, because by 1951 he had lost the copy book, which was discovered behind a file cabinet in his library only after his death.

A third possibility exists: that Gardner, like many folklorists of the nineteenth century, sincerely believed he had stumbled upon an ancient tradition in the practices of the Crotona Fellowship, and set about documenting it and contextualizing it. Given his interest in folklore and anthropology, and the reigning myth-ritualist interpretations of the day, it is not unlikely that he might have decided to "reconstruct" certain elements that he surmised might be missing or lost. He based his interpretations and reconstruction on Frazer's survivalist theories, and on the conjectures of Margaret Murray and Charles G. Leland. The result, of course, was not an ancient religion at all, but a brand new one that perfectly fit the spirit of the times and would gain unprecedented diffusion in the late twentieth century. If this hypothesis is true, Gardner was working in the tradition of nineteenth-century folklorists, who, in the attempt to restore ancient traditions, forged new ones that led to reclamation of national cultures. Gardner's *Witchcraft Today*, then, must be considered next to Elias Lönnrot's *Kalevala*, James Macpherson's *Ossian*, and the Grimms' *Kinder- und Hausmärchen*.

Ultimately, the question of whether Gardner invented revival Witchcraft, or merely discovered a group of English occult practitioners whose rituals he interpreted and publicized, is moot. What is clear is that by the early 1950s Gardner had started a coven of his own; new versions of his Book of Shadows were being copied by his initiates as early as 1953. Some among them shaped the material to their own tastes as well as adding their own embellishments. Gardner's findings were already becoming a tradition; instead of disappearing, as he had feared it would, Witchcraft was taking on a vibrant new life. It is also evident that the disciplines of folkloristics and anthropology had an enormous impact on the interpretation Gardner gave to the occult materials he either came upon or elaborated for his own purposes. All later changes and developments in revival Witchcraft have been based on his interpretations, or in reaction to them.

## Poaching in the Stacks

In *The Practice of Everyday Life*, French sociologist Michel DeCerteau pioneered the notion of consumers as "textual poachers," whose consumption of mass culture subtly undermines the uses for which its creators intended it (DeCerteau, 1984).[20] This idea was elaborated by Henry Jenkins in his study of North American television fan subculture. Jenkins defined textual poaching as "a type of cultural bricolage through which readers fragment texts and reassemble the broken shards according to their own blueprint, salvaging bits and pieces of the found material in making sense of their own cultural experience" (Jenkins, 1992:26) He argues that textual poaching subverts the notion of consumers as passive receptors of cultural productions; the fans in his study emerge as vibrant, creative individuals who seek their own personal meaning in texts meant for mass consumption, and express their interpretations in their own participatory productions (Jenkins, 1992). Mass culture, he concludes, is more participatory than it first appeared to be.

The emergence of Neo-Paganism and revival Witchcraft can be interpreted according to this model as an attempt by small groups of readers to create imaginative, artistic productions (texts, narratives, or rituals) inspired by the survivalist texts of nineteenth-century folkloristics and anthropology. Neo-Paganism's creators were first and foremost readers of history, archeology, anthropology, religion, mythology, and folklore, whose productions were situated primarily on the margins of the academy, putting them in a tenuous position vis-à-vis the academic establishment. Thus, they sought both to construct authenticity for their practices according to academic paradigms, and simultaneously rejected academic authority as the ultimate seal of approval for their productions. Like DeCerteau's resisting consumers and Jenkins's textual poachers, they put academic texts to uses that subverted the intentions of their producers by creating traditions that seemed to demonstrate current theories yet simultaneously belied them.

The creation of authenticity expressed in artifacts such as "Ye Bok of ye Art Magical," or in the books of Leland, Murray, and Gardner, must be seen as a necessary element in the presentation of folklore, according to the narrative paradigms of the late nineteenth and early twentieth centuries. Thus Gardner's fervent avowals of folkloristic and anthropological objectivity, and his portrayal of Wicca as a religion passed down orally from time immemorial, is part of the authenticating process that *all* folklorists and anthropologists once engaged in. It is a narrative style, a way to fit evidence into the master narrative of survivals—a device or trope for creating authenticity for the practices one is documenting.

The process of creating tradition based on anthropological and folkloristic texts continues unabated among American Witches and Pagans today. Pagans are extraordinarily well informed about folkloristics and anthropology. Among them, I have found individuals whose knowledge of folklore and anthropology rivals that of some of my academic colleagues. Yet it is usually not academic theories that interest Witches and Pagans, but ethnographic facts and tidbits, especially material dealing with folktale, myth, ritual, and the year cycle. As Don Frew explained to me: "So many Pagans are anthropologists, or anthropology students, or amateur anthropologists. Part of being a reconstructive tradition is acquiring the skills to do the reconstruction, so you get practically everybody studying folklore and anthropology. . . . The same skills the anthropologist is applying to understand why people are doing things, we're . . . applying to say, 'How can we understand what they're doing so we can do it right?' . . . So [anthropology] has absolutely informed modern Paganism as one of our key tools."

Don also points out, however, that "a lot of folks just aren't up to speed on current anthropology, so they're using nineteenth-century sources. And . . . the very Romanticism that characterizes nineteenth-century stuff lends itself to Paganism." In part, this is because many major reference works continue to reproduce the sorts of survivalist interpretations common one hundred years ago. But, as Don explains, it is also the case that today's anthropological and folkloristic theories do not suit modern Pagans' and Witches' needs as well as those from a century ago.

## Summary

While they are modern religions, Neo-Paganism and Witchcraft are heirs to a venerable pedigree stretching back to Classical times. The Western occult tradition that they inherited has a checkered history, appearing in the Hermetic texts and Chaldean Oracles, reemerging in the grimoires of medieval and Renaissance sorcerers and prescientists, and finding a home in the secret societies of seveneenth- and eighteenth-century Europe. Because of its nature as a marginal discourse after the emergence of the Enlightenment and the scientific revolution, the language of the occult has often been the language of the counterculture as well. During the late 1800s and early 1900s, a number of groups emerged that revived and reclaimed this language in various guises, seeking authentic experience as an antidote to growing urbanization, industrialization, and the disenchantment of the world. The emerging disciplines of folkloristics and anthropology contributed to this search by locating authenticity in the traditions of European peasants and colonized peoples. In some circles, *folklore* became almost synonymous with magic and witchcraft, in that its presence was considered an indicator of a magical worldview. By the mid-twentieth century, a new religion had emerged, steeped in the academic literature on folklore and anthropology, which sought to give adherents a taste of authentic spiritual experience as it was presumed to exist in the cultures of the marginalized and colonized. That religion, which was to migrate to North America by the early 1960s, was Neo-Pagan Witchcraft.

*Chapter 2*

# Boundaries and Borders: Imagining Community

**Field notes, August 5, 1997**

In the process of helping me move, Berkeley Gardnerian elders Don Frew and Anna Korn came across some boxes in my basement that contained the relics of my childhood fascination with troll dolls. In them, we found the remnants of the troll temple, a cardboard structure decorated with childish paintings of earth, air, fire, and water, the principal elemental deities of the troll religion I had invented. Then there were the books I had crafted for the troll library: tiny, hand-lettered volumes that included *The Iliad* and *The Odyssey*, *The Mabinogion*, medieval Welsh poet Aneirin's *Y Gododdin*, as well as made up titles, such as *The Hirlas* (troll epic poetry) and *The Private Lives of Woodland Creatures*. As Anna unwrapped the troll kitchen, she exclaimed in amazement that she could assemble a complete troll altar set: candles, a cauldron, a cup, a broom, even a tiny knife. Don surveyed the toys and said with conviction, as if he meant to settle the matter once and for all, "You're a Pagan. No doubt about it." He explained that these childhood interests were typical of those who then grew up to become Neo-Pagans. Don described Paganism as if it were somehow innate or essential, its seeds already present in childhood. Paganism is understood by many in the movement to be part of a soul's essence, something remembered from past lives and carried on into the future. Witches sometimes use the proverbial expression "Once a witch, always a witch" to imply that attraction to magical practice not only persists throughout a person's lifetime, but is continuous through all of one's past and future lifetimes.

The last chapter traced the roots of Neo-Paganism and revival Witchcraft to a spiritual tradition that has existed as an undercurrent in Western thought since Classical times. This chapter will show how this tradition has emerged in the many forms of Neo-Paganism and revival Witchcraft current in North America at the turn of the twenty-first century: the "branches" of the tree, as it were. In this section, I am concerned with Pagans vis-à-vis the surrounding dominant culture: how they create a sense of identity through which they distinguish themselves from it, as well as from other esoteric groups, and how the various Neo-Pagan traditions distinguish between each other.

In a seminal essay, folklorist Dorothy Noyes has pointed out the dual nature of the concept of "group": it refers, on one hand, to "empirical networks of interaction" in which culture is created and shaped, and on the other, to socially imagined communities in which individuals locate identity, but that, upon close examination, often actually are riven with difference on many levels (Noyes, 2003:11). These parameters are especially useful in understanding the dynamics of the American Neo-Pagan community. To the extent that it exists as a community at all, it is a collection of dense national and international networks of communication whose principal focus is the creation of a new religious culture. It is also a socially imagined community that both distinguishes itself from the surrounding non-Pagan culture, and creates boundaries and borders within itself. From these distinctions, individual Neo-Pagans may fashion an identity which often emerges in the context of performance: that is, at public rituals, festivals, celebrations, Neo-Pagan conferences, and online forums.

Folklore plays a central role in this process of group formation. Just as emerging nation-states turned to folklore for inspiration and answers to questions about their national essence, so Neo-Pagans, an emerging religious group, have created a body of expressive culture that delineates both the boundaries between Paganism and contiguous groups, and those between traditions within the movement itself. This lore both creates distinctions and acts to build a sense of shared identity. In this section, I examine these emerging traditions and analyze them for what they can tell us about points of conflict and confluence within the movement itself.

As the introductory description in this chapter illustrates, the idea of Paganism as something natural or inherent is common in the movement, and is a customary way Pagans narrate their own identity formation process as well as decide who "belongs to" the movement.[1] Yet the use of essentialist terminology is a clear indication of the constructed nature of the Pagan community. Benedict Anderson, writing about the creation of national identities, noted that "in everything 'natural,' there is always something unchosen. In this way, nation-ness is assimilated to skin-colour, gender, parentage and birth era—all those things one can not help. . . . precisely because such ties are not chosen, they have about them a halo of disinterestedness" (Anderson, 1991:143). Anderson was writing about nationhood; but the same arguments apply to ethnic, regional, and in this case religious groups. He argues that most communities are in fact imagined, and that they use the arguments of essence to create and legitimize their existence. Neo-Paganism has particularly compelling reasons for constructing itself in essentialist terms, as its boundaries are in a constant state of flux.

Determining the boundaries of the Pagan community is difficult for a number of reasons. Neo-Pagans do not, for the most part, separate themselves geographically from the surrounding culture. Membership is usually informal and nonexclusive: individuals may belong to a variety of groups, holding multiple initiations and attending some rituals but not others. In some cases, Pagans may think of themselves as belonging to other religious communities simultaneously: for example, I met numerous Jewish Pagans who felt their two religious identities were not mutually exclusive. Neo-Pagans also overlap or are contiguous with a number of other groups: these can include reenactment organizations such as the Society for Creative Anachronism and the Renaissance Pleasure Faire, role-playing gamers, science fiction and fantasy fans, environmentalists, feminists, Goths, folk musicians, and followers of the New Age movement.

Neo-Paganism is not an organized, unified movement, but a loose association of overlapping and interlocking networks stretching across the country and, in some cases, the globe. While there are certainly a number of well-known Pagan authors, there are no charismatic leaders or prophets as such, nor is there a single Pagan authority or unifying organization. The most basic unit of Pagan social organization is the small group, sometimes known as a *coven*, *grove*, or *circle*, consisting of anywhere between three and about fifteen members who meet on a regular basis, usually in each others' homes, to worship and practice magic. These small groups often affiliate with one of many denominations, known as *traditions*, which differ in liturgy, practice, and ritual style. (I will return to traditions later.) Representatives from many different traditions may join together in regional or national networking organizations, such as Pagan Spirit Alliance and Covenant of the Goddess, to sponsor gatherings or engage in social and political actions that benefit Pagans. Through these organizations, Pagans can participate in charitable projects and engage in interfaith dialogue with other religions. There are also numerous Witches and Pagans who choose not to affiliate with a group, but practice apart from covens, traditions, and networking organizations; these are known as "solitary practitioners" or "solitaries." Solitaries may occasionally participate in large public rituals and festivals and become active in social and political networks, but remain essentially unaffiliated with a coven, circle, or grove.

This fluidity of boundaries gives the movement both its great appeal and its essential individualistic character. Yet because of it, knowing who belongs to the Neo-Pagan community at any one time is nearly impossible. Outside the context of rituals, festivals, and other Pagan-centered events, Pagans are largely indistinguishable from other Americans. Although there are an increasing number of second and third generation Neo-Pagans, most are not born into a Pagan family, but become attracted to the religion sometime in early adulthood. Likewise, not all Pagans remain Pagans for life. Some leave the movement for other faiths or practices; others lose interest in it and distance themselves after a time. Within the movement itself, small groups or covens are notoriously unstable. Individuals may join a group, practice for awhile, then "hive off" to form a new group of their own; or they may join a series of different groups in succession, each of which may have a different practice and liturgy; or they may decide to practice on their own for long periods of time. The boundaries of the Neo-Pagan community, if such a thing can be said to exist at all, are clearly complex, shifting, and elastic. The terms "Pagan" and "Neo-Pagan" themselves are contested: most members prefer to call themselves "Pagan," emphasizing the continuity between their own religion and those of both ancient peoples and contemporary tribal and indigenous traditions.

North American Pagans like to emphasize the tremendous diversity within their movement: "For any two Pagans, you get at least three opinions" is an oft-cited proverb, emphasizing the high value they place on individualism, independent thinking, and antiauthoritarianism. This proverb also emphasizes Pagans' ability to hold multiple and even contradictory views simultaneously. These particularly American values suggest that North American Pagans are ambivalent about boundaries in general, tending to interpret them as restrictions on freedom of expression and individualism—a quality also noted by Pike (2001:113). But this lack of boundedness creates a dilemma for Pagans, who also idealize community and strive to create it, whether through covens, traditions, larger networking organizations, the Internet, or at festivals and summer camp-outs, which function as temporary communities (Pike, 2001). The fluidity and range of Pagan groups, as well as their isolation from one another, means that except for small communities such as covens, groves, circles, nests, and shared households, where members engage in regular face-to-face contact, Pagan communities are always "imagined communities" (Anderson, 1991). The tension between the desire for community and the desire for individualism is a central leitmotif in American Pagan culture, reflecting the presence of these twin conflicting desires in the surrounding dominant culture of the United States. It gives rise to the many ways Neo-Pagans separate themselves from mainstream society and from each other.

## Pagans in American Society

Neo-Paganism is one of the fastest-growing religious movements in North America. Its very fluidity, however, makes it difficult to accurately assess the number of practitioners. Estimates range from the relatively conservative five hundred thousand—five times the number Margot Adler found in her 1979 study—and the probably overstated one million. The truth is most likely somewhere around seven hundred thousand (www.religioustolerance.org/wic_nbr.htm, accessed November 15, 2003). Pagans and Witches are found throughout North America and Canada, but are especially concentrated in urban areas and university towns, where relative anonymity and freedom from social controls make it easier for them to find like-minded others and practice without excessive harassment. They belong to all age groups, and there is now an increasing number of second- and even third-generation Pagans who were raised in Pagan homes.

Their ethnic background tends to be predominantly, but not exclusively, Euro-American. While I have met several African American, Asian American, and Latino/a Pagans, the majority of individuals from nonwhite ethnic groups who are interested in spiritual reclamation are drawn to religions to which they feel an ethnic or cultural connection; those who do identify as Neo-Pagan often have special personal circumstances that attract them to the movement. These might be as simple as close friends who are practitioners, as was the case for Darrin Laurelsson, who is African American, or as complex as the cases of "Padma" and "Suzi." Padma's family was the only South Asian one in the small Midwestern town where her father was a college professor. Feeling isolated and misunderstood in high school, she found acceptance and enthusiasm for her Hindu religious heritage among Neo-Pagans. Suzi, whose grandmother had been a *mudang* (shaman) in Korea, saw herself as continuing a family tradition of communicating with the spirit world, albeit in a different form. I will discuss these cases further in Chapter 7.

Surveys demonstrate that Neo-Pagans are better educated than the average citizen (Eller, 1995:21–23; Orion, 1995:66–71). Almost 80 percent of the Pagans I interviewed were college-educated, and about 40 percent had attended graduate or professional school.[2] Higher educations did not always translate into higher incomes, though. As other researchers have observed (Orion, 1995:68), Pagans tend to gravitate toward the humanities and social sciences, disciplines that suffered tremendous cutbacks in the early 1990s; even advanced degrees in these fields left many graduates unemployed or underemployed. My coven mate Pitch, who had completed all coursework for a Ph.D. in anthropology at a research university in the late 1980s, was working in retail by the 1990s, unable to find other employment. Even Pagans with highly marketable degrees generally reject strictly materialistic values, preferring work that allows them to serve others and exercise their creativity. One attorney whom I interviewed (in 1996) chose to work as a public defender, rather than entering a prestigious law firm, because it was more consonant with her values. Many Pagans are employed in the fields of health care and computer science, while others support themselves by working as artists or artisans.

A discussion of Pagan occupations begs the question of Pagans and social class: is Neo-Paganism a middle-class movement, akin to what scholars have found for channeling, firewalking, ritual healing, and other forms of New Age spirituality (Brown, 1997; Danforth, 1989; Hess, 1993)? As the work of Michael Zweig has shown, however, the term "middle class" itself is problematic (Zweig, 2000). The American middle class, which he defines as the class situated between labor and capital, was severely fragmented by the economic transformation of the late twentieth century. Those professionals whose work brought them into contact with the upper classes did well economically, while those who worked primarily with the working class and the poor languished by comparison. According to Zweig, 62 percent of the labor force in the United States is working class, which he defines as nonmanagement workers who have little control over the pace or content of their labor. Viewed through Zweig's perspective, Pagans occupy a very particular niche in the American class hierarchy: while many have the education generally associated with the middle and upper classes, most are in effect part of the working class. Pagans' intellectual sophistication gives them the tools to critique the system of which they are a part, but not the power to opt out of it entirely. Their economic status makes the oppositional discourse of Neo-Paganism particularly appealing.

Gender and sexual orientation are two additional factors that make Neo-Pagans different from the American mainstream. About 60 percent of Neo-Pagans are women (Orion, 1995:60). This is because of the religions' focus on the divine feminine, its positive portrayal of women, and the many liturgical and creative opportunities the movement provides for women in contrast with mainstream Judaism and Christianity. Orion also found that 38 percent of Neo-Pagans identified as other than heterosexual on surveys (Orion, 1995:62), and my field data echoed her findings. Many lesbians, gay men, and bisexuals are drawn to Neo-Paganism because of its accepting attitude toward all sexual orientations, especially compared with the judgmental stance of most mainstream religions. Also, many Pagans are open to sexual experimentation to the same extent that they are interested in experimenting with new forms of spirituality. They may have sexual partners of both genders over the course of a lifetime, and be more willing to openly identify as other than heterosexual. In sexuality, as well as in other aspects, Paganism attracts intelligent nonconformists critical of the dominant paradigms.

## Creating Pagan Identities

If Pagans conceive of their religion as essential, they also put a tremendous amount of creative energy into forging Pagan identities. Perhaps because most adherents come to the movement as adults, Pagan identities are hardly ever taken for granted. Instead, they are performative, in Erving Goffman's sense of a carefully constructed presentation of the self that characterizes most people's social exchanges in everyday life (Goffman, 1959:1–16). Like most of us, Pagans seek to control the impression they make upon others in ways that vary according to the context in which they find themselves. For example, on the job, they may try to minimize any elements that could identify them as members of a misunderstood religious minority and jeopardize their employment. On the other hand, as Pike has lucidly demonstrated, at festivals, the performance of Pagan identities reaches its apotheosis through costuming, the decoration of personal space, and dance performances around the bonfire (Pike, 2001).

I have written extensively elsewhere about Neo-Pagan costuming, jewelry, and body art (Magliocco, 2001). Here I would like to add two observations. First, the costume of Neo-Pagans, whether in everyday life or in a festive context, is a form of coded communication, decipherable by others in the movement, that conveys important information about the wearer's affiliation, proclivities, and identity. For a group of religions that must often operate in secret, it is a powerful form of interaction and a not uncommon method for finding and connecting with others in the movement. Secondly, for Pagans as well as for all members of a consumer society, consumption itself becomes a form of identity: Pagans, like other modern consumers, build identity through their buying habits. Let us examine each of these briefly in turn.

Pagan folk costuming and personal presentations can be understood as a form of coding. Joan Radner and Susan Lanser, examining coding in American women's subcultures, argue that coding takes place in situations of power imbalance when the subdominant group cannot openly express its concerns because of the risk of discovery by the dominant group (Radner and Lanser, 1993:1–29). In Radner and Lanser's feminist study, the subdominant group was gender-based. This is also partly true of Neo-Pagans, a large percentage of whom are women; but the greater danger to them is not only male oppression, but discrimination from non-Pagans who may misunderstand Neo-Paganism as malevolent or dangerous. Coding therefore helps Pagans find each other and communicate without arousing suspicion from unsympathetic outsiders.

Coding can be *explicit,* as when the existence of a code is obvious even to those who cannot understand it; *complicit,* as when group members collectively determine a code drawn from esoteric experiences; or *implicit,* where not only the message but the very existence of a code may be concealed, even to the participants themselves (Radner and Lanser, 1993:5–7). Explicit coding in Neo-Paganism may involve the use of secret magical alphabets such as Theban. According to one anecdote I collected, Allyn Wolfe, a resident of California's Central Valley, a rural, agricultural part of the state with few openly Pagan residents, posted signs written entirely in Theban in Laundromats, grocery stores, and beauty parlors throughout the region. They read: "If you can read this, we might be related. Please call [telephone number, also in Theban]." To his amazement, he received several replies. Because he had used a specific variant of Theban unique to one branch of Craft tradition, he was able to reunite these separated strands of Witchcraft. The explicit code permitted these Witches to communicate in a very public place without arousing the suspicion of their neighbors.[3] An example of complicit coding is Pagan jewelry and costuming. Symbols such as the pentacle, or five-pointed star within a circle, the ankh, or Egyptian symbol of life, and the hammer of Thor are often worn as pendants, and identify the wearers as Witches, followers of Isis or a related form of Egytophile Paganism, or Norse Pagans, respectively. Implicit coding is much more difficult to identify, as it is often opaque even to its performers; in fact, Radner and Lanser argue that its use can be unconscious (1993:6). It is found most commonly in situations where the risk of exposure is greatest, and thus would not be a part of the more public Pagan culture that has developed around festivals and conventions. One could argue that consumption is one type of implicit coding.

Consumption, by which I mean buying habits, is one of the fundamental ways through which contemporary consumers create and perform identity (DeCerteau, 1984; Jenkins, 1993). The examples commonly cited in sociological studies involve the purchase of brand-name or designer products for the purpose of displaying status. This type of consumption is rarely found in the Neo-Pagan subculture, which is generally critical of the values of consumer capitalism and rejects status-seeking through conspicuous consumption. But Pagans are hardly opposed to commerce per se, and often use material culture as a form of identity display, as a casual perusal of any festival or convention reveals. Festivals and cons can resemble medieval marketplaces, jammed with booths and tents selling everything attendees might need to celebrate and display their Pagan identities. Consumers can purchase elaborate ritual costumes, from medieval-looking hooded cloaks to the beautiful, exotic leather masks of California artist Lauren Raine; jewelry to display their affiliation, such as pentacles, ankhs, Paleolithic goddess figurines, and totem animals; henna tattooing and other forms of body art; ritual tools, such as handmade athames (ritual knives), cups, pentacles, incense burners, candles, candle holders, and incense; home altar decorations such as goddess and god statuary; tarot cards and other divination products; tapes and CDs of Pagan music; and, of course, books. Pagans are, as we have seen, avid consumers of books, especially the exploding occult book market, but also in the fields of anthropology, archeology, feminism, environmental studies, history, folklore, and the natural sciences. Pagans define and perform their identity by owning such products, and can "read" the interests of other Pagans by looking at the products they own. Once I found a Pagan dinner guest perusing my collection of books and music cassettes. "I always like to see what people are reading and listening to," he explained, "because you can tell a lot about a person by looking at these things."

Most Pagan worship takes place inside people's homes or in their gardens; there are very few community Pagan temples or spaces, and where these exist, they almost invariably must be shared with other community groups. Paganism is therefore predominantly a domestic religion, one that requires equipping one's domestic space with the requisite ritual tools and accoutrements. In my study of Neo-Pagan altars, I found nearly all the Pagans I interviewed had domestic spaces that reflected their religious practice (Magliocco, 2001). For some, the altar was simply a small table or chest tucked away in a bedroom or a private corner. But a surprising number of Pagans gave their entire home over to their religion, cramming every available space with sacred images, altars, and holy bric-a-brac. For example, Karen Tate, a member of the Fellowship of Isis and founder of the Isis Ancient Cultures and Religions Society, and her husband, Roy, transformed the living room of their Venice, California, apartment into a temple of thanksgiving to Isis. Their walls are painted with columns reminiscent of those at the temple of Karnak in Egypt. There is a large altar with a statue of the goddess Isis, as well as minor altars to Bast, Sekhmet, and Anubis. Each altar is elaborately decorated in an Egyptian style, with bas-relief plaques, gilt accessories, and leopard-print fabric. Many of the items are handmade by Karen herself, or by her friend, local Pagan artist Catherine Farah, whose soft-sculpture cat goddesses figured prominently in my book *Neo-Pagan Sacred Art and Altars: Making Things Whole* (2001). Author Jennifer Reif has similarly transformed her otherwise ordinary apartment into a sanctuary for the goddess Demeter, subject of one of her books (Reif, 1999). She has hand-painted her walls with delicate pomegranate and vine motifs, while the altar, assembled from garden statuary and materials found at yard sales, is decorated with sheaves of wheat Reif grew herself in order to fully experience the agricultural cycle of the Mediterranean on which the mysteries of Eleusis were based. In these domestic shrines, the juxtaposition of images intensifies their sacred associations. For Pagan artists, religion is an all-encompassing passion; their personal, domestic space reflects and performs their religious identity.

As many researchers of the movement have noted, the creative act itself is sacred for Neo-Pagans; transforming one's domestic space into a sanctuary through artistry, craftsmanship, consumption, and a bricolage of found objects is a challenge many Pagans profoundly enjoy. These constantly evolving domestic sacred spaces both define and perform identity, and serve as reminders of the immanence of the sacred in this religious movement.

A third important way Pagans create and perform identity is through the use of sacred names. The adoption of a new name upon religious conversion or confirmation has a venerable tradition; it is common to Jewish, Christian, and Islamic traditions alike, as well as to other religions. In revival Witchcraft, a legend is told explaining the origins of this practice as embedded in "the burning times," as the witch craze is called: practitioners of the "old religion" allegedly used aliases at their meetings so anyone who was captured and interrogated by the authorities could not implicate others by name. Craft names, according to this etiological tale, served as a form of protection and secrecy. Today, the taking of a new name symbolizes the adherent's spiritual transformation, and signals the beginning of a new phase in life. Thus it is not surprising that many Pagans choose to adopt new names as badges of their transformed identities.

"Why would anyone use a magical name? Because a name is a very powerful thing," writes Dream Snake on her Web site.[4]

> Words have power, and a name directly taps into that power. In most cases, our name was given to us by our parents. This means that our name may not fit who we are, or who we want to be. Names affect how we see ourselves, and they affect how others see us. This is an aspect of the psychology of names. There is another powerful aspect of names: the magical aspect. . . . For me, magic is the art of finding, or creating, connections between seemingly unconnected things. This means that a magical name has a connection with you, the name, and what the name means.

Dream Snake goes on to outline three basic ways Pagans may choose a magical name: involuntarily, as when a name comes in a dream, during trance or as a result of a spell or ritual, or when a name is given by coven mates; semi-voluntarily, as when a person has always felt drawn to a particular name, or feels an affinity for a certain animal, plant or deity and wishes to honor the connection; and voluntarily, when individuals choose new names based on their traits, or to bring desired qualities into their lives. "While I strongly feel that names that come to you may have more meaning, I've always felt more comfortable with names I've chosen," she confides.

A subscriber to a Pagan Listserv asked, "I have a question for those who have claimed 'special' names as their own. . . . How did you come about deciding that this was the name you should have? Is it a name that had meaning to you for a long time? Did it just spring upon you one day as 'the one?' And when do you use it? Only with the spiritual crowd or in everyday life? . . . I would like more input about this to see if I too can claim a name as my own." A subscriber named Pandion responded: "Many years ago when i [*sic*] first came home to Wicca—i was told that we take a 'witch name' upon initiation or (in the case of the solitary) self-dedication. This renaming was symbolical [*sic*] of our rebirth into the Craft. My name came to me as I was researching gods associated with the Moon. I read the name and knew that it was to be my Craft name—I just connected with it and felt deeply that that was that." A third subscriber argued: "It isn't a matter of choice; your name is your name. I was told my true name by my Spirit Guides and since it was from a language totally unfamiliar to this incarnation it took years to learn the meaning. When you recognize your name you'll be aware of the 'ring of truth' and you won't question, you'll simply know."

Several readers responded with personal narratives explaining how they came by their magical names in rituals or dreams. These ecstatic experiences are central to Neo-Pagans, and provide them with sources of creative inspiration on many levels. Ilyana wrote:

> I remember my first few years on this path when many of the folks I met had such terrific names. I was searching and searching for a name. I finally decided to relax about

it and see what would happen with time. A few months later I attended my first Witch Camp. . . . during an *incredibly* healing trance we visited the Temple of Love where the Guardians at the gateway greeted me by the name "Ilyana." I was so profoundly moved; I came out of trance, ran to get my journal and wrote it down so I wouldn't forget it. I was shy about using the name for many months after that, but I treasured it in my heart.

A subscriber named Kestrel shared this experience:

My name came to me in a dream about 4 and a half months ago, with a shock of recognition I woke up and wrote it down. I know the feeling of searching for a name, the frustration of wondering why names will not come to one or the unsureness of finding the "true" name but it was crystal clear to me that this name Kestrel was mine. I had never even seen a kestrel before, and I did not know anything about them other than that they were a small hawk like bird. So even though the name came to me in a dream and when it arrived I felt that it was on, I was still a little bit skeptical. About a month later I was out planting wildflowers . . . and a friend I was with, who did not know about my dream or name, said, "Hey Greg, look, there's a kestrel." And there silhouetted against the sky perched on some kind of shrubbery was a kestrel. As I watched it carefully, it caught an updraft from the bluffs which we stood at the base of and lifted with the wind and swung around in a lazy arc. Then the next week I saw another kestrel, this time right by my house, positively identified via a bird book. All this in the space of two months or so. Because of these three sightings I know that Kestrel is my magical name.

Kestrel felt the signs he saw in nature confirmed the validity of the information he had received in his dreams. Natural signs are often interpreted in this way, as they are considered direct communication from the divine world.[5]

Some Pagans choose magical names to bring the qualities of a particular deity into their lives. Priestess and folklorist Holly Tannen, whose creative work includes original music, songs, and plays, chose to align with the goddess Brigid, the goddess of poetry, craftsmanship, and healing, through her choice of magical name. Sometimes this technique can backfire, though, as when artist Katya Madrid took the name of Eris, the goddess of chaos, upon her first initiation, because she liked the idea of spontaneity it evoked. Within a week, her life was in upheaval, as one unexpected event after another confounded her plans. Finally, exhausted, she returned to her initiators and asked whether she could do another ritual to give the name back. She chose instead Polnoch, or "midnight" in Russian, recalling her cultural heritage and a magical game she had played as a child. "Be careful what you invoke!" she concluded in warning. For Pagans, the power of names can be quite literal: Katya interpreted the chaotic events in her life as a direct result of her choice of Eris as a Craft name.

As Katya's example shows, Pagans feel free to change their magical names if they no longer fit. Some opt to take a new name with each initiation or life transition; each name symbolizes some important quality they wish to emphasize in their lives. Others choose instead to imbue their legal names with new meanings that reflect their changing worldview. Another respondent to the Pagan Listserv wrote:

All through my early life my mother called me by my middle name. . . . when I reached 35 I decided to change my name to my first name as it appeared on my birth certificate, "Mary." Later, when I joined the SCA [Society for Creative Anachronism], I called myself "Mary of Thousand Oaks," its [*sic*] the name of the street I live on! And finally in the Craft, I have long ago decided that Mary was a Goddess name because for many centuries women have hidden their love for the Goddess in the persona of the Virgin Mary. So since Mary is just another name for the Goddess, I still keep Mary.

Pagans may use their magical names only in ritual contexts where they remain private, or adopt them as their use names, as have well-known authors Starhawk, Amber K, Raven Grimassi, and Silver RavenWolf. Pagans know their names can sound silly and off-putting to outsiders, though, and this is often the source of self-reflexive humor. A widely circulated, delicious piece of satire on magical names which appears as xerox lore, e-mail lore, and on several Web sites is "Lady Pixie Moondrip's Guide to Craft Names."[6] The essay begins by lampooning the legend of the origin of Craft names, while calling attention to the author's (and presumably the audience's) awareness of the identity-creating purpose of contemporary magical names:

In the Olde Days, when our pagan ancestors were going through the persecutions we now invoke to justify various kinds of current silliness, witches took craft names to conceal their identities and avoid those annoying visits by the Inquisition. In the course of years, it was noticed that these aliases could also be used as a foundation for building up a magical personality. . . . It's clear, though, that these were mere distractions from the real purpose lying hidden within the craft name tradition. It took contact with other sources of ancient, mystic lore—mostly the SCA, role-playing games and assorted fantasy trilogies—to awaken the Craft to the innermost secret of craft names: they make really cool fashion statements.

It's in this spirit that Lady Pixie Moondrip offers the following guidelines to choosing your own craft name. Such a guide is long overdue; the point of fashion, after all, is that it allows you to express your own utterly unique individuality by doing exactly the same thing as everyone else.

The guide continues by offering advice on the selection of names, including such categories as "Starting Off Right" ("Whatever else you do, you should certainly begin your craft name with 'Lord' or 'Lady.' First of all, it's pretentious, and that's always a good way to start"); "Inventing a Name from Scratch" ("The best way to do this is to come up with something that sounds, say, vaguely Celtic, perhaps by mangling a couple of existing names together, and then resolutely avoid looking it up in a Welsh or Gaelic dictionary. . . . It took one person of Lady Pixie's acquaintance only a few minutes to blur together Gwydion son of Don and Girion, Lord of Dale, into the craft name 'Lord Gwyrionin,' and several months to find out that the name he had invented . . . was also the Welsh for 'idiot' "); "Following a Grand Tradition" (that is, "the tradition of stealing things from non-Western peoples. Fake Indian craft names are always chic, especially if the closest thing to contact with Native American spirituality you've ever had was watching Dances with

Wolves at a beer party"), and finally the "Random Craft Name Generator." Like other printed folklore of this kind,[7] this is a list of words that can be combined randomly in twos or threes to create a magical name. The list includes many words derived from nature:

Wolf Raven Silver Moon Star Water Snow
Sea Tree Wind Cloud Witch Thorn Leaf
White Black Green Fire Rowan Swan Night
Red Mist Hawk Feather Eagle Song Sky
Storm Sun Wood Buffalo

On the surface, these appear to be innocent, romantic concepts taken from nature; but combined, they can spawn the likes of "Silver RavenWolf," a popular Pagan author whose name the guide deliberately derides, and the intentionally ridiculous "Squatting Buffalo Firewater." Like other folkloric "random generators," it is a commentary on how a tradition that attempts to be unique and original can lapse easily into triteness and predictability.

The existence of this piece of folklore points to Pagans' high level of self-awareness and ability to comment humorously on the frailties of invented tradition. Some Pagans even found it useful; Dream Snake's Web site recommends it to Pagans searching for magical names as "sarcastic, funny, and yet wisely cautionary." By pointing out common foibles and mocking foolish sounding magical names, Lady Pixie's sardonic piece of wit points out the boundaries and borders of accepted praxis in the emergent Pagan community.

## Internal Distinctions: Traditions

In their efforts to imagine the counters of community, Neo-Pagans distinguish themselves not only from the surrounding dominant culture, but from one another as well. The most common way they do so is according to "tradition," a word they use to indicate denominations within the movement. Traditions are styles of practice that find expression chiefly through ritual. For it is praxis, rather than belief, that is the central rubric uniting Neo-Pagan religions. As Minnesota priest Steven Posch once told me, "Paganism is not about belief. It is about being."

Most American Neo-Pagan traditions share certain general attitudinal contours: a reverence for nature; a view of the universe as interconnected; a concept of divinity that includes a feminine principle; and an ethical precept consistent with "Do as you will, but harm none." They differ from one another chiefly in the deities they venerate, liturgy, historical lineage, internal structure, accessibility to nonmembers, and flavor or ethos. While different traditions may espouse slightly different belief systems, belief is not the most important distinguishing feature between them, as it is not considered necessary for membership or practice. Each tradition may have a sacred text or group of texts, usually known as a "Book of Shadows," yet they are essentially transmitted by direct contact, through oral tradition and by imitation. There are Neo-Pagans who are entirely self-taught, having learned by reading how-to books; whether they can be called members of a tradition in the same sense as those who have learned from direct oral transmission remains hotly debated in the movement. In 2003, the consensus among my consultants is that some form of personal transmission—whether formal (e.g., from a class) or informal—is necessary to become part of a tradition. Thus the term *tradition*, borrowed from folkloristics, is actually quite apropos in the Neo-Pagan context.

While there were numerous North American occult practitioners and almost countless folk healers at the turn of the twentieth century, Neo-Paganism came to the New World from Britain during the 1950s, shortly after the publication of Gardner's book *Witchcraft Today*. The first known tradition-bearers to carry Gardner's Witchcraft to the United States were Raymond and Rosemary Buckland, who came to New York in 1961 with the mandate to begin their own coven in Gardner's tradition (Adler, 1986:92).[8] "Gardnerian" Witchcraft quickly diffused throughout the United States and Canada, aided by the publication of Stewart Farrar's *What Witches Do* (1971), which contains versions of Alexandrian rites (closely related to Gardnerian ones), and *The Grimoire of Lady Sheba* (1971), a version of the Gardnerian Book of Shadows. Because Gardnerian Craft was among the first Neo-Pagan traditions to be described in published sources during the 1950s and 1960s, it has had an inordinate influence on other Pagan traditions, even those that depart from a strictly Gardnerian approach.

As Gardnerian Craft spread throughout North America, it also inspired a number of individuals to develop their own variants of it. Buckland himself, while he had at first railed against the impostors who established their own brand of Witchcraft, split from his tradition in 1973 to create Seax or Saxon Wicca (Buckland, 1986; Adler, 1986:92–93). Because North American society is multiethnic, many innovators injected bits of their own folk magical traditions into the brands of Witchcraft they concocted, giving the American Wiccan landscape a decidedly multiethnic flavor. For example, Leo Louis Martello, the son of Sicilian immigrants living in Massachusetts, was one of the first to identify himself as an Italian Witch, or *strega*. Together with Lori Bruno, another Italian American whose family carried on a tradition of folk healing, he established the Trinacrian Rose Coven, a group whose Witchcraft traditions had a decidedly Mediterranean flavor. Zsuzsanna "Z" Budapest, a feminist Witch whose work was fundamental in the creation of the feminist spirituality movement, borrowed elements from the folklore of her native Hungary in creating a woman-based, goddess-oriented Witchcraft. Other innovators mixed material from their own folk traditions with those of other regional and ethnic groups. Victor and Cora Anderson, founders of the Feri tradition, each grew up in families that practiced forms of traditional American folk magic. Victor, blind from an early age, managed to weave scraps of Sicilian, British, and Hawaiian lore into his mix.

During the late 1960s, the counterculture and second-wave feminism were instrumental in the diffusion of Witchcraft beyond the realm of the esoteric. Young people disillusioned with mainstream religions sought new forms of spirituality, or, lacking that, invented their own; Tim "Oberon" Zell's Church of All Worlds was founded by a group of young people who took inspiration from Robert Heinlein's science-fiction masterpiece, *Stranger in a Strange Land*, the works of Ayn Rand, and the human-potential movement. In the early 1960s, the Reformed Druids of North America (RDNA) was founded by a group of students at Carleton College who resented the school's mandate that all students attend religious worship services. Once the mandate was repealed several years later, the students found, to their own surprise, that the RDNA continued without them, and became a genuine spiritual movement in its own right.

During the same period, many women who felt excluded from liturgical authority in mainstream faiths welcomed the concept of a religion that included a goddess, where women could play central roles as priestesses and healers. Feminists reclaimed the concept of the witch as a symbol of feminine power that stood in contrast to patriarchal authority. Fueled by the writings of Merlin Stone, Mary Daly, and many other feminist writers, feminist Witchcraft was born. Today, new variants of Witchcraft emerge almost daily through the publication of popular books and the creation of Internet sites. The Wicca section of trade bookstores is packed with old and new offerings, as well-known authors and innovators each create their own particular variant of Neo-Pagan religion.

The sheer number of traditions, and their variation across geographic and regional boundaries, makes it almost impossible to give an accurate portrait of all the Neo-Pagan traditions operating in North America today. Rather than attempting to delineate a taxonomy, I would like to give readers a feel for how Pagans themselves construct both difference and commonality among their traditions, and situate themselves on the complex continuum of Neo-Pagan practice. I will briefly outline some general distinctions below, then profile how they existed in the San Francisco Bay Area Pagan community during the years of my most intense fieldwork, 1995 to 2000. I will then examine how Neo-Pagans use folklore and expressive culture to further delineate the boundaries of their community.

## Who Needs a Frog Hanging from the Ceiling? Witches and Nonwitches

> *Q: How many witches does it take to change a light bulb?*
> *A: Only one; but who needs a frog hanging from the ceiling?*

One of the most important distinctions Neo-Pagans make among themselves is between those who call themselves Witches and those who do not. Though

Witches form the largest majority of North American Neo-Pagans, the term *Witch* itself is hotly contested within the movement.[9] For some Pagans, this word is an important tool for reconnecting with a legendary past and for reclaiming positive qualities with which they strongly identify but which are discounted or feared by the dominant culture. The trouble with this word is that, in Euro-American folklore, it has a long history of bad associations. The witches of folktales and legends are not positive figures who wish to subvert the stodgy dominant culture and work for social and spiritual freedom; they practice magic for unabashedly wicked purposes. And while some Pagans will argue that it was Christianity and the Inquisition that gave the word its negative connotation, there is plenty of evidence that throughout Europe witches—people believed to do evil through sympathetic magic—were part of a narrative tradition that long predated the emergence of Christianity and that came to be part of American folklore and cultural history.

Embracing the *W* word may have empowered American witches to validate their intuition, sexuality, and emotions, but it has also made them targets of prejudice, misunderstanding, and even hatred by those for whom the traditional meaning of the word has not changed. It should not surprise us, therefore, to find the *W* word becoming the subject of humor such as that in the lightbulb joke above, which is modeled after the popular jokes of the 1970s and 1980s, and appears similar to other Pagan lightbulb jokes that will be discussed below. However, the witch is an ambiguous figure. One would assume that she is the witch of the Wiccan revision, yet she turns the lightbulb into a frog, just as the witch in the Grimms' tale "Iron Henry" puts a spell on the prince that transforms his appearance. Indeed, while in traditional folktales, witches are responsible for many different kinds of transformations, in the Euro-American popular media, turning people into amphibians seems to be the favorite activity of stereotypical witches. In the film comedy *Monty Python and the Holy Grail*, a man accuses a witch, "She turned me into a newt!" "A newt?" asks his friend skeptically, as the accuser appears thoroughly human. "Well, I got better," he observes somewhat sheepishly. Being a revival Witch who presumably operates according to the Wiccan rede "An it harm none, do what you will," the joke Witch turns her skills on an inanimate object rather than on an individual. The result, however, is puzzling and nowhere near as useful as a lightbulb. The joke seems to be a comment on the many connotations of the *W* word: the Witch may be a positive figure, but her actions link her to the witch of folk tradition in complex and ambiguous ways. The result is that the *W* word, while maintaining a link with tradition and emphasizing the W/witch's powers of transformation, can ultimately be a bit like the punch line of the joke: a frog hanging from the ceiling.

American Witches share the veneration of one or more goddesses, an approach based on ritual magic, and a year cycle of eight sabbats, or holy days, combined with lunar observances, as well as a structure based on the coven, or small working group, as an independent and autonomous unit.

The term *Wicca* (the adjective is *Wiccan*) is preferred by some American Witches because it avoids the negative connotations associated with the *W* word. Wicca has both a broad and a narrow sense: in the broadest sense, it refers to all forms of Neo-Paganism descended from, related to, or influenced by Gerald Gardner—in other words, all forms of modern Neo-Pagan Witchcraft. In a narrower sense, though, it refers only to practitioners of British traditional Witchcraft—that is, the closely related Gardnerian and Alexandrian traditions. Wiccan groups (both broadly and narrowly) have a duotheistic system that includes a god as well as a goddess, a high priestess and high priest in each coven, mixed-gender covens, a shared Book of Shadows with liturgies for eight seasonal sabbats, and a three-degree system of initiation. Among Wiccan traditions, American Gardnerians are the most exclusive: they are lineage-based (that is, they trace descent from Gardner's coven) and oath-bound (much of the liturgy and practice is considered secret, with penalties for those who reveal it to outsiders). Secrecy ensures a fairly high degree of conservatism in the tradition, especially in the liturgy, which initiates must memorize. It also acts as a vehicle to control group boundaries: not just anyone can be initiated, and because Gardnerians keep meticulous records of their initiations, it is relatively easy to determine who is a member and who is not.

American Gardnerians trace their "descent" from the high priestess who initiated them, and regard their ritual lineages as a form of fictive kinship. They keep lineage papers that trace their descent back to Gardner's coven, a tradition that is unique to North America and began when Rosemary Buckland, a British Gardnerian, came to the United States in the early 1960s. Rosemary was given a document by her high priestess (one of Gardner's last) authenticating her initiation and authorizing her to transmit the Craft in America. Lineage papers and narratives are an important way for Gardnerians to construct and maintain a sense of community and continuity in the tradition. When two Gardnerians meet for the first time, discussion of descent becomes a way to establish relations and gain an understanding of the newcomer's background and possible worldview. The permanence of fictive kinship ties keeps the tradition exclusive; high priestesses and priests initiate only those they trust, and they feel a deep sense of responsibility for their initiates. They consider that upon initiation, spiritual power passes directly from the initiator to the initiate, much as a parent passes on genetic material to an offspring.

Besides Gardnerians, there are numerous other types of Witches; in fact Gardnerian Witches are probably a minority among American Witches. Witchcraft traditions sometimes distinguish themselves by the ethnic heritage of their founders; for example, the British traditions, descended from founders in England and Scotland, include (among others) Gardnerian and Alexandrian Witchcraft and the New Wiccan Church. There are also Welsh, Irish, Saxon, and Italian-identified Witchcraft traditions. There are feminist traditions, such as Dianic and Reclaiming Witchcraft; some Dianic Witches practice in women-only covens. There are also a number of eclectic Witchcraft traditions that draw elements from a variety of sources as well as creating their own.

While all Witches are Pagan, not all Pagans are Witches. A number of Pagans practice traditions outside of Witchcraft, though they may have been heavily influenced in form by Witchcraft traditions. San Francisco Witch Deborah Bender has coined the term *Witchen* as an adjectival form of *Witch*; the corresponding term for non-Witchen is *Cowan* (just as among Jews, the term *gentile* means a non-Jew). These terms have now been adopted by many in the San Francisco Bay Area community. Cowan Pagans are a minority within the movement, but are significant nevertheless. They share many aspects with Witchen groups, including the small-group structure (although the term *coven* is characteristic of Witchen groups; non-Witchen groups may use other terms, such as *grove* or *circle*); ritual magic as a central art form; and a concern with historical traditions. While some have adopted the eight-sabbat ritual year, others observe holy days unique to their particular tradition. Examples of non-Witchen groups include the Church of All Worlds, founded by Tim "Oberon" Zell; the Fellowship of Isis, whose members venerate deities from the ancient Egyptian pantheon; Druids and Norse Pagans, of which there are various denominations. Ceremonial magicians—for example, members of the Ordo Templo Orientis (OTO)—may or may not consider themselves (or be considered) to be Pagans, depending on individual preference.[10]

Pagan traditions are not mutually exclusive. Particularly in the San Francisco Bay Area, where I did most of my fieldwork, it is fairly typical for individuals to belong simultaneously to a number of Pagan traditions, and to practice in all of them. Members of my Gardnerian coven had also been initiated into Reclaiming, Alexandrian, Dianic, and Feri traditions, the New Reformed Orthodox Order of the Golden Dawn (NROOGD), and the Church of All Worlds. This should not be interpreted as an endless search for the "right" brand of spirituality, but as a fluid exploration, an openness to many forms of occult discourse. As Anna Korn, who has been active in at least six Neo-Pagan traditions, explained to me, "You find the people that you want to hang out with, and then you get interested in whatever it is they're doing." And while traditions differ from each other in style, they share enough of an underlying framework that cross-initiation is generally not problematic for the individual.[11] Clearly, this fluid contact between members of a variety of Neo-Pagan groups also creates a matrix in which ideas spread quickly, be they ritual elements, narratives, or magical techniques. There is a tremendous amount of influence between and among traditions, even while each tradition retains its own unique distinguishing features.

Another important distinction Pagans make among themselves is that between "traditional" and "popular" Craft—that is, between those traditions that have a coherent body of traditional lore, generally handed down in a Book of Shadows, and those that have evolved in a more free-form fashion. Witches say that traditional Craft is spread through oral tradition directly from a trained individual to her or his coveners, while popular Craft is often diffused by individuals—through books by well-known Pagan authors, the Internet, films, television, and by word of mouth—without a consistent body of tradition. Of course, the earliest books on the Craft were written by Gardnerians and Alexandrians, who are considered the very epitome of traditional Witches. Don Frew drew a more specific distinction by pointing out that Witchcraft and Neo-Paganism first took root and expanded in North American urban areas and university towns, where practitioners had access to research libraries, bookstores, and liberal communities in which to practice relatively unmolested. This meant that the first generation of American Neo-Pagans were mostly middle-class intellectuals and bohemians, imbued with the spirit of critical thought and antiauthoritarianism that permeated liberal areas during the late 1960s and 1970s. Paganism's expansion in the 1990s and turn of the century, however, took place through the Internet and popular publications, venues which do not cater primarily to intellectuals, but to a much broader, less critical audience. Thus the nature of American Neo-Paganism is changing from an esoteric form of cultural critique to a more popular, and at times anti-intellectual, movement. "Our myth of identity is being challenged [by these changes]," explained Don. "We like to think that all Witches are equal. It's becoming increasingly clear that there are great disparities—in knowledge, in rigor, in talent, . . . pointing out differences that were there all along, but that we didn't realize, or chose not to look at."

The easy and rapid diffusion of ideas from one group to another in the Pagan community, as well as through the Internet and popular books, means that practices are constantly being produced, imitated, and passed on to new members with the individual and performative variation characteristic of folklore. Some Pagans interpret this cycle of reproduction and variation as a loss of authenticity. Gardnerian priestess Anna Korn explained, "In many cases [changes in a tradition] represent a real loss of understanding of a tradition, or lead people to cast off what they may not understand, rather than trying to understand it, or to accrue a series of novelties into materials inherited with consequent confusion. An example is the matriarchal [material] that accrued to Gardnerian practice in the Eastern United States in the 1970s, as a partial *Rücklauf* from feminist theory, or the immense amount of poorly conceived ceremony focused on the Queen and her hierarchy" (Interview, 2002). This has led groups to develop a series of strategies to maintain the integrity of traditions; secrecy is the foremost among these. Thus, another important distinction Pagans make is between groups that involve secrecy and those that do not.

Some traditions, both Craft and non-Craft, are initiatory groups whose core teachings are open only to those who have undergone a special rite of passage. These secrets may involve sacred texts, such as a Book of Shadows, as well as material passed on orally or by imitation, such as the content of certain rituals. Membership in these groups is usually by invitation only; a new aspirant must be well known to the group before being asked to join. Initiatory groups often maintain a hierarchical structure, with experienced members teaching newer ones and the final authority resting with a high priestess and/or priest.

Secrecy itself, however, is the subject of much discussion and dissent within groups that observe it. Those who are active in Wiccan rights and in researching the history of the movement often advocate for loosening some of the bonds of secrecy in order to promote greater knowledge and understanding. At the same time, as Anna Korn continues, "we *have* sworn an oath, our mana is bound up in it, and so we must uphold it. Also, the power of certain rituals is preserved through secrecy." Initiations, for example, are thought to have a greater emotional and spiritual impact when the mystery is unknown to the initiate until the moment of revelation.

Nonsecret groups are usually more open to the public, although they too may hold initiations, regard certain aspects as "mysteries" not to be revealed to outsiders, and recognize various levels among their members. Entrance into such groups is often through classes offered by experienced members who act as teachers. Classes are advertised at local bookstores, occult supply shops, and through Internet lists, as well as through Pagan networks operating in urban areas. Unlike secret and traditionalist groups, which may have strictures against the exchange of cash for teaching, many popular groups charge for instruction, though they may have a sliding scale and scholarships so that no one who wants to learn is excluded. They tend to be more egalitarian (at least in theory), having fewer degrees of initiation, and often have less formalized liturgies that allow for a great deal of variation, borrowing of elements, and personal inventiveness.

There are regional differences between traditions in different parts of the United States; like tofu, Paganism tends to absorb the flavor of the surrounding ingredients, or regional cultures. This is particularly striking in Pagan foodways at potlucks and camp-outs, as dishes reflect a strong regional influence, but is present in other aspects of culture as well. East Coast Pagans are often more formal and traditionalist than their West Coast counterparts. Especially along the Eastern seaboard and in the New York area, British traditions predominate, interspersed with Celtic ones and Stregheria (Italian American Witchcraft), reflecting the strong ethnic presence of Irish and Italian Americans. Druidism, in its various iterations, is popular in the American Midwest, where Pagans are also more likely to incorporate material from Native American spiritual traditions. In contrast, on the East and West Coasts, there has been greater cross-fertilization from Afro-Caribbean and Latino religions due to the visible presence of immigrants from these areas in urban centers. In some parts of the United States (but not in the San Francisco Bay), a single tradition may dominate in a geographic or urban area.

NROOGD priestess Laurel Olson suggested a set of correlations between certain Neo-Pagan traditions and regions in the United States, based on a combination of what she called "motive" (existing cultural context) and "opportunity" (locally available Pagan paths and traditions). For example, she described Heathens, Neo-Pagans who affiliate with Norse or Northern European deities and practice, as "essentially post-Reformation Protestants who grew up in the lower Midwest or South with a biblical fundamentalist faith" (interview, 2002). She believes that Heathenism appeals to them because of its textual basis in the Norse and Icelandic sagas and *Eddas*—a textual focus that recalls the biblical literalism already familiar to them through their birth religions. She also remarked on the formal, rather staid nature of many Heathen rituals, relating it to their general discomfort with loss of control and expression of emotion. "Heathens fear losing control because in the sagas and *Eddas* it always brings tragic consequences," she hypothesized, though she later added that it also reflected a broader-based cultural discomfort with emotionalism common to the American Midwest and South. She attributed the racism prevalent in certain strands of American Heathenism to a similar reflection of local cultural norms. Despite her interest in Norse traditions, Laurel refuses to associate with racist Heathens because she does not share their feelings; she has a Cape Verdean husband and African American foster son.

Even the American Gardnerian tradition, among the most conservative in Neo-Paganism, differs greatly from one region to another. Southern Gardnerians, especially those of the Kentucky line, are reputed to be the most formal and traditionalist, followed by East Coast Gardnerians. California Gardnerians, in contrast, are often considered quite radical in their liberal interpretations of the tradition—so much so that some conservative American Gardnerians regard them practically as apostates.

## The San Francisco Bay Area Pagan Community, 1995–2000

During the period I was researching this book, I did fieldwork among Pagans from a number of different traditions and regional communities. I began my explorations in Wisconsin, where I was teaching at the time, with Selena Fox and Dennis Carpenter at Circle Sanctuary, a Pagan retreat just south of Madison. My travels soon took me to California, where I did fieldwork in Los Angeles and Santa Barbara before moving to Berkeley and becoming integrated into the extended Neo-Pagan community around San Francisco. Eventually I returned to Los Angeles and continued to work with local Pagans, while maintaining my contacts in Northern California. My most extensive experience, however, was in the San Francisco Bay Area.

The San Francisco Bay Area Pagan community is unique in North America. It is one of the oldest in the country, with a large number of cooperative, friendly elders who have been active in the movement since the counterculture of the 1960s and 1970s. This gives the community a sense of history that is sometimes lacking in other regions. It is also the birthplace of Covenant of the Goddess (COG), a global networking organization to which many of the area's covens of many traditions belong, and which they all had a hand in establishing, giving them a sense of ownership and investment in the networking process. While some regional communities are beset by "Witch wars," internecine conflicts usually rooted in issues of power, style, and authenticity, the San Francisco Bay Area Pagan community is relatively free from this kind of strife. COG provides a vehicle for members of different traditions across America to cooperate in charitable projects and engage in Interfaith dialogue with other religions; Pagans have found they are more accepted when they pull together, and COG gives them a tremendous incentive to do so.

The local regional ethos is imbued with a liberal atmosphere, countercultural values and a very well-educated population, thanks to the presence of the University of California at Berkeley, Stanford University, the University of California at San Francisco, the University of California at Santa Cruz, the Graduate Theological Union Seminary, Mills College, several branches of the California State University, and countless smaller schools. Not only do the Pagans in this region band together, they also receive a greater degree of acceptance in the surrounding community, freeing up energy for political work. The Pagan community of which I became a part bordered on academia and included numerous artists, musicians, writers, and performers, making it an extremely stimulating context in which to do fieldwork. A spirit of political activism infuses the region; it is no accident that the Bay Area is the birthplace of two separate Neo-Pagan traditions: NROOGD and the Reclaiming tradition, which is one of the most influential Witchcraft traditions of the twentieth century, along with Gardnerian Craft. The peculiarities of this community also skewed my fieldwork, of course—giving me a very large percentage of college and professional school graduates in my sample, for instance.

## Coven Trismegiston: A Gardnerian Group in Berkeley

My experience in the community was grounded in my contacts with the individuals who became my coven-siblings and initiators. Anna, a microbiologist, and Don, a religious studies scholar and bookseller, are the high priestess and high priest of Coven Trismegiston in Berkeley, California. During 1996–97, the coven had four initiated members and three aspirants, of which I was one. The other members included Suzy, a chiropractor, and Katya, a filmmaker and artist. Besides me, the aspirants were Nancy, a molecular biologist, and Pitch, a graphic artist, calligrapher, and retail manager with an ABD in anthropology. Members ranged from their late twenties to their late forties, and almost all had advanced degrees, making it one of the most intellectual Pagan groups I had observed. Almost all members spoke at least one language besides English, and had at one time or another lived abroad. Six were white, one was Asian American; two members were first-generation immigrants who maintained ongoing connections with their cultures of origin, and another was the child of first-generation immigrants with strong linguistic and cultural roots. These elements give the coven an international flavor. The coven met on full moons, new moons, and sabbats, usually in Anna and Don's Berkeley bungalow, which is comfortably cozy and crammed with books, ritual objects, and dried flowers and herbs from Anna's garden.

Coven Trismegiston, which means "coven of the thrice-greatest ones," draws its name from the Greek epithet for Hermes, *trismegistos* or "thrice-greatest." In this form, the figure of Hermes came to incorporate the qualities of an ideal magus. Hermes is one of the protector-deities of the coven; the other is Hecate, goddess of the underworld, the moon, and the dead, and protectress of Witches. It was an intentional pun that the "thrice-greatest ones" could refer to either its patrons, Hermes and Hecate, or to the members themselves. Trismegiston is unusual among Gardnerian covens in its emphasis on Classical deities over Celtic ones. This is a product of Don's scholarly investigations into the history of Western occultism, especially the Corpus Hermeticum and the Chaldean Oracles. These sources have provided scholars with a substantial amount of information about late Classical practices, which Don suspects are at the root of the modern Witchcraft revival. Don and Anna are both very active in researching Craft history; their avocation as historians deeply informs their practice.

Gardnerians are sometimes stereotyped as having rigid gender roles and rituals fixated on the union of the male and female principles in nature. While great regional diversity exists within the tradition, this stereotype is not an accurate representation of Trismegiston's worldview. In Trismegiston, part of the California Gardnerian lineage, gender roles are flexible and fluid. Priests as well as priestesses can initiate new members; covens need not consist of perfectly balanced numbers of female and male participants; ritual roles can be assigned to either gender; several members are lesbian, gay, or bisexual; and participants may ritually embody a deity of the opposite gender. As Anna explained, "The influence of biological thought means we recognize that male-female principles are only one possibility in the diversity of the living world."

Trismegiston's monthly teaching circles usually take place during the new moon. Nancy, Pitch, and I practice casting the circle and take on different ritual roles to familiarize ourselves with the coven's basic Gardnerian outer-court script. Within the circle, Don and Anna give lessons in ritual craft: how to set up the altar, the meaning of each tool, systems of divination, techniques to raise and ground energy. Each month there is a different lesson, and we are expected to read and study and practice between meetings. Sometimes teaching circles consist mostly of discussion, making the experience not unlike a graduate seminar and our relationship to Anna and Don much like that of graduate students to young and enthusiastic professors. We are a group of challenging students. Both Pitch and Nancy have extensive previous experience with the occult: Pitch is active in the Feri Witchcraft community, while Nancy has worked for many years as a psychic healer (separate from her occupation as a molecular biologist). The general tenor of meetings is stimulating and collegial. We all share an intellectual detachment and reflexivity which sometimes erupts in humorous outbursts and self-parodies. Trismegiston members appreciated my professional knowledge of folk customs and traditions, and often asked me about my previous fieldwork in Sardinia to mine them for Classical and pre-Classical elements.

In addition to teaching circles and full moon esbats, Trismegiston also holds seasonal sabbats to which nonmembers and friends of the coven can be invited. These so-called outer-court rituals often have a historical, reconstructionist flavor. Anna and Don frequently turn to Classical sources for ritual material, incorporating foods, incenses, and practices described in ancient texts. Other elements may be borrowed from the works of Margaret Murray, or from British folklore. There is little emphasis on self-help or psychodrama; I was told when I joined the outer court that Gardnerian practice is not therapy. "The assumption here is that you already have your life together," Don explained. While the group is warm and friendly and members participate in each other's emotional lives, and support and encourage one another, there is little discussion of deep feelings or delving into each other's psyches. In Trismegiston, making things whole means closing the gap which separates humans from the gods, and this is to be achieved through ritual, magic, and theurgy.

## The Outer Circle

While Trismegiston is only one small group, its members have had links to almost all the other Pagan traditions in the San Francisco Bay Area. Anna, who of all the members has been active in the movement the longest, also belonged at one time to the Church of All Worlds, and has worked with Feri and Reclaiming Witchcraft as well. Two of her oldest friends are M. Macha NightMare and Holly Tannen; together, all were involved in the early days of the Reclaiming collective soon after Starhawk and her associates founded the tradition in the 1970s. Don's first initiation was in NROOGD, a local tradition whose core ritual was invented by Glenn Turner, Aidan Kelly, Erif dev'dasi and others as the final project for a San Francisco State University class on ritual. Through Don's contacts in NROOGD, I met Rowan Fairgrove, Russell Williams, Laurel Olson, her initiate Darrin Laurelsson, and her husband Andres Mendes, all of whom are involved in NROOGD's public rituals.

NROOGD members Laurel, Darrin, and Diana Paxson, an elder in the Fellowship of the Spiral Path, are also involved in the Ring of Troth, an international Norse Pagan group. I have connections of my own through my neighbors on "Witch Row": Judy Foster, an early NROOGD member, is also a Reclaiming Witch and social activist who runs a food bank from her basement; Mary and Dave are elders in the Fellowship of the Spiral Path, which also has ties to NROOGD, Ring of Troth, and several other covens and circles. All of these individuals are also members of the Northern California Local Council (NCLC) of COG.

One evening Anna drew a Venn diagram to illustrate how the San Francisco Bay Area Pagan community consisted of a series of overlapping and contiguous circles: each circle represented a tradition, but all the circles together constituted the complex and fluid community. While I have already explained the Gardnerian tradition, I will briefly outline some of the traditions I have mentioned and explain how they differ from each other.

### The Reclaiming Tradition

Formed in 1980 by Starhawk and a group of women who had learned Witchcraft and magic from her and other members of her coven Raving, Reclaiming began by offering small classes in basic magic and ritual.[12] It blossomed into a collective community and a separate tradition of Witchcraft. While some scholars have categorized Reclaiming as eclectic Witchcraft, it can also be considered a descendant of Victor Anderson's Feri tradition and of Z Budapest's Dianic feminist Witchcraft, as Starhawk was a pupil of both. It retains Dianic Witchcraft's eco-feminist stance, and shares with Feri tradition a belief in the three souls or selves, an emphasis on certain shared deities such as the Blue God, similarities in the style of circle casting, and an emphasis on trance and ecstasy in ritual. In other ways, however, it has departed from both Dianic and Feri traditions and taken on its own flavor.

Reclaiming's most important distinguishing characteristics are its feminism and its emphasis on the political aspects of magic and ritual. Its spiritual work is among the most clearly and openly oppositional of any Pagan tradition; its aim is the transformation of our current economic, political, and spiritual system. Starhawk writes:

> Much of reality—the welfare system, war, the social roles ordained for women and men—are created collectively and can only be changed collectively. . . . Sexism, racism, poverty and blind accident do shape people's lives, and they are not created by their victims. If spirituality is to be truly life-serving, it must stress that we are all responsible for each other. Its focus should not be individual enlightenment, but recognition of our interconnectedness and commitment to each other. (Starhawk, 1989:207)

Accordingly, Reclaiming initiates must make a pledge to work for political change. Reclaiming members have become forces for political and social activism in the San Francisco Bay Area, manning needle-exchange programs for addicts in San Francisco, running food pantries for the homeless, working to preserve the redwood forests of Northern California, opposing the diffusion of nuclear power, and demonstrating against the spread of global capitalism.

Reclaiming is also characterized by a deep concern with the personal, the transpersonal, and the therapeutic. Starhawk and other Reclaiming Witches argue that in order to make things whole, to heal the oppressive, dysfunctional system we are part of, one must begin by healing oneself; the individual is not separate from the system of which she is a part.[13] Much of this perspective may be due to Starhawk's own background as a psychotherapist. Her greatest talent may be her ability to take traditional material in the form of folk narratives, ballads, and the like, and translate their meanings in terms of the human psyche and the larger political system in the context of ritual. This combination of personal transformation with artistic production and political radicalism is particularly compelling. Starhawk is without a doubt the most influential writer in the Neo-Pagan movement after Gerald Gardner, but there are many other "thealogians" (a term they prefer to the more male-centered "theologians") and ritualists in the group. A great deal of material in Reclaiming arises collaboratively from covens, affinity groups, and Witch camps, worldwide summer intensives that transmit the tradition.

Reclaiming Witchcraft is an example of a more popular, generally nonsecretive tradition. Classes and Witch camps in the Reclaiming tradition are offered all over North America (and Europe as well) by specially trained teachers. Typically, two teachers lead each class, which consists of eight to twelve students. This group works as a coven during the period of the class (usually about ten weeks), and students are encouraged to continue to work together as a coven after the class is over. Since working magic together produces strong emotional bonds, many students do form friendships within these classes, and continue to meet to work magic after the class has formally ended.

Initiation, which is not mandatory for participation, is done by a committee of three instructors chosen by the initiate. Initiations are the only secret part of the Reclaiming tradition. The initiate must request initiation; it is never given as a matter of course, and in some cases takes many years before the committee agrees the aspirant is ready. Unlike Gardnerian Craft, in which initiation follows a script, Reclaiming initiations are crafted to suit the personal quirks and foibles of the individual initiate. Usually the initiate must meet a number of challenges posed by the priestesses; these are tailored to the aspirant's own strengths and weaknesses.

San Francisco's Reclaiming community, like Reclaiming-derived groups in other cities, holds annual public sabbats attended by hundreds of people. The largest and best known is the annual Spiral Dance, held near Samhain (October 31), which can have hundreds of performers, including a small orchestra and choir, and attracts an audience of between one and three thousand. The Spiral Dance involves a group trance experience in which participants journey to the Isle of the Dead, the Witchen otherworld, to commune with their beloved dead—a deeply moving ritual that I will describe in detail in Chapter 4. Starhawk often describes the style of Reclaiming rituals as "EIEIO": ecstatic, improvisational, ensemble, inspired, and organic.

Much of the material from Reclaiming's classes has been published in some form by Starhawk and other Reclaiming authors. Cassettes and CDs are available to those who want to hear the songs and chants taught in Reclaiming classes. The Reclaiming tradition has diffused perhaps more than any single other contemporary Witchcraft tradition, but this wide diffusion has unavoidably created some boundary issues as members try to determine the community's parameters.

## NROOGD

The New Reformed Orthodox Order of the Golden Dawn, or NROOGD, originated in 1967 as a result of a class on ritual at San Francisco State University. Aidan Kelly and Glenn Turner, two of the cofounders of the group, composed a ritual based on the writings of Robert Graves, Gerald Gardner, Margaret Murray, and T. C. Lethbridge (Adler, 1986:163), which they and a large group of friends performed for the class. They later gathered to perform the ritual again, privately, in a local park. The participants were hooked, and from the original group there emerged the first NROOGD coven.

From its inception, NROOGD was a self-consciously created tradition which emphasized the importance of poetry and artistry in ritual. The aesthetic impact of ritual is central to its ability to change consciousness, according to the NROOGD aesthetic. Aidan Kelly, writing to Margot Adler, explained, "I became sure that the Craft could be a religion for skeptical middle-class intellectuals: because it did not require us to violate our intellectual integrity, because it operated nonintellectually, striking deep chords in our emotional roots, because it could alter our state of consciousness" (quoted in Adler, 1986:165).

NROOGD ritual has often unabashedly drawn inspiration from myth and folklore, from the Greek mysteries of Eleusis to contemporary British year-cycle customs such as Padstow's (in Cornwall) May Day hobbyhorse, or "Oss." NROOGD's liturgy, while inspired by Gardner, is more poetic, its meaning metaphorical and open to interpretation. Its rituals are suggestive, dramatic, and aesthetically inspiring, and are often based on European folk customs. NROOGD is also one of the more accessible Wiccan traditions in the Bay Area, holding eight large open public sabbats each year. One of their best known is the annual reenactment of Padstow's May Day customs at Beltane

(May 1). NROOGD overlaps considerably, through cross-initiation, with other major Bay Area traditions, including Gardnerian, Reclaiming, Feri, Spiral Path, and Ring of Troth.

## A Joke Is a Spell: The Role of Shared Humor

Pagans have developed an array of techniques to discuss, determine, and establish the boundaries of their communities. Humor, especially verbal jokes that depend on stereotypes of national and regional character, have long been regarded by folklorists as devices that establish and delineate boundaries between groups, whether regional, national, or in this case religious (Davies, 1990; Bendix and Klein, 1993). Pagans use many different humorous forms, mostly jokes, songs, and parody rituals called "wombats," as a discourse about the boundaries of their own community, both external and internal.

These forms delineate boundaries between traditions and create a common culture around shared knowledge and values. One consultant compared telling a joke to casting a magic circle, one of the primary acts in ritual, which establishes sacred space, keeping the participants' energies inside and undesired energies out. "A joke is a spell. . . . What people do to create a boundary [is] . . . banishing energy and . . . raising energy. The joke has a function of defining in-group and out-group and the values of in-group as opposed to the out-group."

Many jokes take the form of question-and-answer "riddle jokes," similar to those found in mainstream American folklore; they occur in cycles (lightbulbs, road-crossing chickens, etc.) and focus on the supposed characteristics of traditions. Others imitate the kinds of lists popularized by comedians such as David Letterman and Jeff Foxworthy; these are more typically passed through e-mail and photocopied broadsheets. Jokes are most commonly exchanged at festivals, where Pagans from a number of different traditions come together, and on Internet newsgroups and lists, which are usually not limited to a single tradition. In these contexts, stereotypes about other groups humorously convey information about the supposed shared character of members of the tradition. While these jokes may seem to, in the words of one teller, "confer an illegitimacy to the groups we're making fun of," in effect they work to create and maintain a larger Pagan culture. "If you don't understand the joke, you're not in the 'in' crowd," one teller explained. "We're telling these jokes in our community; we can't go somewhere else and make a joke about Gardnerians, 'cause nobody's going to understand."

Pagans often use humor to comment on the differences between themselves, the dominant culture, and groups with which they are sometimes confused, such as the New Age movement. A series of jokes that contrast Pagans with New Agers illustrate how Pagans view their place in the American class hierarchy compared to other, similar groups.

What's the difference between a Pagan and a New Ager?
One hundred pounds and a hundred thousand dollars. [alternately: fifty pounds and five hundred dollars].

What's the difference between a New Age event and a Pagan event?
Two decimal points.

These jokes focus on two presumed differences between New Agers and Neo-Pagans: money and weight.[14] New Agers, according to this stereotype, are wealthier than Pagans, and their events cost more to attend.[15] They are also portrayed as thinner. While doctors estimate that about 50 percent of American adults are over their ideal weight, in American popular iconography weight is generally inversely proportional to social class. Think of the expression "You can never be too rich or too thin." In advertising and popular representation, the wealthy are almost always depicted as slender, while the working class are often portrayed as heavy. Both money and weight can thus be read as markers of class status.[16]

On the surface, the jokes appear to insult Neo-Pagans, identifying them as embodying negative lower-class characteristics, just as certain ethnic jokes may focus on features that allegedly mark a given minority group as being lower class.[17] While the jokes can certainly be told this way, they are more often told among Neo-Pagans about themselves—they are "in-group" jokes. The sort of humor group members make about themselves tends to target characteristics the group considers important or endearing in some way, even if the humor seems self-deprecatory. This suggests that economics—or attitudes about wealth—are an important distinguishing marker for Pagans. Orion's statistics showed that in 1994, 79 percent of Pagans responding to her questionnaire had personal incomes below twenty-five thousand dollars a year, while 50 percent had household incomes below that level; only 3 percent had personal incomes above forty-five thousand dollars a year (Orion, 1995:70). As Orion's research shows, for many Pagans, helping others, artistic and creative pursuits, and employment satisfaction are far more important than earning power in determining career choice. It is not that Pagans devalue income, but that on their general scale of values, accumulating wealth is not a high priority.

This shared value is illustrated by a humorous list circulating on the Internet that offers tips to distinguish yuppie (young, urban professional) Pagans:

You might be a yuppie Pagan if . . .

your BMW stands out among the Toyotas and VWs at the Grand Coven,

the priestess sends the ritual wine back to the cellar,

the ritual wine is more European than your tradition,

you ask your bank for a Visa Gold Card with Stonehenge depicted on its face,

you try to break a hundred-dollar bill in the donation pot at a public circle,

your first-degree initiation had valet parking,

you stop at the 7/11 to buy a cord of firewood for the bonfire,

your ritual bath is a Jacuzzi,

you have to hurry the Yule ritual along, the plane for Aspen leaves in an hour.

The list plays on the incongruity between the egalitarian ethos of contemporary Paganism and the unabashed concern with status and money of stereotypical yuppies. Sam Webster, commenting on the jokes, remarked, "Pagans are more poverty-conscious [than New Agers]," whom Pagans usually consider "nothing but yuppiedom with added hypocrisy" (Purkiss, 1996:31). Pagans generally have an egalitarian ethos, which makes them acutely sensitive to issues of social inequality, and a strong sense of antiauthoritarianism, which leads them to be suspicious of money's power to corrupt. Pagans resist certain forms of consumer culture, especially the commercialization of spirituality. One woman commented on the jokes by saying that for New Agers spirituality was simply a commodity. Yet the proliferation of books, classes, Web sites, products, and workshops with Neo-Pagan themes make it clear that Neo-Paganism is itself highly commodified. Jokes contrasting Pagans with New Agers and yuppies project spiritual commodification onto outside groups, briefly allaying Pagans' anxieties around this issue.

Despite the discomfort many American Neo-Pagans feel about the commodification of their religion, it is impossible to fully separate spirituality from economics in a market economy. While both Pagan and New Age groups are firmly entrenched in the market, Pagans contrast their ethic to that of New Agers, whom they portray as greedy profiteers and hucksters. A related joke expresses this:

How many New Agers does it take to change a light bulb?
You mean you don't know? Why, for just five hundred dollars, that's right, five hundred dollars, we'll send you our complete Power of Lightbulb Changing Course.

Some Pagans suggest that envy and ambivalence may lie behind the hostility toward New Agers. When asked to comment on them, Alison explained, "[The jokes express] envy. They've made it. We've worked so hard for so long, and they got rich in just one weekend!" Another woman, Renee, ventured: "We are concerned with the fact that we're all broke and we'd like to make some money the way New Agers do, just not the way they do it." Yet another commentator suggested the jokes force Pagans to examine their own consciences: "Gee, are any of us slipping into that?"

In raising the issue of economic difference between Pagans and New Agers, these jokes affirm Pagan values, at the same time allowing discourse on difference and ambivalence to emerge. They project exploitive economic practices outside the movement, and emphasize the authenticity and purity of a tradition in which money is not supposed to be the driving force.

Other Pagan jokes attempt to delineate the boundaries between different traditions by playing on humorous stereotypes. Just as national and regional groups share an alleged set of characteristic traits in folklore, Neo-Pagans have developed popular stereotypes (called *blason populaires* by folklorists) about members of certain traditions.

Gardnerians' secrecy and exclusivity makes them a frequent target of jokes among other Pagans, who generally distrust both elitism and hierarchy. Some of this ambivalence is expressed in jokes about the tradition, such as:

> How many Gardnerians does it take to change a lightbulb?
> Sorry, that's a Third Degree secret.

The joke implies that the tradition makes secrets out of obvious or mundane matters. The fact that many Gardnerians also tell this joke about themselves illustrates that they recognize the tremendous emotional charge secrecy carries for them. Gardnerians are sworn to secrecy as part of their initiations; their word is their bond, and breaking it carries serious magical and social consequences. It is natural that they should feel attached to it as an important trait that distinguishes them from popular forms of Paganism.

Like Gardnerians, ceremonial magicians (members of groups such as the Ordo Templo Orientis, or OTO), who may or may not be considered part of the Pagan community, have a reputation for formality and hierarchy. In addition, their alleged character includes the arrogance and pomposity often attributed to their most famous member, Aleister Crowley. The following joke reflects these stereotypes:

> How many ceremonial magicians does it take to change a lightbulb?
> Just one to hold the lightbulb while the universe revolves around him.

Dianic Witches, many of whom worship in women-only covens with a feminist theaology, are targets of some of the same jokes as feminists in the dominant culture. Because of the earnestness of many Dianics in their efforts to create nonpatriarchal traditions, they are portrayed as humorless in this riddle-joke:

> How many Dianics does it take to change a lightbulb?
> Just one, and that's not funny!

These examples of folk humor depend on shared understandings regarding traits allegedly associated with certain traditions: Gardnerians are secretive; ceremonial magicians are said to be self-important; Dianic Witches are supposedly humorless. Similar jokes are told outside the Neo-Pagan community targeting mainstream groups about whom tellers share stereotypes—Harvard professors, for instance, or radical feminists. For both Pagans and non-Pagans, these shared understandings ultimately reflect more about common values than about any real characteristics of the targeted groups. Tellers of these jokes presumably value altruism and humor, and see themselves as possessing these desirable qualities. The jokes create boundaries by emphasizing shared values and shared understandings about the supposed characteristics of outsiders.

A piece of folk humor that circulated on the Internet and on Neo-Pagan e-mail groups entitled "Understanding Traditions" plays on the popular riddle-joke "Why did the chicken cross the road?" In this bit of whimsy, each tradition gives its own answer to the eternally unanswerable question, revealing (to those in the know) stereotypical traits associated with its style and ideology.

> The eternal question "Why did the chicken cross the road?" has many answers.
>
> Alexandrian/Gardnerian: to reveal this would break my oath of secrecy. I can say, though, that it *really* is an ancient rite, dating far back in time, and I have learned it from an unbroken lineage. As Gerald said, it takes a chicken to make an egg.
>
> Asatru: First, we don't believe in a "One chicken" or a "Hen and Rooster." We believe in many chickens. Second, "crossing the road" is part of three levels or worlds, and the chickens simply crossed from one level into another. Hail to the chickens!
>
> British Traditional: The word *chicken* comes from a very specific Old English word (*gecheckken*), and it only properly applies to certain fowl of East Anglia or those descended therefrom. As for the rest, I suppose they are doing something remotely similar to crossing the road, but you must remember that traditional roads are not to be confused with modern roads.
>
> Celtic: In County Feedbeygohn on Midsummer Day, there is still practiced St. Henny's Dance, which is a survival of the old pagan Chicken Crossing fertility rite. Today, modern pagans are reviving the practice, dedicated to the Hen and the Green Rooster.
>
> Ceremonial: "Crossing the road" is a phrase that summarizes many magical structures erected and timed by the chicken to produce the energy necessary for the intention of travel across the road. For example, the

astrological correspondences had to be correct, the moon had to be waxing (if the chicken intended to come to the other side of the road) or waning (if the chicken intended to flee to the other side of the road), and the chicken had to prepare herself through fasting and proper incantations.

Dianic: The chykyn (*chicken* is a term of patriarchal oppression) sought to reclaim for herself the right to be on the other side of the road, after it had been denied to her for centuries. By doing so, she reawakened the power of the Hen within herself.

Druid: To get to the sacred grove, of course! Keep in mind that 99 percent of everything written about chickens crossing the road is pure hogwash, based on biased sources. Yes, there were a few chicken sacrifices in the past, but that is now over.

Eclectic: Because it seemed right to her at the time. She used some Egyptian-style corn and a Celtic-sounding word for the road, and incorporated some Native American elements into her Corn-name, Chicken-Who-Dances-and-Runs-with-the-Wolves.

Feri: In twilight times and under sparkling stars, those properly trained can still see the chickens crossing the roads. Reconnecting with these "fey-fowl" as they cross is crucial to restoring the balance between the energies of modern development and living with the earth.

Family Traditional: Growing up, we didn't think much about "crossing the road." A chicken was a chicken. It crossed the road because that was what worked to get her to the other side. We focused on what worked, and we worked more with the elders of the barnyard and less with all this "guardians of the chicken coop" business. We didn't get our concepts of "chickens" or "the other side" from Gardner, either. You can choose not to believe us since we did not "scratch down" what was clucked to us orally . . . , but that doesn't change the facts: there *were* real chickens, and they *really did* cross the road!

Kitchen Witch: The chicken crossed the road to get food, to get to a rooster, or to get away from me after I decided to have chicken for dinner!

Solitary: The chicken didn't want to be part of a coven, or an oven.

Like "Lady Pixie Moondrip's Guide to Pagan Names," the road-crossing chicken humor pokes fun at the ways traditions create authenticity for themselves, legitimating their own existence while at times disparaging that of other traditions. The chicken and the act of crossing the road become symbols that each tradition interprets according to its own style; the piece is humorous to Pagans because it parodies the recognizable styles of each tradition. As we have seen in other jokes, Gardnerians and other British traditionalists are lampooned for their conservatism and obsession with lineage and origins, while ceremonial magicians are derided for their insistence on precise relationships and procedures in performing magic. The Celtic traditions are ridiculed for their (mis)use of survivalist theories about fertility rites, while the Druids use the chicken to address the issue of their reclaimed history. Asatru, a tradition based on Norse mythology, reflects the old Norse conception of the world as multileveled—derided, in this instance, by its association with the mundane chicken. Dianics are made fun of for their feminist principles, while eclectic Witches suffer for appropriating everything in sight from a variety of cultural sources. Family traditionalists—those who insist that they carry on a folk tradition of Witchcraft that owes nothing to modern authors—are excoriated for their fixation with oral transmission; the Feri tradition, with its emphasis on ecstatic states, is made to seem and silly and flaky.

Other jokes create community without projecting undesirable qualities onto outsiders or targeting shared stereotypes of traditions. The following plays with one of the most frustrating but broadly recognized aspects of the movement: the tendency for organized events to begin later than their stated starting time. This is sometimes euphemistically called "Pagan Standard Time."

How do the Witches know it's midnight?
The eight o'clock ritual is starting.

Pagans overwhelmingly find this joke very funny. While it appears to target Witches, it applies broadly to an experience almost all Pagans have had: the boredom and frustration of waiting for a ritual to begin—or, conversely, the panic of the ritual organizers as they realize important elements are missing and the ritual cannot possibly start on time. Like the joke about the frog hanging from the ceiling, it plays with the audience's understanding of the word *W/witch*: witches are supposed to do mysterious things at midnight, a liminal time, and may have arcane knowledge that helps them determine the timing of rituals. The Witches in the joke, however, turn out to be quite human after all: the punch line is not about arcane knowledge or mysterious rites, but about disorganization and poor planning.

In a similar vein, a piece of e-mail lore modeled on popular stand-up comedian Jeff Foxworthy's use of the list "You might be a redneck if. . . ." enumerates ways to tell whether one is a Pagan:

You might be Pagan if . . .

when you're sworn into court, you bring your own grimoire.

you've been seen talking to cats. They talk back. You know what they're saying.

when asked whether you believe in God, you ask "Which one?"

you have a frequent-buyer card at your local used bookstore. The owner picks up anything to do with Celts and saves it for you.

on Halloween, you yell "Happy New Year!" at passers-by.

you commit blasphemy in the plural.

you know that Christmas trees were originally Pagan; that's why you bought one.

your guests say, "My, that's a nice . . . altar you have there."

you know there are exceptions to the laws of physics. You've caused them.

in Religion 101, you're disappointed because they didn't cover YOUR gods.

you understand the symbolism behind a maypole.

you've ever ended a phone call with "So mote it be."

you're reading this list. You understand what it's talking about. You have more to add.

Like other pieces of in-group humor, the list works by mentioning features most Pagans recognize and claim as their own. It lacks the divisiveness of the road-crossing chicken humor, focusing instead on elements that all Pagan traditions have in common. As the final item suggests, only a Pagan would read the list, understand it, and be able to think of additional items to add.

Pagans use jokes much as they cast circles that separate them from the mundane world and keep out unwanted influences. Who is "in" and who is "out" is largely a matter of context. Traditions may use humor to caricature themselves and each other; but on the whole, Pagan humor has more uniting features than divisive ones, and serves as a vector of cohesion in a community whose boundaries are shifting, flexible, and imagined.

## Summary

American Neo-Paganism exists both as a community in which religious culture is created and shaped, and as an identity performed for both insiders and outsiders. As new religions form and develop, disagreements arise over a number of issues, and these cause factions to diverge in various directions. Neo-Paganism, as a movement which is antiauthoritarian, critical of the dominant culture, and invested in the idea of individual spiritual authority, has spawned an almost endless number of denominations; in fact, one of its appealing features for individualistic, freedom-seeking Americans is that it leaves a great deal of space for difference. It is broadly accepting of differences in gender, sexual orientation, class, and ethnicity, as well as individual differences in the interpretation of belief. Belief, in fact, is not the primary rubric that unites the movement; Paganism is more orthopractic (concerned with practice) than orthodox (concerned with doctrine or belief). Don suggested that an even more accurate term might be "orthognostic: we recognize the same core spiritual experience in each other." One of the Covenant of the Goddess's definitions of a Witch is "It takes one to know one"; this brings us back to the essentialist arguments at the beginning of this chapter. The problem for Neo-Paganism, then, is how a practice- and experience-based movement that consists of shifting, complex networks can achieve a degree of cohesion that allows traditions to be transmitted.

Pagans have come up with numerous strategies for creating community and identity. Some embody the human impulse to standardize, codify, record, and explain through story, while others diverge in new directions, based on individual experience and preference. The result is the existence of multiple, overlapping traditions, each based on heterogeneous borrowing from different texts that differ from one another primarily in terms of style. Neo-Pagans distinguish among themselves by contrasting between traditions, but also through forms of folklore that draw a magic circle around the community, emphasizing its boundaries and borders. The common thread that unites them all is experience, the subject of the next section of this book.

# Part II
# Religions of Experience

*Chapter 3*

# Making Magic: Training the Imagination

**Field notes, November 16, 1996**

The members of Coven Trismegiston have gathered at Don and Anna's house for an evening of teaching and learning magic, held monthly at the new moon. We have pushed the furniture against the walls, creating a tight space between the sofa, the fireplace, the front window, and the bookcases where we can cast a circle. The altar has been set up on the coffee table, stacks of books hidden underneath: in the center is the Maiden Candle, from which the other candles are always lit. On either side are the statues of the goddess and god: Hecate and Hermes, guardians of the paths to the otherworld, mentors of magic, they are our primary teachers. Before them are salt and water, incense and charcoal. Anna mixes the consecrated salt into the water using her athame, or ritual knife, and lights the coal so the incense will burn. These acts of transformation—the dissolution of the salt into the water, the metamorphosis of the incense into purifying, fragrant smoke—symbolize how every act that takes place in the magic circle ("between the worlds," Witches say) is a transformation, a change. Then Anna walks around the circle holding Don's sword, chanting:

> A meeting place of love and joy,
> A shield that none would dare destroy;
> A rampart to contain the power
> Within our Lady's hidden bower.
> And so by fire and water be
> Consecrated, and by me.

Katya and Nancy follow her, sprinkling salt water and blowing incense smoke around the perimeter of the space. One by one, Anna and Katya sprinkle us with salt water and cleanse us with smoke from the incense burner. The circle is cast.[1]

Tonight's lesson is about energy. Don asks us to imagine our feet growing roots that stretch deep into the ground, bringing up the earth's energy, drawing it up into our bodies. Witches call this exercise "grounding," because it makes them aware of their enduring connection to the earth. He asks us to feel the energy as it courses up our legs, into our thighs, filling our torsos and arching out into our arms. Together we pull it up into our heads until we can feel it tingle right at the top of our skulls.

Now we break up into pairs. We are instructed to pull up energy from the earth and send it to our partners, then describe what we feel. My partner for this exercise is Katya. We stand facing each other, and she puts her palms over mine, close but not touching. At first I feel only her breath and the slight warmth from the skin on her palms.

"I don't feel anything," I complain.

"Stay with it," says Don. "Be patient." After a bit my palms start feeling slightly numb and tingly.

"I can really feel your energy," says Katya.

"Really? My hands are starting to feel sort of numb," I reply. I have been so focused on trying to feel Katya's energy that I have forgotten all about sending my own energy to her.

"That's it, that's how it's supposed to feel," she says. She moves her palms up and down over mine. "Put your hands on top," she suggests. We switch hand positions. Suddenly I can feel a gentle resistance between our hands. It feels warm and springy, and we can bounce it by moving our hands up and down in synchrony.

"Whoa! Did you feel that?" I ask. Part of me wonders whether this is just a trick of my imagination: I've been told to feel something, and now my brain has created something for me to feel.

"Yeah, that springy, bouncy thing," says Katya. "That's energy."

I am astounded. If Katya feels the same thing, does that mean it's real? Or did our imaginations somehow work in synchrony, creating parallel impressions? After a while I don't care; I am having too much fun. The feeling reminds us of playing with a spring toy. "It's Slinky, it's Slinky!" Giggling, we chant the refrain to the commercial jingle as we bounce the energy back and forth between our palms.

"Okay, switch partners," says Don. Katya and I have a tendency to get very silly when we're together, and Don wants to return a semblance of seriousness to the lesson.

This time I partner with Pitch. Like me, Pitch loves cats. By now my imagination and sense of play have been awakened. When he places his palms over mine, I feel fur and large, warm pads, like enormous cat paws. "Paws," I exclaim. "Your hands feel like giant paws."

"I was just channeling a jaguar, one of my totem animals," he says. Somehow this coincidence seems profound.

Eventually we all get to partner with each other and create the sensation of sending and feeling energy. Each partnering experience is slightly different and yields a different set of sensations; Witches say this is because each person has a different energy signature, just as we all have different voices. Our energy will also feel different to different people, as each individual senses energy slightly differently: Anna, for example, described my energy as "strong and muscular, like snakes," while to Don it felt "like cold running water."

As we saw in the previous chapters, what unites Neo-Pagans is not a common belief or faith, or even a unified practice, as is the case for many other religions. There is no single deity or set of deities whom they worship, theological/thealogical principles to which they cleave, or tenets with which they all agree. The single rubric that unites Neo-Pagan and Witchen groups is experience.

Magical practice is an experience shared by nearly all Neo-Pagans. In this chapter, I explore how Witches and Pagans conceive of and practice magic. I explore magic first as a set of principles for organizing the universe—a pattern that Neo-Pagans see as underlying all of life, rather than a separate, esoteric, and occult category of phenomena. I will argue that in this religious culture, belief in magic represents a reclamation of traditional ways of knowing that privilege the imagination, rather than an escape from rationality. In this context, I am using *imagination* to refer to a broad spectrum of thought processes, from memory to creative problem-solving to artistic expression, that rely primarily on internal imaging, rather than on discursive verbal expression or linear logic. Imagination is central to human thinking and expression. Rather than being irrational—that is, not rational, or the opposite of rationality—the imagination possesses its own inner logic that complements or enhances linear thought. Imagination is central to human creativity, whether expressed in verbal, visual, or performing arts; it is no accident that so many Neo-Pagans are also artists of one kind or another, and that the creative act is one of the movement's central metaphors: for Pagans, the artist is fundamentally a magician (Magliocco, 2001; Orion, 1995:58). In this chapter, I will spin out some of the implications of this metaphor, suggesting that if the artist is fundamentally a magician, then perhaps it may be fruitful to examine magic as a form of art.

The practice of magic is one of the venues through which the logic of the imagination finds expression. The language of ritual allows the human imagination to express itself and communicates between the unconscious and rational consciousness. This process seems to be central to many Neo-Pagan artists, who use insights and visions gained from the imagination as inspiration for their craft (Magliocco, 2001); but Pagans argue that anyone can benefit from it. In the Reclaiming tradition, the self-knowledge gained from a disciplined use of the imagination becomes a vehicle for achieving personal wholeness, which Reclaiming Witches see as necessary for attaining social and planetary healing, as well. Learning magic involves learning to discipline the imagination, and in this chapter I examine how that is done.

## The Academic Study of Magic

Magic has attracted scholarly attention from the time of the emergence of the disciplines of folklore and anthropology; yet paradoxically, both disciplines have struggled to delineate the concept. "Magic" has been used to refer to both practice (the performance of charms and spells) and belief (faith in their efficacy), often without distinction between the two; both are assumed to be irrational and ultimately false, according to the scientific paradigm. But as anthropologist Stanley J. Tambiah, who has written the most thorough critique of the anthropological study of magic, *Magic, Science, Religion, and the Scope of Rationality* (1990), reminds us, "A narrow yardstick of 'rationality' misses the theatrical and illocutionary aspects of ritual performance" (1990:24). Tambiah dates the cultural construction of the concept of "magic" as separate from religion to the time of the Protestant Reformation, which, as we have seen, sought a direct link between the individual and God free from "accretions" and "contaminations" of both Catholicism and ancient paganism. Protestant reformers attributed magic to Catholic dogmas such as transubstantiation, as well as to peasant practices containing pagan elements. Tambiah argues that the distinction between religion as faith or belief, versus religion as praxis—prayer, spell, ritual, magic—is a legacy of the Protestant Reformation that continues to haunt anthropology (and, I would add, folkloristics) (Tambiah, 1990:19). He traces this concept through the works of Edward B. Tylor, Sir James Frazer, Bronislaw Malinowski, and Lucien Lévy Bruhl.

Tylor's unilinear evolutionary schema established an anthropological tradition of distancing magical practice from religion. It projected magic into past (pagan) practices, or relegated it to the lower classes, women, and "savages." Magic was supposed to characterize the prerational "savage" or "primitive" stages of human development; when it occurred among "civilized" people, it was interpreted as a survival. Because Tylor believed magic to be false, he gave a great deal of attention to the question of why humans continued to practice it, even though it did not work. His conclusions continue to influence anthropologists today in their assumptions that magic works psychologically, as "self-fulfilling prophecy," "placebo effect," "psychodrama," or "secondary rationalizations" (Tambiah, 1990:46).

While they rejected nineteenth-century theories of unilinear cultural evolution, early twentieth-century anthropologists continued to struggle with the problem of magic. Frazer, while he granted magic the legitimacy of a logical system, nevertheless saw it as an early, and erroneous, form of science (Frazer, 1959). French sociologist Emile Durkheim, continuing the tradition of separating magic from religion, perceived magical practitioners as antisocial, acting against the interests of the larger social group, in contrast to religious practitioners, who worked in the interests of group solidarity (Durkheim, 1947).

Anthropologist Bronislaw Malinowski, who studied the magic of Trobriand islanders for many years, understood its central role in the islanders' social and economic lives to a much greater degree than his predecessors; yet, he, too, ultimately saw magic as faulty technology, and attributed to it a psychological function. Malinowski theorized that human beings resort to magic when their technology reaches its limits, and the resulting situations are dangerous or risky. In one of his classic examples, he found that lagoon fishermen, who fished using nets and poison, used very little magic in their enterprise, while deep-sea fishermen, who sailed on the open ocean for weeks at a time in log canoes, practiced many magic rituals. He saw magic as working to reduce anxiety and compensate for what humans could not control through technological means: deep-sea fishermen had more rituals than lagoon fishermen because the outcome of their enterprise was both less certain and more dangerous. But Tambiah critiques Malinowski's thesis by showing how in the Trobriands, magic also had important social roles. Deep-sea fishing was indeed dangerous, but it also yielded shark—a very high-status food with important emotional and affective associations for the islanders. Taro and yam cultivation involved magical rituals because yam and taro exchange was central to Trobriand social prestige. Tambiah suggests that social valuation may be more closely associated with magic than either danger or technological insufficiency (Tambiah, 1990:72).

Tambiah also calls our attention to Malinowski's documentation of the importance of what folklorists today would call magic's performative qualities: its inherent drama, use of the body and voice, manipulation of sacred material objects, and heightened language. The language of magic, according to Malinowski, differed from everyday language in its sacred character, "coefficient of weirdness" (in other words, its very strangeness gave it power and set it apart from ordinary language), and the belief that it had inherent power, present from the very creation of the universe. Use of this speech in and of itself deeply affected people, much as modern English speakers may be moved by the use of Shakespearean language, or language from the King James Bible. Ultimately, Malinowski believed magic functioned not objectively, by affecting causality, but subjectively, by affecting human witnesses and creating change in them (Tambiah, 1990:81). As we will see, this is essentially how many Neo-Pagans believe that magic works.

Many anthropologists and folklorists today are critical of earlier approaches to magic and their ethnocentric, value-laden terminology. Research during the twentieth century illustrated that in most cultures, magic and religion are closely intertwined: all religions have magical aspects. Still, in many contexts within the dominant North American culture, the legacy of nineteenth-century anthropology and folkloristics continues: belief in magic continues to be thought of as irrational, and magical practice as a defective technology whose results are, at best, psychological. Magic is central to the practice of Neo-Pagan religions, yet it is part of what makes them seem alien, marginal, and either frightening or ridiculous to outsiders. As Margot Adler pointed out, to most North Americans, magic means "superstition or belief in the supernatural" (Adler, 1986:6). In psychology, "magical thinking," the belief that we can influence events through thought, is thought to be characteristic of very small children, and is considered pathological when it occurs in adults. Understandably, then, many scholars who have studied the movement have had to grapple with the question of how a group of well-educated, middle-class people, many of them employed in scientific fields, can believe in magic (Luhrmann, 1989; Pike, 1996).

In her study of a Gardnerian coven in London, anthropologist Tanya M. Luhrmann argued that rational, well-educated, middle-class Witches came to believe in magic through a process she called "interpretive drift." Luhrmann showed how continued participation in coven activities and exposure to narratives and interpretations that emphasized magical explanations pushed new practitioners to interpret more of their own experiences as magically caused. My own work both builds upon and departs from Luhrmann's. While I see the sharing of personal narratives with a sympathetic group as important elements in constructing a Pagan or Witchen worldview, I also see many Pagan beliefs as experience-based. Witches and Pagans believe in magic for two principal reasons: their definitions of magic make their beliefs rational and logical, and their personal experiences, both before their "conversion" to Neo-Paganism and within the Neo-Pagan praxis, support a magical worldview.

The process of becoming a Witch or a Pagan is essentially a process of training the imagination. The instruction Witches and Pagans receive in initiatory traditions prepares the imagination to experience religious ecstasy, and facilitates the occurrence of "psychic" and "paranormal" events (Adler, 1986:154). For those who have a history of experiencing these events before their association with Paganism, it also provides a framework within which to understand and control these experiences, and prepares individuals to create rituals that impart these experiences to others. Extraordinary experiences, within the context of Neo-Pagan ritual, should not be seen as aberrant, but rather as the product of a particular set of cultural, social, and religious circumstances that encourage, channel, and perhaps even create them. As I suggested earlier, it might be helpful to think about magic in this context as an art form. Like art, the goal of much magic is to bring about an emotional or affective reaction that effects a change in consciousness. We do not question the rationality of either artists or of individuals who are profoundly moved by art—who may leave an exhibit of paintings in tears, or experience a personal epiphany during a concert—because we expect art to affect human emotions, to bring about reactions that ordinary, everyday experience cannot because of its very ordinariness. In understanding magic and its sometimes surprising results, such as the ones described by Edith Turner, Bruce Grindal, and Raymond Lee in the Introduction, we might think of it as a kind of performance art aimed at producing extraordinary experiences.

## Defining Magic

There is no single definition of magic shared by all Neo-Pagans. Some, drawing on early twentieth-century magician Aleister Crowley, define it as "the capacity to alter consciousness at will." This definition, like Malinowski's above, does not require the transformation of anything outside of the individual's consciousness. Others prefer a definition that allows for the possibility of effecting changes in external reality; for them, magic is the ability to harness existing natural forces in conformity with one's will in order to bring about transformation. Pagans see this potential as natural, rather than supernatural, and inherent in all human beings: we all have the capacity to do magic. Margot Adler, a pioneering researcher of the movement, describes a memorable anecdote in her own study of Neo-Pagans that provides an excellent illustration of this principle at work. Adler was working on a communal farm in Colorado run by a Pagan family. She and several other volunteers were given the task of collecting dying fish from an evaporating stream bed, loading them into a truck, and taking them back to the farm to use as compost. The group struggled with the task for hours: the day was hot, the stream bed oozed with mud, and the slippery fish flopped about, eluding everyone's grasp. They were making no progress; the job seemed impossible. Then Michael, the group leader, suggested the workers imagine themselves as hungry bears that needed to catch the dying fish for their own survival. The volunteers began to think of their hands as great paws; they brought them together to grasp the fish and toss them over their heads into the truck's bed. Within an hour, the truck was filled with fish (Adler, 1986:7–8).

In the above example, only the participants' consciousness—the way they imagined the task—changed. The day was equally hot, the mud did not magically harden into concrete, the fish did not leap willingly into the truck, and the workers did not actually change into bears. But by changing their own consciousness, by utilizing their imaginations, the volunteers were able to change their approach to the problem and actually solve it. That, a Witch or Neo-Pagan would say, is magic. "Magic is simply the art of getting results," Michael explained to Adler after this incident (Adler, 1986:6).

At the same time, magic is more than simply changing one's attitude. Few Pagans would say that simply changing our personal consciousness of a problem makes it go away, although most troubles do benefit from a change of perspective. Many also believe that magic can have a real effect on the world—that magic, properly applied, can change material reality as well. I will take up the issue of how Pagans believe magic works later in this chapter. It is worth bearing in mind, in this context, Tambiah's remarks on this issue: "There might be principles of thought in earlier or pre-modern socio-cultural contexts, that have internal connections and 'logics' of their own and these thought systems . . . differed from our own dominant forms of modern thought to such a degree that our own cognitive theories and logical systems might be powerless to explain them" (Tambiah, 1990:87).

In other words, it is possible that ideas of rationality are limited by cultural bias; that rationality itself is a cultural construct; and that other societies may possess ways of knowing that are challenging for us to understand because they defy our own culturally bound systems of logic.

## Magic as an Organizational Principle: The Interconnected Universe

What makes possible a practical definition of magic is a concept of an interconnected universe that most Pagans and Witches share. According to this rubric, magic is set of principles, underlying the universe, by which all beings and phenomena are interconnected. All objects and events are suffused with meaning, which can be discerned by observing the symbolic correspondences between them. The view of the universe as an interconnected whole is quite ancient, as I illustrated in Chapter 1; it can be traced to the third millennium B.C.E., and continued to exist in some form well into the twentieth century in rural areas of Europe, and among minority populations, as a counterdiscourse to the Enlightenment concept of a mechanical universe.

Recent work by a number of folklore scholars has demonstrated that in many cases, what appears to outsiders as supernaturalism or magical belief is in fact a set of organizing principles that regulate the cosmos.[2] Timothy Lloyd, writing about Ohio farmer Lloyd Farley's practice of farming "by the signs," or according to the position of the moon in the heavens, suggests that magic and "supernaturalism" be reconceived as "the realm of the fundamental patterns and rhythms—of time, space, growth, and decline, for example—which connecting, give governance and purpose to life. . . . These patterns and rhythms are expressed in the natural world in the life cycles of the individual and family . . . , in the annual round of the seasons, in the division of space into directions and dimensions, and the like" (Lloyd, 1995:60). Belief in magic, therefore, should not be interpreted as an irrational faith in processes that violate the rules of nature, but as a fundamental way of organizing and understanding the patterns and workings of the cosmos.

For Neo-Pagans, the universe operates according to a set of laws that they call magic. Magician and Druid Isaac Bonewits synthesized these into twenty-four principles, which he outlines in his book *Real Magic* (1989:1–17). Holly Tannen refined and synthesized Bonewits's principles, with input from Don Frew, and came up with the following list of laws, some of which I have explicated further based on Holly's and Don's oral comments.

1. **Magic follows natural laws.** Magic cannot violate natural laws; thus, magic intended to enhance the natural tendencies of a subject (e.g., making seeds grow) is more likely to succeed than that which violates natural

laws (e.g., turning people into toads).[3] The more simple means are available for accomplishing something, the less successful magic will be. If one is hungry, for example, it is much easier to order a pizza than it is to make one appear by magical means. Making pizza magically appear is in fact unlikely to be very successful. No magical act can be static or permanent; all things go through cyclical change. No magical act is permanent. Thus if I perform magic to find a job, there is no guarantee the job I find will be permanent, or will forever satisfy my needs.

2. **Unity or sympathy.** All phenomena are linked, directly or indirectly. The universe operates as an interconnected whole. This principle can be further broken down, as the rest of this list elaborates.
3. **Contagion.** Things once in contact continue to influence each other, even after the contact has ended. This works like the children's game of "cooties": essences, like cooties, can be transferred through touch or proximity. A magician can transfer the essence of one person or thing to another through touch: healing energy, for example, can be transmitted to another by the laying on of hands (among other methods).
4. **Homeopathy.** "Like causes like." Things that look alike *are* alike, act alike and can substitute for each other.[4] As Starhawk says, "Ritual is thinking in things." Thus one way of making something happen is to enact that change using symbols in ritual space.
5. **Commonality controls.** If two or more things have elements in common, the things are linked through the elements, and can be controlled through that link. For example, in the United States, paper money is green; a spell to bring financial prosperity might use green candles, a green altar cloth, and other green objects to attempt to enhance wealth through that common characteristic.
6. **Microcosm/macrocosm.** "As above, so below." Larger patterns (e.g., movements of the stars) can reflect or influence smaller ones, and vice versa. So, for example, a tarot-card divination pattern can reflect larger patterns in the querent's life; the position of the moon and sun in the sky can affect rituals performed on earth.
7. **Synchronicity.** Coincidences are meaningful. Often, beginning magicians interpret their early successes as coincidental. "There are no coincidences," they are told. Pagans and Witches also interpret natural signs as meaningful, as in the case of Kestrel in the previous chapter: the appearance of a kestrel became a sign that he had selected the right ritual name.
8. **Knowledge is power.** The more you know about something, the easier it is to control it. This usually manifests in the following related principles:
   (a) The power of names. Pagans generally say that names contain the essence of a thing; this is one reason why choosing a magical name is

an important act. Some Pagans do not reveal their magical names outside the ritual context for fear that they could be used against them in a form of magical attack.

(b) the power of words. some Pagans say that certain words and formulas have intrinsic power. Formulas used to cast the circle, call in the elements, and draw down the essence of the deities into the bodies of worshippers are powerful in and of themselves.

9. **Animism or personification.** Any phenomenon can be considered to be alive and sentient. Thus is ritual Pagans may address a personal fear, asking that it depart; or request that the weather patterns change in order to bring much-needed rain.
10. **Invisible entities.** "Just because it's invisible doesn't mean it's not there." For many Pagans, the world is filled with invisible, spiritual entities, and it is possible to communicate with them.[5]

Another key concept in understanding Pagan notions of magic and conceptions of reality is "energy" (Orion, 1995:106). Many Pagans base their notions on the scientific theory that all matter is composed of energy, and on the related law of physics according to which energy can neither be created nor destroyed. But the Pagan concept of energy goes beyond the laws of thermodynamics; to Pagans, energy is the "underlying fabric of the material world" (Orion, 1995:108). Like the Chinese concept of *chi*, it is a life force, but one that is present in all things in the universe, animate and inanimate alike. Pagans conceive of energy as a force that can be raised from the earth, channeled through the physical body, shaped and directed to perform actions in the material and spiritual worlds, and "grounded," or sent back into the earth (cf. Orion, 1995:109). Manipulating energy is the essence of magical practice. Learning to do magic involves learning the techniques to manipulate energy, the fundamentals of which I described in the first sequence in this chapter. To do so necessarily involves changing consciousness: becoming aware of energy flows and patterns in our own selves and in the world around us that are usually not evident on the surfaces of things.

## The Sacralization of Time and Space

For many traditional cultures, the world itself is suffused with sacredness and meaning, such that each landmark, place, or direction has sacred narratives associated with it that link it to the culture's religious, scientific, and moral systems. In traditional societies the seasons were associated with specific activities that related directly to the maintenance of life: sowing and harvesting, the migration of herd animals, the coming of the rains, and so on. Without an awareness of these relationships, human beings would certainly not have survived for long. Cultures marked these changes in the year cycle with holy days that connected people's everyday economic activities with the realm of the sacred. But modern urban dwellers are much less aware of these patterns, as their lives do not depend on them; ways of knowing intimately connected to the seasons and the landscape are unusual in the city. It is difficult to conceive of shopping malls, auto dealerships, and supermarket lots as having meaning or sacredness beyond pure commercialism, and for many urban dwellers, especially in California where the seasons are much less marked than they are in the rest of North America, the year is a succession of days that differ little from one another. Even traditional holidays have become occasions for the marketing of themed products and foodstuffs (Santino, 1996), rather than celebrations that link humans to the seasonal cycles of the natural world, and through them, to the sacred. Yet contemporary Pagans manage to reinfuse their worlds, urban as they may be, with sacredness and meaning through the magical division of time and space. Rituals are one way to mark these passages. Starhawk explains: "Ritual is a way of marking and intensifying value. The moon waxes and wanes, and we may barely notice. But when we mark her changes with ritual, we identify with her cycles. We are reminded at the new moon of our own power to begin. At the full moon, we remember and intensify what it is in our lives that we are bringing to fulfillment. As the moon wanes, we let go. The moon cycle takes on a new depth of meaning, and the changes in our own lives become integrated with the forces around us" (1990:98).

For Pagans and Witches, yearly and monthly cycles are sacred, symbolic keys to understanding many of life's processes as well as the relationship between life and death. Most scan the year into four seasons and eight sabbats, or holy days:

Samhain, the night of October 31

winter solstice, or Yule, approximately December 21[6]

Imbolc, or Brigid, February 2

spring equinox, or Eostar, approximately March 21

Beltane, May 1

summer solstice, approximately June 21

Lammas, August 1

fall equinox, or Mabon, approximately September 21

Winter solstice and Imbolc are the winter sabbats; spring equinox and Beltane, the spring; summer solstice and Lammas, the summer holy days; and Mabon and Samhain the autumn ones. The year begins and ends at Samhain, with the final harvesting of the crops and the decline of vegetation in the northern hemisphere.[7] This year cycle, or "wheel of the year," as many

Witches call it, is rooted in European popular year-cycle celebrations linked to agricultural and pastoral economies. Gerald Gardner first articulated eight yearly ritual occasions in *The Meaning of Witchcraft* (1959), four of which were sabbats; the remaining four consisted of the full moons closest to the solstices and equinoxes. During the 1960s and 1970s, the solstices and equinoxes began to be observed as separate sabbats by many Witchcraft traditions, giving us the modern eight-sabbat year cycle.

Gardner's interpretation was rooted in Frazer's survivalist theory, which interpreted year-cycle rites as enactments of the myth of the death, and rebirth of the divine king. The metaphor of birth, development, death and regeneration is essential to the Neo-Pagan worldview. It is enacted ritually in each celebration of the sabbats, as participants observe and celebrate the changes in the natural world around them. But beyond that, it serves as a metaphor for stages in the individual life cycles of the goddesses and gods, and by association, in the women and men who worship them. There is a multiplicity of metaphorical narratives that Pagans use to organize the wheel of the year. One common myth is that of the earth as a goddess and seasonal vegetation as the god, who is both her son and her consort. The goddess gives birth to the god during the dark of winter, on the winter solstice. As the light increases, his strength grows, and on the spring equinox he bursts forth as vegetation everywhere grows and blooms. The sacred marriage of the goddess and god is celebrated in the rituals of Beltane, which often involve sexual metaphors such as the maypole, with its hoop of flowers at the top, being thrust into the earth. Their union continues through the summer solstice, but already the god begins his decline. At Lammas, his body is harvested with the grain, and sacrificed in the making of bread, which some covens consume as part of the celebration. The old god's decline continues through Samhain, when he returns to his realm in the otherworld, where he remains until his rebirth at the winter solstice. The god is also associated with the sun, whose cycle he follows.

No single myth symbolizes the year cycle in all Witchen or Pagan traditions. Some of the most widespread include the myth of Demeter and Persephone, in which the goddess Persephone enjoys nine months out of the year above ground in the company of her mother, Demeter, then returns to the otherworld during the winter months, when Demeter mourns, bringing the decline of vegetation and cold weather; the alternation of the god and goddess's rulership over the earth, with the fruitful goddess ruling from Beltane to Samhain and the god from Samhain to the following May; and the somewhat similar Oak and Holly King narrative, in which the Holly King rules from the winter solstice to the summer solstice, when he is defeated by the Oak King. Tremendous variation is possible even within a single tradition: for example, it is not unusual for Gardnerian Craft to celebrate both the rebirth of the sun/son at midwinter and the return of the goddess from the otherworld at the spring equinox. Dianic traditions, which focus solely on a goddess as creatrix of the universe, often adapt the goddess-centered myth of Demeter and Persephone as a symbol of their year cycle. The goddess conceives by parthenogenesis in winter, matures at Beltane, fruits through the summer, and declines into the autumn. Pagans do not attempt to homogenize their myth cycles. The existence of multiple sacred narratives about the year cycle, sometimes within a single tradition, is an example of Pagans' ability to hold mutually conflicting views simultaneously. The stories are not perceived as competing against one another, or as mutually exclusive expressions of truth, but as complementary metaphors through which they narrate their relationship to the natural world and its cycles.

In all these myths, the unifying factor is the cycle of life itself, and its harmony with the growth and decline of light in the northern hemisphere. Pagans and Witches use the circle and the spiral to symbolize this never-ending, ever-renewing cycle. When they dance in a circle or spiral, they dance in concert with this flow of energy, both to harness it for the ritual they perform and to help move the energy along its natural path.

In many traditions, the goddess is also associated with the moon, a trait that dates from the worship of Hecate, Diana, and Persephone in late antiquity. In her lunar aspect, the goddess undergoes a life-cycle transformation each month. At the new moon, she is the maiden goddess; when full, she represents the mother; and in her waning aspect, the crone. As Starhawk explained at the beginning of this section, each stage corresponds to different activities: the new moon to beginnings; the full moon to maturity and fruition; and the dark moon to decline, death, and the possibilities for rebirth. As in the solar or vegetative year cycle described above, the dark of the moon, like the dark of the year, is a necessary part of the cycle without which new beginnings, spring, renewal, and rebirth could never take place. Pagans and Witches thus do not fear the dark or equate it with evil, but celebrate decline and death as necessary parts of the life cycle—central aspects of the natural world, and therefore sacred. Many Pagans and Witches carefully time not only magical spells, but worldly projects according to these cycles, preferring, for example, to begin working on a new project at the new moon, bringing it to fruition around the time of the full moon, and using the days of the waning moon to revise, adjust, and correct the project before its completion. Large-scale projects are said to move more smoothly when they are coordinated with the year cycle. Thus in many traditions, initiations of new members are conducted during the period of waxing light between Imbolc and the summer solstice. Some Pagan friends advised me to time my research leave so the writing of this book would harmonize with the seasonal cycle.[8]

Just as time is rendered sacred by its association with sacred narratives, so is space. The four cardinal directions (east, south, west, and north) are fundamental to the casting of the circle, the Pagan creation of sacred space. Each direction corresponds in turn to an element, a season of the year, a quality or essence, and an animal:

east / air / spring / new beginnings, thought / bird or eagle

south / fire / summer / courage, will / lion or cat

west / water / autumn / imagination, intuition, emotion / fish

north / earth / winter / stability, embodiment, the material world / bull or bear

Holly Tannen drew this wheel of the year, with its symbols, for use in a class of mine she guest-taught, and I reproduce it here (see Figure 1).

Specific deities may be associated with each of the elements and directions—occasionally with more than one. Mercury or Hermes, for example, is an "airy" deity whose realms include communication, ideas, thoughts, intellectual work, travel, and "easterly" things; while Venus or Aphrodite, who rose from the waves, is considered "watery," emotional, intuitive, and associated with the west. Even ritual tools and objects are linked to this symbolic system: for example, the athame or ritual knife is associated with fire and the direction south; the wand with air and east; the cup with water and west; and the pentacle with earth and north.[9] These four objects also correspond to the four suits of the tarot deck, and their symbolic significance extends to divinatory work.

Magical training involves a process of learning "correspondences" that link dimensions of time, space, the physical world, and the sacred. For example, each planet corresponds to a particular deity, constellation, cardinal direction, natural element, season, gender, gemstone, and mineral, as well as to several colors, herbs, plants, and animals. Pagan and Witchen books often include tables that list these correspondences for initiates to study. Correspondences are essential to magic because through a process of metonymy, any one link may stand for any other in a ritual or spell. Thus a spell for successful communication might incorporate any of the elements associated with Hermes or Mercury, the Greco-Roman god of communication: the element air; the direction east; the metal quicksilver; the color yellow; the number one; the herbs fennel, dill, fenugreek and lavender; the ash tree; and the serpent, jackal, ibis, or crane.[10] Such a spell might be most effective if performed on a Wednesday, the day of the week sacred to Mercury, as well as during the hour of the day ruled by Mercury.[11]

Correspondences are consistent, but not meant to be rigid; there is considerable leeway for personal variation as well as variation among traditions of Paganism. Thus if a spell for prosperity involving the planet Jupiter calls for the use of purple candles (purple being a color associated with Jupiter), but the individual magician prefers to use green ones because of the color's association

The Wheel of the Year

and its concordances in Neo-Pagan thought

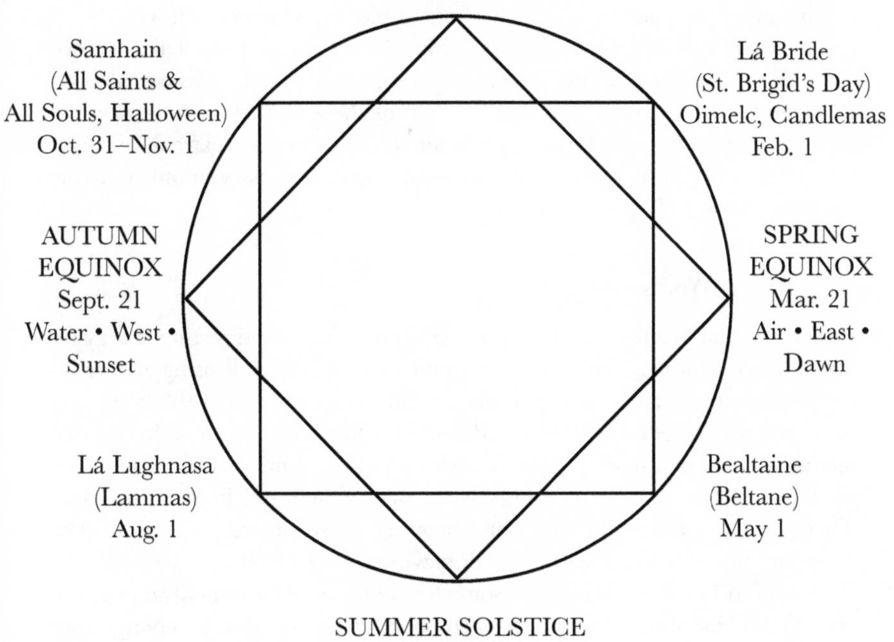

with money, the substitution is easily made. What is important is that the elements all be linked in the magician's imagination, since magic is essentially a mental activity.

The process of becoming a Witch or Pagan thus involves training the imagination to perceive the links connecting the elements in the universe. Soon, the process of seeing these connections becomes almost second nature, so that the sight or thought of any one link automatically evokes all of the others. A Pagan looking at the ivy plant in my office, for example, might associate it with the element earth, the direction north, the winter solstice, the constellation Capricorn, the planet Saturn, and so on. As a result of this, the universe takes on many additional layers of meaning. The use of these symbols in rituals and altars, and their interpretation in dreams and omens, becomes extremely evocative, stimulating participants' memories, emotions, and associations in a way that, according to Pagans, raises and moves energy.

## How Magic Works

Pagans say that magic works by raising, concentrating, and directing energy toward a particular goal, and by invoking the help of deities. Raising energy involves using the imagination, stimulating emotions, or moving the body, and preferably all three. Isaac Bonewits describes it this way: "Emotion is aroused, increased, built to a peak. A *target* [italics in original] is imaged [*sic*] and a goal made clear. The emotional energy is focused, aimed and fired at this goal. Then there is a follow-through; this encourages any lingering energy to flow away and provides a safe letdown" (Bonewits, 1989:159–60).

Most Neo-Pagan traditions use some form of bodily movement to raise energy. Gerald Gardner's Witches danced naked in a circle to raise energy from their bodies, a practice to which Gardnerian Witches still adhere; they say bodily movement heightens the flow of energy. Reclaiming Witches use the Spiral Dance in much the same way, to raise energy, imagined as a cone rising from the participants' bodies, which is then directed toward a particular goal. Energy can also be raised through meditative techniques such as the one described in the initial example in this chapter, drawing it up from the earth and down from the sun, moon, or stars, and into the body. "We do lots of earth protection work because the earth is being depleted; we give excess energy back to the earth [at the end of rituals] to renew the planet," explains Anna. Energy flows through human bodies and back into the earth in a never-ending cycle of reciprocity.

In order to raise energy for a particular magical spell, or working, as Pagans and Witches prefer to call it, symbolic correspondences are manipulated in a way that stimulates emotions, solicits a mental or visual image of the goal, and suggests the effects the magic should bring about. As Starhawk is fond of saying, "Magic is thinking in things." At the heart of this process is the act of transformation: magic is intended to bring about a change or metamorphosis in a situation, condition, or person. The type of magic performed depends entirely on the change desired. In this chapter, I will concentrate on what Pagans call operative magic—spells or thaumaturgy. Magic to "turn the wheel of the year," or celebrate the seasons, and to align with the gods operates on the same basic principles, but will be dealt with in Chapters 4 and 5.

The simplest magic can be performed without ceremonial parameters, such as casting a circle and calling in the deities. When Trismegiston Coven member Nancy broke her foot, Don, Katya, and I went to Nancy's house to perform some healing magic. First Don had us hold our hands over Nancy's healthy foot, without touching it, until we could feel its energy patterns. Then he had us do the same over Nancy's broken foot, which she rested on a foot stool in front of her. "Notice any differences in the energy flow," Don said. "You might feel them as temperature changes." After some time, I could feel the energy over Nancy's broken foot as somehow more jagged and uneven. "Now, drawing energy up from the earth, let it flow out of your hands and make it match the energy over Nancy's healthy foot," he explained. "Make it normal." Katya and I worked over Nancy, smoothing the energy flow until we could feel it changing, becoming smoother and cooler. Nancy affirmed that she felt much less pain in her foot after our healing, although of course it would take many weeks before the bones would knit again. Pagans on the whole do not avoid allopathic medicine, but may employ magic alongside both conventional and alternative medicine to heal the whole patient.

Other magical workings make use of the system of magical correspondences. Pagans use amulets and talismans to bring good luck, strength, healing, and other qualities they desire into their lives. These charms might incorporate a number of symbols associated with the essence the user seeks; for example, a spell for prosperity might incorporate imagery related to the planet Jupiter, the number eight, the colors purple and dark blue, the aspen tree, the horse, and the minerals gold and potassium. When Anna, a microbiologist, was learning RNA blotting techniques, she purchased a fused glass amulet inscribed with a bind rune (a combination of runes) meaning "skill." She liked the look of the piece and felt it would help her concentrate on learning the skills she needed in her new job. When Don was about to engage in a debate, he made a talisman incorporating symbols from the kamea of Mars, a magic square historically associated with the planet of triumph and kingship. He attached it under his lapel with a carnelian pin, because carnelian, a red gemstone, is traditionally associated with Mars. The pin appeared innocuous and attractive to his opponents, but concealed the talisman, which reminded him of his goals and gave him added confidence to achieve them.

Pagans disagree over how much magic can influence the external, material world. While there are some who say that magic works only by altering consciousness—in other words, magic is a psychological tool to change people's attitudes and states of mind—most Pagans and Witches believe that magic has some influence on the material world, as well, although how much is a matter of debate. In theory, according to Don, all things should be possible through magic, but the amount of energy and time this would take makes it impractical to use magic in most everyday situations. As we discussed this, we were sitting in Don and Anna's living room after a ritual, and I was feeling hungry. "You mean, I could magic up a pizza or a roast chicken right here, right now if I wanted to?" I asked incredulously.

"In theory, yes," Don replied. "But considering the amount of time and energy it would take, it's faster to go to Andronico's [a local grocery store with a rotisserie] or call up the pizza place. You could change your consciousness to produce the image of a roast chicken—but it wouldn't be very satisfying."

For practical, everyday problems, Pagans and Witches find it easier to use material rather than magical solutions. In fact, according to the first law of magic, the more simple means are available for accomplishing something, the less successful magic will be; so conjuring a roast chicken is unlikely to be successful when Andronico's is just around the corner. Despite this, magic permeates the everyday lives of Witches and Pagans. They use magic to help find houses and apartments, jobs or cars, they bless new houses and cars with spells and amulets, they use healing spells in addition to allopathic and naturopathic medicine on themselves and their companion animals, they bless seeds and transplants before planting them, and blast weeds with more than herbicide before pulling them from the ground. However, like Evans-Pritchard's Azande (Evans-Pritchard, 1983:22), few of them would say magic alone is enough to produce results in these cases; most agree that it is necessary to work in the material world as well. Magic enhances one's efforts in the material world, but does not replace them. "You can usually tell good magicians because their lives are generally working pretty well . . ." explained Don. "The more you practice magic, the less you need to."

This puzzled me, so I persisted in my questions. "Okay, but think of some of the people we know in the [Bay Area Pagan] community. If they're such powerful magicians, why are their lives such a mess?"

"Well, maybe they're not such powerful magicians," suggested Anna.

"Look, shit happens in everyone's life," said Don. "Magic is no guarantee that nothing will ever go wrong. What you look for is the overall pattern of their lives. Is this a temporary thing, or is there a persistent pattern of lousing up? If it's the latter, well . . ." Don proceeded to tell the story of a well-known couple in the Pagan community, emphasizing the many good things that had happened to them over the years, partly as a result of their magical workings. However, they had consistently made bad decisions about their good fortune, and were now in serious financial trouble. Their personal lives were also marked by strife. His conclusion was that despite their considerable ritual skills, they were in fact poor magicians. In Don's worldview and that of most Neo-Pagans I interviewed, magic and rationality are complementary rather than contradictory forces.Pagans say that while magic is a natural force that anyone can learn to use, people differ in their capacity to use it. Don compared it to a talent for music or sports. While anyone can learn to play tennis or the piano, some people have greater talent in these areas than others. With both talent and skill, one can become a champion tennis player or a concert pianist; but talent alone, with no knowledge or skill, will not yield results.[12] Similarly, some individuals have more talent for certain kinds of magic than others: some excel at herbal magic, for example, while others are inspired ritualists, and still others specialize in divination.

## The Ethics of Magic

Pagans consider magic to be a real and powerful force in the world, but they agree that it is morally neutral. Like electricity, it can be used either to great benefit or great detriment, to improve lives or to harm others. Thus most Pagan traditions have developed ethical principles that are intended to guide practitioners in their use of this force. The most commonly cited ethical principal around the use of magic, known as the Wiccan Rede, is "An it harm none, do what you will." This is usually interpreted to mean "Do what you believe is right, as long as it harms no one." This principle is usually traced to Gardner, who wrote in *The Meaning of Witchcraft*, "[Witches] are inclined to the morality of Good King Pausole, 'Do what you like so long as you harm no one.' But they believe a certain law to be important, 'You must not use magic for anything which will cause harm to anyone, and if, to prevent a greater wrong from being done, you must discommode someone, you must do it only in a way which will abate the harm' " (1959:127).

Good King Pausole was the eponymous character in Pierre Louÿs's 1901 picaresque novel, *The Adventures of King Pausole*, in which the main character distills two principles from his ancestors' book of customs that guide him in his travels: "Do no wrong to thy neighbor" and "Observing this, do as thou pleasest" (Louÿs, 1926:321). It is not clear whether Gardner's Witches borrowed their ethical principle from the work of Pierre Louÿs, or whether Gardner, being familiar with both the Wiccan Rede and Louys's novel, made the comparison between the two.

A related principle is sometimes known as the "Threefold Law": one's actions in the world are returned in kind three times over, implying that evil or irresponsible acts will ultimately bring the actor negative consequences, just as good acts eventually will have positive consequences. While widely supposed to be Gardnerian, and thus to date to the earliest extant Witchcraft texts in the twentieth century, this principle actually appears in none of the Gardnerian

Books of Shadows I have seen. Instead, some texts do contain the dictum "As thou hast received blessings, so art thou bound to return three times over." Anna and Don interpreted this to mean that becoming a Witch entails certain social responsibilities—a kind of Wiccan *noblesse oblige*, whereby Witches are bound to give back to the gods, their communities, and the larger society the good they have received, times three.

Because Pagans do not always agree about such fundamental questions as the nature of human nature, there is some debate in the community over magical ethics. At a workshop on this topic at Pantheacon 2002, a Neo-Pagan conference, a number of discussants maintained that Neo-Paganism presumes that human beings are fundamentally good, and will do good if they follow a spiritual path. Others disagreed, arguing that history demonstrates the contrary. For these discussants, "An it harm none, do what you will" seemed inadequate as a moral code, as there was little in it to encourage people to do good and discouraging them from doing harm. The Law of Threefold Return at least promised consequences as a result of actions. But Don contended that this principle is inadequate as an ethic, because it is essentially based on a punitive principle rather than on a broader sense of moral responsibility. He argued that Pagan and Wiccan ethics are based more on a belief that the natural world and its manifestations are sacred; that sacredness is present in every living thing, and in inanimate natural objects such as stones, trees, rivers, and the earth itself; and on the sense that all things are interconnected. Internalizing this principle leads, ideally, to considering the impact of one's every action upon one's immediate and not-so-immediate environment, asking the question "How do my actions affect the world around me?" This can become an ethical impulse to change society for the better, beyond just a sense of individual enlightenment. Magician Sam Webster suggested, "All rites of magic should be rituals of compassion."

Traditions differ in how they interpret these ethical principles. At one end of the continuum are the many popular Craft books that suggest all magic be done "for the good of all, according to the free will of all," with this dictum recited as a formula at the end of each spell or ritual (Weinstein, 1991:216–18). This is intended to stop any possible negative consequences the spell might have, even those unforeseeable by the magic worker. According to this school of ethics, even a healing spell done without the express request and permission of the person needing healing is unethical, because no magical act should violate another person's free will. Any type of coercive magic is unethical under these parameters, even a spell whose intent is to do good. Some Pagans were critical of what they saw as a kind of oversolicitous popular magic. "Every day, your immune system fights off thousands of microbes, viruses, and parasites, without your even being aware of it," explained Anna. "If you literally could harm nothing, you wouldn't live very long." Witches and Pagans who feel this way say that working only for the good of all weakens magic, essentially guaranteeing that it will never succeed. While critical of misapplied magic that harms innocent people, Don stated that there are few works of magic that can really benefit everyone and everything in the universe. If one is successful at an enterprise—say, buying a house or getting a job—then by definition, others were unsuccessful. And there are times when causing short-term harm is justified in order to serve a greater good: for example, when a physician vaccinates a child, the vaccine causes some temporary pain so that a long-term positive goal, which overrides the temporary, minor nature of the pain, can be met. Pagans and Witches must therefore chart a difficult course between causing as little harm as possible through magic, while at the same time ensuring that their work will be effective.

In keeping with their predecessors, the Renaissance magi, many modern Pagans feel the will of the magician is central to the ethics of magic. Here, the concept of will has to do not only with volition and determination, but also with character and synchrony with the universe. The ethical magician operates under a principle not unlike philosopher Immanuel Kant's dictum "Act such that the maxim of thy will may serve as a universal law." Honesty and consistency are an important part of this ethos. After my initiation into their Gardnerian coven, Don and Anna took me aside and suggested that I needed to modify my practice of cursing behind the wheel, as it was detrimental to the development of my magical will. Like many Italian drivers, I had acquired the habit of not just swearing at, but actually cursing annoying motorists with a colorful range of invectives, of which my native Roman dialect has an imaginative selection. Don's and Anna's concern was not so much that my words could actually harm other drivers, but that in the practice of magic, it is imprudent to make pronouncements one cannot fully endorse. A Witch's word is her bond; as we have seen, words have power. When at the end of a magical working, a Witch says, "So mote it be," she is asserting her will. By cursing trivially, out of habit, I was undercutting my will and weakening my powers as a magician.

Both Anna and Don felt that it would take a great deal more than curses uttered in frustration to harm someone magically. While, as Starhawk says, "It is fashionable in some occult circles to proclaim piously that 'Thoughts are things, and therefore we should think only positive thoughts, because the negative things we think will come to pass,' " (1986:126), I actually met very few Neo-Pagans or Witches who adhered to that point of view. Starhawk's critique of this belief is too biting not to cite in its entirety:

> Directing energy is not a matter of simply emoting. . . . Were it true, the death rate would rise phenomenally. Overpopulation would be the least of our worries—no elected politicians would survive long enough to be inaugurated. If thoughts and emotions alone could cause things to happen, thousands of my contemporaries would have married the Beatles in 1964. And I would not be writing at this desk—I would be sun-

ning myself in Tahiti, where the crowds would undoubtedly be fierce. (Starhawk, 1986:126).

While I did not meet any Witches or Pagans who admitted to practicing aggressive magic against others, I did meet individuals who felt they had been on the receiving end of a magical or "psychic" attack. They described experiences that ranged from a vague sense of discomfort to a life-threatening illness, attributing them to the actions of someone within the community with whom they had had a disagreement. The accused always denied the allegations. In these cases, claims of psychic attack function very much like accusations of witchcraft in traditional societies: they follow the lines of social conflict and attempt to stigmatize the accused for performing aggressive magic, while drawing sympathy to the accuser. These strategies were often unsuccessful, though, since many feel that people are too quick to attribute any unpleasant symptom to psychic attack, and are therefore skeptical of such claims. Anna is fond of saying that some people in the occult community cannot distinguish between psychic attack and indigestion. Most Witches and Pagans I spoke with thought that claims of psychic attack were evidence of social rifts, and true cases of psychic attack quite rare. They pointed out that a good magician should be able to defend against psychic attack with a technique called "shielding," in which energy is pulled up from the earth, and then pushed around the entire body (or house or other object) to form a shield to deflect extraneous psychic forces.

## Essence and Form

Gardnerians teach that because magic is a powerful force, it must be very carefully and specifically applied. The most difficult part of magic is identifying the precise goal or target toward which one is working; this, in turn, determines the strategies, tools, rituals, and even timing of the magical work. This is important because magic misapplied at best will not produce results, but at worst can actually hurt innocent people. One Witch did magic to stop a company from spraying malathion, a toxic insecticide, in his area. Soon after, a large storage tank filled with the chemical ruptured, spilling quantities of the poison into the environment. The company indeed was forced to stop spraying, but not in the way the Witch had intended, and with far more negative consequences. A more targeted, precise approach to the magical goal might have led to a more desirable outcome, one in harmony with the ethical principle "Harm none."

While British traditionalists and most ceremonial magical groups attempt to focus magic quite specifically in order to ensure its efficacy and ethics, Reclaiming Witches take a somewhat different approach. Reclaiming Witches distinguish between magic that works for "forms," or material things, and that which works for "essences," or feelings. Generally, working for essences is thought to be much more effective, because it is easier to change perceptions and feelings than it is to create forms. But working for essence has other implications which are often overlooked or misunderstood by critics of the movement. The process of isolating essence is itself an exercise in altering consciousness, and can be an impetus for social critique. It forces the magic worker to figure out exactly what she really wants or expects to get from the ritual. In doing so she can unpack some of the more insidious effects of consumerism, or become aware of alternative solutions to her needs that are difficult to perceive if she is focused on a single material goal.

Were I to do magic to get a car—a red convertible Mazda Miata, say, with standard transmission, overdrive, and a powerful sound system—I would be focusing my energies on a specific form. Magic is sometimes successful in obtaining forms, but Reclaiming Witches would recommend that I ask myself instead exactly what essences, or feelings, I was after. In the case of my desire for a roadster, asking these questions would force me to focus beyond the specific form, on the feelings I would like to derive from having the car. This exercise brings me face to face with my deeper psychological needs: do I wish to be admired and thought stylish? Do I seek thrills and excitement, the rush of the wind in my hair as I zip down the freeway? Or do I simply need transportation? In each case, a number of different scenarios might fulfill my needs, none of which is necessarily the form I originally thought I desired. In each case, the magic I might do to arrive at those essences would be different. Focusing on essence draws the magic worker's attention to the many ways that needs and desires might be fulfilled, and away from specific consumer products that in many cases provide only temporary palliatives for deeper needs.

This approach is ultimately critical of consumerism by placing emphasis away from objects and onto larger issues and values. It also typifies Reclaiming's idea that in order to bring about social change one must first achieve inner healing. According to this principle, one cannot work politically or spiritually to bring about better wages for workers, a cleaner environment, a more just society, and a more peaceful world if one believes that security, desirability, and personal worth are measured by social status or consumer products. Working for essence is magic as cultural critique: not waving a wand to get a desired result, but a focused process of self-examination, reflexivity, and creative problem-solving.

In the spring of 1997, after nine years of a peripatetic academic career in search of a tenure-track appointment, I decided that I wanted to have a more permanent situation in California, where I had spent the previous year and a half. I invited Holly, Don, and Anna, the members of my coven, and other Pagan and academic friends to participate in a ritual to keep me gainfully employed in the state I had grown to love. Rather than working for a particular position at a specific university—a form—we decided to work instead for essence. The ritual I designed with help from Don, Anna, and Holly involved transforming me from a stranger to a native, from an outsider to an insider, from a position of insecurity and rootlessness to one of security, prosperity, and belonging, through a series of symbolic transformations. The essences I was seeking were feelings: security, prosperity, belonging, rootedness. We worked with symbols to bring about this desired transformation. I entered wearing heavy clothing from my previous employment in a frigid Midwestern state; at each quarter, I shed an item of clothing and gave up a token that stood for feelings I wished to leave behind, and received from participants a small gift that stood for the new essences I wished to bring into my life. From one I received hawk feathers, symbols of intellectual freedom and my ability to soar; from another, soil which he rubbed inside my blucher mocs, to ground me and give me stability. The ritual participants fed me native California foods—artichokes, blood oranges, local cheeses, and wine—to incorporate regional elements into my body, transforming me into a native. Together, we planted a rose bush to stand for rootedness, growth, and prosperity into soil I had prepared. The ritual acts of transformation stood for the transformation of essences I desired; the ritual was a piece of performance art that enacted, through the use of symbols and actions, changes I wanted to see in my own life.

Two weeks later, I received a call for an interview from the university where I was ultimately hired. Of course, I had already applied to a number of positions in California when I did the ritual; most Pagans say that one must work in the material as well as in the spiritual realm to attain a goal. While this outcome may well be considered a coincidence, my Pagan consultants did not see it as such. Coincidences, as we have seen, are meaningful.

## Reclaiming Vernacular Magic

Many elements of Neo-Pagan magic are grounded in the beliefs and practices of vernacular magic brought to North America by the people who came from Europe, Africa, and Asia. Vernacular magic was organized around the principles identified by Sir James Frazer under the rubric *sympathetic magic*; the two main operating principles were homeopathy, or the idea that like causes like; and contagion, or the axiom that two objects once in contact continue to influence one another even when separated. Correspondences were thought to exist between certain natural objects and processes: for example, in Italy, red stones were thought to stop bleeding because of their common color; geodes with particles trapped inside were believed to protect pregnant women, since both "contained" something. In addition, a broad knowledge of herbal properties, both actual and putative, came into play in the creation of magical cures.

Most traditional rural cultures had a range of magical practitioners: from learned specialists, to cunning men and women, who were often at least partly literate and incorporated some learned traditions of ritual magic into their work, to local healers who specialized in love spells, removing the evil eye and the like, to family-based practitioners who might charm warts or make amulets to keep evil away from children, livestock, and homes.[13] Some forms of magic, such as "planting by the signs," or coordinating sowing and harvesting with the phases of the moon, were widely known among agriculturalists in Europe and the Middle East, and are still practiced in parts of North America (see Lloyd, 1995). In many cases, vernacular magic was closely intertwined with religion: almost all spells collected by Italian ethnographers, for example, contain some reference to saints, the Virgin Mary, or God. Though religious officials may have found them inappropriate, even blasphemous, practitioners seldom saw themselves in opposition to official religion. In my own fieldwork in Sardinia, for example, I observed a number of magical practitioners who were also heavily involved in local religious traditions, such as the fraternities and sororities that maintained saints' cults and chapels throughout the year. They perceived their practice of folk healing and their religious activities as complementary.

Neo-Pagan magic both draws from this rich tradition and departs from it in significant ways. Some Gardnerian Books of Shadows contain versions of vernacular magical spells that have changed very little from their earlier forms. Many contain charms similar to those documented by folklorists. An example is the Meresburg charm, one of the oldest healing rhymes extant in the English language:

Our Lord rade
His foal's foot slade;
down he lighted,
His foal's foot righted:
bone to bone
sinew to sinew
blood to blood
flesh to flesh
heal in the name of the Father, Son and Holy Ghost. (Storms, 1975:109)

Like many European healing charms, this one is in narrative form. It tells the story how Jesus took a fall after his horse slipped, and how he "righted" the horse's foot. In this form, it has no overt pagan content; but Storms, who collected similar healing rhymes from Scotland, Denmark, Germany, Norway, Sweden, the Netherlands, Estonia, Finland, and Hungary, traces it to a Germanic charm that mentions Wotan, Frija, and other Norse deities. In this version, it is Wotan who falls from his horse, and Frija, Volla, and Wotan sing over the horse's sprained leg to heal it. The rhyme concludes:

ben zi bena, bluot zi bluota
lid zi geliden, sose gelimda sin

bone to bone, blood to blood
limb to limb, so they belong together
(Storms, 1975:110)

In these cases, modern Witches and Pagans simply remove the Christian content of the charms, sometimes substituting the names of their own deities. In other cases, they reinterpret and recontextualize the spells, transforming them into something quite different from magic in its earlier context. One example is the witch bottle: a glass bottle filled with nails, pins, and human urine that, in European and American vernacular magic, was buried at the boundaries of a property to keep witches away. For contemporary Witches, in contrast, they are tools used to keep away those who would victimize them. The materials and processes are the same; what has changed is the interpretation: vernacular magical practitioners are recast as W/witches who made use of traditional ways of knowing to protect themselves and their families. In still other cases, Pagans may reinterpret and reclaim spells intended as harmful magic, turning them toward a worthier cause. New York Witch John Yohalem described how his high priestess used a spell from the ballad "Willie's Lady" to prevent a miscarriage:

> The priestess who taught me subscribed to a whole bunch of folklore journals and had bought the complete publication in four volumes of [Francis James Child's] *The English and Scottish Popular Ballads*. And I found a number of interesting magical techniques from looking through this. The one where he brings his bride home to his mother, and his mother's a witch, and she can't have a child because it turns out the mother's been tying knots and throwing them under the bed. Anyway the way it was used was this. When Julie was pregnant and had a false labor early on, they put her to bed and so forth and were very worried. Judy sent them the ballad, and very night they would tie another knot and put it under the bed; and then when the ninth month was up, they untied all the knots, and a couple of weeks later she had Ned, who's sitting over there having lunch! So it was a great success.[14]

As in the witch-bottle example, the priestess turned the harmful witch image on its head: instead of using the binding spell to cause barrenness, she used it to stop a threatened miscarriage. The essence of the practice, however, remains the same.

Unlike vernacular magic, Neo-Pagan magic is a self-conscious attempt to revive and re-create a sense of interconnectedness in the world, a sacredness of time and space that Pagans locate in preindustrial cultures. Like Max Weber, Pagans see the world as having been progressively "disenchanted" by the developments of modernity. Weber's notion of *Entzauberung der Welt* hypothesized the premodern world as a magic garden where humans and nature coexisted with supernatural beings and forces that were not perceived as separate from nature itself.[15] The gradual marginalization of magical beliefs, accompanied by the emergence of state-linked world religions and the general recession of religion from its previously central place in social life, contributed to the disenchantment of the world. By resacralizing notions of time and space and reclaiming magical ways of knowing, Neo-Pagans are reenchanting the world, creating a complement to the mechanicistic philosophy of the post-Enlightenment era. Magic becomes a form of cultural critique, as well as a training of the imagination to perceive patterns and meaning where the dominant culture no longer sees them. These skills are crucial in the design and actualization of ritual, the movement's preeminent form of artistic expression.

*Chapter 4*

# Ritual: Between the Worlds

**Field notes, October 29, 1995**

Reclaiming's Spiral Dance in San Francisco, California, may be the largest public sabbat in North America. Held yearly to celebrate Samhain, the Witches' new year near October 31, it draws between fifteen hundred and three thousand participants, not all of whom are Witches or Pagans. Because of its size, it is in many ways atypical of Pagan rituals, which tend to be small, intimate, and participatory. Members of Reclaiming perceive this public sabbat as their "offering" to the San Francisco Bay Area community; they "put on" the performance for an audience. The Spiral Dance has a marked separation between performers and audience. It has a producer and director, a choir and musicians who perform on a stage, acrobats and dancers who are hired to "dance" the four directions, and a crew to manage lighting, props, sound, setup, and cleanup. Some Reclaiming members act as "snakes," monitoring the audience's energy throughout the performance; "dragons," controlling disturbances; "graces," welcoming newcomers and seeing to their physical and emotional needs; and "anchors," keeping the energy grounded.

This year's performance takes place in the cavernous Herbst Pavilion at Fort Mason, an ex–military hangar now used as a public park and recreation area. Pagans from all over the San Francisco Bay Area are gathered in the lobby, waiting for the doors to open. Some are wearing fanciful costumes: feathered or leather masks, ornate clothing that looks medieval or tribal, or traditional black witches' garb; others simply wear street clothes against the chill. As a priestess welcomes and purifies us with incense, we enter the giant ballroom through a labyrinth of veils painted with images of skulls and fetuses—leitmotifs that symbolize death and rebirth, the themes of this holy day on which the Witches remember their dead.

Inside the pavilion, Reclaiming houses and covens have set up four altars, one to each of the cardinal elements and directions. These communal creations are intended to evoke the emotions and correspondences associated with the elements and directions according to the magical worldview. The air altar has chains of origami cranes suspended from the ceiling, amid sheets and veils fluttering in the breeze created by hidden fans. We can literally feel air blowing on us as we admire the other objects on the altar: images of birds, feathers, and ritual knives, symbols of the mind's ability to cut, discern, and create categories and boundaries. The earth altar, for many years assembled by my neighbor Judy Foster,[1] pays homage to the Witches' ancestors, the Mighty Dead. It includes traditional images of witches from medieval woodcuts, juxtaposed with dried flowers, fruit, and seed pods, all symbols of the earth, and skeletons drawn from the celebrations of Halloween and El Dia de los Muertos in the surrounding community.

The ritual begins with all participants forming an enormous circle around the perimeter of the hall. Then the choir begins to sing the "Lyke Wake Dirge," a traditional English folk requiem; in place of the original line "May God receive my soul," Witches sing "Let earth receive my soul," repaganizing what they feel was originally a pre-Christian song. M. Macha NightMare, a Reclaiming priestess whose magical work focuses on death and dying, makes some introductory remarks explaining the ritual to newcomers and non-Pagans present. Then priestess T. Thorne Coyle leads us in a grounding and centering, and the circle is cast. Now, as we, the audience, settle down on the cold, hard floor, acrobats and dancers appear from the four directions to dance in the quarters. The air dancers lower themselves from the ceiling on ropes; the fire dancers actually breathe fire; the water dancers are on tall stilts. Now the goddess and god appear, also as groups of dancers, although Reclaiming is playing with the standard sexual polarity of Wiccan-derived liturgy by having same-sex dancers dance together. These are wordless, dramatic performances, accompanied by music, song, and drumming, whose intent is to evoke emotions and engender a quality of otherworldliness—an elaborate preparation for what is to follow.

At last the dancers have gone backstage, and the choir and orchestra are silent. Macha steps into the center of the circle and, to the sound of a muffled drumbeat, begins to call out the names of those who have died during the year—crossed over, Witches say, to the other side, the world of the dead and yet unborn, the Summerland, a term they have borrowed from Yeats's Celtic Revival a century ago. All year, Macha collects messages on her answering machine from Witches and Pagans whose loved ones have died, and who wish their names to be read at the Spiral Dance. Tonight, she is reading them. The list seems endless. It mixes names of the well known with those known only to their loved ones; even pets' names are called out, as Pagans believe animals and humans, being made of the same essence, are united in death. Around me people sigh and cry out when they hear a name they recognize. Entire families are here, mourning in community; some are weeping and comforting one another.

Now the time has come that many have awaited all year. For the core of this ritual is a trance journey in a spirit boat to the Isle of the Dead, during which Pagans commune with their beloved dead. "Set sail, set sail," the choir chants,

Over the waves where the spray blows white, into the night, into the night;
Set sail, set sail!
Turn your face where the veil grows thin, beyond the rim, beyond the rim;
Set sail, set sail!
Follow the twilight into the west, where you may rest, where you may rest;
Set sail set sail . . .
Over the dark of the sunless sea, where you are free, where you are free;
Set sail, set sail;
To the shining isle where the heart is led, to meet the dead, to meet the dead.[2]

Starhawk, in that nasal, breathy voice that always takes me into trance, asks us to step onto the ship that will take us over the sea of tears and to the shores of the Summerland, the Isle of Apples, the land of the dead and yet unborn. I see the ship before me: a wooden vessel with sails the color of blood, creaking and pitching in her moorings. I step aboard. Despite the crowd all around me in the hall, I am alone on the ship's deck, looking out at the waves of this gray-black sea of tears—tears of mourning that humans have wept for their dead since there were humans on this earth. The moorings are loosed and the anchor raised; slowly the shoreline recedes as the wind blows into our sails. In time, I see a shadow on the horizon. It grows larger and darker until we arrive at last on the banks of the Isle of Apples. All around me people disembark and greet their loved ones who await them; I look around and see no one waiting for me. I disembark anyway and make my way inland. As I walk, I see that in this land I have become a child again: a girl of seven or eight with long dark hair and skinny legs sticking out of a white shift.

The light in the Summerland has an almost purple cast; it is as if it were always twilight. I find myself in the apple orchards of the goddess, where the trees are at once in bud, bloom, and fruit. The air is fragrant with the smell of apple blossoms, and their petals fall in soft showers around me. A young man comes toward me, smiling. He has sandy hair and green eyes, and is wearing a black frock coat in the style that was popular in Europe during the 1920s. He holds out his hand to me, and I take it; we begin to dance. He is much bigger than me; I put my little girl feet on top of his shoes and he whirls and spins me around as the trees shower us in blossoms. We do not speak, but I am happy. Then he takes me by the hand and leads me away. I understand he wants me to meet someone: a tall, dark man in a military uniform. This second man I recognize from old photographs I have seen; it is my paternal grandfather, killed in 1936 in Italy's Ethiopian campaign. I never knew him, since he died when my father was a boy, and he apparently has no idea who I am. "I am Bruno's daughter," I tell him. "Bruno has a daughter!" he exclaims. He had no idea he was a grandfather. "You have four other grandchildren and a great-grandson," I say. He is delighted. The two men each take one of my hands; I skip between them as they lead me back toward the shores of the Summerland, where the ship is waiting to take me back. "You know," says my grandfather to the other man, "this is my granddaughter." "Yes, I know," replies the young man; "she is mine, too." And from his voice I recognize him at last: Andrew Vázsonyi, "Bandi," as I called him—the husband of my dissertation advisor, a dear friend and surrogate grandfather figure from my graduate school days. It moves me profoundly that he remembers me, that he danced with me, though I am not his blood kin.

But now I must say farewell. The drumbeats are calling us back, back to the land of life. Still my child-self, I reach up to hug and kiss my grandfathers; but they are becoming incorporeal shades as we near the landing. "Go back, go back," they motion me. "One day you will return, and we will be here to meet you again." I run down the gangplank and jump onto the ship, and in a moment, we are at sea.

I open my eyes to see that around me others are returning from their own personal journeys. The man next to me is crying; I reach my hand out to him. "Are you okay?" I ask. He nods. "I understand now that I had a happy family," he says. "All my life I've tried to distance myself from them, but tonight I understood that they loved each other and loved me too, in their own way."

Now a singer begins to sing, a cappella:

A year of beauty, a year of plenty
A year of planting, a year of harvests
A year of forests, a year of healing
A year of vision, a year of passion
A year of rebirth
This year may we renew the earth.

We all, all two thousand of us present, join hands to form an enormous circle and are pulled into the Spiral Dance, chanting counterpoint to the singer and the choir:

Let it begin with each step we take
And let it begin with each change we make
And let it begin with each chain we break
And let it begin every time we awake.

The crowd is so large that the dance continues for almost an hour before it has wound in on itself, unfolded, then wound in again. Dancing and chanting, I feel my energy ebb and flow; at times I sing out, harmonizing with the choir and the other dancers; other times, my energy must be carried and sustained by the group. The chanting and dancing build to a crescendo until we are all tightly packed in against each other, no longer chanting words but merely singing out, "Oh!" and "Ah!" as we reach for the sky, releasing the energy. "There is no end to the circle, no end; there is no end to life, there is no end," we chant as we unwind the circle. We have been to the otherworld and returned, bringing back the seeds of renewal.[3]

## Ritual as Praxis

Ritual is a form of practice that unites all the Neo-Pagan traditions. As we have seen in the previous chapter, Neo-Pagans rely on a shared concept of the magical, interconnected universe as one determinant of community membership. Ritual is the practical expression of the magical worldview. The concept of the interconnected universe finds its most complete expression in the practice of ritual. It is ritual that creates common experiences that bind American Neo-Pagans together, linking them to the past, to each other, and to the larger cosmos, as well as expressing the community's hopes for the future. This chapter examines Neo-Pagan ritual as group praxis and artistic expression: its most important form of art.

Ritual plays a central role in Neo-Paganism. As I have argued elsewhere, it is the movement's most important form of expression, one that can legitimately be called an art (Magliocco, 1996:95). It often subsumes other art forms, such as narrative, music, drama, costume, and crafts, which are used to create elements for use in rituals. Like other forms of folklore, ritual is "artistic communication in small groups" (Ben Amos, 1972:13). Its fluid, improvisational nature is built around a common framework, and it is subject to constant innovation and variation according to the personalities, traditions, and circumstances surrounding it. While rituals can be diffused through publications and seminars, or copied from Books of Shadows, most American Pagans learn them informally, through observation, imitation, and experimentation. In many cases ritual performances are the product of collaborative planning and decision making.

## Reclaiming Ritual

Pre-Reformation Europe preserved a tradition of year-cycle customs linked with the agricultural (and thus economic) calendar, overlaid with Christian theology. These were occasions for the performance of community identity, as well as for festivity and symbolic inversion—the temporary reversal of everyday norms of behavior. Celebrations were characterized by Rabelaisian overindulgence and the eruption of the fantastic into everyday life. In contrast to the everyday privation of peasant life, there were food and drink aplenty; and dramas, games, and popular entertainments enacted the Christian liturgy and allowed people to participate in it through revelry. Ecstatic elements were often present in religious observances—for example, groups of male devotees would carry heavy saints' statues throughout the town, sometimes in competition with each other; individuals on pilgrimages and prayer vigils would camp for days around rural sanctuaries, praying, singing, sharing stories, and hoping for spiritual rapture. The presence of the tragic as well as the comic provided an affirmation of life in the face of death, pain, and political oppression, and linked participants to the larger cosmic forces in life. These celebratory occasions were important to the community because they permitted the expression of creativity and popular fantasy, and allowed through the use of symbolic inversion, the conceptualization of a different kind of social order free from the hardship of feudal relationships.

The Reformation brought an end to many of these customs in Protestant Europe. The Puritans who first settled in North America not only brought few festive customs with them; they also carried into American culture a general disapproval of the licentiousness, ecstasy, and release that characterized these festivals. This disapprobation was further strengthened by the values associated with developing industrialism and capitalism, and the emergence of the Protestant work ethic, which frowned upon license and leisure. While later immigrant groups brought with them the memories of festive traditions that persisted in parts of Europe relatively untouched by the Protestant Reformation, and some of these took root in parts of North America (for example, Mardi Gras in French-dominated New Orleans and surrounding Acadian areas), carnivalesque traditions on the whole did not become a part of American folklore. The exception to this pattern is Halloween, a holiday that has included elements of symbolic inversion since the late nineteenth century (Rogers, 2002). This means that for American Neo-Pagans, in contrast their European counterparts, the link with ecstatic festivity and celebration is more tenuous and countercultural, and must be reconstructed from scratch.

Some scholars have argued that the loss of these traditions had a damaging impact on American culture. For example, Harvey Cox, a professor of religion at Harvard Divinity School, wrote in *The Feast of Fools* (1969) that the loss of medieval European festivals of inversion represented a grave detriment to all Western societies. These celebrations, he argues, allowed people to spoof the power hierarchy and imagine a more egalitarian social order. More importantly, the loss of celebratory folk traditions weakened Western culture's capacity for festivity and fantasy. It is through ritual and the imagination, Cox contends, that humans situate themselves vis-à-vis their history, and link themselves to larger spiritual and cosmic forces (1969:13–14). He calls ritual "social fantasy" (71) and "embodied fantasy" (73), in the sense that ritual enacts in a social milieu the shared dramas of history and culture. Cox calls for a return to the ethos of the Feast of Fools, a reclamation of festivity and fantasy, in order to enrich contemporary spiritual life.

American Neo-Pagans are among the groups that have reclaimed ritual as a vehicle to heal the rift separating humans from the natural and the divine.

However, because they lack the direct historical connections with the old year-cycle, they must construct these links themselves. They usually do so by borrowing material from cultural traditions that preserved elements of festivity and fantasy in year-cycle and other rites. The Pagan reclamation of ritual is part of the Romantic impulse that characterized early study of folklore. Nineteenth-century scholars of ritual were among the first to project authenticity onto the rites of Classical pagans, European peasants, and colonized peoples, and to contrast these with the sedate, impoverished nature of urban religious life. The idea of the modern world as "disenchanted," and of ritual as a form that would reenchant the world and heal it of alienation, found expression in the works of many thinkers, and from there, into the cultural register of American Neo-Pagans.

There are several reasons why Pagans have chosen to reclaim ritual in the context of a dominant culture in which ritual expressions are becoming both less frequent and less formal. Pagans perceive ritual as a vehicle for personal and planetary healing and transformation. They believe ritual can work in metaphorical ways, by changing consciousness, and in physical ways, by transforming the material world. They base their worship on pre-Christian religions; ritual becomes a primary way of enacting and maintaining the presumed historical link between contemporary and ancient paganism that is at the root of Neo-Pagan teleology. This connection is central even to those who realize its construct nature. Steven Posch, a priest from Minnesota, explains:

> I don't really believe that modern Paganism in the form it's in now, or Wicca, to be specific, has come down to us from most ancient times in a hands-on succession from the woman who sculpted the Willendorf Mother; I really don't think so. [But] people have been celebrating these folk festivals all along. . . . The rituals stay the same; the interpretation of rituals varies from generation to generation as each is reinterpreted. These are things people have been doing for thousands of years, and we are the current incarnations of those people doing just what they did in a new way.

The link with the past is one ritual vehicle for inducing feelings of timelessness and liminality that make ritual experiences transcendent. Steven continues:

> There's a grove by the Mississippi River where Witches have been doing ritual for thirty-five, forty years. . . . There was a big ritual going on there one night: the bonfire was going, and people were dancing and singing, and the sun was setting, and the dogs were barking, and the children were running around. That was one of those things where I just stepped back from myself and I had a very strong feeling of . . . timelessness. Suddenly we had stepped out of time, because what we were doing then is what [people had been doing] forever. And what we will always do.[4]

Creating connections to a historical past presents special problems for North American Neo-Pagans. In North America, historical links are often shallow compared to other parts of the world; written history goes back four hundred years or so at most, to the time of European colonization, leaving no connection to the pre-Reformation European world Pagans idealize. Much of North America lacks the historical depth of other cultures, where the past has not been obliterated by commercial development and the ever compelling search for the new. Even personal histories are often lost as families splinter and relocate. The mobility and rootlessness of American society mean that many Pagans did not grow up in same place as their families, and may live thousands of miles away from where they were born. Others have chosen to distance themselves from families they perceive as dysfunctional or dogmatic in their religious and moral views. In cases where roots have been severed or lost, the invention of links to the past becomes a way to compensate for their loss. In seeking their history, Pagans often must forge their own connections, and ritual is one compelling way they do so.

## Ritual in the Neo-Pagan Community

Ritual life is central to the American Neo-Pagan community. Rituals serve as the principal occasions for social interaction and exchange, both within the coven and the larger community. Covens meet at full moon rituals, called esbats, where they conduct business and perform ritual. Teaching circles—meetings during which aspirants and initiates receive training—are held monthly during the new moon. Non-Witchen Pagan groups also meet for monthly rituals, although they may or may not coordinate their meetings with the phases of the moon. These intimate meetings are generally closed to nonmembers, and also serve as occasions to share food and drink and catch up on news and gossip. In the San Francisco Bay Area, members of the same coven or circle often socialize with each other outside these scheduled meetings as well, getting together to eat at a restaurant, see films and performances, hike, and browse the many bookstores. The coven or circle is a social network for the individual, as well as being a place for magical training and ritual. Some Pagans and Witches build their entire social lives around overlapping covens and circles to which they belong, meeting now one group of friends, then another, to plan, execute, and discuss a series of rituals throughout the year.

Sabbats are usually more public than monthly meetings. In Coven Trismegiston, members were free to invite friends to the sabbat celebrations. These events are ways for the coven to reach out to the larger Pagan community, both to teach them about Gardnerian Craft and to include them in a network of reciprocal relationships with Witches and Pagans of other traditions. They are also a way to screen potential new coven members. Large group sabbats organized by traditions such as Reclaiming and NROOGD may draw together hundreds of participants from all over the San Francisco Bay Area. These, too, provide ways for interested outsiders to evaluate a group or tradition before making deeper commitments. For members, they renew ties of friendship and acquaintanceship, both within and across traditions. Rituals, therefore, have an important social function in the Neo-Pagan community: they build social bonds by creating powerful, shared emotional experiences. They bridge the different traditions and unite the community through networks of reciprocity and common experience.

Pagan definitions of ritual can be exceptionally broad. "It's art, it's theater, it's sacrament—it's so many things," explained Lhianna Sidhe, a priestess from the Midwest and a well-known organizer of large group rituals at festivals. Adler cites one Witch's personal definition: "It's sacred drama in which you are the audience as well as the participant, and the purpose of it is to activate parts of the mind that are not activated by everyday activity" (Adler, 1986:141). Lyra, a Rhode Island Witch, said to me, "Anything can be a ritual." As an example, she gave an animal sound she and her partner made to soothe each other when they were feeling stressed. "That's a ritual," she explained. Pagans ritualize many aspects of life, and are reflexively aware of this, using it as a source of in-group humor. At a 1993 Pagan outdoor festival, a member of the cleanup crew announced, "We have a new ritual: please crush your aluminum cans before recycling them!" He demonstrated the technique by stomping on a can as though he were performing a dance.

## Types of Rituals

It would be nearly impossible to arrive at a taxonomy of Neo-Pagan ritual that accurately represents the range of ritual artistry in this movement. It is helpful, nevertheless, to attempt to categorize some of the different types of rituals Pagans perform in order to better understand the aesthetic appeal of the movement, and how rituals work on the psyche and emotions of participants. In anthropological terms, Pagan rituals may be divided into three categories: year-cycle rites, which mark important seasonal transitions in the calendar; life-cycle rites, which mark important transitions in the lives of individuals; and rites of crisis, in which the community unites to bring about a transformation as a result of some necessity. These categories should be treated as guidelines rather than rigid classifications. They sometimes overlap: for example, it is not unusual for Reclaiming rituals to combine the observation of a sabbat with magic to bring about political change in response to current events.

## Turning the Wheel of the Year: Year-Cycle Rites

In the previous chapter on magic, we saw how Neo-Pagans resacralize the year, by scanning it into various holy days that correspond to natural cycles, and metaphorically recall changes in the human life cycle and psyche. Witchen and some Pagan traditions observe eight sabbats, or holy days, that correspond to the solstices, equinoxes, and the days between each equinox and solstice, or the "cross quarter days." This calendar, based on European folk practice and nineteenth-century survivalist interpretations, is by no means universal; other Pagan traditions may follow calendars with roots in different seasonal cycles. The Fellowship of Isis, for example, schedules feasts based on an ancient Egyptian calendar that corresponded to the flooding of the Nile; Jennifer Reif, a Los Angeles priestess of Demeter, developed her own calendar of observances based on Classical texts and her personal experience planting, growing, and harvesting wheat in Southern California, whose climate mirrors that of the Mediterranean Eleusinian cults (Reif, 1999). The Witchen eight-sabbat calendar is nevertheless the most widespread one in Neo-Paganism.

Sabbat celebrations range from small, intimate gatherings to large public celebrations, such as Reclaiming's Spiral Dance. Sabbats are generally the most theatrical and performative of the three types of rituals Pagans observe. They are also the most likely to make use of material from European folklore and calendrical rites. By observing the sabbats, Pagans attune themselves more closely to seasonal cycles, and thus with the sacred. Pagans call the celebration of the sabbats "turning the wheel of the year."

The year cycle most commonly observed in the American Neo-Pagan movement begins and ends with Samhain, October 31. Situated roughly midway in the autumn season, between the fall equinox and the winter solstice, Samhain is one of the most important holy days in the Witchen year. All over North America, signs of the changing season are present in the decreasing light (made even more dramatic in certain areas by the shift from Daylight Savings Time to Standard Time), the falling leaves, the decay of plants and growing things, the annual migration of birds, and the chill in the air. Mainstream Americans are celebrating Halloween, a holiday in which skeletons, ghosts, and weird creatures—images of death, decay, and supernaturalism disowned by American culture—are publicly displayed and embraced. American Neo-Pagans have incorporated the seasonal concern with the dead in a holy day that celebrates the cyclicity of life, death, and rebirth.

In keeping with European, and especially Irish folk beliefs, Pagans say that on this day, the veil between the world of humans and that of the spirits is thin.[5] This allows spirits and deities to visit humans on earth, but, more importantly, facilitates humans' movement across the boundary as well. On this sabbat, Witches remember their dead, reclaiming European Catholic practices surrounding All Saints (November 1) and All Souls (November 2), which they say were Christianizations of earlier pagan customs. Witches may erect altars in honor of their ancestors, both actual and spiritual; they may hold dumb suppers, inviting them to enjoy in complete silence the earthly pleasures of food and drink now denied them in spiritual form (Lafferty, 1998); and they hold rituals during which they journey in trance to the otherworld, the Summerland, where the dead and yet unborn live, to commune with their beloved dead.

Sometime near December 21, North American Pagans observe the winter solstice. The theme of this sabbat is the death and rebirth of the light, sometimes personified as the birth of the deity. The symbols of this holy day are similar to those of the Christmas season in the dominant American culture: evergreens and wreaths, emblems of the continuing vitality of vegetation despite the cold temperatures and dark days, and candles, which signal the rebirth of the sun. Pagans use these elements freely because they understand them as ancient pagan fertility symbols Christianized by early missionaries in an attempt to persuade pagans to observe the birth of Christ. Some contemporary Pagans even decorate evergreen trees, calling them "solstice trees." Another favorite practice during this sabbat is the lighting of the Yule log with a bit of the previous year's log, carefully preserved for this purpose. Any folk custom that can be understood as a Christianized pagan survival can be adapted and reclaimed, including the practice of wassailing (a form of luck visiting) and the singing of Yule carols with pagan themes, such as "The Holly and the Ivy." Pagans understand the reference to vegetation in this song to be a remnant of an earlier fertility religion.

The celebration on February 1 or 2 of Imbolc or Oimelc, known in some traditions as Brigid, has its roots in the Irish observations of the beginning of the lambing season (*Oimelc* is sometimes translated as "ewe's milk," but this is a dubious etymology) and St. Brigit's Day, a Christianization of an earlier holiday in honor of the pre-Christian goddess Brigid.[6] On the Continent, Catholics celebrated Candlemas, the blessing of the candles, or St. Blaise's Day. Some Wiccan traditions bless all the coven's candles at this time of year, when the growing daylight first becomes apparent. In other traditions, Brigid is the season for initiations. These rites of passage are timed to coincide with the earliest stirrings of spring, to harmonize with the concept of beginnings. Reclaiming Witches use this time to make pledges for the coming year; they plan what they will accomplish and promise publicly to deliver. Brigid, the goddess of poetry, smith craft, and the healing arts, is especially beloved in Reclaiming, as well as by many other traditions in the San Francisco Bay Area.

The spring equinox, like the autumn equinox opposite it on the wheel of the year, marks a time of balance between the day and night, the light and the darkness. Witches and some Pagans observe this state of balance, and the return of spring, by celebrating this juncture. In some traditions, this sabbat is known as Oestre or Ostara, for the Germanic goddess of the rising sun from whom the Christian holiday of Easter derived its name.[7] Pagans reclaim her symbols of fertility and returning life: the egg, the rabbit and the chicken. Some color eggs using natural dyes and incorporate them into the seasonal celebration. In other traditions, Witches celebrate the return of Jack in the Green, a figure from English folklore whom they associate with vegetative fertility, or of Persephone from the underworld.

May 1, or Beltane, exactly opposite from Samhain on the wheel, marks the beginning of the summer season, just as Samhain marks the beginning of the winter. In Wiccan symbology, Beltane marks the ritual union of the goddess and the god, the feminine and masculine forces in nature—harbingers of the crops, fruits, and plenty that follow at midsummer.[8] Many Witches erect a maypole and dance around it to celebrate this sabbat, interpreting this act as a visual symbol of the divine union they solemnize. NROOGD's May Day celebration is unique in its incorporation of both the hobbyhorse theme and the ritual battle between the May Queen and the Winter Queen; this is, in part, the result of the combination during the late 1980s of two covens' different Beltane rituals. Just as Pagans say the veils between the worlds are thin at Samhain, so too are they at Beltane; only on this sabbat, it is the fairy folk, broadly conceptualized as nature spirits, who are said to appear. The light half of the year is theirs; fairies are thought to be active throughout the summer and to become less so as the year darkens, until at Samhain they give way to the souls of the ancestors.

The summer solstice, around June 21, marks the sun's highest point in the year cycle and the longest day of the year. Pagans and Witches often celebrate this sabbat as their European ancestors did, with great bonfires in open spaces. This is the time when many Pagan camp-outs and festivals take place; dancing around the bonfire is an important part of the celebration as well as the performance of identity at these gatherings (Pike, 2001). Some traditions also mark the fading of the sun after this date, as the Sun King yields to the Winter King, who will reign until his descent into the underworld at Samhain.

The last cross-quarter day of the Witches' year is Lammas, observed on August 1. Also known as "First Fruits," in higher latitudes this sabbat marks the harvest of summer's earliest bounty. In the southern half of North America, where the earth has already been yielding her fruits for many weeks, this is the harvest of the winter wheat planted after the previous Samhain. All over North America, Pagans and Witches give thanks for nature's bounty by decorating their altars with newly harvested fruits and vegetables and enjoying a feast. Many traditions in the San Francisco Bay Area bake bread to honor the harvested wheat. Borrowing from Frazer's concept of the sacrificial god-king, wheat is interpreted as the body of the deity who sacrifices himself so that life may continue, and so that he may be reborn in the spring. Sometimes, in recognition of this metaphor, the bread is shaped into a human figure (with greater or lesser detail, depending on the proclivities and artistic abilities of the ritualists) and consumed as part of the sabbat. Raisins and other fruits may be incorporated into the bread as symbols of the earth's bounty. This sabbat also marks projects Witches and Pagans may have begun around Brigid that are coming to fruition at last. At one Trismegiston Lammas, coven members baked and consumed many individual breads in the shape of books, papers, and artistic creations to help bring about the completion of their academic and artistic projects.

The autumn equinox on September 22 signals the definitive end of summer and the beginning of the fall season. In Northern California this is also the time of the grape harvest, while in other parts of North America the last of the crops are harvested from the fields. Witches observe the changing seasons by celebrating Mabon. For traditional Wiccans, this is the final descent of the sun-god figure who was born at midwinter, into the otherworld for a period of rest before his return at Yule. In only six weeks, Witches themselves will make the journey to the otherworld to commune with the dead and contemplate the cyclical nature of all life on earth. As with Lammas, harvest symbols predominate at this relatively minor sabbat.

In addition to the sabbats marking the wheel of the year, Witches observe the full moons each month. These rites, known as esbats, are more private and subdued than sabbats, and are usually used for conducting the business of the coven and for the practice of magic. There are between twelve and thirteen esbats per year. The observation of the lunar as well as solar cycles constitutes a complementarity that balances the wheel of the year.

## Rites of Passage: Initiations

Rites of passage recognize transitions in the individual's life cycle. French ethnographer Arnold van Gennep first recognized that these typically occur at birth, puberty, marriage, and death. American Neo-Pagans mark these occasions with special rituals; some are adapted by those who formerly had other religious affiliations and seek to create Pagan alternatives to less satisfying mainstream models. The Pagan handfasting, for example, is a celebration of marriage that can be legally binding when performed by Pagan clergy holding ministerial credentials; but it is just as often performed for same-sex couples who do not have the right to a legally recognized marriage in the eyes of the dominant culture. "Wiccanings," or baby-blessing celebrations (the term is a transformation of *christening*), are held after the birth of a child to welcome it into the larger community. In keeping with their reclamation of ritual, many Neo-Pagans design special puberty rituals for their children. These can include "first blood" rituals to celebrate a girl's menarche. Books such as Starhawk and Anne Hill's *Circle Round* (1998) give parents suggestions for developing personalized rites of passage for their teenagers. Many Neo-Pagans are also experimenting with alternative memorial and funeral services; some examples of these are described in Starhawk and M. Macha NightMare's *Pagan Book of Living and Dying* (1997). They may also devise personal rites of passage to mark transitions they consider important in their lives, such as divorce, coming out, menopause, or the completion of a project.

The most important rites of passage for Witches and Pagans are initiations. Traditions differ in their attitude toward this rite. Gardnerian Wicca and other traditional Craft groups are initiatory; members undergo three initiations into graded ranks: first, second, and third degrees. Each rank signals a higher level of expertise and experience in magical work; third-degree practitioners may form independent covens and pass on the entirety of the tradition to new members. In contrast, in Reclaiming and other feminist traditions, initiation is optional, and must be requested by the postulant who usually selects three priestesses to oversee the process.[9]

In all traditions, obtaining an initiation raises a participant's status in the group. French anthropologist Pierre Bourdieu has noted that a principal function of initiations is to separate those who have undergone them from those who have not yet undergone them, and, ultimately, from those who will never undergo them (Bourdieu, 1991:117). Bourdieu was discussing rituals tied to class hierarchy, such as royal coronations; but Neo-Pagan initiations also separate initiates from those of lower ranks, in hierarchical traditions, as well as from non-Pagans who will never experience them. Like classic rites of passage in anthropological literature, Neo-Pagan initiations often feature tests, trials, or ordeals. These may involve answering a set of questions, learning a body of material, or meeting "challenges" posed by initiators. Challenges are not intended to be dangerous or intentionally injurious, but to teach initiates to confront their weaknesses. Jone Salomonsen describes how a man who drank heavily and habitually was challenged to give up drinking for a year and a day; a woman who had strong prejudices against non-Pagan religions was challenged to seriously study another religion (Salomonsen, 2002:250). Don stressed that it is the responsibility of the initiators to monitor tests and keep the initiate out of trouble; one of the test's intentions is to demonstrate the initiate's trust in the initiators. At heart, though, the initiation is not primarily about trials or tests, but about the revelation of a spiritual mystery and the ongoing process of self-transformation.

Initiations are usually oath-bound: the initiate promises not to reveal their contents to others. Because I took such an oath myself upon my initiation into Trismegiston, I will not discuss the details of my own experience here.[10] Oaths of secrecy in part prevent postulants from learning the nature of the rite in advance; much of the ritual's power is in its unexpected nature. But even when the mechanics of the ritual are accessible to novices, the heart of the initiation—the revelation of the mystery, the ecstatic state, the personal communication with the spiritual world—remains ineffable and unique to each individual. The Pagans and Witches I interviewed all felt deeply transformed by their initiations, and often described them as special and magical; yet when pressed to describe the nature of the revelations, they called them "indescribable," "beyond words," "mystical," and "transcendent." The initiatory experience is about giving oneself over to the deities, and to the will of the initiators through whom they communicate; it epitomizes the Wiccan maxim "Suffer to learn," in the sense of submitting to learning.

Pagans say that initiations effect actual spiritual transformation in initiates, rather than just recognizing it. The ritual is not pro forma, but involves an actual transfer of spiritual power from the deities to the initiate. Initiators are merely vehicles in this process. Because power is thought to come directly from the spiritual world, it is also possible for Witches to initiate themselves.

## Rites of Crisis

Rites of crisis, in anthropological theory, are designed to address a crisis or state of spiritual imbalance in the community, and to bring about a change by engaging the help of deities and spiritual entities. In American Neo-Paganism, rites of crisis are the most "magical" of rituals. While Witches and Pagans are perfectly aware that the wheel of the year will turn without them and that individuals will undergo life transitions minus magical help, rites of crisis employ operative magic to have an effect in the material world.

A striking rite of crisis I observed was the magical healing of Susan Falkenrath, a Reclaiming Witch, elementary school teacher, jazz singer, and mother of two who was diagnosed with an aggressive form of breast cancer in the December 1996. She immediately had a double radical mastectomy and began radiation and chemotherapy treatments; but her doctors felt an experimental therapy called stem cell rescue offered the best hope for recovery. This risky treatment would cause Susan to stay in the hospital in isolation for an extended period of time as stem cells were removed from her bone marrow, treated, and reimplanted.

This type of health crisis is a challenge to anyone's faith. How would magical belief deal with such a crisis, I wondered? Witches repeatedly told me that magic could do anything. But could it stave off death? Exhausted from the treatments, Susan did not have the strength to perform magic. Her friend Vibra Willow, also a Reclaiming priestess, came up with a ritual Susan could do to sustain her sense that she could survive. Each day, she would move a pebble from one basket to another, one for each day that she was alive. Vibra collected enough colored glass pebbles to last five years, the length of time doctors said Susan would need to live cancer-free before being declared cured. The pebbles were incorporated in a healing ritual that drew together Susan's friends, colleagues, and the parents of her students.

The ritual, which was designed to be simple and accessible to the many non-Pagan participants, was held outdoors at a park overlooking San Francisco Bay. It was sunny, but very windy and cool. I was surprised that there was nothing in the ritual about fighting an enemy or defeating a scourge. Instead, it focused on healing the earth, building community and communication, and weaving a web. Susan saw her illness metaphorically as a failure on the part of some cells to communicate effectively with other cells, and related it to the broader problems that have afflicted the earth, such as pollution and habitat degradation. She spoke of how before her illness, she had felt a sense of alienation and isolation from her communities. Her illness made it possible for her to perceive herself as part of an extended web of friends, colleagues, and associates, all of whom had rallied around to support her. There was no sense that the cancer was a form of punishment or "karma," or that it was a "gift" or part of a message or greater purpose. Pagans and Witches usually avoid searching for deep meaning in sicknesses, seeing them instead as part of the nature of existing in corporeal form. Susan simply stated that as a result of her illness, she was able to feel a sense of belonging and interconnectedness.

For this ritual emphasizing the connections between humans and the planet, individuals and communities, Susan chose to invoke Arachne, the goddess of weaving. The working focused on the pebbles, which Vibra, who facilitated the ritual, encouraged us to think of as cells. Each participant took a basket full of these and directed energy into them; these were then given back to Susan, who would work with them for the next five years, moving one each day to affirm her life. "We're not superstitious," Vibra remarked as participants were scooping up the pebbles. "If you drop one or it breaks, it's not symbolic of anything." For Vibra, meaning resides in natural laws, rather than in the individual's magical ability; in this case, if a pebble fell to the ground, any "meaning" was to be found in the law of gravity: if you drop something, it will fall. Rosemary sprigs, symbolizing healing, were then passed around the circle for participants to take home with them to anyone who also needed healing, or to give to the earth for its healing. The ritual culminated in a beautifully harmonized chant intended to support Susan:

Listen, Susan, listen to my heart song.
Listen, Susan, listen to my heart song.
I will always love you; I will always be with you.
I will never forget you, I will never forsake you.

The participants danced a Spiral Dance to raise the cone of power, weaving a web of life and interconnectedness around Susan to heal, create, and bring about change, singing:

We are the power in everyone.
We are the dance of the moon and sun.
We are the hope that will not hide.
We are the turning of the tide.

Despite terrible odds, Susan did survive her harrowing treatment, and at this writing, five years later, is cancer-free. I saw her the following Samhain at Reclaiming's Spiral Dance in San Francisco. She stood, alone and proud, in the center of the cavernous ritual hall with eyes that had seen death and come back to tell about it, and sang an a cappella solo of her song "Spirits":

Spirit of the waters, soothe away my anger
for I am soon to leave here in great fear and pain.

Surround me with thy beauty if it please thee
that I might lose my fear of the flames.

Spirit of the fire, hear me when I cry
For I am soon to die and leave a daughter to mourn.
Let me burn brightly if it please thee
that she might see my light and be warned.

Spirit of the air, lift my ashes, quietly
high above that gathering, then let them fall again.
And this shall be a sign if it please thee
that I shall be returning on the north wind.

Spirit of the earth, I give my body to thee.
Oh, let my bones, scattered, be among the growing things.
Then let the forest grow if it please thee
o'er this place of death and suffering.[11]

In this is a song, a woman about to be burned for practicing witchcraft invokes the four elements to watch over her, to take her back into them, and to look after a daughter she leaves behind. I wondered how many times Susan must have thought of her own children as she faced surgery, chemotherapy, radiation, and stem cell rescue treatments during the year; and I thought that whatever the final result, the rite of crisis had done its magic.

## The Structural Framework

Regardless of their intent, Pagan rituals share a structure that is common to all the Neo-Pagan traditions. This structure constitutes a kind of grammar that allows ritualists both to reproduce rituals they have experienced and to generate new ones that improvise on the framework and insert new elements at appropriate times. It also allows Pagans from widely divergent traditions to participate in one another's rituals with relatively little difficulty.

The basic structural framework was first alluded to by Gerald Gardner in *Witchcraft Today* (1954:24–25), and "Ye Bok of ye Art Magical" gives outlines for several Craft rituals; but it was elaborated in published form by Farrar and Farrar (1981) and Buckland (1986). Wisconsin priestess Selena Fox pointed out that North American Neo-Pagan ritual structure probably owes as much to the social movements of the late 1960s as it does to Gardner and his followers. Books such as Alicia Bay Laurel's *Living on the Earth* (1971) and (with Ramon Sender) *Being of the Sun* (1973) combined ritual techniques with concepts from popular psychology to design "happenings" that emphasized ecological, spiritual, and psychological goals. These in turn influenced second-wave feminists searching for liturgical roles and ritual models empowering to women. The writings of anthropologists such as Victor Turner, whose classic work *The Rit-*

*ual Process* (1969) became a core text in anthropology classes of the 1970s and 1980s, also inspired some groups, such as the founders of NROOGD. These models passed into the countercultural matrix, and from these into the folklore of the American Neo-Pagan subculture. The composite model of American Neo-Pagan ritual is thus a combination of Gardnerian parameters and ceremonial magic with principles culled from anthropological studies of ritual, popular psychology, and the quest for self-actualization. Today, many Pagans learn ritual structure informally through participation in open rituals, festivals, and contact with other Neo-Pagans.

At its core, Neo-Pagan ritual has a tripartite structure first expressed by French ethnologist Arnold van Gennep in 1909, and elaborated by Victor Turner in 1969. It shares this structure with rituals from numerous other religious traditions, including Judeo-Christian ones and those of ancient pagan religions. This basic structure consists of entering (or, in the case of Neo-Pagan ritual, creating) the sanctuary, invoking the deities, magical acts, and a recessional. Neo-Pagans often refer to the three-part structure as "beginning, middle, and end," or "casting the circle, doing the work, and taking down the circle." These can be interpreted according to van Gennep's categories of separation from the everyday world, testing, and reintegration. The transformative part of ritual, the ritual's core, is equivalent to van Gennep's "testing." Ritual is hard work. Because it is participatory, it requires each participant's undivided attention and tests the strength of the circle. Many Pagans say that rituals fail when one or more participants are unable to dedicate their energy to the task. Certainly, rituals are less than successful for participants if they are distracted, bored, or inattentive.

Because Witches and Pagans worship in their homes, backyards, and public outdoor spaces, they create sacred space each time they do a ritual. This often begins with a process of purification: both the space and the participants must be purged of outside influences. While in Gardnerian ritual, this process conserves the outlook of ceremonial magic in which spiritual impurities must be banished from the circle in order to protect participants, most American eclectic Pagan and Witchen traditions interpret this as the shedding of participants' worries and concerns so that they can give their full attention to the ritual. Thus most rituals begin with a process called "grounding and centering," in which participants imagine themselves connected to the earth by roots or cords growing from their bodies. Using their breath, they draw energy up from the earth into their bodies through their "roots," and, in some traditions, down into their heads from the moon. When performed correctly, this exercise yields a relaxed and tingly sensation throughout the body that some Pagans describe as "running energy." When all participants are running energy, they are said to be grounded and centered. In some traditions, participants are then purified by sprinkling with water and censing with incense. In Gardnerian Craft, the elements used in purification—the water, salt, charcoal, and incense—must themselves be purified using verbal formulas, then combined (salt stirred into water, incense placed on a lit charcoal) in the first acts of transformation of what is to be a transformative experience.

The creation of sacred, liminal space continues with the casting of the circle: a circle is drawn—sometimes physically, by drawing a stick or chalk on the earth, other times by an individual holding a sword or athame—that encloses all the participants and delineates the space in which the ritual is to take place. The drawing of the circle separates the actions that follow from ordinary time and space. It is said to be "between the worlds"—literally midway between the world of human beings and the world of the gods. Pagans meet their gods halfway. Casting the circle is followed by "calling the quarters": an invocation of the four cardinal directions and, in some traditions, the spiritual guardians associated with them. Some traditions add a fifth direction and element, center and spirit, to the tetrad. Originally a further precaution against any unwanted spirits that might molest ceremonial magicians, in American Neo-Paganism this is often interpreted as a way to connect with the natural forces of wind, fire, water, and earth.

When the circle is cast and the quarters have been called, Pagans invoke the deities. Gardnerians and traditional Witches invoke a goddess and a god; their identities may vary from one coven to another and from ritual to ritual, but traditionalists usually attempt to ensure they are at least from the same cultural pantheon, whether it be Celtic (Brigid and Lugh), Greek (Hecate and Hermes), or from some other corner of the world. Deities need not be linked as a couple in mythology in order to be invoked together. In some eclectic groups they need not even be from the same culture; some Witches may call the Greek Athena and the Hindu Ganesh into the same circle together. What is considered most important is that the deities be matched to the intent of the ritual; thus, in a ritual for academic endeavors, it may be considered quite appropriate in to call upon the Greek goddess of wisdom and craftsmanship and the Hindu patron of scholars and writers. The Feri and Reclaiming traditions and a few others may also call upon the ancestors and the fairies—spirits conceptualized as intermediaries between humans and the gods—to be present at a given ritual. Most traditions have formulas of some sort for all the activities surrounding "constructing the temple": grounding and centering, casting the circle, calling the quarters, and invoking the gods. In some traditions, these are fixed-word formulas that do not vary; other traditions are more free-form and may use new formulas each time, or even sounds, dancing, or colors for this purpose.

What follows next is the core of the ritual, the content of which depends greatly on the ritual's intent, the sabbat being celebrated, and countless other variables. It is the part that is least formulaic and most open to creative variation and therefore planning; it may include instruction, magic, theatrical performance, dancing, singing, trance, religious ecstasy, and sacred possession.

The key element is the transformation of consciousness. During this phase, Pagans enter a liminal world in which surprising shifts of consciousness may take place; the singing, dancing, storytelling, and other activities move participants out of ordinary consciousness and into the magical world of ritual. Witches "raise the cone of power," or consolidate the combined energies of the participants in a cone that rises from their bodies and is directed into the universe to transform it. In Gardnerian Witchcraft, the transformation culminates in a symbolic Great Rite, the union of the female and male principles in nature symbolized by the priestess plunging her athame into the cup held by the priest.

After the main actions of the ritual are accomplished and the energy raised during the ritual's climax has been directed toward a goal, Pagans say the energy must be "grounded" so the participants can safely return to everyday consciousness. Rituals that end abruptly without any closure are said to be potentially dangerous, since participants may still be in an alternate state of consciousness, not fully ready to return to ordinary activities. Grounding is usually accomplished through the act of physically touching the ground, or, in the case of NROOGD rituals, another member of the group who is touching the ground; but it is also assisted through a ceremony known in traditional Witchcraft as "cakes and wine," in which the group shares food and drink. While bread and wine are used in traditional Craft because they embody the transformative processes of rising and fermentation, in practice any breadlike substance and drink can be used. Many rituals in the San Francisco Bay Area are "clean and sober," using no alcohol of any kind out of respect for participants who may be recovering from addictions. Trismegiston sabbats, on the other hand, often featured vintage wines from Don and Anna's cellar, imported ciders and ales, and exotic nonalcoholic beverages, reflecting both the availability of gourmet foodstuffs in the San Francisco Bay Area and the relatively high degree of culinary sophistication of Trismegiston members. After sharing food, the spirits invoked earlier are saluted, thanked, and dismissed, and the circle is ritually opened using a formula.

The tripartite structure of rituals serves several purposes in Neo-Pagan culture. Its clear beginning and ending provide a container for ecstatic ritual practices, marking them as framed experiences during which participants feel free to suspend disbelief and become absorbed in the activities. The frame itself is important, because it prepares participants for what follows and furnishes a transition to everyday reality when the ritual has ended. A lack of framing is disastrous to ritual. I once attended a Pagan camp-out during which the organizers cast an opening circle that was intended to create sacred space for the entire duration of the festival, thus avoiding the need to cast a circle each time a ritual took place. The results were desultory at best. The rest of the rituals that took place during the weekend were aimless and disorganized; no one could manage to leap directly into the body of ritual without preparation. The tripartite ritual organization also ensures that Pagans of any stripe can easily participate in the celebrations of other traditions with only a little adjustment. While each tradition has its own unique liturgical style, everyone knows what it means to cast a circle, call the quarters, and invoke the deities. In this way, elements diffuse easily from one tradition to another, leading to a standardization of certain practices across traditions.

While some researchers have interpreted this trend as "routinization," a decrease in creativity and originality in the movement (Berger, 1999:100–104), it could represent instead a crystallization of core features in an emergent folk tradition. As folklorist Henry Glassie has observed, "The usual critic, because he is not an artist, can find excellence in artwork only when it displays obvious originality, so he has difficulty in apprehending the qualities in folk art" (1975:64). The "repetitiousness, simplicity and seeming unreality" of folk art "come out of its authors' sincere attempts to express a resonance between a spiritual inner sound and an outward materiality" (Glassie, 1975:64). Folklore is repeatedly winnowed and refined by its bearers; what emerges is a core of essential parameters within which the tradition bearer must operate. Ritual structure creates such a framework in Neo-Pagan culture; within it, artistry and creativity can more easily flourish.

## Ritual and Folk Narrative

Folk narratives—myths, legends, ballads, and especially *Märchen*, or magic tales, furnish Neo-Pagans with much of the source material for their rituals. The reasons for this are varied, and are partly rooted in Neo-Pagans' interpretation of nineteenth-century folklore theories. Like the myth-ritual theorists, some Pagans see myths as the narrative form of rituals; since rituals, in their view, enact myths, it is fitting and proper to model reclaimed rituals on well-known sacred narratives from ancient times. Both the Greek myth of Demeter and Persephone and the Sumerian story of the descent of Inanna into the underworld realm of her sister Erishkigel are popular ritual themes because they recall Frazer's myth of the divine king, only with a goddess protagonist. But Pagans' use of folk narrative is hardly limited to myths: ballads and folktales also turn up in rituals. Reclaiming's Witch camp is often organized around one particular myth or folktale. In *The Twelve Wild Swans* (2000), Starhawk and Hilary Valentine explain why they have chosen to use the eponymous tale (AT 451, "The Girl in Search of Her Lost Brothers") as a template for the transformative process of Witch camp:

> In the Goddess tradition, we have no sacred text other than nature herself. We have no bible, no Koran, no Bhagavad Gita, no official compilation of myth and story. What remains of the stories our ancestors told are passed down to us as fairy tales and folk tales. These have been told for centuries. . . . When politics or religion changed, form and heresy were redefined, dangerous aspects of the stories were hidden or given a Chris-

tian gloss. . . . In the Reclaiming tradition, we approach the stories in a unique way. We do not analyze them for archetypal elements, in Jungian fashion. We do not take the characters, Goddesses or Gods, as role models for how we should be as women or as men, nor do we see the tales as morality plays. Instead, we look for the true form. . . . We find clues in the colors, symbols and actions and their historical associations. When we encounter an aspect of the story we find problematic, we welcome it as an opportunity to work fully with the material it evokes through meditation, reflection, and ritual. As we do so, the story evolves and transforms. We may never know what the original intention of the first tellers was, but we can know what our intentions are and how the tale can work for us. (Starhawk and Valentine 2000:xx–xxi)

Starhawk and Valentine see the tale as "contain[ing] within it the instructions for a transformative journey" (Starhawk and Valentine, 2000:xx). This recalls Vladimir Propp's theory of the shamanic roots of magic tales. Propp theorized that the classic European magic tale was once a template for a rite of passage for a shaman or healer (Propp, 1977:383–84). The magic tale especially lends itself to this interpretation because of its structure: at the core of the tale is a loss, and the tale's plot broadly concerns the actions of a hero or heroine to remedy that loss through magical transformation (Propp, 1968). This structure exactly parallels the Neo-Pagan worldview. Pagans experience the world as enchanted; they see magic in the cycle of the seasons and the waxing and waning of the moon; they personify the elements and natural phenomena and feel the sacred present within them. Yet this experience contrasts vividly with the view of the world they receive from the dominant culture: one in which the world is instrumental to material and economic goals, a complex machine that exists to exploit and utilize. This loss of enchantment is the central problem for Neo-Pagans. It leads them to see the earth, and all life forms that are connected with it, as in need of healing, and to see themselves as the healers. The structure of the magic tale, with its initial loss and final restoration, lends itself to manipulation and interpretation in ritual, which acts as a vehicle for reenchanting and healing both self and other. Starhawk writes: "Encoded in 'The Twelve Wild Swans' is a set of instructions for becoming a healer, a shaman, an artist, a Witch: one who can walk between the worlds and retrieve lost souls, one who can restore balance and justice to a world made ill" (Starhawk and Valentine, 2000:xxii). The transformation of an ordinary individual into a Witch, a healer, an artist who can, in turn, transform the world is the central unifying theme in many Neo-Pagan rituals. It is especially salient in initiations, and the experience of Witch camp is essentially that of a rite of passage: participants are isolated for a week at a campground, and participate in daily magical exercises and rituals that culminate in a large group ritual on one of the final nights of camp. Thus it is particularly fitting that Reclaiming Witches have structured the camp experience around a single folktale and its interpretations.

In another Reclaiming production, the ballad "Tam Lin" was used as a template for a ritual in which participants imagined themselves as mediators between the enchanted world of faery and the everyday world. The ballad tells the story of a young woman (Lady Margaret or Fair Janet) who trysts with a mysterious lover in the forest. When she discovers she is pregnant, she returns to the glade where she met her lover to try to discover his identity. There she meets Tam Lin once again; he confesses he was stolen by the fairies as a youth, but that Janet can free him by taking him from his horse as he rides in the fairy rade on Halloween, and holding him tightly through a series of fearsome transformations. Using William Butler Yeats's poem "The Stolen Child" (1886), which also has the theme of fairy abduction, Reclaiming members added verses to the ballad expressing the theme of mediation and transformation:

Come away, o human child
To find a world unseen;
Know the wonder and the wild
And be a bridge between.

Come away, o human child
Back to the earth so green;
Know the hearth and know the wild
And be a bridge between.

As participants danced the Spiral Dance to raise the cone of power, they chanted:

We are alive, as the earth is alive.
We have the power to fight for our freedom.
If we have courage we can be healers
Like the sun we shall rise.

Just as the story "The Twelve Wild Swans" was interpreted as a template for an initiatory ritual, the ballad "Tam Lin" was transformed from legend to participatory drama. Janet became a mediator between the human world and the world of faery; like participants, she could be "a bridge between" the hearth and the wild, culture and nature, the ecstatic world of faery and the everyday world. The final, energy-raising chant expressed many of the most important tenets of this practice-based religion: that the earth is alive, animated with magical forces, just as humans are; that Pagans can heal the earth; and that there will be a rebirth of ancient wisdom and practice: "Like the sun we shall rise." While the goal of healing self and earth is a difficult one to achieve, attaining it involves many difficult transformations, just as Tam Lin was transformed into a series of fearsome creatures in Janet's arms before taking his true form as a human being. To be fully human, the ritual suggested, means holding on to one's heart's desire in the face of obstacles and frightening changes.

## The Aesthetics of Ritual

Pantheacon, 1998, San Francisco, California. The Magical Acts Ritual Theater is giving a workshop entitled "Acting for Magicians." I arrive punctually at the appointed time, but the workshop appears to be in a state of disorganization. The performers seem to be preparing for a ritual, but a very strange one: the priestess is nowhere to be seen, the other participants stroll in late, and the facilitators are still arguing about the ritual's purpose. Finally they begin to make sacred space by calling the quarters. But the calls are incompatible with each other as well as with the elements they are invoking. The priestess invoking the direction south, which corresponds to the element of fire and the qualities of passion, courage, and will, was a tiny wisp of a thing who delivered her speech in a flat, barely audible monotone. Darrin, a tall, powerfully built man, called in west and water, which symbolize intuition, the imagination, reflectiveness, and creativity, by waving his athame around carelessly and shouting, "West, yo! Here! Now!" Thankfully, magician Sam Webster put a stop to the "ritual" before things could get much worse, and revealed to the audience the group's intention: articulating an aesthetics of ritual.

Like all art forms, Neo-Pagan ritual has a set of aesthetics recognized within the community. But this shared aesthetic can be difficult to articulate. Styles vary according to tradition; even individual ritualists have their own recognizable styles. Non-Witchen styles differ considerably from Witchen ones, and eclectic Wicca diverges in flavor and character from more conservative traditions. Few Pagans agree on the essence of ritual aesthetics. Some feel rituals should be varied each time, to keep them spontaneous: "I don't want to do the same ritual week after week," said Toraine, an eclectic Witch from the Midwest. "If I wanted that, I'd be Christian." Others prefer more formality and continuity: "I think it's wonderful that people can rattle off the Lord's Prayer without even bothering to think about it," said Steven Posch, a Gardnerian priest. "I aspire to a time when Pagans can do things without having to be so conscious about them."

Gardnerian rituals tend to be more scripted, because all Gardnerians share basic liturgy for all their rituals that derives from Gardner's coven in the early 1950s. While they have undergone significant changes and some Gardnerian covens encourage creative reinterpretations of the scripts, their liturgy is more fixed and textual. Reclaiming Witches, on the other hand, favor more ecstatic, dramatic rituals that raise energy through song, dance, chanting, and trancing. Their proclivity for this type of ritual performance has earned them the sobriquet of "Pentecostal Witches" from those whose aesthetic style is more staid. They, in turn, tend to criticize rituals they perceive as static, boring, and undynamic as "high church," "middle-class," or "mainstream"—"the worst insulting language thinkable in this particular community" (Salomonsen,

2002:206). The rituals of the Fellowship of the Spiral Path, a kabbalistic group led by Diana Paxson, who once trained as an Episcopalian minister, are often humorously described as "High Episcopagan" because of their formal, churchlike style.

Even those initiated in the same tradition may have widely differing views on ritual aesthetics. NROOGD, for example, emphasizes poetic license and creativity to such an extent that each coven modifies material over a period of time. This leads to tremendous variation over a short generational time span, and renders compromise difficult, as individual ritualists become attached to their own creative variations. NROOGD's case is an interesting example of the conditions under which certain ritual forms change or crystallize. The most stable NROOGD rituals, according to members, are the institutionalized sabbats—those that have become fixtures in the San Francisco Bay Area Neo-Pagan year cycle, such as the celebration of Beltane and the Eleusinian Mysteries in September. Much of this stability is due to the rituals' longevity (both the NROOGD Beltane and the Eleusinian Mysteries are among the group's oldest, and thus have been performed repeatedly over a period of time). Fixed phrasing of ritual text also contributes greatly to a ritual's stability over time: in the case of NROOGD's Eleusinian Mysteries, the text is taken from Aristophanes and cannot be altered, as its intent is to re-create the Greek original. A similar textual stability is characteristic of Gardnerian rituals. Next in order of stability are the initiations and elevations. Innovations for these occasions happen slowly and deliberately; changes become part of a pool of variation from which initiators may draw, but the pool of motifs remains relatively small. Other sabbats have the greatest leeway for innovation and change, allowing room for individual input and creativity.

Conflicting aesthetics are one of the primary reasons why covens split apart. A Santa Barbara, California, coven I briefly observed in 1995 typified this process. One faction preferred a light-hearted, humorous, playful style manifest in free-form rituals to honor chocolate or comic-strip characters, while the other sought greater discipline and depth in rituals that explored personal feelings and spiritual themes. As members bickered over details and refused to compromise aesthetic principles, friendships became strained. Those who longed for rigor were characterized by the opposite faction as rigid, authoritarian, and lacking in imagination, while those who wanted social occasions and levity were typecast in turn as shallow and lazy. Riven by simmering conflict and resentments, the coven eventually split in two.

Despite these divergences, the responses I received from Pagans all over the country to my questions on ritual aesthetics were remarkably similar. "Ritual should be a transformative experience," said Lhianna Sidhe, a Witch from Ohio. "If we don't know more on an internal level after we've left the circle, as well as on a cerebral level, then something has not happened." Rituals are educational tools, but must also move participants on an emotional level in order to be considered successful. All my respondents believed ritual should be more than a meaningless rote performance. "I want to learn something, I want to be moved, I want to feel renewed, I want to feel like I've had some kind of participation in something bigger than myself," Steven explained. As he described for me the sense of timelessness and transcendence that the ritual along the banks of the Mississippi had induced in him, I became so moved that I developed gooseflesh, and I called his attention to it. "That's it!" he exclaimed. "That's how you know a ritual's good."

Not all rituals are equally successful for all participants in this respect, and what moves some individuals does nothing for others. Since ritual is primarily an internal experience, its success or failure often depends on the qualities each individual participant brings to it. Certain images and activities resonate with some, but not others; I was repeatedly amazed by how rituals that seemed to me lackluster and boring could induce ecstatic states in other participants. Ultimately, the qualities that move individuals remain ineffable. However, most Pagans agreed on features that guaranteed a poor ritual performance. These included rituals that went on for too long, losing participants' attention; scripted presentations with little spontaneity and few participatory elements; rituals with invocations that were incomprehensible to those present, either because they were recited in a foreign language such as Old Norse or Gaelic, or because they were delivered in a whisper; and disorganized rituals, in which no one was sure what was going on and there seemed to be no direction. These negative examples indicate the existence of a shared aesthetic that embodies important American Neo-Pagan values: a strong participatory ethic, resistance to hierarchical esoterism, and an emphasis on spontaneity and creativity within an organized framework. "I think that's the art form: being able to include that spontaneity and sincerity in worship in a piece . . . that isn't totally chaotic," concluded Toraine.

Despite the great divergences of aesthetics in different traditions and among individuals, the performance of Magical Acts Ritual Theater described at the beginning of this section suggests that Neo-Pagans share a set of parameters to determine what folklorist Richard Bauman calls "performative competence" in a tradition (Bauman, 1984:30). Magical training develops performative competence in initiates within the particular aesthetics of that tradition. But emic concepts of performative competence may transcend the boundaries of traditions, in that Neo-Pagans recognize successful ritual even when it occurs in a tradition not their own or not to their liking. They certainly recognize elements of "performative incompetence," as the pseudoritual example I gave earlier suggests. Performative competence includes skills such as organization, the ability to coordinate a group and to raise energy, determining the intent of the ritual, and a thorough understanding of the system of magical correspondences such that each element of the ritual remains in harmony with the qualities being invoked and evoked.

Good ritual demands planning and organization, as Toraine suggests, in order to achieve just the right mix of artistry and structure. The ritual facilitator must at once play the part of a good host, providing an attractive setting, beautiful props, and delicious food and drink, yet at the same time strive to give participants a transcendent experience. In many ways, ritual is a collaborative performance between the facilitator and all of the participants. Lhianna, who often facilitates large rituals, explained, "I like to make sure that not a lot is left to chance, although I don't want to inhibit creativity on the part of participants, either. . . . Flexibility is essential. I want people in the group to find the deep places within themselves and feel the freedom of expression." Ritual planners must take into account the size of the ritual, its setting, and its primary participants in designing a successful series of actions; what works in an intimate coven becomes impossible in a large group ritual, and vice versa. While small group rituals often play on the intimate relationships between participants, large group rituals become more theatrical, as issues such as visibility, audibility, and space take precedence over the subtle interplay of emotions. Reclaiming's Spiral Dance, which I described at the beginning of this chapter, is by far the most theatrical ritual I have witnessed; song, dance, and dramatic action in it replace the verbal formulas for quarter calls and invocations.

## Ritual as Art

Rituals move participants toward greater understanding and transcendence chiefly through their aesthetic charge. This is achieved not through words, or cognitive meaning, but through dramatic action—affective meaning (Smith, 1975:7). Pitch, a graphic artist and retail manager with graduate training in anthropology, explained, "Neo-Pagan rituals produce their effects as a result of their aesthetic impact rather than their content or their declared intention. . . . It's not so much about what they are as thealogical statements as what they do as performances that brings about a response and perhaps an enduring change in the participants."

Ritual, then, is seen within the community as a form of art (Adler, 1986:141). Steven Posch, one of the most gifted and skilled ritualists I encountered in my fieldwork, told me, "Ritual is my chosen art form." Master ritualists are highly regarded within the community; demonstrating one's ritual abilities significantly raises one's status. Likewise, those who never seem to get the hang of organizing ritual, or those whose aesthetics do not mesh with their coven or group, can be marginalized: one Los Angeles woman was denied initiation because her initiators considered her ritual skills weak.

Selena Fox likened ritual to performance art. In part this is because ritual often has in common with theatrical productions the need for scripts, staging, set design, and elaborate prop and costume construction. But it also points to a deeper issue in the movement's aesthetics: the importance of individual creativity. Pagans value creativity to an unusually high degree; they believe that "an effective artist or craftsperson is, or has the potential to be, a magician" (Orion, 1995:68). Both ritual magic and art involve transformation, the creation of a new product or feeling in accordance with one's will. Both artists and magicians use imagination and the resources of the unconscious to manipulate objects and symbols to make manifest a vision. As anthropologists and ritual scholars Victor and Edith Turner have noted, the recombination of divergent symbolic elements in an aesthetically significant way startles people "into thinking anew about persons, objects, relationships, social roles, and features . . . hitherto taken for granted. Previous patterns of thought, feeling and action are disrupted" (1982:205).

Continuing his musings on ritual as an aesthetic form in a e-mail letter (10 October 1996) to me, Pitch elaborated:

> My notion of aesthetics was shaped by the influence of thinkers like Susanne Langer, who holds that works of art provide symbolic replications of patterns of human experience. As I recall, that means art pares down and condenses our experiences to their essential patterns, then represents those patterns back to us symbolically. Art is virtual experience. In this series of metaphors, I suggest that rituals are virtual dreaming (as dreaming is widely valued by Neo-Pagan ideology). Neo-Pagans consider dreams important and potentially transformative experiences, sources of insight, contact with divine forces, and formally coherent and meaningful. Dreams have meaning, and their meanings are discussed and interpreted. The meaning of a dream may be refractory and not immediately comprehensible, so that for Neo-Pagans, the experience of a dream provides (requires) follow-up process work by the individual and perhaps those others involved in interpreting the dream. Neo-Pagan rituals may be seen as opportunities for a group to engage in collective dreaming via a group performance. The actions of the ritual are not necessarily obvious; there is a certain openness to the performance—twists, turns, and surprises. Adaptability on the part of the participants and officiants is required and expected. Individuals are encouraged to access the subconscious content of their own psyches, and to undertake acts of choice and decision in regard to those contents. There is in many rituals a feeling of suspension or flying or intensification of experiencing selfhood which has a dream-like feeling. Participants are invited to feel vulnerable and reveal their vulnerability, at least to themselves in inner visualizations or inner dialogue. . . . Neo-Pagan rituals provoke an "aesthetic response" which is a holistic emotional experience that is different from common states of mundane consciousness.

In other words, when Neo-Pagans say that the goal of ritual is to change consciousness, they do not only mean raising consciousness about spiritual, social, and personal issues. They also include transcendence and ecstasy—altered states of consciousness that differ, as Pitch explains, from ordinary, everyday consciousness. Rituals are works of art intended to bring about such shifts in consciousness chiefly through an aesthetic charge.

While Pagan ritual aesthetics vary widely, most Pagans agree that a ritual that succeeds in inducing ecstasy is successful. Trance and ecstasy do not happen to all participants at every Pagan ritual; in fact they are considered relatively rare, and for that reason are more prized and valued. Whether or not individuals experience ecstasy depends on a number of factors, including their state of mind when entering the ritual, the aesthetics of the ritual itself, and the interaction between the two. Rituals are designed in part to bring about a state favorable for the emergence of ecstasy. Yet even for those who do not experience ecstasy, good rituals are expected to have deep and lasting effects.

Neurologists Andrew Newberg and Eugene D'Aquili have studied the physiology of spiritual experiences, including what I am calling here "religious ecstasy." According to their findings, ritual may play a central role in bringing about spiritual experiences by changing the physiology of the brain (Newberg and D'Aquili, 2001:87). Among the most important ritual elements that influence brain chemistry are what the authors call rhythmic behaviors: the dancing, swaying, singing, drumming, and chanting that are often found in the middle part of Pagan rituals. These rhythmic behaviors can affect the flow of neural information to various areas of the brain, including one area the researchers have studied intensely, the orientation association area, or OAA, a part of the brain that controls how we distinguish ourselves from the surrounding environment. Intense rhythmic behaviors, whether frenzied or slow and deliberate, can alter the way the OAA perceives where our bodies end and our environment begins, bringing about what Newburg and D'Aquili call "unitary" transcendent experiences, or ecstatic feelings of union with the world around us and with a greater spiritual force. Rituals, however, do more than simply prescribe a set of motions that disorient the OAA. They combine the content of sacred narratives with neurological reactions; in fact, ritual's power comes from this synthesis of neurological function with sacred content (Newburg and D'Aquili, 2001:95–96).

In this chapter, we have seen how the structure common to all Pagan rituals is designed to facilitate ecstatic states and bring about the spiritual transcendence that Newberg and his colleagues have documented. Neo-Pagan ritual is, to borrow Turner's term, a liminal experience (V. Turner, 1968)—"time out of time" (Falassi, 1987). For this reason Pagan rituals usually begin with grounding and centering, an exercise in visual imagery, during which participants are encouraged to breathe deeply, temporarily put their worldly cares aside, and imagine themselves rooted in the ground. Worry about mundane concerns inhibits ecstasy, regardless of the nature or beauty of the ritual. Bad aesthetics can be jarring; participants feel irritated or bored, or begin to criticize the ritual in their minds. A poorly conducted, badly planned ritual will seldom produce ecstatic experiences. Part of the appeal of religious ecstasy for Pagans is its ability to silence for a moment the thinking, analytical part of the mind and to give the individual over wholly to experience. The creation of sacred space, the separation from everyday reality through formulaic actions and codes, the invocation of deities, the running of energy through the body, the channeling of that energy through movement, dance, singing, and chanting are all tools to help bring about changes in consciousness—changes that create a state of suspended disbelief during which magic can happen. Pagans use elements from folktales and European calendar customs in ritual because they carry a strong affective and aesthetic charge that helps move them "between the worlds." In the next chapter, we will examine more closely how ritual and narrative work together to bring about ecstatic states.

*Chapter 5*

# "The Juice of Ritual": Pathways to Ecstasy

**Field notes, May 11, 1997**

"I can't believe they have to write books about 'Why do these weird people do these weird things,'" says Don, alluding to my presence, tape recorder in hand, at the gathering. The room erupts into laughter. We are at Anna and Don's place along with members of NROOGD's Dark Star Coven, unraveling the maypole ribbons from the previous week's Beltane celebration, and the talk has turned to visions and ecstatic states. One by one the members share stories of their visions and trances, connecting them with the reasons they were originally drawn into the religion, their initiations, and their experiences of healing and union with the divine. One would think the mood would be solemn, but it's not. Anna has ordered pizza and everyone munches away as they work on unraveling the tightly braided maypole ribbons and carefully rolling and taping them so they can be used again next year. The narratives are moving, personal, and intimate; yet people laugh and joke, interrupting each other with humorous comments and asides. The presence of the maypole, a symbol of male sexual energy to Neo-Pagans, adds another source of humor.[1]

Pagans often experience powerful visions and trances during rituals. These can range from very personal images that resemble vivid waking dreams, to experiences of actually embodying deities. Not all rituals engender these experiences in all individuals; what moves people is highly idiosyncratic. But the experience of altered or alternate consciousness that reveals a previously hidden, spiritual reality is the core of the Neo-Pagan movement, uniting Pagans and Witches even beyond shared practice. One interviewee called it the "juice" in ritual—"It's the whole reason I go to ritual; it's what I strive for," he explained. This is the deepest form of magic: theurgy, or communicating and aligning with the gods.

While I collected a number of narratives about ecstatic experience from my consultants, often in a group context where members could share them with each other as well as with me, several felt that I actually created these occasions by soliciting the stories. "Pagans don't testify as Christians do," explained Don.

"You got a lot of these [stories] because you asked for them." Thus I am cautious about assuming that Pagans construct a sense of common experience only by sharing these narratives. At the same time, ecstasy is the heart of ritual, and a core value in the Neo-Pagan community. It would be equally naive to assume that Pagans only talk about ecstatic experiences to the ethnographer who requests them. Specific rituals in certain Pagan traditions—for example, the Reclaiming ritual in honor of Brigid that I described in the Introduction—actually make time for participants to break into small groups so they can share their experiences of ecstasy in sacred space. Therefore it is safe to say that even if I created the occasions on which my consultants told me their experiences of religious ecstasy, occasions also exist within the Neo-Pagan community during which individuals may share some of these experiences with each other.

Linda Dégh and Andrew Vázsonyi have shown how individuals with a particular interest in the numinous form "legend conduits," networks through which they share narratives about their own experiences and those of others (Dégh and Vázsonyi, 1975; Dégh, 2001). The telling of these stories provides a forum in which beliefs are formed and debated. In fact, networks may coalesce around a particular experience and a set of beliefs associated with it (Dégh, 2001:296–97). While it is clearly more than a simple network of narrators sharing numinous personal experiences with each other, Neo-Paganism functions in some ways as one of the conduits described by Dégh and Vázsonyi, in that it provides a context in which ecstatic experiences are shared, analyzed, and understood. Neo-Pagans' beliefs emerge from these experiences and their discussion of them.

For Pagans, ecstasy is ordinary, in that it is an expected part of religious experience and something which everyone can achieve. At the same time, it is the central religious experience, the goal of much ritual, and, as Don humorously suggested above, one of the primary reasons why many Pagans begin their involvement with the movement. Some Pagans are first drawn to the movement because of a spontaneous spiritual experience of alternate consciousness. In Paganism, they find a context that normalizes such experiences and privileges the imagination. For educated, urban intellectuals who grew up without a knowledge of trance and ecstasy, and often with a fear that such experiences were tantamount to insanity, Paganism provides a context in which a spontaneous vision can be understood and integrated into the individual's experience. This was the case for Laurel, high priestess of a NROOGD coven, who had trained for many years as a classical soprano. It was in the context of a musical performance that she had her first experience with ecstasy, an experience she related at the gathering at Anna and Don's on May 11, 1997:

All my life, I loved the music from Handel's *Messiah*, and I always wanted to sing the soprano recitatives and the "Rejoice greatly oh daughter of Zion" in a church service before a large group of people. . . . A few days before Christmas, the woman who was the premiere soprano at the Methodist church was struck mysteriously ill and could not sing. And all of a sudden, this woman says: "You've been studying [this piece] in your voice lessons; you can sight-read the recitatives; sing them." And I did. And it was one of those experiences where the organist was a true musician, and it stopped being the organ and the voice and it became the music, as happens when music is really good. . . . I sight-read the recitatives and it was beautiful; and then I got to sing "Rejoice greatly O daughter of Zion." And when I hit the part [sings] "He is the righteous savior and he shall speak peace unto the heathen," I left my body. I rose up to the top of the church, and there was this node of white light, and it had a consciousness, and it said, "Finally!" And it slammed into my body and out through my voice. And this is really embarrassing because this is another New Age term, but I was translated into light. . . . I remember this power flowing through me and flowing through the music and flowing through the organist. . . . At the end when we finished I was trembling, almost crying. I could barely walk back to my seat; and the first three rows of the church were sobbing, I mean, crying loud. People all over the church were crying. I realized then that something had happened.

Laurel's experience puzzled and worried her. Her Methodist pastor did not provide her with a framework in which to understand it,[2] yet she knew it was important in her life and felt certain she was not insane. She sought the advice of a friend who knew about many spiritual traditions, who gave her Starhawk's book *The Spiral Dance* (1979), one of the fundamental texts of modern Neo-Pagan Witchcraft. Laurel began to read it, but after a few chapters she put it aside, bored; she felt it had little meaning for her. But then she had another extraordinary experience:

I was laying [*sic*] down in the room that had been my bedroom as a child. . . . I was looking at this picture my mother had put up in my old bedroom of a hillside on a summer day with the golden light and trees and a path coming out of the trees. . . . This woman comes walking out of the picture with her head on fire; it was flames making a crown. And she said, "He's had you for twenty-seven years of your life; I believe it's my turn now" [audience laughs]. . . . And so I ended up going to this newly forming women's circle, and the group was called Brigid's Fire.

In this vision, Laurel experienced a goddess telling her that "He" (Jesus) had "had" her for long enough and that now it was the goddess's turn to have Laurel as a devotee. As a result, Laurel decided to explore Pagan spirituality through a women's group. The woman with the flaming crown is recognizable to most Pagans as Brigid, Irish goddess of craftsmanship, poetry, and healing. Laurel felt it was significant that the first group she joined was named Brigid's Fire, in honor of the deity who had appeared to her, although it was not until much later that she was able to identify the woman in her vision as the goddess Brigid.

Neo-Paganism provided Laurel with a context in which to understand her unusual experiences, and with an explanation that her church had been unable to provide. As Laurel deepened her involvement with Pagan groups, she acquired the skills to experience visions and trances voluntarily—skills which gave her control over the experiences, so she was no longer at their mercy, but could use them deliberately in ritual, their appropriate context. Today, Laurel is recognized as one of the Bay Area Pagan community's most gifted trancers.

Ecstatic experiences are typical of Neo-Pagans in the early stages of experimentation with the religion. Individuals often feel they confirm the rightness of their new spiritual path. Many Pagan narratives about ecstatic experiences emphasize the completely unexpected and unpredictable nature of the event. Narrators emphasize their skepticism, naiveté, and agnosticism before encountering Pagan ecstasy. Darrin, high priest of a NROOGD coven, had been earmarked for ministerial training in an African-American Lutheran church; but as a teenager he became increasingly agnostic and eventually abandoned that road to enlist in the military. It was then that he first experienced trance, as he told the gathering at Anna and Don's:

> I was in the military at the time and I was just coming off a reserve drill. Here I am, nineteen, fairly thick-headed, fairly skeptical. And I decided I'd go visit my friend Ian. . . . He told me, "Well, you know, it's great to see you, but there's a class tonight." "What kind of class?" "Oh, it's in this thing called the Kabbalah, a filing system for the gods. You wouldn't be interested." I said, "Oh, I dunno about that; let me check this out. I don't have anywhere else to go; I may as well hang out here." . . . The class begins and at this point I'm pretty solidly agnostic. . . . But I know that these people, as they're talking, sound really insane. They're talking about energy points and ley lines and the various energies of a place. I'm going, "Why am I here?" Suffered through that, went into the ritual. Then we get to the meditation, which is the main portion of the working for the ritual. . . . During this meditation, I, who tried [meditating] before . . . and failed, just *disappeared.* I was completely gone into trance during this meditation. Never had been able to do this before in my life. I saw a great many strange and wonderful things. . . . The class for that evening was centered around a particular sephiroth, which was Malkuth, which is the realm of earth. Before this we were each given a token: a stone. So we all had these stones as we went through the ritual. Went through the meditation, came out the other end of it; sat up, blinked; the stone was in my hand. I looked down in my hand, and found that the stone was in pieces all over my hand. Looked up and said, "Did anyone else's stone break?" [audience roars with laughter]. In a living room that was about thirty [feet] by ten [feet], . . . they found fragments of this stone at the other end. From there, I said, "You know, I think I better take a closer look at this."

Darrin describes his state of mind before the ritual as bored and rather disgusted with the "insane" talk of the ritualists. He describes himself as skeptical and agnostic, even thick-headed—not the sort of person who is usually drawn to spiritual things. This makes the story's conclusion even more dramatic, especially emphasized by his understated remark, "Did anybody else's stone break?" The broken stone would be considered a sign of tremendous magical power by the other ritualists; but Darrin portrays himself as innocent of its significance.

On a separate occasion, Gus, a political scientist and author of *Pagans and Christians* (2001), told me this story of his first, transformative experience with religious ecstasy:

Before this experience, I was not practicing Craft. . . . [Then Don Frew] invited me to a Midsummer Sabbat in Tilden Park. . . . I got there and I was filled with both anticipation and some fear; very rapidly, they were replaced with enormous boredom. . . . [The ritual] is supposed to start at a certain time, and time passes and time passes and time passes. Almost two hours passed. I was compulsively punctual. All fear and anticipation has long since left, and I'm just wishing I could get out without embarrassing my friend Don, who had invited me. Then they finally get started. . . . We formed a circle, and there was something sort of nice about that circle . . . but I was mostly thinking about it with relief, that finally something was happening. And the circle is cast and they prepare to invoke the gods, and I'm sort of standing there, curious, but not much of anything else, not really expecting much to happen. The goddess is invoked, and all of a sudden as quickly as switching a light switch, there was a presence that was not visible, that was not auditory. But the presence was feminine, powerful, beautiful, and loving—all four of those categories far beyond anything I had ever experienced in my life. It was the most beautiful experience of my life, up until that time. I remember thinking, "My God, here's a religion where they ask their god to come, and she does!"

Up until then, my primary interest in magical phenomena, besides being a curious soul, was that I was interested in powers, pizzazz, things to demonstrate that in fact there is another dimension to reality. After that, my interest in magic in that sense of the term evaporated as quickly as dry ice on a hot sidewalk. There was not even a puddle left. . . . So it was transformative not only in terms of the way I look at the nature of divinity—I have no doubt—but in addition, it was transformative in that it led to a fundamental restructuring of my values.

Gus's story is structurally similar to Darrin's: he presents himself as curious but skeptical and bored before the beginning of the ritual. Once the ecstatic experience begins, his attitude changes dramatically. He becomes convinced of the reality of the goddess through his own experience of her. Unlike Darrin, Gus was already interested in exploring "another dimension to reality"; yet his story shares with Darrin's an emphasis on embodied experience as a catalyst to a fundamental change in consciousness and values. Stories like Gus's and Darrin's stress the unexpected nature of ecstasy, the fact that it can happen to anyone if the time is right and the gods are willing, as well as its transformative nature. They also establish and reinforce belief, especially in the early stages of religious experimentation. For Gus, the experience radically changed his belief system: he now has "no doubt" about the existence of divinity. The stories illustrate that in many cases, belief arises from embodied experience; as the well-known Pagan song says, "my skin, my bones, my heretic heart are my authority."

Gus's and Darrin's tales are narratives of conversion; but for other Pagans, ecstatic experiences only confirm what they have long known about themselves. Like many Neo-Pagans, Don had a long-standing interest in magic going back to childhood. Soon after he began attending NROOGD rituals in college, he had a vision during a meditation session that seemed to confirm that he was on the correct path, a path he had been on all his life.

When I came to [the University of California at] Berkeley, in the dorms, I met somebody else who was very interested in magic . . . and we started studying ritual magic together; but it was entirely in a secular context. I was not terribly interested in the spiritual or religious side of any of it. Actually for me it was more experimental magic. I was interested in how magic worked. At that time what we were doing was actually summoning spirits and sending it to the other for the other to then . . . contain and observe, and report back what kind of spirit it was. So we were supposed to do this at midnight, jointly. . . . My ritual preps were done, so I just thought I'd meditate. So I lay down on the floor and I started singing that chant from the [NROOGD] sabbat I'd been to: "We All Come from the Goddess." So I'm like [sings] "duh-duh-duh-duh-duh," singing this chant to myself, when suddenly the darkness behind my eyelids parted, like curtains. And I was looking out on a scene that looked every bit as real as everyday life; it was a sunlit, grassy, rolling hillscape with woods off to my left, and a path coming out of the woods and going off towards the hills. And this beautiful golden summer light. So I thought to myself, "I guess this must be the Summerland.[3] Cool!" And there's other voices singing the chant with me, and I look to my left and there's this woman coming down the hill with this trail of children. And she has long dark hair, and she's wearing a white robe, and the children are all in white robes with white cords and sandals. And I go, "Oh-oh, that must be the goddess! Now what am I supposed to do?" I think I'm supposed to say something profound. I can't think of anything profound! [audience laughter]. So I said, "Well, OK, I have to say something." So I stepped forward one step as she came by, and I said, "Lady, would you watch over me and my workings tonight?" And she looked at me and gave me this very interesting smile, like, "You really couldn't think of anything else to say, could you?" And said, "Of course. Are you not already one of my children?" And she gestured back to the children behind her, and there in the group of children was me, at the age of twelve.

When Don was about twelve years old, he and some friends had played at being Witches, experimenting with magic and even forming a coven. Don's interpretation of his vision was that his earlier involvement in a children's group actually constituted the first step in his lifelong commitment to his religion, a first degree initiation in practice if not in fact. "I definitely see my involvement in Craft as a series of steps, each one building on the one before," he explained.

Ecstatic experiences are particularly characteristic of initiations and the times surrounding them, when the individual is making, or deepening, a commitment to a practice. Initiations are, to a greater extent than other kinds of rituals, designed to give initiates the opportunity for ecstasy. Initiates are told to expect a life-changing experience, and they often get it. This is true even if the initiators botch the ritual or perform it awkwardly: the nature of the ritual itself, and the expectation of an ecstatic experience, is enough to induce it. Sometimes these experiences will not happen in the initiation itself, but during events leading up to or immediately following an initiation. Don's case is especially striking. At the age of seventeen, shortly before he began to attend the University of California, he was involved in a motorcycle accident, suffered a concussion, and experienced amnesia, some of which lasted for several years. He regained his memories just before his NROOGD initiation. He explained:

I found [having amnesia] to be the most illuminating experience, . . . not the least bit frightening. It was a very important turning point in my life. . . . I found it to be endlessly fascinating and tremendously liberating; . . . it created a sense of "Well, I'm whatever I want to be; I'm what I choose to make of myself." . . . What did come back after a few days was my memory of everything after about the age of sixteen; everything before that was still gone. . . . That lasted for two or three years, which was very embarrassing in college because my friends would talk about their past, but I didn't remember mine. . . . I lived with that until the night of my first degree with NROOGD. Before the first degree, I was meditating. . . . I was just sitting in my room, looking at the moon—and suddenly, all my memories came back. I was just meditating on the goddess, and this being a transition point, when suddenly there was this weird kind of rapid-fire, you know, my eighth birthday party in the garage, where they made the garage look like the Bat Cave; Uncle so-and-so, who I'd forgot; just this whole flood of things going bam-bam-bam-bam-bam through my head. . . . It definitely left me in a very altered state going in, because it was like a part of my brain had been turned back on. . . . It's hard for me to say [it was a] coincidence. A singularly dramatic event in my life that made a huge difference happened as a consequence of my NROOGD initiation.

For "Rhiannon," the shift in consciousness that sharpened her perception of the natural world occurred on the eve of her initiation.

We had planned for my first-degree initiation to occur on a particular day. I had done all this research why I wanted that particular day, and it had to do with one of the people in Salem (Massachusetts), from the witch trials. A week before this event was supposed to happen, the high priest and high priestess called me and said, "We can't do it that night; we've got a conflict. We have to reschedule for a week later." And I was . . . very upset, because there were reasons that this day was important for me; but without them, I really couldn't go through this initiation. So my husband and I were driving down the freeway . . . going over to a friend's house. And all of a sudden there was this *click* that just happens; and I look and I'm like, "Wow! Look at the sky!" And he's like, "What do you mean, look at the sky?" "Look at the color!" It was like every color that I have perceived since then is different. Everything shifted. My whole way of looking at everything was now different. And that's when my initiation happened. A week later, it was just sort of a confirmation. I cried through the whole thing. It was really a confirmation that, yes, I was making the right decision.

Rhiannon described her change in perception as "crisper . . . the difference between seeing the sky through sort of a haze, and seeing it on a very crisp autumn morning," suggesting that in some ways her previous perception of the world had been incomplete.

Dennis Carpenter, in his study of Pagan mystical experiences, notes that many Pagans report experiences of ecstatic union with nature to be the core of their religious identity (Carpenter, 1994). For many Pagans, the interconnectedness of the universe is not a matter of speculation, but of lived experience. Many in fact are drawn to Paganism because of its emphasis on the interconnectedness of things and of humans' basic link with the natural world.

For Melissa, a NROOGD initiate, musician, and administrative assistant, a feeling of oneness with all of nature was fundamental to her attraction to the religion. She had been drawn to Neo-Paganism first through an interest in astrology, which led her to read about the ancient Greek gods and goddesses for whom the planets are named. Eventually she developed an interest in Egyptian mythology, especially the goddess Ma'at.

> Ma'at to me is the symbol of truth. When you strip away everything else, and there's nothing left but the actual truth, that truth that exists in some kind of pure form. And I was trying to work on kind of absorbing that, working very physically and doing a lot of hiking and backpacking. . . . The previous day I had done this hike and gone to my special spot: this really steep, steep hill when you end up on top of the cliff that overlooks this huge valley, and you can see Hayward [California] and everything. You can see the entire [San Francisco] Bay Area. And there's a dead tree and a big stone, and I was just doing circles right there. And that was the day I dedicated myself to her. I didn't have a flash or anything; it was more of a mellow feeling. Next day I'm walking around at lunch, at work—and it was like, all of a sudden I couldn't perceive any difference between me and the stop sign, and the building, and the computer in the window, and I felt how everything is composed of the same element. It's hard to put into words, but it was there. It lasted for about ten minutes or so. But it was like this really intense perception . . . and I can kind of summon that back now. To me, that epitomizes that particular goddess. She doesn't take on a form to me.

About a week later, Melissa came to the defense of a total stranger whose husband was beating her in the middle of the street. The couple was on their way to see a divorce lawyer. Melissa intervened on behalf of the woman, linking arms with her and walking her to the lawyer's office to prevent the husband from continuing his assault. She connected this episode to her experience with Ma'at—"this whole taking risks and everybody is linked. There was no fear, there was none of that 'don't get involved' thing. Ever since then I've been able to do that: put myself forward and connect with people."

The visceral feeling of connection between all things and their inseparability is an important factor that motivates many Pagans to undertake political action in a personal way. It is at the root of Reclaiming's thealogy of political commitment. For Pagans, ecstasy is not about escaping the world, but about realizing one's connection with it and responsibility toward it. If everything is connected, then, according to Pagan thealogy/theology, we all bear a responsibility for making the world a better place.

These narratives suggest that ecstasy comes unannounced, that it is somehow unpredictable and not subject to human manipulation and control. While this may sometimes be the case, ecstasy is not random; it requires a certain state of mind and set of externals, which may well be different for each individual, but nevertheless share some common threads. While it is difficult to describe exactly the state of mind conducive to the ecstatic experience, a certain openness and contemplativeness is helpful. For Don, Rhiannon, and Melissa, the experiences came at significant moments in their spiritual lives: as Don was contemplating his upcoming initiation; after Melissa had dedicated herself to the goddess Ma'at, the universal principle of truth; and as Rhiannon was preparing for her first-degree initiation. For Darrin and Gus, as well as for me in the example I gave in the Introduction, the ecstatic state of mind was more the result of a willingness to suspend disbelief for the moment, to explore an unfamiliar experience.

## The Nature of Ecstasy

What I am calling "religious ecstasy," from the Greek *ekstasis*, meaning "a state of being outside the self," corresponds to a range of states that might be classified as altered or alternate states of consciousness, a "qualitative alteration in the overall pattern of mental functioning, such that the experiencer feels his [*sic*] consciousness is radically different from the 'normal' way it functions" (Tart, 1972:94). According to many researchers, these states are biologically based and measurably different from ordinary waking consciousness, in that they are accompanied by specific changes in brain-wave patterns, as well as observable physical changes such as an increased heart rate, a drop in blood pressure, a decline in the presence of stressor hormones (adrenaline, noradrenaline, cortisol) in the blood serum, and an increase in the body's production of endorphins (Tart, 1972; Lex, 1979; Goodman, 1988:39). As my research did not involve physiological studies of Neo-Pagans experiencing religious ecstasy, what is important in the context of this study is that the narrators *felt* their consciousness shift, and experienced their visions and trances as different from ordinary consciousness. I am assuming that many of those who told me their experiences actually underwent some physiological transformations, as well.

The term "altered" or "alternate state of consciousness" implies an ordinary consciousness that differs from these said states. While it can be argued that we cannot know whether our usual state of consciousness is, in fact, normal or ordinary, in practice people perceive a difference between their usual waking states and what they experience during an alternate state of consciousness. The most commonly reported differences center around the sense of identity and self-control that characterize ordinary waking consciousness, which seem to be diminished or absent during ASCs (Evans, 1989:230; Newberg and Aquili, 2001: 87; Sturm, 2000: 288–89). While ASCs also differ from one another in intensity and form, they share a set of characteristics that occur throughout the continuum of alternate states. These include:

> a decreased awareness of one's surroundings, subjects become absorbed by the experience;
>
> a decreased sense of control, in the sense that the experience seems to have its own trajectory, and the beings that may appear in it seem to operate independently of conscious thought;
>
> a heightened sense of reality, the experience seems unusually real;

time distortion, a short period of time may seem lengthened, or hours may pass in what feels like a minute;

increased suggestibility, the subject loses the ability to question the reality of the experience, at least while it is happening;

improved performance at certain tasks, for example, spontaneous religious oratory, or the biofeedback skills acquired under hypnosis;

depersonalization and role-playing: subjects feel unlike their usual selves, and at times seem to take on the role of a different person or entity;

personification: other people and objects are interpreted as part of the ASC by the experiencer, and may be given a symbolic role to play in the drama of the vision.[4]

Alternate states of consciousness range in intensity from a light trance, which most of us have experienced while daydreaming or driving on the freeway, to full-fledged states of dissociation, in which subjects may feel distanced from their bodies or not fully in control of their actions. Individuals in a light trance are conscious and aware of their surroundings, but are fully "engrossed" in what Erving Goffman has called a "framed" experience (Goffman, 1974)—for example, watching a film or listening to a story. This state of light trance is common to most Neo-Pagans who have participated in a ritual. They shift easily out of their engrossed state once the experience ends. In a deeper state of trance, experiences may be dreamlike, but vivid; there may be visual, auditory, or sensory hallucinations. Sounds, sights, smells, and sensations are experienced as in real life, but have a particular intensity, and are remembered fully when the individual emerges from trance. The experiences of Darrin, Gus, and Don, cited above, probably fall into this category. Melissa's and Rhiannon's, on the other hand, resemble the "unitary" experiences of mystics across many cultures and religions, in which the ordinary sense of self is replaced by feelings of transcendence and unity with a greater spiritual force. On the far side of the spectrum are experiences of ecstatic possession, which some Pagans call "aspecting," which I will describe below. In these states, individuals may feel they have become a different being. They may dance, fall to the floor, or move about in unexpected ways, performing actions that would be difficult under ordinary circumstances, taking on the role of the being they are impersonating. If they speak, they may produce rhythmic nonsense syllables (glossolalia), unusual vocalizations, poetry, or even song. Individuals sometimes do not recall what has transpired during these deep states of ecstatic possession once they return to ordinary consciousness; or, they may recall it in a detached way, as though they had observed themselves from somewhere outside their bodies. All ASCs may be accompanied by other somatic presentations, such as shivering, sweating, or weeping; Neo-Pagans often call these "moving energy," and describe them as a flow of energy coursing through their bodies that causes them to shake, sweat, or cry.

ASCs are part of the human experience; they are neither unusual nor difficult to bring about. They can occur spontaneously or deliberately. While Western medical explanations have tended to emphasize the role of drugs, fever, and organic disorders in causing them, they can also be induced by certain "triggers": sensory overload, sensory deprivation, repetitive rhythmic behaviors, fatigue or exhaustion, pain or injury, and altered body chemistry (e.g., insulin shock). Triggers can also be psychological in nature—for example, stress, fear, and personal crisis. Individuals can learn techniques to induce altered states in themselves and others and seek them voluntarily through use of alcohol and drugs, meditation and spiritual disciplines, and hypnosis.

Altered states of consciousness are quite common in non-Western societies. Of 488 non-Western societies studied by anthropologist Erika Bourguignon, 92 percent were found to make use of some kind of altered state (Bourguignon, 1976). In most of these, ASCs were an institutionalized part of a religious system. This very high incidence suggests that ecstasy is what David Hufford has called a "core experience": a somatic experience with a stable set of perceptions (often due to a physiological cause) that occurs cross-culturally without regard to a subject's preexisting beliefs, and because of which the subject refers to a spiritual world for explanation (Hufford, 1995:28). Core experiences may be human universals, in that all human beings have the potential to experience them. However, their explanation and insertion into the cultural register differs greatly from one culture and religion to the next.

The West has its own traditions of altered states, ranging from the ecstatic trances, in which the Pythia made her predictions at the Delphic oracle in ancient Greece, to Jewish and Christian mysticism, in which subjects reported feelings of ecstatic union with God. Reports survive from the Middle Ages of folk traditions from various parts of Europe, in which individuals, often healers, entered alternate states of consciousness through which they communicated with spirits that would help them to cure clients.[5] Many European folk traditions preserved ecstatic states associated with both healing and religious practice well into the twentieth century: for example, the *tammurriata* and *tarantella* traditions of southern Italy, which featured intense drumming and dancing during which practitioners achieved ecstatic states; the ecstatic dancing of Romanian *calusari*; vernacular traditions associated with various saints' cults in Europe, in which participants undertake great physical challenges on behalf of the saint; and the healing traditions documented in southern Italy by ethnologist Ernesto DeMartino and his students, in which folk healers entered trance states to diagnose and cure illness (DeMartino, 1961).

Two important historical watersheds brought about a sea change in the way Europeans perceived ecstatic practices and altered states of consciousness: these were the Reformation and the Enlightenment. "Since the onset of the

Age of Enlightenment . . . and even earlier, there has been a trend away from religious experience in all Christian denominations, and towards a *thinking about* religion instead," writes anthropologist Felicitas Goodman (Goodman, 1988:35). As part of its effort to purify Christianity, the Reformation banned many of the ecstatic practices associated with saints' cults and the Catholic year cycle. These were condemned as outdated remnants of pre-Christian practices, and rejected.[6] The new way of relating to God was altogether more intellectual and verbal, based on the recent availability of mass-printed translations of the Bible into vernacular European languages. For Protestants, the Bible became the way to God.

The second crucial historical development in the European conception of altered states was the Enlightenment. The Enlightenment created a discourse of rationality by devaluing and excluding what folklorist Marilyn Motz calls "traditional ways of knowing"—including the beliefs and practices associated with ecstatic states (Motz, 1998:341). With its exaltation of human reason, the Enlightenment denounced manifestations that defied rationality, including states that transcended rational consciousness, as primitive, ignorant, superstitious, and insane. In *Madness and Civilization* (1965), French historian and cultural critic Michel Foucault traces the construction of the idea of madness, or insanity, in explicit contrast to reason. While Renaissance concepts of madness included transcendence—the possibility that the insane were experiencing "some happy mental aberration [that] frees the soul from its anxious cares and at the same time restores it by the addition of manifold delights"—for Enlightenment philosophers, madness became not only the enemy of reason, but a manifestation antagonistic to new ideas about production.[7] Simply put, people preoccupied with ecstasy and transcendence of any sort were not amenable to the discipline and regulation inherent in an emergent industrial economy. In order to create "docile bodies," the state had an interest in suppressing experiences that could be personally empowering, disruptive of social norms, and critical of emerging paradigms. Ecstasy represented a blot on bourgeois order, and it had to be suppressed. Part of the suppression of ecstatic traditions involved their pathologization: they were reinterpreted as manifestations of mental illness.

Almost as if in reaction to the suppression and pathologization of altered states during the eighteenth century, the following century saw a burgeoning of new religions in which ecstasy was a prominent feature. Throughout the eighteenth and nineteenth centuries, religious minorities emerged for whom trance and possession were an integral part of religious knowledge and experience. The Shakers, a mid-nineteenth-century religious community, similarly were characterized by ecstatic states during which participants danced and shook with the Holy Spirit. Pentecostal Christianity, a collection of Protestant sects in which adherents seek eternal salvation through faith in Christ, spread throughout North America by itinerant preachers, and gained many adherents during the nineteenth century. Pentecostals are still known derogatorily as "Holy Rollers," because of their ecstatic services during which members may twitch, shake, shout, speak in tongues, and fall on the floor as they are baptized by the Holy Spirit. In the mid-nineteenth century, Spiritualism, a movement in which mediums in a trance communicated directly with the spirits of the dead, swept through North America and quickly spread to Europe and other parts of the world. Each of these movements originally incorporated trance or religious ecstasy as an important part of their services. While the Shakers gradually disappeared because of their practice of complete celibacy, yesterday's Spiritualists have become the channelers of the late 20th century, and Pentecostalism, or charismatic Christianity, is one of the fastest-growing religious movements in the world. Trance and religious possession are also an integral part of Afro-Caribbean syncretic religions, such as Lukumi (Santería) and Vodun, now practiced throughout North America in areas with a high population of Afro-Caribbean immigrants. In many cities, these practices also draw the participation of other ethnic groups.

An individual's experience and understanding of religious ecstasy will vary according to cultural and religious background. Channelers, for instance, speak of contacting entities from other planes of existence, or communicating with the spirits of the dead; practitioners of Vodun speak of being "ridden" by a particular *lwa*, or deity; *santeros* about an *orisha* (deity) being "mounted" or "seated" in the head of the possessed; charismatic Christians about getting baptized by the Holy Spirit. Beliefs about the causes of trance and ecstasy in turn shape the nature of trance behavior and experience: *orisha*s and *lwa*s do not show up at Pentecostal revivals, nor do *santeros* experiencing *el santo montado* suddenly speak in tongues or praise Jesus. Ecstatic behavior, in other words, is learned behavior, and as such conforms to cultural expectations and patterns. Societies that incorporate trance and ecstasy as an institutional part of religion have procedures for dealing with spontaneous occurrences of trance that channel the subject into a particular religious path. Trance and ecstasy have specific roles which are managed by experts.

In contrast, mainstream Western explanations have tended to pathologize trance when it occurs outside the rehabilitative setting of a therapist's office. Psychiatric explanations have called trance and possession experiences "dissociative," theorizing that they distance individuals from their experiences and create alternate realities for pathological reasons. Few Western medical professionals espouse the idea that trance and ecstasy can be part of the life experience of a healthy individual. Until quite recently, medical explanations have concentrated on organic causes of alternate states of consciousness: drug use, disease, either physical or psychological, and hypnosis, a technique intended to bring about trance for therapeutic purposes. Outside of the hypno-therapeutic setting, there are no roles for trance in Western institutionalized systems. Therefore, Western culture's ecstatic traditions tend to occur in settings outside the cultural mainstream, often among groups that are stigmatized for their perceived "backwardness." The spontaneous occurrence of trance or religious ecstasy can be a disquieting and disturbing experience for most mainstream Americans, who are likely to interpret it as a symptom of insanity.

Neo-Pagans are reclaiming a Western tradition in which trance, healing, and possession are important parts of spirituality. They provide a context that normalizes and explains such experiences when they occur spontaneously, and teach practitioners specific techniques for achieving and controlling them.

## Trance Journeys and the Art of Narrative

### Field notes, March 3, 1997

In the ritual room at Don and Anna's house, the members of Coven Trismegiston lie on the floor in a circle, our bodies radiating out like spokes from a wheel from the center of the circle. There Don sits, lightly and rhythmically beating a *tar* (an Indian frame drum) as we relax and get comfortable. We have just completed a Hecate's Supper, a ritual offering of food to the Greek goddess of crossroads, transitions, magic, and the otherworld, and Don will now lead us on a trance journey to meet Hecate's devotees on the night of the dark moon.

"Take a deep breath in . . . relax . . . and when you feel ready, begin to walk down the path to the Witch's cottage in the woods that you have visited before." I imagine it as a classic storybook cottage from nineteenth-century children's book illustrations: half-timbered, with a thatched roof and large stone chimney. Inside, the walls are lined with shelves packed with ancient tomes; drying herbs hang from the ceiling rafters. There is a rag rug and a comfortable reading chair by the fireplace, and a heavy table where I have found, in past trances, a red elixir that magically eases the gnawing pain that grips my stomach in the midst of anxiety. This time, Don directs us to the fireplace and to the brooms that are waiting there for us. "Find your broom and sit astride it. Now it's time to say the words that will take you safely up the chimney and to the sabbat." My broom is the smallest one—it's like the folktale "Goldilocks and the Three Bears," the smallest one is always just right for me, I think with irony in my lulled state. I mount the broom and push off with my right foot, and along with the others I rise easily up the chimney and find myself flying through the night sky. I can feel the wind against my body as the broom rushes forward, but I'm not cold. Above me the sky twinkles with unfamiliar stars; even the constellations are alien in the world of the imagination.

"Now you find yourself approaching a clearing where the sabbat is going to take place. Find a place to put your broom so you can find it again when it's time to return. Now begin to walk around the circle; notice who is here.

Look east . . . and notice what you see. Look to the south . . . and notice what you see. Look to the west . . . and notice what you see. And now you look to the north . . . and notice what you see. And now you look into the center of the circle . . . and notice what and whom you see there. Give yourself some time to meet and greet the others in the circle."

I am back in Monteruju, as I often am in trance, going up toward the rural chapel of Santa Maria, over the fields and hills to a crossroads. I see many others going there: Efisia, the storyteller; Basiliu, the wart charmer; Tiu Dominigu, who can take off the evil eye and, some say, give it as well; Witches I have known in other covens, and people I have never met at all. At the gathering place, a bonfire is burning in the center of the circle, and around it people dancing wildly. There is drumming and a *launeddas* (Sardinian bagpipe) player makes raspy music that accompanies the frenzied dancing. On a thronelike chair surveying the scene is a *mammuttone,* a costumed sheep-man from Sardinian carnival masking traditions. I keep scanning the assembled throng for my friend E.T., but I do not see her. I see another friend instead, and I ask her whether E.T. is coming. "She is not one of us," the woman says, and as she speaks I see it is not my friend at all, but the goddess Hecate herself. She draws me into the dance; soon, everything is spinning around us as we are pulled along in the frantic spiral. The dance suffuses my entire body; I feel alive, aflame, part of the dance. "We are on the edge of love and death," she whispers; "this is the fulcrum of all existence." Then I hear the quickening drumbeats calling me to go back. I want to stay, to continue to feel the ecstasy, but I must return. I find my broom and push off again, riding through the night sky to the witch's cottage, following the drumbeats and Don's voice until I am back in the ritual room with Anna, Don, and all the others. We sit up, rub our eyes, stretch, and begin to tell each other about our experiences.

For most Neo-Pagans, the ecstatic state is the essence of magic. When they define magic as the intentional changing of consciousness, they mean experiencing religious ecstasy, which is achieved through alternate states of consciousness. Neo-Pagans distinguish between several types of alternate states of consciousness, and traditions teach special techniques designed to bring them about. The most frequently made distinctions differentiate between pathworking, sometimes also called trance, journeying, or guided meditation, a form of trance in which individuals experience a kind of directed vision; and aspecting, in which participants embody deities. Reclaiming priestess Macha NightMare explained to me: "I do think trancing takes place along a continuum, . . . from a light trance to a full trance state; but aspecting is a sort of branch off the continuum. . . . In trance and meditation the idea is to go more fully or deeply inside yourself. . . . But aspecting involves making space inside yourself for the divine to manifest through you."

Trance is the easier of the two states to achieve. Starhawk describes it as "any state of consciousness when we are focused inwardly rather than outwardly" (Starhawk, 1990:109). Pagans often achieve trance during rituals using a technique called guided visualization or guided meditation. In this process, described in my field notes above, a designated storyteller tells a tale or describes a scene, inviting the participants to imagine themselves as part of the story and add their own details and characters. Starhawk explains: "Story, myth, drama all take us into the collective landscape. What we often call guided meditation or guided fantasy can perhaps best be thought of as a particular form of storytelling, an improvised oral poetry that creates a collective story we all tell together" (Starhawk, 1990:109). This form of oral performance has its own particular aesthetic. Storytellers often speak in a "trance voice," a rhythmic, resonant, lulling cadence that soothes listeners and draws them into the tale world. Another important key is using just the right amount of description so participants can imagine details to fit their own life circumstances. Flooding the story with too much detail leaves no space for individuals to personalize the experience. The storyteller must also allow plenty of time for participants' imaginations to go to work, creating internal imagery. Rushing the story or leaving too many gaps both destroy the magic of the experience. Storytellers also use repetition in these tales, for example suggesting that listeners look east, then south, then west, then north, with formulas that introduce each of the directions. Repetition creates patterns within the tale that listeners can follow; it also creates space listeners can fill with their own personal details.

Storytellers may have different intents when they take ritual participants on a trance journey. When leading the trance I described above, Don strove to create an imaginary experience based on traditional descriptions of a witches' sabbat that the entire coven could share. His narration was both specific enough to incite images in our minds, and general enough for each of us to interject details from our own experience that would make the scene real for us. Once we arrived at the sabbat, his instructions were simply to look in each of the cardinal directions and notice what we saw there; it was my own imagination that took me to Sardinia and added the various participants and details based on what was familiar to me. The goddess Hecate, of course, was a natural, since the ritual was dedicated to meeting her. Other narrators may have different intentions and styles. Starhawk's guided meditation during the Brigid ritual described at the beginning of this book was at once more general and more personal. Since the point of that journey was an inner exploration to discover what was sacred to each participant, she spent less time describing landscape and more time encouraging participants to delve into their own psyches: "Does Brigid have you on her anvil? Is she working on you?" These kinds of questions stimulate self-searching, and bring on the kinds of experiences I had during that ritual. A skilled narrator can manipulate the narrative so that most, if not all, participants actually share similar trance experiences. On a different occasion, Don led the coven on a trance journey into the heart of an other-world tree. While he did not describe to us what we would see there, each of us independently saw a glowing, steplike, twisting, spiral pattern that went endlessly up the center of the tree, which we interpreted as the double helix of DNA during the discussion that followed the ritual. (It didn't hurt that we had two biologists in our coven.)

In other circumstances, participants in the same trance journey can have radically different experiences. In a ritual created by a small affinity group at Reclaiming's Witch Camp 2001 in Mendocino, California, a trance journey to meet an ancestor led each of us to have our own unique visions. Erin, a union organizer and mother of three, saw a large treelike being who told her he was a fungus who helped with recycling in the forest. His message was simple and direct: "Clean it up," he told her, which she interpreted to mean cleaning the environment. In my own vision, a cougar appeared to me and communicated wordlessly, through image and sensation, about her life in the forest: hunting, mating, raising her kits, drinking at the river. At one point I *became* the cougar, and experienced the forest as she did, through smell, taste, and feel. She showed me how her kind was threatened by continuing human encroachment into their territory. Erin's and my visions, with their environmental cast, were not unexpected in the context of Reclaiming's wilderness camp, with its eco-feminist flavor. But Jim, a corporate vice president in search of a new kind of spirituality, and Melusina, an artist and dancer of Native American extraction, had more personal visions. Melusina communicated with a spiritual guide who appeared to her in the form of an owl, affirming her choice to continue her spiritual seeking. Jim saw a third- or fourth-century Scot who bore his grandfather's name, MacBride. He wore a kilt and carried a great broadsword strapped to his back. Jim's mother had always explained the surname to him as meaning "son of the bride," or an illegitimate birth; but Jim had recently learned another explanation of his name's origin in which the "bride" was Bride or Brigid, the goddess to whom some of the clan traced their ancestry. Jim's vision was pivotal to him, in that his ancestor confirmed that his new spirituality was reclaiming something his ancestors had once practiced—something that was part of his birthright.

We learned of one another's visions after the ritual, when we shared our trance experiences with each other. Sharing one's visions after the trance is an important part of the ritual. It is through sharing Pagans arrive at interpretations of their experiences that insert them into a context of emergent belief. For example, a consensus emerged in the Witch camp group that the fungus in Erin's vision had been a fairy or nature spirit, creatures understood as guardians of the earth in Reclaiming Witchcraft. I learned from Melusina and Erin, who had attended earlier Witch camps, that a female cougar had been seen wandering through camp several times in previous years. My vision was interpreted as a special form of communication from her. As James McClenon found in the case of individuals who had shared extraordinary spiritual experiences, exchanging personal narratives helps shape belief and negotiate the nature of reality (McClenon, 1994:60), a finding documented more generally by Linda Dégh (2001). Folkloric motifs, such as fairies, animal spirits, and ancestors, emerge because they are a fundamental part of the cultural register, and help people categorize and organize unusual experiences.

Brian W. Sturm has commented on the power of storytelling to move participants into alternate states of consciousness. He demonstrates how while listening to stories at storytelling festivals and events, people "enter a qualitatively different state of consciousness" (Sturm, 2000:289). This state is characterized by a lack of awareness of one's surroundings; an absorption into the reality of the story, which is experiences "as if" it were real; deep identification with the story to the point of experiencing physical reactions to the plot, characters, and emotions described; a perceived loss of conscious control, in which listeners allow themselves to become absorbed by the story; a distortion in perception of time, so that brief stories can seem to last a long time if many events are being described; and a particular sense of "placeness," of being in an alternate world, "sucked in," as one woman described it (Sturm, 2000:294). Sturm compares storytelling to hypnosis in its power to absorb listeners and take them into different states of consciousness. His hypothesis is confirmed by Andrew Newberg and his colleagues, who have studied the neurological and physiological effects of ritual described in the last chapter. Commenting on the power of the sacred narrative in a ritual setting, they write: "[Its use] allows the worshipper to enter a mythic story metaphorically, confront the profound mysteries the myth embraces, and then experience the resolution of those mysteries in a powerful, possibly life-changing way" (Newberg and D'Aquili, 2001:95). Narrative, in other words, is as powerful a tool as rhythmic behaviors and stimulation of the senses in bringing about a change of consciousness.

The world of trance journeys is in many ways similar to the world of the traditional folktale, or *Märchen*: an enchanted world in which animals speak, objects have magic powers, humans fly and perform other amazing feats, and deities interact with humans. Neo-Pagans are no strangers to this world; as we have already seen, many of them report childhood fascinations with myths, legends, and folktales, and an attraction to contemporary literary forms, such as fantasy and science fiction, which make use of the devices of *Märchen*. It is this world that skilled narrators try to re-create in their trance journeys, and which Pagans construct through communal events such as rituals and festivals.

The folktale world also appears in traditional ballads, stanzaic narrative folksongs that were once diffused throughout western Europe and North America. For some, ballads provide the entrance point to religious ecstasy.

Holly Tannen described how ballads became for her not only a way to ecstasy, but a road that led her to the performance and study of traditional folk song, which has been the center of her life. She explained:

> The seminal moment . . . was hearing Martin Carthy sing "The Famous Flower of Serving Men." The rolling drone of the guitar, and the imagery of the song—the white hind, the singing dove—transported me. I was in deep trance; I experienced the reality of another world—the world of ballads . . . where characters shape-shift, as in "Tam Lin" and "The Two Magicians," animals talk, otherworld beings interact with people. It was not just that the songs talked about this other realm; a strong singer could take me to that place where I felt I was living in it. I determined to learn how to sing this way, and it has remained the focus of my life.

It may be that the nature of the tale world itself encourages listeners to identify with the story, drawing them into its magical web.[8]

## Other Roads to Ecstasy

Both trance-journey narratives and ballads represent highly verbal forms of trance induction that lead to a particular type of ecstatic experience: one characterized by strong visual images and the feeling of being part of a story. They can be successful for many Pagans, but others respond better to nonverbal stimuli that lead to a different, more diffuse kind of trance experience, one that is closer in character to Melissa's description of merging with the sacred. The flooding of the senses from music and drumming can cause the onset of altered states. Neo-Pagan rituals may use chanting, music, and drumming to induce trance. Farida Fox, a priestess in the Church of All Worlds, described her experience:

> I've been to circles or rituals where at three or four in the morning the truth is being told, and it's being told in song; and people are weeping, reaching out for one another and holding one another. . . . It's a transcendent experience, and it's being facilitated through music. . . . First of all, the heart opens, so that feelings are really flowing freely, and you're totally intent on feeling them deeply. Then there's a transcendent moment in which you suddenly realize that you're in this state with all these other people who are also in the state. And there's a sudden sense of—it's more than kinship; you're truly connected. Deeply connected. That's an amazing experience.[9]

In this case, the sense of union many Pagans experience with the universe is specifically felt in connection with a group of people who are singing together.

For others, movement is necessary in order to bring on alternate states. In critiquing a spring equinox ritual I had conducted for Coven Trismegiston and other Berkeley Pagans, Macha commented on the importance of a dance we had performed around the statue of the goddess Persephone/Hecate in the "underworld" (my basement) before bringing her back upstairs to celebrate spring. We had joined hands and danced around the statue, chanting Starhawk's

She changes everything she touches and
Everything she touches changes.

"Dancing is real important," Macha explained. "It always 'sends' me [into trance] . . . it gets me out of my head, away from 'talking self.' " In the Reclaiming tradition, "talking self" is the conscious mind. Dancing is in fact one of the touchstones of ritual in both the Gardnerian and the Reclaiming traditions, and in NROOGD, most rituals begin with a "meeting dance," a spiral dance in which each participant greets every other participant.

Gardnerian Witchcraft also uses scourging—ritual flagellation with a scourge, a whip with multiple lashes—to induce religious ecstasy. Scourging has multiple, layered meanings in Gardnerian Craft, some of which are revealed only to initiates. Don explained scourging as a trance tool that symbolizes, among other things, the Gardnerian proverb "Thou must suffer to learn"—in this case, he said, "to suffer" does not mean to endure great physical pain, but recalls the earlier meaning of the word, "to allow oneself" or "to submit." Scourging symbolically acknowledges that the initiate must allow herself to learn by submitting to the learning process, which often takes an ecstatic turn; by becoming humble, in the sense of not becoming arrogant about her knowledge; and by embracing the "perfect love and perfect trust" that characterize (at least in theory) relations between members of a coven. Scourging also recalls the suffering of the witches during the Burning Times, and symbolizes the turning of adversity to one's advantage. I have never seen scourging done to cause pain in a Gardnerian ritual. Rather, it is one of several techniques that help move participants outside their ordinary consciousness by focusing attention on the body, and, through the body, on a reality beyond the physical realm.

For a few Pagans, though, pain can also be a road to ecstasy and alternate consciousness. Processes of body modification such as tattooing and piercing can be used as a source of religious ecstasy and a form of connection to the divine. One Northern California festival featured the Ball Dance, a ritual in which participants were pierced with weighted balls that hung through the piercings. Participants danced ecstatically until the balls ripped out of their flesh. For the participants, overcoming the pain was a gateway to religious ecstasy, an altered state of consciousness in which they felt joined with the sacred. About such trends, Farida theorized, "I would say that probably some of the impetus behind the current S and M and the piercing and body scarification groups among us, is one way of making an alliance with the darkness. We're a culture . . . that's hidden from the dark for all these centuries. And there have been terrible things that have run rampant in our society and have been covered up, or ignored, or not paid attention to. Well, this stuff has to go somewhere."[10]

Pagans celebrate sexuality as a central aspect of the life force. Sexuality is sacred to them, and is celebrated as the root of creative energy. Gardnerians and several other Wiccan traditions include in their rituals the Great Rite, a metaphoric union of the female and male principles in nature that is enacted symbolically when the priestess plunges her athame (ritual knife) into the chalice held by the priest. While Pagans love to tell stories about covens in which the Great Rite was enacted by the priest and priestess in the flesh, I have never actually witnessed such an occurrence. Some of my consultants commented that the spread of sexually transmitted diseases, including AIDS, has stemmed this aspect of the subculture in the San Francisco Bay Area, although sexual contact between coven members may still occur in other parts of the country. Committed couples who practice and worship together have reported experiencing sexual ecstasy in their private enactments of the Great Rite. In these cases, participants actually embody the goddess and god (or in some cases the same-sex union of deities) in their lovemaking, resulting in an experience of deep emotional connection to the partner as well as to the sacred. Experiences of sexual or erotic union with deities during trance journeys are not unusual, and are considered positive and sacred in this group of religions.

Discussions about religious ecstasy and altered states of consciousness inevitably beg the question about drug use in ritual. Most Pagans with whom I have spoken discourage the use of drugs to achieve alternate states of consciousness at public rituals; in fact, the majority of public rituals in the San Francisco Bay Area are conspicuously advertised as "clean and sober," meaning no drugs or alcohol are permitted out of respect for those who may be recovering from addiction. However, some admitted to experimenting with drugs, especially during their college years: "A lot of us were hippies," one commented. A few Pagans I talked with expressed an interest in the ritual use of psychedelics, and admitted to using them to enhance a ritual experience. One Pagan practitioner described an elaborate, three-day rite in which he enacted his descent into the otherworld and rebirth. He used a potent herbal mixture to induce a torpor that mimicked death, from which he then awakened for the rebirth part of the rite. He emphasized that this use of drugs was not recreational, but an intended part of the ceremony, and that his coven-mates closely monitored him during the ordeal. Others reported that their drug-induced highs paled before the ecstasy they experienced during ritual, or that they preferred the relative control of the ritual trance experience to the lack of control they felt while under the influence of drugs. The point of most Neo-Pagan ritual is to induce a change in consciousness without using mind-altering substances.

## Religious Possession: "Aspecting"

Aspecting differs from pathworking in that the subject actually embodies a goddess or god in physical form. It is considered much more difficult than trance work, and Pagans say that those who tend to be analytical, critical thinkers have difficulty achieving this state. More so than trance journeys, aspecting involves renouncing conscious control over one's actions and surrendering to the imagination. Macha spoke with some envy of another priestess whose facility with aspecting is well known throughout the entire Bay Area community: "She just rolls her eyes back and she's gone." But, she confessed, "It's definitely not my best skill, in that it's hard for me to get away from all the head-tripping." She described an instance in a ritual in which she embodied Atropos, the Greek Fate whose task it is to cut the thread of life. "I could feel myself hovering just behind [Atropos], not really conscious of what I was saying, but not fully gone, either. I kept nudging myself away, telling my conscious [*sic*] to leave, but I wasn't ever fully able to do it."

There is no single technique that all practitioners use to embody deity; techniques differ according to tradition and the needs of individual practitioners. Don described how his role as the Beltane hobbyhorse, a comic figure, helped him release enough conscious control to learn possession skills. Kevin spoke about imagining the deity standing behind him, then slowly merging with it until his feeling of being an independent entity was gone. For some practitioners, movement is the key. Diana, a member of Ring of Troth, a Norse Pagan group, had been working on embodying the god Odin, but was having difficulty even feeling the god's presence. Once she began to move as she imagined he would move, taking heavy, long strides and walking with stately, masculine steps, she began to feel his presence in her body and was able to let go. Rachel commented on the importance of dance and movement in trance induction: in the course of moving in a particular style, according to the traditions of a specific culture or ethnic group, she was able to access information about a particular deity and feel more like her or him. These remarks confirm the observations of neurologists Newberg and D'Aquili regarding the importance of rhythmic movements in inducing the blurring of personal boundaries (Newberg and D'Aquili, 2001:87–88).

It is clear that for some Pagans, trance and possession are very physical experiences. Laurel described how her body felt the presence of different deities: "[When I am possessed by] Coyote, my nose itches and my hands cramp. Coyote wanted everyone to have paws, so when he comes you have trouble using your fingers. With Brigid, the lady of the holy well, the lady of tears—when she is present, the water [tears] just flows. When Hecate is present, it feels like someone punched me in the gut." According to Laurel, each deity has his or her own unique signature that she feels within her body. "Each deity that you work with has its own little niche in your body," explained another Witch.

The physical acts of putting on costumes and taking up props are also important cues for some Pagans. This is one reason that costumes and props are such an important part of Neo-Pagan sacred material culture; through them, participants can literally take on new identities. In Gardnerian Craft, the goddess makes an appearance at full moon rituals in an act known as "drawing down the moon"—the goddess, identified with the moon, is believed to be drawn into the body of her priestess. For this ritual, the high priestess wears a circlet bearing a moon symbol while the high priest wears a matching one decorated with horns or antlers, symbols of the horned god of death and rebirth. The very act of putting on the circlets signals to the participants that the deities are about to make their entrance, and communicates to the hgh priestess and high priest that they must enter the proper state of mind to embody the gods. Some traditions use a verbal formula as a cue. The Reclaiming tradition uses different techniques. Macha described an initiation she did with Vibra, another Reclaiming priestess, in which the initiate was stripped of all her clothing and jewelry and dressed in the clothes and jewels of the goddess. These props and procedures are helpful to those who have trouble letting go, because they are signals that give the wearer permission to enter into an alternate state of consciousness.

Pagans discern various levels of trance and possession. The Reclaiming tradition teaches that the physical host is like a glass of water: she can choose how much of the deity she wants to fill her. Reclaiming Witches distinguish between full-blown or "amnesic" possession, in which the host is unconscious and unaware of the passage of time, and the much more common "shadowing," a lighter form of possession in which individual consciousness hovers around the edges as the host opens herself to the deity.

Many Pagans recognize a connection between aspecting and acting, in that both involve inviting another character into the body or consciousness of the practitioner. When coaching initiates on aspecting, elders sometimes encourage them to engage in imaginative, playful acting, for example doing humorous imitations of people and animals. "When you're doing that, you're halfway there," Don explained. Yet there are also important distinctions between acting and aspecting. In acting, the subject is still fully present in her/his body, and is consciously engaged in imitation or evocation. In contrast, aspecting involves giving up conscious control and surrendering the body to the deity. Pagans say that when aspecting is genuine, the subject's voice changes, familiar mannerisms and movements fall away and are replaced by very different ones, and it becomes clear that the individual is not "there" anymore. The subject's eyes often take on a glazed appearance, or they roll back into the head so that the whites are visible. When these signs appear, Pagans usually say that the deity is present in the body of the subject; the words and actions may appear to come from the subject, but are actually divinely inspired. Pagans recognize that immersing oneself deeply in a role can lead to a state of ecstatic possession, and that some individuals who are gifted actors have a particular facility with alternate states as well.

Aspecting sometimes occurs as a result of acting when it is not a part of the plan or intent of the ritual. Laurel Olson told this story about the first time she was possessed by the goddess Brigid:

> I got asked by [priestess] Diana Paxson to portray the goddess Brigid in a NROOGD sabbat. I said, "OK, I'll do that [laughs]. I have lots of acting experience, and I memorize very quickly." She gave me some stuff to memorize and I memorized it all, I didn't even think about it. Then all of a sudden they were putting this crown of *fire* on my *head*. . . . there were these foot-tall dinner tapers on my head, and they were none too steady but I went out and answered the invocation and said, "The Goddess will be with me; I know I can do this." And all of a sudden, I was sort of in this fog. The words were coming out, but they weren't the way I'd practiced them, and then I'm walking around the room, and I'm going, "Oh my god, they're going to kill me! I'm not supposed to do this yet!" [laughs]. Then I started touching people. And there was this one woman, and I *knelt* to her. And I touched her. And I felt this power come out of me like I'd felt it come into me in the Methodist church. . . . This was a woman who was crippled with arthritis. And I ran into her later, and she said, you know, "For three days after you touched me, all my joints just popped." . . . Then I figured out who this goddess was who had come to see me all these years ago and how she kept showing up, whether I [wanted her to or not]. . . . It was Brigid, and she had come to get me.

In this narrative, Laurel makes a sharp distinction between acting and aspecting. While she started out in her role thinking she was acting (she memorized the lines, was self-conscious when she was being costumed in her crown of tapers), soon she felt "in a sort of fog," and she realized she was no longer following the script. While a part of her continued to be conscious and present, she was seemingly no longer in charge of her movements, words, or actions. When she healed the arthritic woman with her touch, listeners understood that Laurel was not taking personal credit for the miraculous healing; it was believed to have come from the goddess herself.

Because words and actions performed during possession are believed to come directly from the deities, Pagans take the pronouncements of aspecting individuals very seriously. Occasionally, this belief can be exploited by individuals for personal and political gain, for instance, by making pronouncements in ritual that are interpreted as coming from a divine source because they seem to occur in the context of embodiment, but are actually politically motivated. In these cases, there is often an underlying conflict in the group, and the gods, embodied in the priestess or priest, appear to support one opinion or faction over another. Such statements often lead to heated arguments about the authenticity of aspecting in that particular instance, as each side seeks to justify its own perception. Experienced Pagans realize the explosive potential of ecstatic pronouncements, and are generally cautious about interpreting such statements. Anna and Don commented that deities very seldom make political statements. Both felt that while the gods often communicate about specific personal and spiritual matters to their devotees, they do not concern themselves with coven disputes or choose one faction over another. Likewise, they believe deities never ask adepts to do anything dangerous or harmful to themselves or others. Don told the story of a fellow Witch who, during a guided meditation, encountered a spirit who told him he could have either great worldly success, or great happiness, but not both; he had to choose. The Witch's response was

"Get away from me, false spirit!" The Witch knew from experience that the gods love humans and would never ask them to make such a choice. "That's not how the gods communicate. You can safely ignore those kinds of statements," Don advised. "If they don't come from the gods, where do they come from?" I asked. "From [the speaker's] unconscious, or from their own desire for power," explained Anna. "Or from other kinds of spirits. Not from the gods," added Don. Both Anna and Don believe firmly in the deities' benevolence, although they see the gods as part of a broader spiritual reality that also includes other kinds of beings, not all of which are benign. "There are both sheep and sharks in the spirit world," Don cautioned. "Just because something comes from the spirit world, it doesn't mean it's necessarily good or enlightened, or that it's telling the truth."

Don's statement suggests that aspecting is not completely without risk, and many Pagans agreed. This is one reason why all my subjects emphasized the importance of undertaking these mind-altering exercises only in the course of ritual. The ritual framework, with its magic circle, supportive members, guardians, benevolent deities, and clear framing in time, sets conspicuous parameters around trance, aspecting, and possession. It ensures the boundedness of the experience: any spirits called in are also dismissed at the end of the ritual. Unfriendly or dangerous spirits are kept out by the presence of the gods and the guardians, who are known to be loving and benevolent. The presence of others guarantees that the possessed individuals do not endanger themselves or the group. In spite of these precautions, problems do occasionally occur. "When there's a problem, I feel it in my solar plexus—like a tightening," Laurel explained. A problem might be "the priestess is afraid, or there's something in the room that doesn't belong there," according to Laurel—a spirit that is not necessarily evil or dangerous, but simply unwanted by the participants at that time. When I asked her how she could tell the difference between the goddesses and gods, or what she called "large" spirits, and the "small" spirits, the flora and fauna of the astral plane, Laurel replied: "How can you tell the difference between [the music of] Mozart and Charles Ives?" She compared the spiritual awareness of a trained practitioner to the knowledge of a person trained in music: just as each composer has a unique, recognizable style and level of importance, so do spiritual beings. When she feels the presence of unwanted entities, Laurel invokes the goddess: "Calling the goddess will send unwanted entities skittering away," she assured me.

Another problem that occasionally presents itself is the reluctance of the priestess or priest to come out of trance. In these cases, experienced practitioners recommend calling the trancer's name, or giving them food or water to bring them back in touch with the material world. This, explained Laurel, is most commonly a problem of inexperienced trancers. "It is not the deity who is the problem when someone doesn't want to come out of trance. The letting-go process is more about the priest or priestess than about the deity."

Nevertheless, Pagans do share cautionary tales about what can happen when trance and aspecting get out of hand. Both Laurel and Don told a story about two teenage girls who invoked the spirit of Darth Vadar, a character from George Lucas's *Star Wars* films, and found they could not get rid of him. One of the girls became possessed, and an experienced elder had to be called in to banish the spirit. What is interesting about this case is that Darth Vadar is a fictional entity. Apparently, it makes no difference whether a spirit originated as part of a religious system, or as a character in fictional story; both types can be invoked and, under the right circumstances, can become possessing entities.

While they recognize the existence of a wide variety of spirits, including ancestor spirits or ghosts, Pagans do not as a rule fear them. They honor the dead on Samhain, and some do work regularly with the spirits of their dead relatives or ancestors. Don told a story about a Samhain sabbat in a San Francisco Bay Area park, in which the ancestors were summoned. A participant approached the high priestess, concerned because she saw a spirit in a corner; but the priestess was not worried or impressed. After all, she reasoned, they had summoned the ancestors; she expected them to show up. But spirits of the dead are also believed to be potentially dangerous, especially if they are unknown to the practitioner—that is, not their own ancestors—because they can occasionally pull a priest or priestess into the otherworld; thus Pagans exercise caution in working with them to make sure there are clear boundaries and parameters around the ritual. The structural features of ritual which I discussed in the previous chapter are in part designed to make sure that participants keep the spirit world separate from the everyday world, and that helpful, protective spirits such as the gods and goddesses are present to oversee any magical working that takes place, including the invocation of other types of spirits that might become bothersome. Closing formulas at the ritual's end, in which entities present are thanked and dismissed, reinforce these boundaries, emphasizing the division between spirit and material worlds and preventing spirits from hanging around. As priestess Holly Tannen cautions in one of her humorous songs, one of the most important principles in Witchcraft is "Don't invoke what you can't banish."

## Interpreting Ecstasy

Pagans have deeply personal visions that reflect both individual concerns and group ideology, and which they experience as healing on some level. How can we interpret such personal material without, on the one hand, losing sensitivity to emic experiences and interpretations, or, on the other, accepting acritically the reality of tradition-bearer's interpretations? In an attempt to answer this question, I apply the concept of the *autonomous imagination*, a phrase coined by anthropologists Michele Stephen and Gilbert Herdt. Stephen and Herdt propose "the existence in the mind of a continuous stream of imagery that operates mostly outside . . . conscious control" and ordinary consciousness (Stephen, 1995:99). This stream of imagery can enter ordinary consciousness through dreams, waking visions, and trance experiences, and with special training, individuals can learn to control its occurrence and unfolding. Stephen and Herdt argue that shamanic trances, spirit possession, meditation, hypnosis, and similar phenomena all draw upon the autonomous imagination. The autonomous imagination often emerges as vivid hallucinatory images, augmented by strong sensory impressions that can include smell, sensation, taste, and auditory dimensions. It is more freely creative than ordinary thought processes, and responds readily to outside cues and cultural contexts. The autonomous imagination is particularly active in individuals with a religious or spiritual role in society; in these specialists, Stephen argues, it mixes material from the religious and cultural registers with elements from the immediate, everyday environment, allowing them to create or re-create ritual experiences that powerfully affect participants. Stephen believes that it enables communication between the conscious and unconscious mind without conscious awareness; it is not simply a mechanism for producing wish-fulfillment fantasies, but part of the mind's complex system of information processing (Stephen, 1995:99, 106).

This is strikingly similar to what Neo-Pagans themselves say about religious ecstasy. Reclaiming Witchcraft, drawing from the teachings of Feri founder Victor Anderson, who based his insights in part on the works of Max Freedom Long, calls the unconscious "younger self," while the conscious mind is known as "talking self." "Because they function through different modes of awareness, communication between the two is difficult" (Starhawk, 1989:35). Younger self experiences the world through sensation, emotion, and intuition, and communicates through dreams, visions, art, and physical sensations and symptoms. Talking self organizes, interprets, and explains experience, and communicates through language, concepts, and formulas. Feri and, in turn, Reclaiming Witchcraft also recognize a third self, "deep self" or "sacred self," which does not correspond to a psychoanalytical construct, but refers to the presence of the sacred in each human being. Deep or sacred self does not communicate directly with talking self, but can do so through younger self. Feri and Reclaiming Witchcraft teach communication among the various selves; ritual, with its panoply of aesthetic experiences, and ecstasy, with its powerful sensations and images, are tools in this process (Starhawk, 1989:36–37).

The images emerging through ecstasy are traditional, in that they are drawn from folktales, legends, ballads, myths, and other products that form a part of the cultural register of most North Americans, and thus exist, as Stephen postulates, as a stream of mental imagery and information. Yet they also incorporate a great deal of personal material from each individual's psyche in order to create imaginative inner landscapes. Through the autonomous imagination, these two streams of imagery combine in trances and religious possession to produce the effects described in the narratives in this chapter: effects which are both culturally significant and intensely personal for practitioners.

Most scholarly explanations of religious ecstasy emphasize how such states both conform to cultural and religious expectations, and function to confirm the existing beliefs of adherents. This applies to the visions and experiences that Neo-Pagans have during ritually induced altered states. As we have seen, trance and possession experiences grow out of the context of Neo-Pagan ritual, and feature well-recognized deities and elements from the Pagan narrative landscape: witches' cottages and sabbats, beloved goddesses such as Brigid, creatures that exhort greater environmental awareness and respect for the earth. Having such a vision or experience can establish or deepen belief. By sharing these visions and experiences, Neo-Pagans negotiate the nature of reality.

Anthropologists and folklorists have usually assumed that belief is grounded in social reality: Pagans experience Brigid because she is a deity who incorporates values and attitudes important in their culture; they have environmental visions in trance because they sacralize the earth and work politically for ecological causes. David Hufford has argued, however, that some beliefs are grounded in somatic experience—that experience itself, rather than wishful thinking, delusion, or misperception, is the source of some widespread beliefs. As both folklorist and physician, Hufford first worked with what he calls the "mara" or "nightmare" experience: usually lying in bed, but not asleep, subjects feel a heavy weight pressing down on their chests and are unable to move or dislodge the weight for several minutes. The subjects may have the impression that an evil force or spirit is responsible for the oppression, and most find the experience unpleasant if not downright terrifying (Hufford, 1982:47–170ff.). He concluded that the phenomenon, which is due to temporary sleep paralysis, is found cross-culturally, and that most cultures have spiritual explanations for it. Hufford's conclusions led him to hypothesize that some spiritual beliefs are based on real somatic experiences that occur cross-culturally regardless of a subject's prior beliefs, knowledge, or intentions. These experiences can be subdivided into distinct classes with sets of stable perceptual patterns—that is, subjects from divergent cultures report the same pattern of physical sensation and perception (although their explanations of the experience may vary greatly). He calls such occurrences "core experiences" (Hufford, 1995:28). Core experiences commonly refer intuitively to the existence of spirits and an alternate spiritual reality qualitatively different from ordinary, everyday reality. While Hufford does not necessarily accept the existence of spirits as factual, he argues that belief in spirits may be based on experiences such as the "mara" attack, the near-death experience, contact with loving presences, and other core experiences with wide cross-cultural distribution (Hufford, 1995:35–36).

The "unitary" experiences documented in a variety of religions and cultures by Newberg and D'Aquili (2001) can also be understood as "core" experiences according to Hufford's paradigm. In this case, widespread religious beliefs about the oneness of the universe, the pervasiveness of the sacred, and the interconnectedness of humans with both material and spiritual reality may be grounded in neurological experiences involving the orientation association area of the brain. Understanding the physiological and neurological features of spiritual experiences should not be interpreted as an attempt to discredit their reality or explain them away. Rather, it demonstrates their physical existence as a fundamental, shared part of human nature. Spiritual experiences cannot be considered irrational, since we have seen that, given their physiological basis, experiencers' descriptions of them are perfectly rational. On the other hand, as Newberg and D'Aquili assert, the physical basis of some spiritual experiences is not meant to be a denial of the existence of a spiritual dimension to reality. All human perceptions of material reality can ultimately be documented as chemical reactions in our neurobiology; all our sensations, thoughts, and memories are ultimately reducible to chemistry, yet we feel no need to deny the existence of the material world; it is no less real because our perceptions of it are biologically based (Newberg and D'Aquili, 2001:146–47). Therefore, until further evidence is available, it is not rational to assume that the spiritual reality of core experiences is any less real than the more scientifically documentable material reality.

Core experiences may underlie some contemporary American Neo-Pagan beliefs. It is unclear whether all instances of Neo-Pagan religious ecstasy, including both trance-journey visions and possession or aspecting, qualify as core experiences. However, the manifestations experiencers describe—"journeying" or flying to distant or imaginary locales, a feeling of ecstatic merging with the universe, the presence of loving and benevolent deities—have a long and well-documented history not only as part of Western mysticism, but cross-culturally as well. In many cases, Neo-Pagans begin having these extraordinary experiences before their first contact with Paganism. Neo-Paganism and revival Witchcraft may serve as cultural contexts in which these experiences are discussed, framed, normalized, and interpreted. They also provide a set of tools with which practitioners can regulate the experiences, bringing them on at will and stopping any that are perceived as dangerous or harmful. These tools—magic and ritual—in turn bring about additional spiritual experiences that help shape and consolidate an emergent American Neo-Pagan belief system.

It remains a difficult business to tease out the complex relationship between belief and experience, because they are intricately entwined in human culture. It is clear that some beliefs do have an experiential basis; stories such as Laurel's, Darrin's, and Gus's illustrate how skeptics can become believers as a result of experiences that point to the existence of a spiritual realm. The re-sacralization of the everyday world—the magical worldview, in other words—provides a context in which extraordinary experiences become part of the ordinary world, a world full of meaning and enchantment. At the same time, rituals are designed to bring about extraordinary experiences through the use of trance journeying and cues that help participants embody the deities. All three elements work together to create a cultural context that normalizes and privileges ecstasy.

Part III

# Beyond Experience: Religion and Identity

*Chapter 6*

# The Romance of Subdominance: Creating Oppositional Culture

For many mainstream Americans, the words *witchcraft* and *paganism* have ambivalent associations at best. In the eyes of most people, witches are make-believe figures from folktales and children's literature, though some subcultures consider them dangerous agents of the devil who traffic with the supernatural in unsavory ways.[1] The term *pagan*, in turn, conjures up images of indulgence and dissolution from Hollywood B movies. Yet contemporary Pagans and Witches have embraced these terms as emblems of identity. By doing so, Neo-Pagans accomplish two important goals in the creation of a new religious culture: they reclaim terminology previously devalued by the dominant culture, and they create an identity in opposition to certain aspects of mainstream society. In this chapter, I will explore how these processes take place.

## Revival Witchcraft and Neo-Paganism as Oppositional Culture

Witches and Pagans construct their identity in contrast to that of the dominant American culture. Oppositionality is part of the process of identity creation; it operates in the lives of individuals as well as in larger groups and polities. At its most basic level, it involves adopting an identity antithetical to that of some other individual or group in order to differentiate self from other. In the case of social groups and movements in complex societies, however, oppositionality is more complicated, in that within any given society, symbol systems correspond to social inequalities. These tend to center around gender, class, race, ethnicity, kinship, age, and sexual orientation, although other characteristics may also play an important part in the creation of symbolic systems. Usually, one side of the symbolic continuum is accorded higher status than the other, which is coded as negative, taboo, dangerous, or ambiguous, therefore justifying social disparity. However, this less valued side emerges regularly in numerous forms of expressive culture—such as ritual, drama, parody, satire, and play—that reverse or invert the established social order, valuing, however temporarily, the very emblems that are devalued by the dominant system. Various scholars have used different terminology to refer to this process: Mikhail Bakhtin has called it the "carnivalesque" (1968); to Victor Turner, it is "anti-structure" (1969); Barbara Babcock calls it "symbolic inversion" (1978), while James Scott describes it as the "hidden transcript" (1990). All these terms refer to a similar process of oppositionality.

Oppositionality is important because it offers possibilities for cultural critique and renewal; artistic trends, cultural revitalizations, and revolutionary movements all tend to draw their iconography from this devalued symbol set. Many scholars who have studied resistance movements have paid great attention to the role of oppositional expressive culture in sowing the seeds of social change. The Italian socialist Antonio Gramsci was extremely influential in the development of twentieth-century ideas about power and resistance. Gramsci, who grew up in rural Sardinia, witnessed firsthand how certain forms of folklore allowed peasants and workers (the "subaltern classes") to protest the elites' control over production and cultural capital. However, Gramsci also saw folklore, particularly folk beliefs, as part of a system that kept subalterns trapped in a situation of powelessness by ultimately reinforcing the values of the hegemony. French historian and cultural critic Michel Foucault greatly refined and expanded upon Gramsci's ideas by examining systems of power and knowledge: how power and its ideologies affect the production of knowledge. His focus was on the development of modern European states and their symbolic systems of social inequality. Foucault wrote the now famous maxim "Where there is power, there is resistance"—meaning that no system of power goes completely unchallenged, in that any act or system of power necessarily creates resistance (Foucault, 1984:300). Even the most miserable victims of power find subtle ways of resisting. However, like Gramsci, Foucault saw resistance as ultimately bound up with the very systems of power that produce it. Forms of resistance are often not perceived as resistance by those in power; in fact they often reinforce the same systems of power they attempt to subvert. Power and resistance are therefore closely intertwined in a perpetual dance, where each begets the other but neither is fully autonomous.

Power and resistance have usually been studied in terms of social class, gender, and race. Following Gramsci, a number of scholars have seen folklore as a voice of resistance and opposition among economically and racially marginalized populations. (Lombardi-Satriani, 1974; Limon, 1994; Scott, 1990). Neo-Pagans and Witches, however, do not fit this cultural profile. My fieldwork confirms the findings of earlier researchers (Eller, 1995; Orion, 1995; Pike, 2001; Berger, 1999; Salomonsen, 2002; Hutton, 1999): the Neo-Pagans I studied are predominantly white Euro-Americans who range from working class to upper middle class in their families of origin.[2] In other ways, though, they differ considerably from mainstream American culture, as we saw in Chapter 2. Most Pagans are better educated than average; 80 percent of my sample completed college, and another 40 percent earned a postgraduate degree.[3] Higher education does not always translate into higher income, however (cf. Eller, 1995:21–23; Orion, 1995:66–71). For many Pagans and Witches, job satisfaction is more important than earning power in their search for careers; they tend to choose occupations in which they can serve others or exercise their creativity. Many are employed in the health-care and computer industries, while others make their living as artists, artisans, and small-business owners. They also differ from average populations in gender and sexual orientation. Orion described Neo-Pagans as "the inverse of the larger population . . . [a] minority in a democracy whose traditions and policies are shaped by the majority" (1995:75), and my data confirms hers. While Neo-Pagans clearly differ from the norm in important ways, they are not on the whole a minority group marginalized because of race, ethnicity, class, colonialism, or any of the other conventional categories around which resistance movements have tended to develop.

In early twenty-first-century America, however, the discourse of oppositionality, resistance, and identity creation is firmly rooted in social movements of the twentieth century that sought civil rights for oppressed and marginalized groups. African Americans, Native Americans, women, and other minorities who suffered egregiously at the hands of the dominant culture created, through their struggle for recognition, a model that linked suffering and oppression to the emergence of a movement for cultural renewal and political recognition (Abrahams, 2003:215). This model has become central to the process of identity creation in the late twentieth and early twenty-first centuries. In creating an oppositional identity, Neo-Pagans have crafted a history for themselves that specifically links them to the marginalized and oppressed.

Neo-Pagans and revival Witches suffer real discrimination because of their religion, which is sometimes feared and misunderstood by mainstream culture. Especially in small towns and areas with a high concentration of conservative groups, they may be considered dangerously deviant. Because of this prejudice, they have had their businesses and homes vandalized or destroyed, lost custody of their children, been dismissed from jobs, and had their religious services disrupted by harassers. In most cases, the prejudice against them comes not from mainstream religious groups, but from charismatic, conservative Protestant sects who view any form of contact with the supernatural outside Christianity as dangerous diabolism (Ellis, 2000:171–75). Sarah Pike has shown how, by sharing personal narratives of persecution, Pagans create a sense of common experience and mutual support, tightening the boundaries of their communities (Pike, 2001:104–6).

Some Pagan oppositional narratives, however, concentrate on the distant historical past, casting Neo-Pagans and Witches as victims of a legacy of discrimination of which contemporary insults are only a small and recent part.

By telling these stories, Pagans contextualize their experiences of discrimination in a way that galvanizes an identity oppositional to Christianity as a whole.

## Oppositionality in Song and Story

Neo-Pagans usually do not isolate themselves from those outside their religious communities through obvious signs, such as separate residences, distinctive everyday dress, work, or social activities, or rejection of technology, as other religious minorities sometimes do. Instead, they create a religious culture that flourishes whenever they get together: to celebrate seasonal rituals in small or large groups, at summer festivals, camps and gatherings, in Pagan publications, and increasingly on the Internet. Neo-Pagan culture is literate and literary; much of it is created in, and transmitted through, texts; but there is no single text considered authoritative to Paganism. Because of this, the face-to-face interaction of small groups and festivals is fundamental in the creation and transmission of Pagan culture. At coven meetings, at festivals and camp-outs, and increasingly online, Pagans exchange chants, songs, and narratives that tell their story as a group and construct an emergent culture in contrast to the "mundane" or "Cowan" world of non-Pagans. Sacred stories are one of the most important vectors for the creation and diffusion of Neo-Pagan and Witchen identity.

Most religions have myths, by which I mean sacred narratives believed to contain hallowed truths about the origins of things as they are today.[4] Neo-Pagans and Witches are no exception. Two principal, interrelated narratives can be considered core Neo-Pagan and Witchen myths, in that they are widely regarded as true and explain the origins and development of the religions. I will call them the myths of Paleolithic Origins and the Burning Times; but I present them as intertwined, as they exist within the movement.[5] The first refers to a story about the origins of pagan religions in a Paleolithic Eden where many goddesses and gods were worshipped, people lived in harmony with nature, and gender relations were egalitarian; the second, to the idea that the witches persecuted during the witch hunts were the practitioners of ancient pagan religions, and that revival Witchcraft descends from them actually or spiritually. Many Pagans and Witches first encounter these narratives in texts: both appear in rudimentary form in Gardner's *Witchcraft Today*, as well as in Starhawk's *The Spiral Dance*, two of the most influential books on revival Witchcraft. Since Gardner's version is scattered throughout his book as an interpretation, rather than a single coherent narrative, I will paraphrase Starhawk's version here. Starhawk's version has a feminist cast that is common to many, but not all, Neo-Pagan traditions, in that she emphasizes the importance of goddesses (or a great mother goddess) in ancient pagan religions, and postulates a time when women were accorded tremendous authority and respect because of their associations with the divine feminine. In order to emphasize their mythic nature, I have set them off from the rest of the text in italics.

*The roots of Neo-Pagan Witchcraft lie in Paleolithic Europe, at the time of the last great Ice Age, among bands of foragers who followed herd animals across Europe. These foragers had a shamanistic religion; their religious leaders, both male and female, created rituals to honor the deities and ensure plentiful hunting. These deities included "the Mother Goddess, the birthgiver, who brings into existence to all life; and the Horned God, hunter and hunted, who eternally passes through the gates of death that new life may go on" (Starhawk, 1989:17). During this period, humans lived in harmony with the earth and its natural cycles of birth and death. They conceptualized a cosmology in which "life and death were a continuous stream; the dead were buried as if sleeping in a womb, surrounded by their tools and ornaments, so that they might awaken to anew life" (17). Worship took place in caves, the wombs of the earth, personified as the goddess portrayed in Paleolithic figurines and bas-reliefs familiar to us from introductory anthropology textbooks.*

*As the Ice Age ended and the glaciers retreated, human beings began to live in more permanent settlements and to domesticate plants and animals. Agriculture and pastoralism replaced foraging as subsistence strategies. These economic changes led to a shift in the conceptualization of the goddess and god: "The Hunter became Lord of the Grain, sacrificed when it is cut in autumn, buried in the womb of the Goddess and reborn in the spring. The Lady of the Wild Things became the Barley Mother, and the cycles of moon and sun marked the times for sowing and reaping and letting out to pasture. . . . The year became a great wheel divided into eight parts: the solstices and equinoxes and the cross quarter days in between, when great feasts were held and fires were lit" (Starhawk, 1989:18). Still, humans were deeply attuned to the rhythms of the natural world, as their survival depended upon it. Shamans and priestesses now held knowledge about when to plant and when to harvest. They erected dolmens, menhirs, and megalithic monuments to mark sacred places in the landscape, serve as temples, and preserve astronomical knowledge that signaled the important times in the year cycle. Cultures developed knowledge of mathematics, medicine, poetry, music, and the arts. Women and men lived in egalitarian communities where both genders had access to power and authority, sacred and secular.*

*But during the Bronze and Iron Ages, these peaceful cultures were destroyed by chariot-driving warriors who drove them into the hills and imposed on them their own martial religion, with a pantheon dominated by male gods. As the new deities merged with those of the Old People, this resulted in different syncretic religions in various parts of Europe: the Greek pantheon in the Mediterranean, Druidic mysteries among the Celts, Norse gods and goddesses in the north, and so on. Eventually the new, syncretized religions became dominant. Some of the Old People went into hiding, and became known as fairies; others intermarried with their conquerors.*

*Christianity, with its myth of the Virgin Mother and her sacred, reborn Son, at first was understood as simply another version of the story of the goddess and her divine child and consort. Early Christians preserved in the liturgical year many of the sacred feasts of the earlier goddess-centered religion. But as famines, plagues and wars ravaged Europe and the Crusades brought new ideas from the East that threatened the Church's power, the Church began to per-*

*secute those who still worshipped the old gods, calling them witches and heretics. Because women were believed to be inherently susceptible to temptation, witch hunters often focused on them, especially if they were elderly, mentally ill, ugly, handicapped, "uppity," or different in any way. "Homosexuals and freethinkers were caught in the same net" (Starhawk, 1989:21). Victims were considered guilty until proven innocent; confessions of witchcraft were extracted through brutal tortures. All in all, nine million innocent people were executed during the Burning Times.*[6] *Yet despite these persecutions, some practitioners of the Old Religion survived. Some even came to the New World; Starhawk suggests that the ideas of freedom of speech, government by representation, and individual rights central to the drafters of the United States Constitution were grounded in Witchcraft, and that members of the distinguished Adams family were practitioners of an ancient mystery cult (1989:21). The Enlightenment brought new assaults on the Old Religion: disbelief in the power of magic and a rejection of witches as ridiculous and grotesque. Only in the late twentieth century have Witches reclaimed their history; according to Starhawk, "'Witch' carries so many negative connotations that many people wonder why we use the word at all. Yet to reclaim the word 'Witch' is to reclaim our right, as women, to be powerful; as men, to know the feminine within the divine. To be a Witch is to identify with nine million victims of bigotry and hatred and to take responsibility for creating a world in which prejudice claims no more victims. A Witch is a 'shaper' who bends the unseen into form, and so becomes one of the Wise, one whose life is infused with magic" (1989:22).*

There is little doubt that the reclaiming of the word *witch* is a powerful act of opposition and identity creation for many in the movement. Anith, a California Witch, explained to me why she liked the word and what it meant to her: "I was raised Baptist, but not Fundamentalist. Yet there was still a feeling that the intuitive, the powerful, the sexual . . . belonged to 'the dark side.' I want to embrace the dark side, the intuitive, the emotional. The word 'witch' is a powerful way for me to do that—to reclaim and validate those attributes which were regarded as sinful or bad for so long." She continued by summarizing the plot of a novel she had read in which a girl in seventeenth-century Salem, Massachusetts, felt the stirrings of sexual and emotional awakening. Yet her Puritanical upbringing assigned those qualities to the devil. The young girl became convinced that because she felt these stirrings, she, too, must be "of the devil," and therefore a witch. Anith does not believe her intuition and sexuality are sinful, but by reclaiming the word *witch* and recasting it as positive, she feels she is subverting a dualistic system, which proposes a strict opposition between good and evil, male and female, rationality and intuition, purity and sexuality to which she no longer subscribes.

Even though embracing the word *witch* has disadvantages, many Neo-Pagan Witches feel empowered by its connotations. Don explained that while calling himself a Witch might cause some people to fear him, on the whole he prefers being feared to being considered silly: "If they fear me, they'll listen to what I have to say and I can allay their fears. If they think I'm silly, they'll just dismiss and ignore me."

Neo-Pagan and Witchen sacred stories, which Starhawk presents as "our legends," recognizing their fundamentally folkloric character, did not originate with Starhawk, or even with Gardner, but are an amalgam of interpretations and theories from the eighteenth and nineteenth centuries that have become part of an oral discourse about world history. As we saw in Chapter 1, they reflect a Romantic primitivism rooted in the writings of Rousseau and authors from the post-Enlightenment Romantic revival that locates spiritual authenticity in the practices of "savages" and ancient peoples, often equating the two along unilinear evolutionary schemes of cultural development. The idea that early cultures were matriarchal can be traced to Johann Jakob Bachofen's *Das Mütterecht* (1858). Bachofen postulated that the rule of women ended in Classical times, when it was defeated by the ancestors of the Greeks, whose superior technology and knowledge of human reproduction trumped the power of the matriarchs. Bachofen's theory had an intrinsic evolutionary bent: its premise was that patriarchy was superior to matriarchy—a step up the ladder of cultural evolution. Because of this, it was picked up and reproduced in the writings of many of his anthropological contemporaries who espoused a model of unilinear, universal cultural evolution, including William Robertson Smith, Herbert Spencer, Lewis Henry Morgan, and Edward B. Tylor (Eller, 2000:31). Fifty years later, just as anthropologists were beginning to reject unilinear evolutionary schemes, Friedrich Engels used the theory in *The Origin of Private Property, Marriage, and the State* (1884), from which it became a sort of socialist myth of origins (Eller, 2000:32). It was also adopted by some early feminists, whose work, as we shall see later, was instrumental in inspiring its revival by second-wave feminist writers in the 1960s and 1970s.

The idea of fairies as a cultural memory of earlier inhabitants of Europe developed as a result of early archeological and linguistic research, which postulated that northern Europeans belonged to a racially and culturally superior branch of the Indo-European family that had conquered the racially and culturally inferior indigenous inhabitants of Europe and driven them into marginal areas. These indigenous peoples were, according to theories of the time, dark-skinned and small in stature; they lived in caves and mounds, and made use of the very small implements often found around these archeological sites. The main exponent of what came to be called the pygmy theory was David MacRitchie. In his *Testimony of Tradition* (1890), he attempted to establish connections between European fairies and circum-Arctic peoples such Lapps and Eskimos, whom he believed to be living exemplars of the earlier indigenous races of Europe. Tales about magical fairy powers, he argues, are really examples of how Europeans misunderstood certain elements of the earlier peoples' technology. MacRitchie's theory was heavily criticized by W. Y. Evans-Wentz, who pointed out that most bearers of fairy legends considered the fairies to be spiritual in nature, not human; that his hypothetical connections between peoples of vastly different cultures and linguistic groups, such as

Lapps and Eskimo, were not supported by any evidence; that there was no evidence of their ever having inhabited Britain or any other part of Europe; and finally, that small-statured peoples themselves often hold beliefs about smaller-statured spiritual beings (Evans-Wentz, 1966:234–35). In any case, few scholars have ever taken it very seriously; but it apparently made an impression on popular culture, as Gardner cites it in *Witchcraft Today* (1954).

The myth that Pagans themselves call the Burning Times developed out of the same cauldron of Romantic fantasy and wishful scholarship that characterized the mid-nineteenth century. Ronald Hutton, in his survey of the history of Neo-Pagan Witchcraft, has already pointed out how by the mid-nineteenth century, European and American historians of the witch hunts had cast the Catholic Church as the principal culprit; they said the Church had fabricated a demonology that seemed to explain the crises of the Middle Ages, then searched for scapegoats to blame for its problems (Hutton, 1999:132–36). But it was Frenchman Jules Michelet who, out of his own anticlerical and anti-monarchical bias, pioneered the idea that the witch hunts constituted a crusade against the practitioners of an ancient pagan religion that had preserved the ideals of liberty, equality, and fraternity through the Dark Ages, so they could be revived by the French Revolution. In *La Sorcière* (1838), Michelet painted a picture of the witch as a symbol of popular resistance—a healer, visionary, and "natural rebel," whose sabbats, dedicated to fertility rites in honor of Pan, who was misinterpreted by Christians as the devil, were actually appeals for the liberation of serfs. Michelet believed women were born enchantresses, whose menstrual cycles put them in touch with the natural world and mystical powers (Hutton, 1999:139). While *La Sorcière* was never taken seriously as scholarship, its risqué, melodramatic content, replete with scenes of sabbat fertility rites, made it an instant best seller. It inspired two works by American writers, which in turn became important in creating the Neo-Pagan myth of the Burning Times: feminist writer Matilda Joslyn Gage's *Women, Church, and State* (1893), and folklorist Charles Godfrey Leland's *Aradia; or, The Gospel of the Witches* (1890). It was Gage who married Michelet's story of witchcraft as pagan religion to Bachofen's theory of early matriarchal societies, giving us the earliest version of the Neo-Pagan and feminist mythos (Hutton, 1999:141). Gage's writings were rediscovered by second-wave feminists Mary Daly, Andrea Dworkin, and Merlin Stone during the 1960s and 1970s, from which they diffused into the blossoming women's spirituality movement, itself an offshoot of both feminism and revival Witchcraft. Leland, on the other hand, claimed to have discovered in Tuscany the remnants of a religion of sorcery and peasant resistance.[7] While clearly influenced by Michelet's work, it was *Aradia*, more than *La Sorcière*, which shaped the Neo-Pagan mythos, spawning several works of Pagan literature and a whole branch of Italian American revival Witchcraft, which I will describe in greater detail in Chapter 7.

The Pagan mythos has been heavily critiqued within the movement. Isaac

Bonewits, who holds a Ph.D. in anthropology from the University of California, Berkeley, was among the first to point out its problematic nature, as early as the 1970s; Starhawk began to move away from some of the assertions of *The Spiral Dance* (1979) in her later works *Dreaming the Dark* (1982) and *Truth or Dare* (1987), which present the story of early matriarchy as legend, rather than fact. As better historical scholarship on the European witch hunts has emerged, it has in turn influenced Pagan writers, who have begun to critique and revise their version of the Burning Times.[8] Today most well-read Pagans and Witches realize the symbolic nature of their origin stories, and no longer accept them as fact. Yet these stories continue to have a powerful effect on individuals, even when they understand their metaphorical nature.

Pagan sacred stories are such a central part of the Neo-Pagan cultural register that they are seldom recited verbatim; it is taken for granted that most people are familiar with them. Instead, the principal way these myths circulate in oral tradition is as songs performed at rituals, festivals, song circles, and concerts by Pagan artists. Pagans can purchase tapes and CDs of the songs from alternative bookstores, by mail order, and on Internet sites. Listening to the recorded music reinforces the song learning that took place at the earlier event; often by the next gathering, the song has become part of the individual's repertoire, and is performed at a new song circle, continuing the cycle of dissemination.

One of the most widely known Pagan songs is Charlie Murphy's "The Burning Times," also recorded by numerous other Pagan artists. Its refrain is one of the most commonly used chants in rituals from the larger Neo-Pagan to the Womanspirit communities; in fact it is sometimes jokingly called the Pagan National Anthem. The refrain, a litany of goddess names, originally existed as an independent chant, and may have been grafted into the song by Jamie Sieber, an instrumentalist in Charlie Murphy's band and its possible author.

In the cool of the evening they used to gather
'Neath the stars in the meadow circled near an old oak tree
At the times appointed by the seasons
Of the earth and the phases of the moon.
In the center often stood a woman
Equal with the others and respected for her worth
One of the many we call the Witches
The healers and the teachers of the wisdom of the earth.
The people grew through the knowledge she gave them
Herbs to heal their bodies, spells to make their spirits whole.
Hear them chanting incantations
Calling forth the wise ones, celebrating in dance and song.

*Refrain (twice):*
Isis, Astarte, Diana, Hecate, Demeter, Kali, Inanna.

There were those who came to power through domination
And they bonded in their worship of a dead man on a cross.
They sought control of the common people
By demanding allegiance to the Church of Rome.
And the Pope declared the Inquisition
It was a war against the women whose powers they feared.
In this holocaust against the nature people
Nine million European women died.
And the tale is told of those who by the hundreds
Holding together chose their deaths in the sea
While chanting the praises of the Mother Goddess
A refusal of betrayal, women were dying to be free.

Now the earth is a witch and men still burn her
Stripping her down with mining and the poisons of their wars
Still to us the earth is a healer, a teacher, our mother
The weaver of the web of life that keeps us all alive.
She gives us the vision to see through the chaos
She gives us courage; it is our will to survive.[9]

This song contains the core elements of the Pagan sacred narrative: that European Witches were the practitioners of an ancient goddess-worshipping Pagan religion; that they met at night according to seasonal and lunar cycles; that covens were democratic, egalitarian, and led by a woman whose position was based on merit; that witches were healers, teachers, and herbalists who worked for the good of the people; and that the Inquisition was specifically a "war against the women" and an attempt by the Catholic hierarchy to impose control over "the common people." "The Burning Times" explicitly compares the witch persecutions with the German genocide of Jews during World War II through its use of the word *holocaust,* and promulgates the idea that nine million women were killed during the Burning Times. The final verse compares the destruction of the environment to the witch burnings: "The earth is a witch, and men still burn her"—and describes the earth as a nurturing mother, "weaver of the web that keeps us all alive." The words *we* and *us* in the final verse suggest a historical continuity between witches of old and contemporary Witches and Pagans.

The refrain, a litany of goddess names—"Isis, Astarte, Diana, Hecate, Demeter, Kali, Inanna"—collapses the distinctions between widely different cultures and historical periods, implying that these deities are aspects of a single mother goddess. These tenets are central to the Pagan, and especially Witchen, thealogy, with its Neoplatonic-like emphasis on the ultimate oneness of all sacred manifestations.

While among the most popular, "The Burning Times" is also among the most controversial of Pagan songs. Much of the controversy surrounds the historical authenticity of the myth of the Burning Times, which has been heavily critiqued in Pagan publications, and has both passionate adherents and staunch detractors. Political scientist and Pagan Gus di Zerega described to me the first time he heard the song: "I had just barely begun involvement [with Neo-Paganism]. . . . I was by myself in my apartment and I put the music on. I was in a pretty good mood, sort of a quiet mood, and by the end of the first verse I was sobbing uncontrollably. It took playing that song probably twenty to thirty times before I wouldn't sob uncontrollably when I heard it." While he was clearly emotionally affected by the imagery in the song, this did not prevent Gus from critiquing its historical accuracy. "The part that really bothered me [was the] the nine million European women, which is bad history, both because some of them were men, . . . and there was [*sic*] nowhere near nine million." For Gus, the song retains symbolic power, even as he recognizes the historical untenability of its claims.

Like many other Pagans with whom I spoke, he also felt that while opposition to Christianity might have been important in the early stages of Neo-Paganism, it is something that Pagans, both individually and as a movement, need to outgrow. "We too often define ourselves against the Christian religion. And I think we have enough going for us spiritually that we don't need to do that, . . . because so long as you define yourself by what you're against, what you're against is still defining you." Gus's book *Pagans and Christians: The Personal Spiritual Experience* (di Zerega, 2001), is an attempt to bridge the gap between the two religions by examining the core spiritual experiences, as well as the ethical and theological/thealogical principles of each.

For Kate Slater, a Canadian Witch, the song evoked a similar mixture of feelings: "I love the music, rhythm, passion of this song. However, it contains the Pagan myth about 'the Pope declared the Inquisition, nine million European women died.' This has become perniciously widespread. . . . The problem is that it is so wrong, whether it represents a lack of realistic scholarship, innumeracy, or the desire to identify with victimhood. It is propaganda."

The late Gwydion Pendderwen, well known in the California Pagan community as the movement's bard, is the author of another favorite song of resistance, "We Won't Wait Any Longer."

> We have trusted no man's promise, we have kept just to ourselves,
> We have suffered from the lies in all the books upon your shelves
> But our patience and endurance through the burning times and now
> Have given us the strength to keep our vow.
>
> *Refrain:*
> We won't wait any longer
> We are stronger than before
> We won't wait any longer
> We are stronger.

You have grazed away the heather and razed the sacred groves
You have driven native peoples from the places that they loved
Though your greed has been unbounded, still you felt the pangs of shame
Every time you trod upon the Mother's name.

Though you thought you had destroyed the mem'ry of the ancient ways
Still the people light the balefire every year on solstice day
And at Beltane eve and Samhain you will find us on the hill
Invoking once again her triple will.

Through the ages many races have risen and have gone
Yet dispersed among the nations of the earth we linger on
Now the time has come to take the sacred cauldron of rebirth
And renew our ancient promise to the earth.[10]

Like "The Burning Times," "We Won't Wait Any Longer" contrasts colonizers, degraders of the environment, and by implication Christians and academics, whom it lumps into a single category ("you"), with [Neo-]Pagans ("we"), survivors of a series of oppressions who continue to worship according to the "ancient ways," albeit "dispersed among the nations of the earth." It creates continuity between early earth-worshippers and present-day Pagans, hinting at kinship between all polytheistic nature-worshippers, regardless of race, culture, or nationality. In it, Neo-Pagans are survivors, who will rise again and reclaim what is theirs, calling for political action—"we won't wait any longer, / We are stronger than before. . . . / Now the time has come to . . . / renew our ancient promise to the earth." The song's ideas are also repeated in a popular Pagan chant that works its way into rituals:

We are the old people
We are the new people
We are the same people
Stronger than before.

A large number of Pagans find such songs stirring. Darien Delu, a political analyst from Sacramento, offered this explanation for her feelings: "I am most moved by [songs] that express connection with nature and . . . resistance to oppression and to attacks on nature, songs that express sadness about what is happening to the earth. I think it's because there's so little public expression of this grief that the songs offer an outlet for my grief, plus an affirmation of its legitimacy. Through our songs, we claim our (Pagan) history. We declare our common culture. When I hear such a song, I feel strengthened, heartened, renewed."

As Kate Slater astutely observed, songs of resistance and opposition create identity by partly through a "desire to identify with victimhood." Pagans identify with two specific oppressed groups: indigenous peoples whose environment have been destroyed, and witches whose persecution is likened to Hitler's holocaust of the Jews. The first metaphor, according to Chas Clifton, "turn[s] the literate, often college-educated modern witch into a noble savage" (Clifton, 1998:61), while the holocaust has become "the paradigmatic narrative for understanding atrocity in the late twentieth century" (Purkiss, 1996:17).

While many of my respondents were critical of the Pagan myths of the Burning Times and Paleolithic Origins, they nevertheless found these songs deeply moving and inspiring, identifying with them on a deeper level. But why would college-educated, white middle-class seekers identify with oppressed indigenes and witches burned at the stake? Why create an oppositional identity by linking with the marginalized and oppressed? What are Neo-Pagans and Witches resisting?

To answer this question, it may be useful to apply Lila Abu-Lughod's inversion of Foucault's dictum "Where there is power, there is resistance" into a diagnostic: "Where there is resistance, there is power" (Abu-Lughod, 1990:314). In other words, when we find forms in a culture's symbolic system that hide, oppose, invert, parody, and otherwise resist power, we can gain insights into the power system that creates them by asking what is being opposed or contested. What ideas, concepts, and values does the existing system of power exclude by definition? Neo-Pagan subculture reveals specific values and patterns which suggest that what is being resisted is a dominant discourse about the nature of reality, which marginalizes certain kinds of spiritual and imaginative experiences as irrational and irrelevant. This construction of reality, rooted in the Enlightenment, contradicts the embodied experience of many, if not most, Neo-Pagans and Witches—experiences that, as we saw in the last chapter, lie at the core of the movement's rituals.

Another popular song of resistance, "The Heretic Heart," expresses the essence of this embodied experience. Set to the tune of an Episcopal hymn, the song juxtaposes Christian symbols and turns of phrase with Pagan ideals. Pagan writer Margot Adler used it as the theme song of her WBAI radio show "Hour of the Wolf," and titled her autobiography, *Heretic's Heart: A Journey through Spirit and Revolution* (Boston, 1997), after the song.

Two versions of the song exist. The original, written by Catherine Madsen in about 1982, was revised and recorded by Holly Tannen in her 1985 release *Between the Worlds.*

| The Heretic Heart<br>by Catherine Madsen | The Heretic Heart<br>as recorded by Holly Tannen |
|---|---|
| I am a bold and a Pagan soul<br>A rattlin' through this land.<br>I judge the world by my own lights<br>And I come by my own hand. | I am a bold and a Pagan soul<br>A-rattlin' through this land.<br>I judge the world by my own lights<br>And I come by my own hand. |

And if you ask where I learned
To live so recklessly
My skin, my bones, my heretic heart
Are my authority.

My mother was a spinner of tales
My father a dreaming man.
And I have swung on the dragon's
tongue
And danced on holy land.
I have sung the seed up out of the
ground
And the bird down from the tree
My skin, my bones, my heretic heart
Are my authority.

I once was found, but now I'm gone
Away from the faithful fold
The ones who preach that holiness
Is to do what you are told.
Though law and scripture, priest
and prayer
Have all instructed me
My skin, my bones, my heretic heart
Are my authority.

Now they tell me Jesus loves me,
But I think he loves in vain,
He must go unrequited
On me he has no claim.
For the man who would command me
Must wear the horn and let me be;
My skin, my bones, my heretic heart
Are my authority.

Then while I breathe this glorious air
An outlaw I'll remain,
My body shall not be subdued
And I will not be saved.
And if I cannot shout aloud
I'll sing it secretly:
My skin, my bones, my heretic heart
Are my authority.[11]

And if you ask me how I've learned
To live so recklessly
My skin, my bones, my heretic heart
Are my authority.

My mother lived her life in fear
My father's a broken man.
But I have sung in the ancient
tongue
And danced on holy land.
I sing the seed up out of the
ground
And the bird down from the tree
My skin, my bones, my heretic heart
Are my authority.

I once was found, but now I'm gone
Out of the faithful fold
Of those who teach that holiness
Is to do what you are told.
Though priest and scripture, man
and law
Have all instructed me
My skin, my bones, my heretic heart
Are my authority.

They tell me Jesus loves me
But I fear he must love in vain,
For what can any man-god know
Of woman's secret pain?
My healer is the lady Moon
Whose tides run deep in me.
My skin, my bones, my heretic heart
Are my authority.

So while I breathe this glorious air
An outlaw I'll remain.
My body shall not be subdued
My soul shall not be saved.
And where I may not shout it loud
I'll sing it secretly:
My skin, my bones, my heretic heart
Are my authority.

The two versions are similar, but Holly made significant revisions in the second and fourth verses to bring the song in harmony with her own experience. In the second verse, Catherine Madsen describes her mother as "a spinner of tales" and her father as "a dreaming man." These descriptions are important, because they valorize folklore and the role of the imagination, and locate the singer within a family pedigree that legitimizes their expression. But Holly, whose family devalued folklore and the imagination and derided her experiences, changed the words to reflect her own perception of her parents. In the same verse, the reference to swinging on a dragon's tongue may refer to imaginary or visionary experiences that are central to Pagan identity. In Holly's version, this becomes "But I have sung in the ancient tongue," because of her knowledge of Latin, Hebrew, and Gaelic, and her feeling that dragons were peripheral to her experience of Witchcraft. In the fourth verse, Madsen's version rejects any claims that Jesus might have on her, stating "The man who would command me / Must wear the horn and let me be." Originally a mocking reference to cuckoldry, this has been interpreted by some Pagans as a reference to the high priest who in some Craft traditions wears a horned crown in ritual. Holly has once again changed these lines to resonate with her personal experience: "I refuse to sing a song which suggests that any man might 'command me,' " she explained. "A Witch is a free woman." She also added words that addressed her personal experience of illness and healing.

"Heretic Heart" creates identity by repeatedly contrasting Christian and Pagan ideals and worldviews. The singer describes herself as a heretic, in that she is bold and reckless, responsible for her own judgments and her own sexual satisfaction ("I judge the world by my own lights / And I come by my own hand"). Many of the phrases and images in the song are variations or inversions of Christian ones. "I once was found but now I'm gone" plays on the line "I once was lost, but now I'm found" from the Christian hymn "Amazing Grace." "Out of the faithful fold" alludes to Christians' self-definition as sheep whom Jesus shepherds. They are instructed by "those who teach that holiness is to do what you are told." Holly felt that "They tell me Jesus loves me / But I fear he must love in vain" juxtaposes two very different songs: "Jesus loves me, this I know / 'Cause the Bible tells me so," a children's Sunday school song, portrays a loving Jesus who "suffers the little children to come unto Him." But in "I fear he must love in vain," Holly heard an allusion to Robert Johnson's "Love in Vain," a song popularized by Mick Jagger. This line eroticizes the love of Jesus, and then rejects it, suggesting a parallel between the sexual and the religious domination of women. Jesus' love is rejected because, in Holly's version, he cannot understand women's embodied experience: "what can any man-god know / Of woman's secret pain?"

"Heretic Heart" locates authority in the [female] body: "My skin, my bones, my heretic heart / Are my authority," specifically in women's embodied experience, which is in harmony with natural and cosmic cycles: "My healer is the lady Moon / Whose tides run deep in me." This personal, embodied authority is contrasted to the religious and secular authority of "priest and scripture, man and law" which attempt to subdue not only the female ("My mother lived her life in fear"), but the male as well (My father's a broken man").

In the final verse, the singer identifies herself as an "outlaw" who rejects external authority of any kind: "My body shall not be subdued / My soul shall not be saved." This balanced set of phrases implies that for the soul to be saved, the body must be subdued as well—something the singer will not accept. The song underscores the importance of the personal, the experiential, and the individual in Neo-Pagan thought. It also sacralizes the body, which is presented as in syntony with the cycles of nature, and rejects any form of authority imposed on the body from without. Many Pagans, especially women, identify strongly with this song. Reclaiming tradition priestess M. Macha Nighmare asserted: " 'Heretic Heart' perfectly expresses my worldview and philosophy of life."

Embodied spiritual or imaginative experience is the core of Pagan identity. It is what allowed Don and Anna to assume that I was somehow essentially Pagan when they discovered the relics of my childhood troll house: many of my Pagan subjects described having been very imaginative children who constructed elaborate make-believe worlds for themselves based on books, and spent a great deal of time living in those imaginary worlds, spinning out plots and characters and interacting with their creations, which seemed, at times, more real to them than the everyday world of school and family. Sometimes these children were physically smaller than their peers, or younger than the rest of the children in their class; others reported suffering from illnesses or disabilities that made them different from other children. A few individuals I interviewed were culturally and ethnically different from their peers, but lacked an ethnic community in which they could find a sense of identity; or, as children of refugees, had lives marked by frequent migration and instability. For these "bookish children," as I came to think of them, reading and imagination provided a refuge from the slings and arrows of childhood. Sarah Pike has described another frequent pattern in the life stories of Neo-Pagans: the "magical child" who saw fairies and ghosts and may have had psychic or spiritual experiences from an early age (Pike, 2001:157).

Both "bookish children" and "magical children" reported feeling ostracized by their peers and misunderstood by adults. Bookish children experienced rejection by other children, while the unusual experiences of magical children were ridiculed and considered evidence of mental illness or even intrinsic evil by religiously conservative parents (Pike, 2001:175). Sometime during adolescence or young adulthood, these young people decided to capitalize on their difference. They began to construct identities that were oppositional in the cultural register of American high schools, where conformity is key to social acceptance, becoming punks, "Goths," Dungeons and Dragons players, artistic or theatrical types, musicians, or writers. I suspect that this experience of rejection and difference is what lies at the core of Neo-Pagan identification with subdominant Others.

There is a strong tradition of imaginative and psychic experiences in Western folk culture; yet these "alternate ways of knowing," as Marylin Motz calls them (1998), were marginalized and silenced by the rationalist discourses of the Enlightenment. This silencing was particularly strong in the lives of the bourgeoisie, the class that produced and consumed science and capitalism, as both require a rejection of the symbolic, the metaphorical, the spiritual, and the transcendent (Lyotard, 1984:77). In the United States, this rejection combined with Puritan ideals to effect what science fiction author Ursula K. LeGuin has called "a fear of dragons." LeGuin argues that Americans are fearful and distrustful of a particular kind of creative imagination, "the free play of the mind, both intellectual and sensory," because of a "secular Puritanism" that rejects whatever is not useful or profitable as escapist and probably sinful (LeGuin, 1985:41–43). Neo-Pagans not only are not afraid of dragons, they are enamored of them; dragons and other fantasy themes are prominent motifs in Neo-Pagan artwork and iconography. On a more abstract level, Pagans have a particular kind of creative imagination that delights in the fantastic. This is a different kind of creativity from that which is praised by modern managers and CEOs; it is playful, sensory, and blessedly free from any apparent practical use. But as LeGuin comments, this sort of creativity has always been suspect in American culture, particularly in certain sects of Protestantism, in which anything smacking of fantasy is equated with the work of the devil. It is no accident that right-wing Christian groups foment stories about the dangers of fantasy role-playing games, about science-fiction literature and Harry Potter books leading to the practice of satanism, and that such groups have also labeled Neo-Paganism as "satanic."

The anti-imagination discourse relegates the numinous to a state of unreality. Since according to this paradigm, numinous experience is unreal, those who claim to have experienced it are considered outside the norm and out of touch with the culture's constructs of reality. They are marginalized, their voices are silenced, and narratives of their experiences are delegitimized. Neo-Pagans resist this construction of reality based on materialism, pragmatism, and rationalism (as distinct from rationality). Neo-Pagans do not reject rationality, but rather the exclusion of certain ways of knowing and operating in the world deemed "irrational," and thus inferior.

In broader terms, some Neo-Pagans may consciously resist power itself, especially what Starhawk, the most prominent founder of the San Francisco group known as "Reclaiming" and one of the most influential writers in the movement, calls power over (Starhawk, 1988: 2–3). By power over, she means domination, especially the forces of the state, with all of its discourses and institutions, and their impact on the environment, society, and the individual.

Starhawk urges Pagans to overthrow the paradigm based on power over and replace it with one based on "power from within," a term she defines as closer to its root meaning in the Latin verb *possum*, "I am able," and akin to the concept of "spirit," yet not separate from the corporeal world (1988:4). In contrast to the power of the state, of social institutions, and of mainstream religions, "power from within is the power of the low, the dark, the earth; the power that arises from our blood, and our lives, and our passionate desire for each other's living flesh" (1988:4). Like many Pagans, Starhawk sees power-over as responsible for the current "estrangement" [her term] of human consciousness, which she defines as a failure to perceive the interconnectedness of the world and our part in it. Humans are estranged from nature, from other human beings, and from parts of themselves. As these separate parts are objectified and rendered inanimate, the only possible relationship between them, in a materialistic conception of the world, is one of manipulation or domination among things. Starhawk sees estrangement and commodification as the cultural and spiritual bases for capitalism's exploitation of resources, whether human or natural. In turn, when the natural world and human beings are emptied of spiritual meaning, only what can be calibrated, scaled, graded, counted, exchanged, or bought is real. Everything else is illusion, nonreality (Starhawk, 1988:5–8). It is in opposition to this worldview that Neo-Pagans construct their culture.

By choosing to identify as such, Neo-Pagans and revival Witches are knowingly and consciously constructing themselves as the opposite of right society—part of the dark, the irrational, the primitive, and the possibly dangerous. But as we have seen, from their point of view, there is nothing "right" about right society when its institutions are responsible for environmental degradation, human exploitation, violence, alienation, and (in the words of Starhawk) nothing short of "the destruction of the world" (Starhawk, 1988:5). Words such as Witch and Pagan define identity by allying the user with groups that are outside the power structure. A kind of intentional marginalization is inherent in these constructions.

Those who question whether it is in the best interests of any group to identify with the marginal miss the touchstone of identity in the postcolonial, postmodern world, in which marginality has become a source of power and creativity. The cultural critique of feminist and postcolonial authors such as Gloria Anzaldua, Cherrie Moraga, and Homi Bhabha have identified cultural borderlands as loci of hybridity and the emergence of new cultural forms. Long the wellsprings of popular resistance movements (Scott, 1990:123), the margins emerged in the late twentieth century as sources of hybridity, creativity, and cultural critique. As James C. Scott observed, "the negation of a dominant religious ideology requires an off-stage subculture in which the negation can be formed and articulated" (Scott, 1990:118). Max Weber, in *The Sociology of Religion*, outlines the importance of the marginal "pariah-intelligentsia" in spreading resistance movements: "Groups which are . . . altogether outside of the social heirarchy stand to a certain extent on the point of Archimedes in relation to social conventions. . . . Since these groups are not bound by social conventions, they are capable of an original attitude towards the meaning of the cosmos" (quoted in Scott, 1990:124). For most American Neo-Pagans, who grew up in mainstream culture, intentional marginalization is essential to their ability to critique the dominant paradigm and come up with creative alternatives.

This distancing could be interpreted as a refusal to accept responsibility for the sins of the dominant culture; but most Pagans see it as a form of cultural critique. Just as anthropology itself has from its very inception turned to the primitive and the Other as an inspiration for how to right the wrongs of Western society, so contemporary Paganism represents a continuation of this critical impulse in Western culture.

Pagans are neither the first nor the only ones to have critiqued the modernist paradigm of detached consciousness. In this sense, the movement's emergence as a cultural force in North America during the late 1960s, and its subsequent growth and diffusion, are part of a larger that which some scholars have called postmodernity. Postmodernity is notoriously difficult to define, but it can be useful to understand it as a reaction against certain developments of late modernity. If modernity was characterized by concern with the rational, the analytic, the linear, the centered subject, and the search for truth, the postmodern proffers "the religious, the synthetic, the holistic, the ritualized." (Schechner, in Grimes, 1990:25), as well as the decentered subject and the multivocality of experience. A number of scholars have remarked on the centrality of ritual in the postmodern landscape. Schechner in fact proposes that while narrative was the primary performative genre of modernity, ritual becomes the principal performative genre of postmodernity, a kind of "religious and cultural entertainment" (Schechner, in Grimes, 1990:25). Thus Neo-Pagans' preoccupation with ritual as a central expressive art form, as well as their concern with holism, community, and reflexivity, can be understood as part of the historical movement from late modernity to postmodernity.

Philosopher Morris Berman suggests that it is exactly such a worldview which is necessary at this historical juncture to "reenchant the world" (Berman, 1984). Borrowing from Max Weber's prediction of the progressive "disenchantment" of the world as a result of the diffusion of scientific understanding, Berman argues that the central metaphor of modernity has been one of progressive disenchantment: "non-participation, . . . a rigid distinction between observer and observed. Scientific consciousness is alienated consciousness. . . . Subject and object are always seen in opposition to each other. . . . The logical endpoint of this worldview is a feeling of total reification: everything is an object, alien, not-me; and I am ultimately an object too." (Berman, 1984:3). It is perhaps more precise to identify this belief system *not* as "scientific," but as *scientistic*—a popular understanding of scientific consciousness which has become a folk belief system in its own right.

Like Starhawk, Berman blames this worldview for many contemporary problems, from nuclear proliferation and environmental degradation to increasing violence and alienation. As an antidote, he suggests a reenchantment of the world, a politics of consciousness which would reconnect the individual to the community and to the larger world. While the sacred narratives of the Burning Times and the Paleolithic Origins of Matriarchy are not literally true, like all myths they have a kernel of metaphorical truth: experiences and ways of knowing that belonged to a pre-Enlightenment, interconnected view of the universe have been banished from modern Western consciousness. In conjuring an oppositional culture, contemporary Pagans seek to reclaim that worldview.

*Chapter 7*

# "The Heart Is the Only Nation": Neo-Paganism, Ethnic Identity, and the Construction of Authenticity

**Field notes, May 4, 1997**

On a sunny afternoon near the first of May, Pagans from all over the San Francisco Bay Area are gathered in Berkeley's Live Oak Park for NROOGD's Beltane celebration. At the center of this year-cycle ritual is the hobbyhorse, or "'Oss," borrowed from a May Day tradition in Padstow, Cornwall, documented in a 1953 film by American folklorist Alan Lomax. To NROOGD Pagans, the 'Oss is an ancient spirit of the land, symbolizing its cyclical fertility and ability to sustain us. It consists of a large round frame covered in black fabric, on which is attached a long pole with a brightly painted horse's head at the end. The whole contraption is worn by a hooded dancer. For now, the 'Oss, played by Don Frew, remains hidden behind the bushes.

Like all NROOGD rituals, this one begins with a "meeting dance": we all join hands to form an outward-facing chain, which then winds in on itself so each participant greets or kisses every other participant. We then form a circle; Melissa, who is priestess today, stands over a large bowl that has been placed on the altar and charges the water, oil, and salt inside it. Then, turning toward the circle, she calls on the elements to be present. Picking up the bowl and asperging the circle, she chants, "Three from me, of five alive, by nine makes mine." She takes the athame from the altar and holds it extended toward the circle, moving clockwise, and casts the circle: "Athame draws the circle round about; power stay in, world stay out." Next, she purifies the circle by the powers of the elements. First she carries the incense around, saying, "Around, around, it shall be as sound as it were bound." She performs the same act carrying a pentacle: "Three times around, three times about; a world within, a world without." She carries the bowl of water around the circle, aspersing the participants with a sprig of herbs, chanting: "Three from me, of five alive, by nine makes mine." Then she seals the circle with a staff, calling, "Avante, avante, maleficum defense. Honi soit qui mal y pense. [Shame to who thinks ill of it.]" Finally she declares the circle sealed, and turns the staff as if to lock the gate. "As I will, so mote it be. Chant the spell and be it done. This circle is closed."

Darrin is the priest, known in the NROOGD tradition as the "Black Man." Striking in his black attire, moves to the center of the circle carrying a great sword, which he holds vertically. He faces east, and calls, "Merlin, be our wand." He turns to his left, to face south, "Prometheus, be our sword." He turns once again to face west, and declares, "Morgaine, be our cup." At last he faces north and says, "Gudrun, be our pentacle."

Now Darren invokes the May Queen, a young woman dressed in green and white, with flowers in her hair, who is brought into the circle by her two attendants. The participants chant:

Lady, come, come in, come through
Lady, join the work we do.
Come down, Lady; now she is near.
She is coming, she is coming,
She is here!

Suddenly the Winter Queen, dressed in snowy white tulle and lace, enters with her two attendants, crying, "And so am I!" Laurel, the Teaser, who has been trying desperately to get everyone's attention to warn them about the presence of the Winter Queen, says in a stage whisper, "Oh-oh. We're in big trouble."

The priestess tries valiantly to persuade the Winter Queen to leave, but to no avail; everyone knows she won't give up her reign easily. She and the May Queen must fight for sovereignty over the land. The two queens and their attendants square off in the center of the circle, clacking their staffs together in a mock fight. At last the Winter Queen yields, as she must every year, and the crowd erupts in cheers.

The triumphant May Queen calls in her consort, Jack-in-the-Green, a young man dressed in fabric leaves, who runs into the center of the circle and kneels at her feet. He whistles, and his attendants arrive, bearing the maypole, decorated with ribbons and garlands; as it passes by, many hands reach out to touch it, to gain for themselves a little of its power. The pole is erected in the circle's center, and soon we all take a ribbon and begin to dance the maypole dance, weaving the ribbons over and under. As we dance, we sing:

For she will bring the buds in the spring
And laugh among the flowers
In summer's heat her kisses are sweet
She sings in leafy bowers.
She cuts the cane and gathers the grain
When fruits of fall surround her.
Her bones grow old; in wintry cold
She wraps her cloak around her.

Meanwhile the May Queen and Jack-in-the-Green hold the maypole between them as they kiss and caress each other. To the crowd's delight and amusement, Jack occasionally strokes the maypole, which appears to be rising from his groin. For Pagans, Beltane is the celebration of the union of the male and female energies in nature that leads to the fruitfulness of summer's bounty, and the actors take their assigned roles quite seriously. Soon, the whole maypole is sheathed in a bright braided covering of ribbons. The May Queen calls the drop, and we all move forward toward the pole, willing the energy into the earth for the fruitfulness of the soil and crops.

Now Laurel, the Teaser, moves into the center of the circle. "You know what time it is, don't you?" she teases the crowd. "It's time to call him in—the 'Oss! 'Oss, 'Oss!" She calls.

"Wee 'Oss!" the crowd roars in response. " 'Oss, 'Oss! Wee 'Oss!

'Oss 'Oss! Wee 'Oss!"

Suddenly, from the far end of the meadow, the 'Oss emerges from his hiding place. He moves majestically over the green grass, black skirt and mane streaming in the breeze. Although up close the heavy wood and metal frame is cumbersome and awkward, from a distance, he looks powerful and otherworldly; there is something profoundly chthonic and moving about him that makes the hair on my arms stand on end. The crowd is hushed, and I feel a thrill as the circle opens to let him in.

Now the 'Oss and Teaser begin their mirroring dance. Don, inside the 'Oss costume, cannot see past the end of the large frame he carries on his shoulders, so Teaser's crucial role is to guide him by moving as she wants him to move, ensuring that he does not strike people with the heavy hoop or trample small children who dart in and out between his legs—for it is good luck to be caught under the 'Oss. It is Teaser who tells the 'Oss when to twirl, when to go forward and back, dodge or feint, and this is done entirely through body movements.

The performance of the 'Oss and Teaser is accompanied by the sound of the choir Gaia's Voice singing Padstow's traditional May song:

Unite and unite and let us all unite
For summer is a-come in today;
And whither we are going, we shall all unite
In the merry morning of May.

Oh where is King George? Oh where is he now?
He's out in his long boat all on the deep salt sea.

When the chorus sings the "King George" verse, which has a slower tempo than the other lively verses, the 'Oss stops and settles to the ground. Teaser pretends to coax him, and finally in exasperation kicks him. At last a little girl is called forth to kiss the 'Oss, and only this persuades him to rise again. But he exacts revenge by butting Teaser and knocking her down several times, much to the crowd's delight. Finally a bucket of water is brought in for the 'Oss; he dips his "beard" into it and twirls, spraying the crowd. People eagerly rush forward to catch the droplets, which are considered a blessing.

Suddenly, after the 'Oss has drunk and sprayed the crowd, Laurel comes up behind me and grabs me by the shoulders, hurling me under the 'Oss's skirt. "Here's for your book!" she shouts. "Wait, wait!" I cry; but it's too late; I am tumbling in the dark. Don is so tall I can stand upright beneath the hoop and I discover I can dance with the 'Oss—dancing is in fact the secret to avoid being crushed. We dance for a moment or two, until I emerge again into the May sun and the cheering crowd.

At last the ritual is winding down. Jack and the May Queen bless the bread and ale, and carry them around the circle so all can have a taste. The priest salutes the spirits attending, and the priestess unwinds the circle, saying: "Around, around, it shall go to ground and not rebound." All gather around the staff in the center of the circle; those who can, reach out to touch it, and those who are too far away touch someone next to them who can touch another person whose hand is on the staff. The energy is driven into the ground with a chant:

Let the power pass from me to end where it was begun
As I will so mote it be, chant the spell and be it done.

The priestess opens the circle with the formula "The circle is open, but unbroken. Merry meet, and merry part, and merry meet again."

## Neo-Paganism and Ethnic Identity

In the last chapter, I examined how Pagans use their embodied experiences to create an identity oppositional to both mainstream-secular and Christian cultures. In this chapter I explore how Neo-Pagans create authenticity by using material from a variety of cultural sources in their rituals and folklore. I am particularly interested in how Neo-Paganism and revival Witchcraft interact with notions of ethnicity and identity in the surrounding culture: how Pagans and Witches perceive their own cultural heritage and its relationship to their magical practice. What is the relationship between Neo-Paganism, Witchcraft, and ethnic identity? How do Neo-Pagans and Witches construct or express identity through their use of folklore in a ritual context? And how does the movement intersect with broader cultural trends, such as the twin processes of globalization and localization, and the hybridity that results from cross-cultural contact?

These questions lead into a thicket of issues around the definition of culture as commodity or property, cultural ownership, transnationalism, and transculturation—all part of the American cultural landscape of the early twenty-first century. As we have seen throughout this work, Neo-Pagans are bricoleurs, who may combine material from a number of different cultural and historical traditions within a single ritual to construct an aesthetically pleasing whole. It is an aesthetic impulse, rather than a commercial one, that motivates Neo-Pagan cultural borrowing: the poetics of ritual involve creativity, imagination, variation, and improvisation. Neo-Pagan notions of spiritual authenticity locate this quality in the folklore and customs of historical or contemporary indigenous peoples. Their appearance in ritual is often in order to enhance a sense of the sacred as "authentic." Because Neo-Pagans are overwhelmingly middle-class Americans, they have at their disposal, through books, college courses, the Internet, and television, a wealth of information about the folklore and ritual practices of other cultures and historical periods, and they make use of this information to create a new culture. This practice has led to accusations that Neo-Pagans borrow, appropriate, or steal from other cultural traditions. In this chapter, I hope to examine these issues, laying bare the complexity of the relationship between ethnicity, identity, authenticity, and practice in American culture.

In defining *ethnicity* and *identity*, I draw from the literature that emerged from the postmodern historical critiques of cultural categories previously understood as "natural" or essential (Anderson, 1983; Hobsbawm and Ranger, 1983; Sollors, 1989). According to this theoretical current, categories such as race, nationality, and ethnicity, which at first glance appear essential or inherent, can be regarded as "inventions," in the sense of "widely shared, though intensely debated, collective fictions that are continually reinvented" (Sollors, 1989:xi). By adopting this stance, I am neither denying the existence of real cultural differences between groups, nor asserting that expressions of ethnic identity are not genuine for tradition bearers. Instead, I posit that ethnic groups, as we think of them today, are not static, stable entities with a set of essential characteristics that exist relatively unchanged through time. Instead, as Werner Sollors proposes, ethnicity as a construct emerges in situations of cultural contact as a strategy of self-definition through opposition (Sollors, 1989:xiv). What we take for granted today as America's ethnic groups emerged during the nineteenth century, as the American nation was shaping itself; identity crystallized in an atmosphere of intercultural contact. Our assumptions about ethnic groups carry the legacy of European Romanticism, with its emphasis on authenticity reflected in a group's folklore and other cultural productions (Sollors, 1989:xiv; Bendix, 1997:4): we tend to imagine ethnic groups as natural, eternal, stable entities with ties based on blood and kinship, each with its own set of traits, myths, and cultural capital. But in fact, as anthropologist Michael Fischer suggests, "ethnicity is something reinvented and reinterpreted in each generation [and] by each individual," often in ways that remain fairly obscure and impenetrable even to the artists and recreators themselves

(Fischer, 1986:195). While I view ethnicity as a construct, a process that involves constant reinvention and reinterpretation, this view is by no means shared by either my Neo-Pagan and Witchen subjects, nor the general American culture of the late twentieth and early twenty-first century. Instead, as I will illustrate below, many popular notions of ethnicity and identity are rooted in nineteenth-century ideas about blood and origins. American Neo-Paganism both embraces and presents alternatives to these ideas.

Neo-Paganism, by definition, attempts to reclaim, reconstruct, and experiment with the pre-Christian traditions of European indigenous peoples. But American Neo-Pagans face special dilemmas in the construction of culture and identity, in contrast to their European cousins; for it is not easy to practice folklore reclamation in a multiethnic society. Most European nations today also include a variety of ethnic groups, and have since their formation in the eighteenth and nineteenth centuries. But European nations developed under the aegis of Romantic nationalism and Herder's ideal of the *Volksiele*, the national soul, which presumed, at least theoretically, that all inhabitants of a nation were united by a common language, culture, and ethnic identity. These shared traits were in fact the impetus for the formation of many European nationalist movements that strove for independence and self-determination. The nations of North America—Canada and the United States—developed under strikingly different conditions. Historically, the presence of numerous ethnic, racial, religious, and even linguistic groups has been a given. American society has been made up not only of European immigrants from various nations, but by native American peoples from a variety of different ethnic and linguistic families, Africans brought to the New World as slaves, and Asians initially enticed to the Pacific coast to work low-wage jobs. The United States motto, "E pluribus unum" (Out of many, one), referred not only to the issue of states' rights in a federalist republic, but to the necessity of constructing a common identity among immigrants who hailed from a variety of cultural and religious traditions. Cultural and religious pluralism has always been a feature of American society. At the same time, the emergent American ideology emphasized the importance of the individual in society; self-determination and development are the leitmotifs that form a counter to the melody of American pluralism: as historian Robert Kelley explains, the American cultural pattern includes the "paradoxical idea that unified peoplehood emerges from the exercise of individual liberties" (Kelley, quoted in Griffin, 1998:2). Both strains—individualism as well as notions of pluralism—are reflected in American Neo-Paganism.

Throughout their history, Americans have developed various tropes to address this cultural paradox. Edward Griffin identifies three, which he calls "melting-pot," "vegetable soup," and "martini cocktail" (Griffin, 1998:1). The melting-pot trope, which emerged already in the late eighteenth century, emphasizes the transformation of the immigrant in the crucible of the new nation into an essentially new man, completely separated from the customs and worldviews of the old world. Old-world forms disappear in the process of fusion that characterizes the melting pot. The melting-pot metaphor faced successive challenges from new waves of immigrants who initially appeared "unmeltable," but it persisted as the principal metaphor of unity through transformation in America until the 1960s. The civil rights movements of that decade exposed the fact that the "new man" that emerged from the so-called melting pot excluded African Americans, Native Americans, Latinos, women, homosexuals, and many other marginalized groups, whose American experience did not include a shared identity with the mainstream (Griffin, 1998:3). New scholarship focused on the so-called unmeltable ethnics, southern and eastern Europeans who maintained cultural, religious, and linguistic traditions through several generations in the urban enclaves of the East and Midwest. A new trope emerged to address changing conceptions of unity and identity: variously called "vegetable soup," "salad bowl," "mosaic," or "tapestry," it emphasized the retention of ethnic and cultural distinctiveness that enriched the American cultural whole (Griffin, 1998:4). This trope became central to multiculturalism, the idea that each culture's unique distinctiveness must be honored in order to protect the legitimacy of the larger American culture, with its respect for the rights of the individual. But multiculturalism drew political fire during the 1990s from both the right and the left. As the right agitated for shared standards, whether in respect to language, merit, or allegiance, that applied equally to all Americans, the left, influenced by the works of poststructuralists such as Michel Foucault, increasingly focused on issues of power. In the emerging view of American culture, plurality was overwritten by the categories of oppressor and oppressed. According to this paradigm, "an entrenched, powerful ruling class calculatedly imposes its cultural and ideological will upon an oppressed minority" (Griffin, 1998:5). Difference necessarily related to power; ethnic, racial, religious, and gendered groups could now be sorted into one of two categories, the hegemony or the subdominant classes. A new metaphor, which Griffin calls the martini cocktail, emerged: society, according to this formulation, was composed on three parts "raw, powerful but colorless gin," one part vermouth (colorful and flavorful, but overpowered by the gin), and the tiny olive garnish (Griffin, 1998:4). According to this paradigm, American plurality exists only within the subdominant groups, whose cultures are "flavorful" and "of color," but victimized by a powerful, white, and flavorless hegemony. All white ethnicities are subsumed under "white" culture. Griffin sees the culture wars within the academic and political left as emerging from the warring paradigms of multiculturalism versus the Gramscian construct of hegemony versus the subdominant classes (Griffin, 1998:5–10).

It is against this larger backdrop of the political and social construction of difference that we must understand the complex relationship between Neo-

Paganism and ethnic identity. In the racially and culturally diverse, left-leaning San Francisco Bay Area, where the bulk of my fieldwork was conducted, Asians, African Americans, Latinos, Native Americans, and Pacific Islanders constituted "marked" ethnic categories during the late 1990s and early 2000s. The category "white" was commonly believed to subsume all other ethnic groups, and to constitute an Anglo-American dominant culture; in fact it was often combined or replaced with "Anglo" on forms that requested an ethnic and racial affiliation.

How do Neo-Pagans situate themselves along this cultural continuum of identity and ethnicity? Quantitative studies of Neo-Pagans have usually described them as white and middle class—clearly within the hegemonic category (Adler, 1986; Orion, 1995; Hartman, 1976; Jorgensen and Jorgensen, 1982; Kirkpatrick, Rainey, and Rubi, 1984; Ludeke, 1989), and my data echoes this. The majority (80 percent, according to Hartman, 1976) are of northern and central European descent; the largest group of these identify as being at least partly of English, Welsh, Irish, or Scottish extraction. Most are several generations removed from immigration and have lost language, verbal folklore, and other overt markers of ethnicity. Because of acculturation and intermarriage, the observance of nonverbal genres, such as music, custom, and ritual, has also decreased.

In response to questions about their ethnic background, many Pagans I interviewed described themselves as "mixed," "mutts," or "Euro-mongrel," indicating that they recognized a variety of European ethnicities in their background. A few answered "I'm nothing," a response that can only be understood in light of current definitions of race and ethnicity in which white ethnics become unmarked in contrast to marked categories of ethnic identification. Thus they may feel they *have* no ethnicity and therefore are "nothing." Some Pagans may also feel that compared to the colorful public traditions of more marked ethnic groups, the traditions preserved in their own families are more mainstream, "nothing interesting." "[White] people in America don't get to be ethnic," complained Laurel, who describes herself as being of mixed northern European heritage. Taking a broader social view, Don mused, "Society has moved away from rituals, creating a situation in which people lose their sense of belonging to a particular culture." Part of the function of rituals, according to this view, is to publicly mark their practitioners as belonging to a specific culture or ethnicity. For Pagans in this category, cultural borrowing may be a form of compensation for feelings of loss of distinctiveness, as white ethnics become increasingly associated with a colorless dominant culture.

However, the composition of this movement cannot be easily reduced to ethnic and racial formulas, and applying this principle to all Neo-Pagans would be an oversimplification. My data suggests that not all Pagans are of northern European extraction, and not all get involved in the movement to compensate for a lack of ethnic rituals and traditions. The Gardnerian coven in Berkeley, California, in which I participated for over a year included a remarkably large percentage of immigrants and first-generation Americans, including individuals of Korean, Russian-Jewish, Irish-German, and Italian descent.[1] These individuals felt strongly connected to their cultures of origin, retaining language, contacts in the nation of ancestry, and many customs and traditions that they continued to practice along with Wicca. Some interpreted their involvement in the Craft as a way of maintaining ties to these customs in a new cultural context.

Suzi, whose grandmother had been a *mudang* (shaman) in Korea, saw herself as continuing a family tradition of communicating with the spirit world, albeit in a different form. She explained:

> I never saw [my grandmother] doing her ritual work because I was too young. By the time I was old enough to understand, she was not practicing anymore due to illness and she died before I really had a chance to know her. . . . There are, however, many family stories about her and the work she did—stories from my mother and her siblings. She had her spirit guides who helped her, . . . four of them. She used to have their portraits. . . . She would go into trance and dance on the sharp edges of big kitchen knives and of course there would be special traditional music playing—the ritual is called a *kut*. Sometimes she would have messages for people, or blessings. . . . I feel very close to my grandmother and I believe she has influenced me throughout my life, especially in my spiritual work and development.

For others, involvement in the movement becomes a way to revive and recontextualize elements from their ethnic heritage which are devalued by the dominant culture. This is clearly the case for many practitioners of Stregheria, or Italian American Witchcraft, as I have argued elsewhere at length (Magliocco, 2003). Beginning with the late Leo Martello in the 1970s, some Italian Americans have interpreted a family practice of vernacular magic and healing as evidence that they belonged to a line of goddess-worshipping Witches stretching back to Leland's Aradia and beyond. This interpretation reached its apotheosis in the works of Raven Grimassi, a California Witch and prolific author of popular Craft books. Born in Pittsburgh in 1951, Grimassi is the son of an American father and an Italian mother. He claims to have been initiated as an adolescent by his aunt into a family tradition of magical practice. His mother's family preserved a number of magical traditions, including removal of the evil eye, the making of curative liqueurs and tonics, divination, and folk healing, which Grimassi's mother brought with her to the United States. Drawing inspiration from the works of Charles G. Leland and of Italian Americans such as Leo Martello and Lori Bruno, Grimassi began to interpret many aspects of his mother's folk culture as evidence that they preserved the ancient religion of Etruria, which he identified as Witchcraft. His popular books *The Ways of the Strega* (1995), *Hereditary Witchcraft* (1999), and *Italian Witchcraft* (2000) detail a system of beliefs, rituals, and practices largely based on Gardnerian Craft, but with an Italian accent: the deities, names of the sabbats, and types of spirits honored are all drawn from Italian folklore books and academic treatises on Etruscan archeology. They also include a small selection of spells for removing the evil eye, finding lost objects, and making protective amulets with many analogues in folklore collections and Italian folklore archives. These books have sold approximately sixty thousand copies apiece, becoming Pagan best sellers, and have spawned a plethora of Web sites and covens dedicated to *Stregheria*.

For Italian Americans whose vernacular Catholicism was often misinterpreted and labeled "pagan" by the Irish-dominated American clergy, and whose healing rituals, evil-eye beliefs, and ecstatic religious practices were branded as "witchcraft" by educators and social workers, Grimassi's concoction is a potent brew of folklore reclamation and ethnic identity creation. Stregheria and other forms of ethnic revival Witchcraft revalue ethnic folklore and vernacular religion that were devalued by progressivist discourses and metaphors of ethnic acculturation and "melting." Instead of being viewed as signs of backwardness, folk magical practices are recast as a complex system of occult knowledge going back to the ancient Etruscans; rather than being regarded as superstitious nonsense, they become evidence of peasant resistance. Even when immigrants have preserved some beliefs and practices, they often exist in the context of a diaspora whose lifeways are radically different from the peasant context in which they existed before immigration. Grimassi offers a new backdrop against which the old practices can be understood. Italian American Witches can now interpret almost any folk practice in their family as a sign that they are the heirs to an ancient mystical religion.

This mechanism, through which family traditions and folklore are interpreted as evidence of perpetuating an ancient pre-Christian pagan religion, is not limited to Italian American Witches, but is one of the fundamental ways Neo-Pagans, especially Witches, create a personal identity and authenticate their practices. Often calling themselves practitioners of "family traditions," American Witches from a variety of ethnic backgrounds look to their own families for folklore that could point to a tradition of Pagan practice. Jenny, an Ohio Witch whose family had come north from the hills of Kentucky after the collapse of the coal industry, remembered that her grandmother had been able to see ghosts and had planted "by the signs." For her, this was evidence enough that her grandmother had actually preserved fragments of the Old Religion. Instead of devaluing the traditional beliefs and practices of her mountain relatives as signs of their "hillbilly" status, Jenny chose to recontextualize them as elements that gave her prestige and authenticity in her new religion. For her, as for Italian American Witches, Neo-Paganism becomes not a compensatory mechanism for a lack of rituals and traditions, but a tactic of resistance against the rhetoric of acculturation and the forces of positivist rationalism that combine to devalue traditional folk beliefs and practices. By reclaiming these,

American Witches also reclaim for themselves an identity as a "marked," and thus "authentic" and significant, social category.

In other circumstances, Neo-Paganism provides a context for Americans who grow up practicing non-European, non-Christian religions to find acceptance in an otherwise hostile setting. Padma, a South Asian American who grew up in a small Midwestern town where her father was a college professor, described her family as "nominally Hindu, but basically nonreligious." Hers was the only South Asian family in the community, and she and her siblings often felt isolated and misunderstood. In high school, she met a classmate who identified as a Witch, who, in contrast to classmates who marginalized her and thought her weird, was fascinated with Padma's polytheistic Hindu heritage. Through her, Padma met other Pagans who were friendly and accepting, and developed a greater interest in her family's customs: "I started feeling more proud of who I was instead of embarrassed that my family did these weird things, had these weird beliefs," she explained. In the late 1990s she was attending university in a city with a substantial South Asian population, and had a wider social network of friends with her own ethnic and religious background, among whom she found support and understanding. Nevertheless, she has maintained her friendship with the woman who first befriended her, and occasionally attends Neo-Pagan rituals and events. "I do think of myself as a Pagan because I practice a non-Christian, polytheistic religion," she said, "although my Paganism is different from [that of American Neo-Pagans and Witches], even though we do a lot of the same things."

Padma's identification with Pagans reflects a broader trend among non-Christian groups in Interfaith movements around the globe. According to the Interfaith representatives from Covenant of the Goddess, a Wiccan networking organization that has participated in global interfaith events since 1993, American Wiccans have been successful in representing themselves to the Interfaith community as practitioners of indigenous European religions. They have forged strong alliances with other indigenous religions from around the world, including a number of African, Asian, and American religions, and now often form voting blocks with representatives of these other faiths. Like Padma, many members of traditional non-Christian polytheistic religions recognize a basic set of shared assumptions and practices common to them and Neo-Pagans; this mutual recognition makes possible Interfaith networking and alliances.

## Neo-Paganism and Cultural Borrowing

At home, however, American Neo-Pagans' relationships with practitioners of indigenous religions has been more problematic. Pagans have often been criticized by outsiders, especially by Native Americans, for appropriating the cultural traditions of other ethnic groups (Eller, 1995:67–81; Pike, 2001:123–54). Pike, for example, describes how Native American critics Martina Looking Horse and Wendy Rose have argued that Native American cultures have become objectified signifiers of spiritual authenticity and spirituality to white people. When whites dress as Indians or borrow Indian customs and practices, they perpetuate colonialism, racism and "cultural strip mining" (Pike, 2001:134–35). Particularly threatening to Native Americans is the commodification of their sacred practices and ritual objects in ways that render them endlessly reproducible and accessible to anyone willing to pay. "These critics are offended by expensive weekend 'vision quests' and by 'bestsellers' with a 'tenuous hold on facts' written by non-Natives. . . . For many American Indians, financial competition and the false assumption of cultural authority by outsiders makes cultural appropriation intolerable" (Pike, 2001:136).

The same parallels between Neo-Pagan and indigenous practices that make networking and alliance-building possible can also create confusion and lead to resentment. In at least one case, the accusers themselves were unclear about which customs were appropriated and which represented parallel developments in separate spiritual traditions. At the 1993 Parliament of World Religions in Chicago, a group of Lakota elders formally declared war on all those engaged in the "abuse and sacrilege" of their sacred traditions. Among the long list of culprits were Neo-Pagans. The Lakota Elders objected to practices such as the use of Native American chants, ritual sweat lodges, and smudging (purification using burning sage) by non-Natives. But they also interpreted the Neo-Pagan practices of worshipping in circle, invoking the four directions, and purifying with burning incense as imitations of their own practices. Members of Covenant of the Goddess also present at the parliament responded to the accusations by personally contacting a representative of the Lakota delegation. They explained that the origin of some of the practices criticized by the Native American delegation lay in European magical practice, and denied the practice of cultural borrowing. While the two groups ultimately performed a public ceremony together to demonstrate their new mutual understanding and alliance, the larger debate over Neo-Pagan borrowing is far from settled. Native Americans and other groups whose traditions have been borrowed have heavily criticized Neo-Pagans for cultural appropriation, while many Pagans continue to justify cultural borrowing as important to their own personal spiritual development (Pike, 2001:137).

In approaching this issue, it is important to point out that terms such as "cultural borrowing," or the more forceful "appropriation" and "theft," presuppose a view of culture as a commodity, a thing that can be possessed, objectified, exchanged, and imitated. This view emerged during the twentieth century as cultural productions increasingly became commodified and copyrighted to individuals. In this paradigm, culture is a limited good: as Mary

Lefkowitz points out in *Not out of Africa*, these "metaphors . . . make it appear that the discussion is about tangible objects rather than about ideas. The confusion obscures an important difference: if I borrow your car, you do not have it until I return it; if I borrow your ideas, you still have [them] to keep and use, whatever I go off and choose to do with them" (1999:188).

There is, however, another view of culture, proposed by Deborah Kapchan (2002), that needs to be considered in this discussion: that of culture as a *possessing*, as well as a possessable, entity. Building on the metaphor of spirit possession, Kapchan argues that "possession requires an alchemical reaction, a transmutation of subtle and dense matter as two different substances encounter and change each other. Culture inhabits us in similar ways. It lives within the confines of our flesh like a second nature" (Kapchan, 2002:4). The concepts of culture as both something that can be possessed and something that possesses us are not mutually exclusive; in fact, culture may come to possess us exactly when we reach out and make it our own. Moreover, as we have already seen, culture becomes evident only by contrast with something that is recognized as "other": "Culture, because it lives in the unconscious recesses of the nerves and organs, comes to light when it encounters difference—as when liquid hits air, or water turns to gas" (Kapchan, 2002:4). In discussing the issue of cultural borrowing and appropriation, it is evident that both Pagans and their critics shift their perceptions of culture as both a possession and a possessing force. It is also important to note that criticisms of cultural appropriation (and defenses of the practice) are not neutral or objective, but like all statements, reflect the positionality of the speakers. Just as Pagans stand to gain from arguments that culture is a possessing entity, that it chooses them, rather than the other way around, so Native Americans and other critics have a vested interest in constructions of culture as a commodity when it affords them legal protection from those who would continue to exploit them.

Having said this, it is evident that, despite their protestations to the contrary, contemporary Witches and Pagans do indeed use folklore from a variety of sources in their rituals and practices. Folklore, as we have seen throughout this book, is construed as a seal of authenticity—a link to pre-Christian European practices, or those of contemporary indigenous peoples who, like indigenous Europeans, are thought to have a more spiritual relationship to the earth and the divine. It might be useful at this point to examine in detail exactly how Pagans in the San Francisco Bay Area community use folklore from other cultural traditions, and how they explain their practices. In exploring these issues, I will argue that Pagans' use of folklore involves two different systems for constructing authenticity: one based on notions of ethnic or blood connections to a particular tradition—Tzvetan Todorov's (1993) "relativist" position—and another based on more universalist notions of human similarities. Both strategies are ultimately based on a desire to return to origins, in the belief that earlier cultures had a relationship with nature and divinity that we have lost.

## Relativist Attitudes: The Celtic Twilight Zone

Wicca and certain Neo-Pagan traditions such as Druidism are usually presented as Celtic in origins and flavor, hearkening back to the religions of the pre-Roman Celts who inhabited much of northern Europe. Given the ethnic composition of the large majority of Neo-Pagans, it is understandable why many would be attracted to a religion which purports to be similar to that of their ancestors.[2] Much of contemporary Wicca draws heavily from Celtic pantheons and constructs itself as Celtic in origins. Yet there is little evidence for the Celtic origins of Gardnerian practice; we have already seen how it was cobbled together from a combination of European ceremonial magic and interpretations furnished by Leland, Murray, and Frazer. What accounts for the notion that the Craft is particularly Celtic?

What we know of the pre-Christian religions of the Gauls, Britons, and Gaels, though admittedly filtered through the eyes of their Roman conquerors, bears little resemblance to either European ceremonial magic or to contemporary Wiccan practice (Fairgrove, 1997; Jones and Pennick, 1995). It is possible that the attribution of a Celtic heritage to Wicca was the contribution of Doreen Valiente, one of Gardner's initiates and his high priestess from 1951 to 1953. Perhaps inspired by Margaret Murray's understanding of the origins of Scottish witchcraft in Celtic fertility religions, Valiente grafted material from Alexander Carmichael's *Carmine Gadelica* (1928) into some of the sabbat rituals. It is difficult to know whether their choice was motivated by aesthetic or by political concerns; in any case, the two may have been intertwined. In wartime England, after Gardner joined the Crotona Fellowship and began to acquire the Wiccan materials, the Greco-Roman flavor of some of its Neoplatonic motifs may have had an unsavory association with fascist Italy in the minds of English practitioners. During fascism, Italy's leader Benito Mussolini drew on Classical images to construct itself as the successor of the Roman empire and justify its colonial expansion into North Africa. It would be understandable if English Witches of that era wished to disassociate themselves from fascist imagery as much as possible. They may have decided to turn to more recognizably British deities in the construction of their rituals. Since the Germanic mythology linked to Britain's Anglo-Saxon heritage was similarly tainted due to its use by Hitler's Third Reich, this left Celtic mythology as a safe choice to be mined for tales, rituals, and deities, which, according to the scholarship of the period, could be superimposed upon Classical deities in more or less a one-to-one correspondence. Celtic cultures had been heavily romanticized and documented by nineteenth-century folklorists, who often compared them to Native Americans. Celts had acquired a cachet as the "noble savages" of Europe. If this hypothesis is correct, it suggests that Wicca's Celtic identity is the result of a splicing of traditions: a Celtic overlay on top of magical traditions that already had gone through a variety of cultural transformations. Neo-Pagan borrowing and identity politics are deeply embedded in the movement's history and tradition.

British traditionalists such as Gardnerians are among those most likely to assert that they have no interest in borrowing the cultural practices of others because they have a well-delineated text-based tradition preserved in Books of Shadows. Gardnerian Books of Shadows are "oathbound"—that is, secret materials available only to initiates, which they swear not to publish or reveal to noninitiates. The exclusive nature of Gardnerian Books of Shadows and the ceremony and conservatism with which they are preserved gives them an imprimatur of authenticity. British traditionalists are culturally conservative, and while they do innovate, they feel little need to draw from the traditions of others. When they do turn to outside sources, it is most often to other British material, to literary and occult texts, or occasionally to sources from Classical antiquity. Gardnerian Books of Shadows already contain quite a bit of this type of material—for instance, songs adapted from the works of Rudyard Kipling and names of deities drawn from the Welsh *Mabinogion*. Many Gardnerians in fact display outrage that *their* traditions, from which other forms of Neo-Paganism draw heavily, have been appropriated by other groups.

## Reactions

The predominance of Celticity in Neo-Paganism has, predictably, spawned a whole spate of new traditions focused on the magical heritage of a different ethnic group or geographic area. Notions of heritage conservation are sometimes at the root of individuals' attraction to these traditions. Raven Grimassi, the architect of Stregheria, or Italian American popular Witchcraft, explained that he was first inspired to develop an Italian tradition in response to Celtic witches who accused him, as an Italian—and thus, in their eyes, a descendant of ancient Romans—of cultural imperialism and the genocide of the Celtic peoples of Gaul and Britain. Some Jewish Pagans have attempted to reconstruct and revive aspects of Caananite religion as a way to maintain a link to their Jewish identity while exploring the roots of the more pagan elements of Jewish ritual. Melissa, who grew up Jewish, found the Celtic emphasis of Wicca unsatisfying, and began to explore the religion of ancient Egypt, reasoning that her ancestors had once hailed from an Egypt-dominated area: "One thing I discovered from reading was that everyone was doing Celtic work, and I'm not Celtic. I wanted to work with my own ancestors, so I started looking at the Egyptian pantheon; and Ma'at really struck me. Themis was another one . . . the goddess of truth and the goddess of wisdom."

San Francisco's Reclaiming tradition draws predominantly from the Celtic pantheon in the creation of public sabbats for the extended Pagan community: the goddess Brigid and the god Lugh are its public tutelary deities. But because Reclaiming also wishes to diversify, drawing in participants from nonwhite backgrounds and cultures, this sometimes causes conflicts. For nonwhite, non-European Witches, the Celtic pantheon is not always the most satisfactory symbol set. Carolina DeRobertis, a Latina Witch and Reclaiming priestess, explained how the development of her feminist political consciousness and her identity as a lesbian alienated her from her family and cultural roots: "From my cultural vantage point, becoming free and liberated has often seemed synonymous with leaving behind the Latina in me, getting 'White-washed,' melting-potted, losing or betraying the culture I come from. . . . Being ME meant being a Witch: working with the Goddess, magic, the sacred elements, the sacredness in all things." (DeRobertis, 1999:4). At first, Carolina found that working with what she calls the "Anglo" deities of Reclaiming (in reality, Brigid and Lugh are drawn from a Celtic pantheon, not an Anglo-Saxon one) was empowering. Ultimately, though, she concluded that "leaving your heritage behind and throwing away the key is not the answer. It is ultimately not empowering because it does not allow you to realize your whole being" (5).

At Reclaiming's Brigid ritual, Carolina had a powerful vision of the Virgin of Guadalupe, who said to her, "*I am Brigid; I am here too. Behold my well! Throughout the ages, across all lands, people have given me sacred names. . . . Every name, every face is part of the story. Do not hold us separate, do not be afraid; where we meet, there is great joy! I too can bring you to this well of healing, these bright fires, this forge of action in my name. Call my name and I will guide you. Through all my names, my love pours out. . . . I am Brigid, I am Brigid too. Que esté benedicida*" (57).

Because of this experience, Carolina became devoted to the Virgin of Guadalupe, whom she interprets as "a . . . Goddess in her own right, based largely on the ancient Aztec Goddesses Tonantzin and Coatlicue" (1999:5). She urged Reclaiming,

> If we truly welcome all races and wish to embrace diversity, it does not make sense to expect people of color to assimilate to working with primarily Celtic deities. Assimilation to a White mainstream is, after all, a perpetual imposition that people of color in our world know only too well. . . . How might such perspectives, once heard and acknowledged, affect the way we do community magic? . . . the four directions called in four languages? A blending of traditions and deities from different cultures into one ritual? Perhaps a summer solstice rite with Amaterasu, Japanese sun Goddess, as she sets into the belly of Yemaya, African Goddess of the seas?

Ironically, however, when Reclaiming has attempted to diversify its cultural symbol set, it has drawn criticism from Witches and Pagans who are sensitive to issues of cultural appropriation and the exploitation of indigenous cultures. In the summer of 2001, Reclaiming's Witch camp in the Mendocino Woodlands was based on a story drawn from the Hindu *Mahabharata*: the princess Savitri's adventure to free her husband Satyavan (Truth) from the grasp of

Lord Yama (Death). This story was adopted in part because of the impetus of Witch camp teacher Beverly Fredrick, who had recently returned from India, where she studied meditation and yoga. It was evident that her experience had deeply affected both her spirituality and sense of aesthetics. The adoption of this tale was also an attempt on Reclaiming's part to honor cultural diversity. However, it provoked some critical responses from Witch camp attendees. One woman wrote:

I generally prefer rituals based on European folk narratives. This is strictly a personal preference, because I connect better with this more familiar material. But on a broader level, the borrowing and adaptation of a living tradition which does not belong to us (and most of us are European Americans) concerns me. In fact I found this whole Witch Camp permeated by concepts borrowed from Hinduism—devotion, prayer, meditation, knowing the deities through contemplative merging—that don't mix very well with Witchcraft. I have spent a lifetime getting away from the ideas of religion as devotion and prayer, and I already had my fling with Eastern religions back in my college days. I am looking for a more active, reciprocal relationship with deity. One of the great powers of Witchcraft is spellwork, which is not devotional but interactional; you don't adore the deity, but work alongside her to bring about change in the universe. This is the kind of Witchcraft I want to practice, not some hybridized, decontextualized Hinduism. (camp evaluation form, Reclaiming Witch camp, Mendocino, California, July 2001)

For this critic, Reclaiming's attempt to include diversity failed on two levels: first, because of her concern over issues of cultural appropriation and decontextualization; and secondly, because she rejected Hindu models of worship in favor of Witchcraft's more interactional, reciprocal ideal. When it comes to the thorny issues of multiculturalism and respect for other cultural traditions, it seems at times that Witchcraft cannot win for trying.

Ultimately, though, ethnic and cultural denominations within Neo-Paganism boil down to differences in flavor, but not in essence. As Pitch put it: "We Pagans use a very strong classification system for Witchcraft based on ethnicity and culture—contemporary or mythohistorical . . . but we tend to use a more or less common tool kit to approach these ethnic varietals. . . . Ethnicity becomes an inflection on a common approach to magic."

For a few Pagans, however, ethnic connections to practice take on a central importance, leading to blood-right arguments with a disturbing cast. A few members of European revivalist traditions argue for the influence of morphogenetic fields, a notion of culture as genetically embedded in DNA, on spiritual practice. According to this argument, religious and cultural information is genetically encoded in each individual based on his or her ethnic and racial heritage; individuals are drawn to, and have genetically encoded knowledge about, the spiritual practices of their ancestors, and conversely are repelled by and incapable of excelling in "noncompatible" traditions. Some members of the Asatru Norse reconstructionist tradition claim that only those of Teutonic heritage can practice Norse Paganism.[3] One member told me that the reason runes, a divinatory device based on an early Teutonic alphabet, did not appear to forecast accurately for me was because I had no Germanic heritage. A few Odinist groups mix the Neo-Pagan reclamation of Scandinavian and Germanic gods and goddesses with racist notions of white supremacy and anti-Semitism. Not surprisingly, such groups do not borrow from other cultural traditions whose practices might "contaminate" the heritage they believe they are reviving. These are, however, a very small percentage of North American Pagans, and are not represented in the left-leaning San Francisco Bay Area.

## 'Oss, 'Oss, Wee 'Oss Redux: A Case Study in Borrowing Folk Traditions

For more eclectic groups, on the other hand, borrowing folk traditions may be a sine qua non. This is certainly the case for NROOGD, which uses European folk traditions as the basis for many of their sabbats, such as the Beltane described at the beginning of this chapter. It may be useful in this context to examine how a May Day custom from the small Cornish town of Padstow was adapted to become an American Neo-Pagan Beltane ritual.

The two principal designers of NROOGD's hobbyhorse May ritual were priestesses Laurel Olson and Leigh Ann Hussey. In the early 1980s, Leigh Ann was associated with the Institute for Celtic Studies, a Berkeley organization dedicated to the study and research of things Celtic. It was through this organization that she first became aware of Padstow's hobbyhorse. The institute had a copy of the 1953 film *'Oss 'Oss, Wee 'Oss*, by Alan Lomax, Peter Kennedy, and Jean Ritchie, a piece of mid-twentieth-century folklore scholarship that interprets the May Day custom, according to classic Frazerian survivalism, as the detritus of an ancient fertility custom. Inspired by the film, Leigh Ann decided to make the hobbyhorse for NROOGD's Beltane. She was aided in this by the excitement of Laurel Olson, who had seen a version of the Padstow hobbyhorse at the Renaissance Faire and, in her own words, "I fell in love with the 'Oss." Along with NROOGD members Don Frew, Andy Mendes and Darrin Laurelsson, the two priestesses built the 'Oss costume. Then NROOGD created a ritual incorporating the 'Oss and other elements of English May Day folk custom, including a maypole dance.

NROOGD's enthusiasm for the Padstow May Day custom was clearly based on notions about its age, authenticity, and connection to pre-Christian customs.[4] Some of these are directly expressed in the film by Lomax's voice-over narration; others were derived from folklorists' explanations. Several NROOGD members mentioned Violet Alford's work on animal mumming and masking traditions in Britain as an important source in the reconstruction of this tradition in America. Leigh Ann saw in the rising and falling movements of the 'Oss the dying and reviving of Frazer's sacred god-king. "These elements are overtly pagan—that's right up there with the Eleusinian mysteries!" she explained enthusiastically. Laurel believed the 'Oss was a direct descendant of pre-Christian Celtic horse cults. She saw the 'Oss as a fertility figure tied to the land, both through his color—black symbolizing the richest possible loam—and his action of scattering the water from his beard over the land and people to stimulate the fertility of the crops. Others were less certain of the connection between the Padstow festival and an ancient fertility rite. Russell Williams, who with Rowan Fairgrove actually traveled to Padstow in 1989 to observe their May Day traditions, expressed disappointment at the lack of overt pagan survivals in the Cornish celebration. "I had envisioned a small folk celebration; what I got instead was something that resembled the Gilroy Garlic Festival—a typical big municipal festival with a carnival and a Ferris wheel and so on."

Although the 'Oss itself is modeled closely on the one portrayed in the film, and the NROOGD ritual incorporates Padstow's May Day songs, the two May Day traditions are quite different. NROOGD chose to emphasize what they interpreted as "overtly pagan" elements in the custom. For Berkeley Pagans and Witches, the 'Oss dances in conjunction with a religious celebration, while Padstow's custom is primarily civic in nature. While in Padstow, the 'Oss dances through the town streets, the Berkeley 'Oss dances only in the context of the ritual; there is no quête or luck-visiting. The Berkeley 'Oss intentionally chases both men and women—a change NROOGD ritualists intentionally made from the original in order to make the ritual more gender-equal. The Padstow belief that a young woman caught under the 'Oss will be married within the year has been reinterpreted in Berkeley to fertility in a broader sense: both fecundity and creative fertility, equally applicable to either women or men.

While NROOGD members of all ethnicities are intimately involved with this custom, for some members of the group, it has a special resonance. "Finding these May games *gave* me an ethnicity," explained Laurel, whose mixed European ancestry includes some Cornish connections. "This ritual is a gift from my forebears, and a gift I give to the community." Russell, whose ancestry is English and Welsh, commented, "I really enjoy the connection with the folk customs of England. . . . I don't have illusions about historical accuracy, but the aesthetic elements give me a sense of continuity and of connection with the origins of seasonal celebrations."

What emerges from these examples is an overwhelming feeling that in the reclamation of folk traditions, blood does indeed matter, as Pike states (2001:121). Many Witches and Pagans feel especially drawn to reclaim folk practices to which they can claim an ethnic link. They may recontextualize family practices as ancient pagan religion, take up contemporary Pagan or Wiccan practice as a continuation of their families' non-Christian spiritual practices, or intentionally revive and reconstruct practices to which they feel linked through blood, ethnicity, or nationality. When reclaimed practices resonated with knowledge about ethnicity and with real or imagined ancestral customs, they created powerful affective states that gave individuals a sense of connection to something greater than themselves—a tradition that had endured through time and space.

## Universalist Arguments

In contrast to relativist arguments about connection to folklore by blood or ethnicity, universalist arguments focus on common elements across boundaries of nationality, ethnicity, race, and gender. As Cynthia Eller, who studied goddess-centered women's spirituality, a group of religions contiguous with Witchcraft and Neo-Paganism, found, universalists who borrow from other cultural traditions see themselves as part of a global community or human family united by beliefs and practices that share many elements cross-culturally. They interpret these similarities across time and place as evidence of a greater spiritual truth underlying all religious traditions, and often perceive the act of borrowing from another culture as a compliment (Eller, 1995:75).

While Sarah Pike found that many Pagans in the Eastern and Midwestern United States made use of traditions from Native American practice, I did not find the same pattern among California Witches and Pagans. Perhaps this was due to the greater political visibility of Native American groups in the state, as well as to the leftist, radicalized politics of many Bay Area Pagans, who are more likely to see cultures in terms of Marxist or Gramscian power relationships. In fact there was often a marked reluctance to incorporate in ritual anything that might be construed as being Native American in origin. At Susan Falkenrath's healing ritual, a woman performed a smudging using burning sage. However, she publicly identified herself as "three-quarters Apache Indian," and warned the assembled crowd, "Don't do this at home. . . . I wouldn't go so far as to say 'don't do this unless you have a Native American present'; just understand the significance of what you're doing, its deeper meaning." She did not, however, elaborate on what the practice's deeper significance might be. Vibra Willow, a Reclaiming priestess who does abortion healing rituals, adapted a Native American chant she heard at a public Pomo ritual after obtaining permission from the Pomo friend who taught the chant. Nevertheless, she worried about appropriation; "I wonder whether this is just another form of colonialism and cultural imperialism," she confessed. While I was living in Berkeley, I heard rumors about a local group that occasionally held sweat lodges in great secrecy, to protect against threats they had allegedly received from local Native American groups; but I was never able to find the location or identity of these practitioners. These instances, along with other conversations, led me to conclude that the Berkeley Pagan community generally avoided using Native American material, out of respect and a fear of being politically incorrect.

This was not the case in other parts of the country to which I traveled. Popular information about Native American customs and practices is widespread and has its ultimate roots in the works of early ethnographers. The contents of these scholarly works, truncated and interpreted for a mass audience, have been adopted by the Pan-Indian movement as markers of Native American identity, and have been made available through a number of popular publications, exhibits, and television documentaries. It is from these sources that many Neo-Pagans cull undifferentiated native terms and practices—sweat lodges, moon lodges, power animals, spirit guides, and such—which are combined with other traditions or applied to cultures (e.g., "Celtic" culture) to which they are decidedly foreign (Jones, 1994). Sometimes this is couched in discourse based on nineteenth-century notions of cultural evolution; as one practitioner explained, "My ancestors were Celts, and they were once at the same stage of development as Native Americans, and they probably wore feathers in their hair and painted their bodies and had shamanic visions; so what I'm doing is not borrowing stuff from Native Americans, but reviving things that my ancestors actually did." Lyra, a Rhode Island priestess, reports drawing ritual elements from documentaries about indigenous peoples shown on the Discovery channel. While many of these films may have been made by ethnographic filmmakers, the information they present is filtered through so many levels of representation that the end result is decontextualized, abstracted, and essentialized. The decontextualization and shallow understanding of other cultures from which motifs are borrowed sometimes leads to humorous misunderstandings: a group of North Carolina Witches called the Lukumi orisha Oya into a circle celebrating lesbian feminism. They interpreted the rainbow, one of Oya's symbols, according to its contemporary significance in the North American gay rights movement, as a sign of a gay, lesbian, or bisexual identity, ignoring the fact that, in Lukumi, Oya is the favorite wife of Shango, the warrior orisha.

Pagans sometimes use arguments of blood or ethnicity to justify their right to certain disputed cultural practices. Selena Fox, a Wisconsin priestess, explained her practice of leaving offerings of tobacco and cornmeal to nature spirits on her land by citing her own one-quarter Cherokee heritage. But she added that the spirits associated with the land in the New World are the deities of Native American peoples, and they should be venerated according to indigenous customs. This involves observing and following Native American sacred practice. In other cases, they may mix the concept of reincarnation with notions of blood right to justify their use of a tradition. One Georgia woman, who runs monthly "moon lodges" and leads shamanic journeys to find one's power animal or spirit teacher, explained that she had always known how to practice these techniques because she had been doing them for six hundred years. She implied that she had been a healer through many incarnations, including lives as a Native American, and had carried the knowledge—and the right to practice a tradition—with her through various incarnations. Significantly, though, I found little of this type of argumentation and identity construction among Bay Area Witches and Pagans.

In the Bay Area, Pagans and Witches most commonly used material from the folk traditions of their immediate neighbors in the larger community: Latinos, African Americans, and Asians. This is a process that Robert Cantwell has called ethnomimesis, the unconscious mimicry through which people take in influence, tradition, or culture (Cantwell, 1993:5). In California, Neo-Pagans live side by side with Americans from many other ethnic groups and traditions. Their Samhain altars for the dead borrow many elements from Mexican American celebrations of El Día de los Muertos altars, such as *papel picado* (paper cutouts), sugar skulls, and vignettes showing the dead at work and play. These products are available in local shops and markets alongside more mainstream Halloween products, which Pagans also adapt for Samhain use. The traditions are easily transferable, since both customs involve setting up family altars for deceased relatives and friends. They may hang *thangka*s and Buddhist prayer flags from their walls because of their sacred nature, or display brass statuettes of Hindu deities on their altars, to whom they offer *puja* at the appropriate calendrical times. These products and information about them are available in the many shops along Telegraph and University Avenues in Berkeley, and in many small neighborhoods of San Francisco and Oakland. Bay Area Pagans and Witches learn about these traditions from friends and neighbors, as well as from reading and scholarly investigation. A few may have training in Hindu or Buddhist traditions.

In some cases, individuals may develop personal relationships with magical practitioners from other cultures that result in the exchange of ideas and techniques. Valerie, a Witch from Palo Alto, befriended the Afro-Cuban owner of a neighborhood botanica where she usually shopped for herbs and candles. They exchanged magical techniques as part of everyday conversation, and he sent her clients for minor thaumaturgical work. When her house was robbed, he recommended a protective spell from Yoruba tradition, which she incorporated into her personal practice. This exchange between magical practitioners, unmediated by outside sources, represents the transmission of folk knowledge as it has taken place historically in instances of cross-cultural contact. Valerie's intent was not to imitate or borrow Afro-Cuban practice, but to protect her home. She followed her friend's magical suggestion in the same spirit in which she followed other friends' advice about installing locks and dead bolts; as a magical practitioner, both approaches seemed logical to her.

A few Pagans seek instruction in a non-Western religion in order to gain a greater understanding of how magic works in cultures with a strong tradition of magical practice. In the late 1990s, several San Francisco Bay Area members of Ring of Troth, a Norse Pagan group, began experimenting with *seidr*, a divination technique described in the sagas that involves religious possession. Some members sought instruction in possessory techniques from Mama

Renee, a local practitioner of Umbanda, an Afro-Brazilian religion that mixes elements of African spirit worship with European spiritualism and indigenous Brazilian practices, because of Umbanda's well-developed tradition of spirit possession. Because European traditions have lost these possessory elements, they turned instead to a tradition that has the requisite knowledge and experience. Their intent was not to become Umbanda initiates, but to better understand and develop their abilities to channel information from spirits.

Afro-Caribbean religions had a high profile in the Bay Area during the late 1990s. Author and Yoruba priestess Luisa Teish and Umbanda priestess Mama Renee had built positive, long-standing relationships with the Bay Area Pagan community, and participated in many local conferences, festivals, and workshops. Thus it was not surprising to discover that some Witches and Pagans had sought further instruction in these traditions.

For David Morris, a classical musician and teacher from the San Francisco Bay Area, the decision to pursue the study of Afro-Cuban religion was tied to his growing dissatisfaction with the Catholic Church's attitude toward gays and lesbians. "I knew I had a vocation," he explained, "and when I was a kid, I assumed it would be the Catholic Church. And then it was clear that was not going to be happening." When David came out as a gay man, he felt ready to explore the nature of his spiritual vocation. He became intrigued by the Afro-Caribbean syncretism of Catholic and earth-based African elements: "I thought it was a way for me to reclaim some of the aesthetics of the Catholic Church—the imagery of the saints, the shrines, and so on, but without having to take on the baggage of Catholic morality. Yoruba theology is concerned with ethical behavior rather than specific sexual behavior, and the main focus in this tradition is to help people figure out what they are supposed to be doing with their lives. That's the whole point of divination and sacrifice—to ask for divine assistance in keeping us on our individual spiritual paths."

David sought training from Guillermo, a local Cuban santero, and eventually, after years of study and dedication to the orishas, became initiated as a priest of Yemaya. Although David is also a Witch in the Reclaiming tradition, he does not mix Witchcraft with Afro-Caribbean religion in his practice, nor does he perceive orisha religion as syncretic. He explains, "Although I personally like the look of the syncretized Afro/Catholic version of this religion (e.g. using both plaster statues of saints and Yoruba carvings to decorate an altar), my actual spiritual practice has nothing to do with syncretism. I happen to like the look of the syncretized version, but not the theological viewpoint it might represent."

For David, initiation into orisha worship represented a furthering of his own spiritual development, as well as an attempt to satisfy his own aesthetic yearnings in a spiritual way. He does not identify as "Pagan" at all, preferring to call himself a priest of Orisha who "happens to have been raised a Catholic and studied Wicca." All three components—his Catholicism, his study of magic through revival Witchcraft, and his initiation into the Yoruba religion—form important but discrete parts of his spiritual identity.

Gus di Zerega wanted to explore magic and spirituality in the context of traditional religions in which spirit belief was part of everyday life. This quest included experimenting with a range of Neo-Pagan and New Age practices. During a vision quest led by a non-Native American neoshaman, he began to twitch and jerk uncontrollably. The instructor informed Gus that his symptoms were not characteristic of a Native American spirit possession, and advised him to seek training in an African-derived spiritual tradition. Gus, who up to that point had no special attraction to Afro-Caribbean practice, began to attend workshops and seminars, and eventually found his way to Antonio, a Brazilian priest of Umbanda who ultimately became a Buddhist after a spirit claiming to be a Lama kept appearing to him. Umbanda is itself a highly syncretic religion in which spirits are believed to have either an African, indigenous, or European ethnic affiliation. Gus studied Umbanda under Antonio's direction and began to channel several spirits: an African woman named Bobo 'Zeffe and a *caboclo* (indigenous spirit) called Wapuri. He now heals people by channeling these spirits, while continuing his practice as a third-degree Gardnerian. He does not, however, mix the two practices in individual rituals.

Gus's unusual experiences have convinced him that "gods do not respect cultural boundaries." Rather than seeing spiritual experience as conforming to cultural expectations, Gus believes that it is the spirits themselves who choose their devotees. "I do not think it is up to human beings to determine who has a right to a spiritual practice, although each is certainly qualified to determine who is able to take on knowledge he or she already possesses. The very question of 'cultural property' with regard to spirituality subordinates the sacred to secular criteria, such as political power relationships. . . . The hubris of such people, claiming to speak for the gods, is amazing."

For both Gus and David, cultural elements, in this case spirits, are clearly possessing, as well as possessable, entities—spirits that can inhabit the body, make it move in particular ways, speak with a different voice and a different gender. Both have spent a considerable number of years studying the religious cultures in which they are initiates, such that those cultures and their spirits now reside in their bodies. Both believe that it is the spirits who choose their worshippers, and not the other way around.

It is easy to dismiss these points of view as convenient ways for whites to justify the appropriation of spiritual tradition. Ultimately, though, as we saw in previous chapters, personal spiritual experience has roots in the autonomous imagination, a part of the unconscious that combines individual memories and psychological material with elements from the surrounding culture. Because of globalization, transnationalism, and the explosion of information on the World Wide Web, middle-class whites now have unprecedented access to information, symbols, and practices from other cultural and religious traditions.

These entities come to possess them, to inhabit their imaginations in ways that would have been impossible a century ago, and they become incorporated into the reserve of symbols from which the autonomous imagination draws in creating spiritual visions.

## Pagan Attitudes Toward Cultural Borrowing

As we have seen from the discussions above, the issue of cultural borrowing has been much debated within the Neo-Pagan movement. A range of attitudes exists, from enthusiastic embracing of the grab-bag approach to spirituality, to concern with the offensiveness of appropriation, to notions of racial birthright and genetic predispositions to spiritual practices, to interchange and communication across ethnic lines between friends. Pagans living in ethnically and racially diverse parts of the United States, who have regular and frequent contact with people of different backgrounds, tend to be more concerned about cultural borrowing than those living in more homogenous surroundings. For them, the problem becomes how to respect, include, and work in concert with minority groups, without engaging in cultural appropriation.

There is a growing feeling within the movement that cultural borrowing and hybridization are problematic, especially if practiced with little regard to the original cultural context and meaning of the material. Wren Walker, editor of *The Witches' Voice*, an online daily news forum for Pagans, wrote an editorial about the dangers of "F-keying," or skimming, through history, a danger she saw as particularly characteristic of Internet searches:

> I think that Pagans and Neo-Pagans today often miss something too when we F-key our way through history. In our efforts to reclaim, retrace or reconstruct the spiritual or magical or cultural beliefs of ancient peoples, we so often just key on a word or a phrase and then lift it out of its original context. We isolate Isis from Egypt or Arianhrod from Wales or The Eddas from Iceland and then either place them into a completely foreign land or leave them dangling out there in magical space somewhere with no familiar reference upon which to rest. And by isolating them such, we not only steal them away from their homeland and culture, we also rob ourselves of an opportunity to grow.[5]

For Walker, the problem is not only the theft of cultural material from other people, but that, in taking it out of its natural context, Pagans cheat themselves out of the kind of depth that comes from deeper study.

Though Reclaiming seeks to form political alliances with members of oppressed minorities, Starhawk cautions strongly against the dangers of cultural appropriation:

> If we are to be allies in struggle with people of different backgrounds, we need to respect different worldviews. The debate about the linking of the spiritual with the political too often takes place in terms that discount or make invisible the experience of the non-dominant world. Such cultural imperialism is itself a form of racism. . . . Or if we do bring ourselves to admit that the dominant description of reality is too narrow, we may run slavishly after other spiritual traditions, eager to acquire experiences of non-

ordinary consciousness as if they were Gucci bags or Cuisinarts, commodities we can use to bolster our status. We become spiritual colonialists, mining the Third world for its resources of symbols and shamans, giving nothing back, in a way that cheapens both the traditions we seek to understand and our own spiritual quests. (Starhawk, 1990:19)

Some felt that borrowing could only be done with the permission of the original performer of the tradition, and even then as part of an ongoing reciprocal relationship in which, for example, a person who feels called upon to borrow a Native American chant develops personal relationships with Native Americans in her area, and works with them for political and social causes to right the imbalance of power. The element of personal contact and relationship is key in these arguments. Many Pagans believed that cultural borrowing was justified if they learned material from native teachers who chose to pass on their traditions to out-group members.

But while most Pagans were critical of cultural borrowing on some level, they continued to engage in it on another. Steven Posch complained, "One of the things that irritates me about too much Neo-Pagan ritual is this blithe assumption that we can just rip anything off, regardless of its cultural roots; that anything we claim is automatically ours." But he explained his attitude toward appropriation by telling me the story of Isis and Osiris. Osiris's body has been torn into a million pieces, and Isis must find them all and reassemble them. She manages to find all except the phallus, which has been eaten by an oxyrhynchus fish; so she makes Osiris a new phallus and breathes life into his body with her wings. They make love, and her son Horus, the Egyptian sun god, is conceived. Steven explained, "It seems to me that rather than taking pieces from other traditions . . . , what I'm actually doing is finding pieces of my own tradition that have been scattered everywhere, and have not been preserved in most places. But the point of the story is that the part which gives the most joy, the part that sparks new life, is always something you have to make yourself."

Songwriter and vocal artist Ruth Rhiannon Barrett is the author of a song entitled "The Heart Is the Only Nation" (sung to the tune of "A Parcel of Rogues in a Nation"), a beautiful and impassioned appeal to overcome distinctions of ethnicity, religious affiliation, gender, and other markers which balkanize us. Like the Pagan songs in the previous chapter, we see in this one references to the Burning Times and oppositionality vis-à-vis Christianity. But the song also contains another, deeper theme: the need for love and compassion to transcend boundaries and borders.

Farewell to all the lies of men,
Farewell to all churches and stations
Farewell to all I thought I'd been
When I accepted prisoner's rations
I served them all with a smile of death

I sold my soul for their praises
And not even I knew what stirrings inside
Said "The heart is the only nation."

I saw the sky turn black as night
With fires from the Inquisition
I saw the people standing by
Waiting for an answer or reason
The homeless, the lonely, the beggar, the slain,
Will they not find their haven?
While borders stand on every land
The heart is the only nation.

You talk with words, you speak in tongues
To tell of revelation
Your deeds speak truer than your speech
When there is no love or compassion
You shake your head and curse the winds
You close your ears to wisdom
The Earth will still go round when you're buried in the ground
The heart is the only nation.

I weave my past into the day
When kindness is the way of the stranger
When children can sleep tucked in their beds
Without a fear of danger
I'll turn my face to the clear blue skies
And raise my arms to the ocean
While I breathe I'll take my stand
The heart is the only nation.[6]

Ruth explained how she came to compose the song: "I was thinking about people's connections to each other overriding national and ethnic . . . boundaries that we put on connection. . . . The idea of 'The Heart is the Only Nation' is about expanding one's personal boundaries to be more inclusive, regardless of artificially imposed [categories]. . . . This is a song about people who would limit their heart because of their thoughts about what's right and what's wrong with other people."

While Ruth was among the most strongly concerned of all my subjects about the problems of cultural borrowing, ultimately she balanced her concern with the recognition of the commonality of human experience and the need to reach out to others, despite differences. Her song suggests that imagination and empathy are primary tools in transcultural understanding, and that an individual can be drawn to the practices of another culture for emotional reasons: "The heart is the only nation."

## Discussion

As Clifford Geertz has noted (1998), religion in a postcolonial, globalizing world is no longer only a matter of individual experience. The presentation of self in everyday life has shifted to a more public sphere, making the relation of self to other increasingly prominent. Religion and culture are two of the many axes around which both identity and power revolve. The increasing mobility of humans and their cultures—what anthropologist Arjun Appadurai (1991) calls "global flows"—have brought people into more frequent contact with others whose religions and cultures differ from their own. Identity, as we saw in the last chapter, is usually constructed through a process of contrasting self with other. Thus, inevitably, growing interreligious and intercultural contact has led to greater differentiation and polarization as identities crystallize around religious and cultural issues, especially those in the public sphere.

Against this context, American society has developed contrasting models of cultural and religious plurality—the vegetable soup and the martini cocktail—that differently describe power relations in a multicultural society. While both recognize plurality, the latter, which dominates social discourse on the California coast, constructs white ethnicity as allegedly unmarked, colorless, and hegemonic, in contrast to marked identities, which are seen as colorful and authentic, but oppressed. But while this discourse may appear to grant whites an overwhelming amount of power over oppressed groups, it has actually shifted the axis of power toward marked categories of ethnic and religious affiliation, and erased the many differences that exist among white ethnics.

Many Pagans seek to disassociate themselves from what they perceive as an alienating cultural heritage, one that has exploited the environment, women, and native peoples, and produced a sterile and vapid mass culture. They do not see themselves as oppressors, but as victims of the same forces that have marginalized indigenous peoples. In the last chapter, we saw how their sacred narratives often portray them as the survivors of medieval European witch persecutions, or of an overthrow of peaceful, matriarchal, goddess-worshipping people by nasty, warlike patriarchs. They often discuss how indigenous European pagan traditions were forcibly eliminated by the expansion of Christianity, much as colonized peoples' religions were destroyed by missionization. This bit of historical revision is a powerful metaphor, which underlies their identification with oppressed or marginalized peoples. Oppression such as that suffered by indigenous peoples at the hands of colonizers becomes an indicator of genuine spiritual knowledge or power—the same kind of spiritual authenticity they imagine pre-Christian European peoples must have had. In reclaiming the folk customs of European peasants, and often those of ancient cultures and indigenous peoples as well, Pagans contest the problematic idea of an all-white, Anglo-dominated cultural hegemony that erases the existence of nuance between the various white European ethnicities. Reclamation becomes a strategy for fashioning a new marked version of the self that challenges existing axes of power by creating solidarity with the other.

Ironically, while Neo-Paganism likes to construct itself as critical of colonialism, racism, and ethnocentrism, its ideology is based on nineteenth-century notions of primitivism and cultural evolution. Authenticity is located in the cultures of the ancient past or of marginalized peoples, who are interpreted as the precursors of contemporary Pagans. Many Neo-Pagans believe marginalized peoples have spiritual wisdom and a relationship with the earth that the dominant culture has lost. In an effort to recapture the lost ethos of the past, Neo-Pagans may appropriate elements of their expressive culture and spiritual practice.

Neo-Pagan universalism stresses the ecumenicity of human practice, what Leslie Jones has called "the monism of most New Age thought, which sees all religions as different versions of the same faith" (Jones, 1994:133). At its best, this approach draws attention to our shared humanity; at its worst, it flattens and homogenizes difference to the standards of white middle-class culture, assuming that all peoples understand the universe as we do and then using "their" understandings to justify contemporary practice.

At the same time, Pagan relativist notions lead some to seek identity in the traditions of their own ancestors. However, strict relativist constructions that depict ethnic and racial boundaries as static and inherent, rather than culturally constructed and relative, are similarly rooted in nineteenth-century Romantic nationalism. Imagining that we can—and should—all stick only to the traditions of our ancestors ignores another kind of reality: that of an American culture that is not only multiracial and multiethnic, but part of a globalizing world where transculturation bring us into daily contact with the cultures of others. Material from these encounters, be they mediated or direct, becomes a part of the imagination, and subsequently may become a part of spiritual experience.

Both the arguments of universalists and those of relativists, whether within or outside of Neo-Paganism, need to be understood against a larger cultural backdrop of cultural commodification and identity politics in the contemporary United States. The idea of culture as commodity is a recent development. Writing about the commodification of folksong, Pauline Greenhill notes that in traditional communities, practices are not commodified: "Ownership of cultural expressions . . . has a different basis in traditional communities. . . . Songs cannot be expressed in terms of capital use or exchange value, but in terms of reciprocity and the creation and maintenance of social ties. . . . Under such circumstances, performers can authentically appropriate the materials available to them by transforming them so that they fit into new contexts" (Greenhill, 1993:154). While this process may look like theft or plagiarism, Greenhill points out that plagiarism is a historically derived concept based more on notions of ownership than on the location or identity of the original creator. What distinguishes new forms of appropriation from old-style cultural diffusion is not the imbalance of power between colonized people and their Euro-American conquerors and oppressors, but that it is occurring, for the most part, through the medium of consumer culture, thus bypassing any form of social exchange or reciprocity between the two individuals or groups. Commodification has allowed interested audiences to experience the wisdom of marginalized peoples through the consumption of consumer goods. This vehicle for cultural diffusion completely surpasses the individual contact which characterized large-scale diffusion in the past, removing the elements of mutual exchange and individual control from the interchange. It also introduces the issue of representation: people are understandably resentful when their practices are being appropriated *because* they are considered "primitive."

Once a practice itself becomes commodified and therefore endlessly reproducible and diffusible, its value, in the language of mercantilism, decreases. The problem for those whose practices have been fetishized becomes how to maintain the value and authenticity of a tradition in the face of its commodification. The answer, in the language of the marketplace, is to create scarcity. Thus the kinds of arguments put forth by indigenous peoples are couched in the discourse of scarcity: authenticity becomes tied to blood right, putting practice out of the range of nonmembers.

The commodification of culture and its conceptualization as property has grown alongside an ethic of heritage conservation that reifies ethnic and cultural identity: certain cultures are thought to belong to certain groups of people. By analogy to other types of property, the right to cultural ownership then becomes determined by descent and genetics—in other words, by blood. And increasingly, only those who are blood members of a given community are thought to have the right to represent it. Yet such arguments too are problematic. The blood-right model is based on the assumption that race, ethnicity, and culture are linked—an idea which has been challenged by physical anthropologists and geneticists, and which, taken to its logical extreme, "gets ugly. It leads directly to twin evils: racism . . . based on an exclusivist argument . . . and essentialized cultural forms and practices" (Abrahams, 2003:215). Yet it remains a powerful model of identity creation for a large part of the American population.

Blood-right arguments are complicated by a general lack of understanding of cultural diffusion and polygenesis, and by essentialist notions of cultural purity rooted in nineteenth-century nationalism. Members of the Lakota delegation assumed that certain Pagan practices such as worshipping in a circle, invoking the four directions, and purifying with burning herbs were imitations of Native American practice, whereas in fact these particular practices developed independently in Europe, an example pf polygenesis.[7] The fundamental hybridity of humankind due to the many migrations of peoples across the ages is also unallowable in essentialist systems. When the Asatruar remarked to me that runes worked only for people of Germanic heritage, I found myself wondering whether he was aware of the many incursions of Germanic tribes into the Italian peninsula and the long domination of Sicily by the Normans, a Germanic people. Besides being a cultural halfie, who knows what variety of genetic material swirls around in my DNA? The study of folklore has taught us that contrary to essentialist notions, rituals and customs, like narratives and their component motifs, are never the exclusive property of any single cultural group, but exist in multiple and evolving variation across broad cultural areas.[8] They change constantly in response to individual human creativity and contact with cultural others. To freeze them, as blood-right arguments are wont to do, is to mummify them as artifacts of a cultural heritage petrified in time and space.

To a movement such as Neo-Paganism, which in its first generation, at least, is so clearly an imagined community, blood-right arguments are unsettling. What is left out is the idea that an individual can be emotionally drawn to cultural practices that are outside his/her immediate experience and scope of knowledge, that imagination and empathy can be useful tools in cross-cultural understanding. As Cantwell suggests, the imagination is in fact the most fundamental human tool in perceiving and processing experience (Cantwell, 1993:6). It might be more useful to understand Pagan borrowings and hybridizations as playing with notions about the nature of difference in a way that subverts their construction in the current cultural climate and points out their ultimately untenable nature. Arguments such as being drawn to Native American cultural practice because of one's identity in a previous incarnation ascribe membership in a different and disturbing way, but they allow more room for hybridization than restrictive arguments of difference in which genetics alone determine membership and access.

Of course, it is relatively easy for Neo-Pagans, coming from a position of privilege, to ignore the power differentials between themselves and those from whose cultures they borrow. I am not arguing here that indigenous practitioners should not have the right to control the dissemination of their cultural practices, and to be compensated fairly for their commodification. Arguments of blood right are understandable and appealing when they come from a subdominant group; it is easy to empathize with Native Americans, whose cultures have already been decimated by colonialism, when they argue against the appropriation of traditions that serve as powerful loci of resistance against white hegemony, and the commodification of their own practices and artifacts. Yet the same arguments become distasteful and racist when made by Asatruars. There is a problem here. Any workable theory of cultural property must be equally applicable to all groups, and must not depend on the relative powerlessness of any particular group, as power differentials among various cultural groups change over time. It cannot be based on specious notions equating culture with race, ethnic origins, or nationality. It is tempting to want to censure Neo-Pagans for appropriating the spiritual practices of marginalized peoples, to want to protect the rights of Native Americans and other minorities to their spiritual traditions. But the consequences of limiting cultural practice to those who have a genetic right to it are also problematic.

In understanding the borrowing and hybridization of magical and spiritual traditions, it might be helpful to remember that they are art forms, as we have established in Part II of this book. Among art forms, they are just as susceptible to cross-cultural influence as other art forms such as foodways and music. To take music as one example, America has produced such classic hybrid genres as jazz, blues, rock, and bluegrass, each of which combines, in different ways, elements from African and European musical traditions. It might be instructive to see how scholars of musical traditions have treated the issues of hybridization and cultural borrowing. Scholars of contemporary music have described many situations of boundary crossing, hybridity, and the emergence of new musical forms as a result of transculturation and global flows (Hebdige, 1979; Feld, 1992; Lipsitz, 1994). Rather than censuring the hybridization of cultural and musical traditions as a result of cultural contact, they offer provocative models for understanding the processes that shape musical change. Dick Hebdige (1979) described how punk and other forms of counterhegemonic rock emerged in Britain during the 1980s as a result of contact between working-class white youth and youth from Afro-Caribbean cultures living in the same neighborhoods. While cross-cultural contact led to the development of some genres of oppositional music and costume, it also led to vibrant and provocative new musical genres. George Lipsitz's (1994) musicians draw not only from their ethnic background, but from their knowledge of other musics, rhythms, and sounds in their compositions. Many of them are halfies, having multiracial, multiethnic backgrounds, and are also influenced by the musical culture of their place of residence. Lipsitz posits that in a postcolonial, multicultural society, where transculturation has resulted in both ethnic and cultural hybridity, ethnicity alone may no longer be a sufficient or satisfactory way of ascribing identity. His subjects drew from a number of models in choosing their musical affinity, blending styles and not limiting themselves to what was determined by their own ethnic background. Ultimately, aesthetic affinity, not blood, determined their choices.

Like musical traditions, magical traditions easily cross cultural boundaries. Practitioners freely incorporate material from other cultures and traditions, adapting it to fit their own styles of practice. Not only spells, but gods and goddesses, chants and songs may be adapted to fit new cultural contexts. In the multiethnic urban environments of twenty-first century America, it is entirely predictable that emergent spiritual traditions would incorporate the influence of both local and global cultures. For white ethnics in America, for whom identity has long been a matter of choice and imagination, affinity for a particular pantheon, a specific magical style becomes one of many ways of imagining identity. And affinity is notoriously difficult to explain simply in terms of identity construction, expedience, or shifting axes of power, because it is in essence an aesthetic and spiritual sentiment. In the end, what moves us may not be a matter of blood or power at all, but of spiritual and emotional longing. The art of magic allows our imagination to transcend the boundaries of blood and geography, to experience, at least in part, other cultures and time periods and feel empathy with other living beings. In the words of Ruth Barrett, "The heart is the only nation."

# Notes

*Introduction*

1. Invocation of the four directions (east, south, west and north) and their corresponding elements (air, fire, water and earth).

2. Usually understood by American Neo-Pagans as the Irish goddess of smithcraft, poetry, healing, and creativity, later Christianized as St. Brigit.

3. "In the middle of our life's journey / I found myself in a dark wood / having strayed from the straight and narrow." Dante Alighieri, *Inferno*, 1. 1–3 (my translation).

4. Funari is a spring located in the territory of Monteruju. It is famous as the dwelling of Sa Rejusta or Sorre Justa, a legendary witchlike figure who is said to live under a large boulder near the spring. Once a year, on the night of July 31, she comes out from under her rock; she makes herself very small, and enters houses through keyholes so she can spy on the behavior of the young women who live there.

5. "E.T.," a schoolteacher in Monteruju, was one of the principal consultants for my Sardinian project and became a close friend. In Monteruju, young people used to formalize friendships by jumping together over the bonfire on St. John's Eve (June 23) while reciting a rhyme; E.T. and I participated in this ritual in Monteruju in 1986. See the preface in Magliocco (1993) for additional information on our friendship and its consequences.

6. At the festival of Santa Maria di Runaghes, Monteruvians dance the circle dance, a line dance in which people hold hands forming a human chain that winds inward, then outward, much like the spiral dance of the Witches. In the process of winding and unwinding, all the dancers are brought face-to-face with each other.

7. *Grounding* is a term Neo-Pagans use to mean the direction of energy into the ground or earth. This concept is explained in detail in Chapter 3.

8. The idea that evolution has a specific goal, whether the rise of *homo sapiens* or the development of Western civilization, was of course *not* part of Darwin's original theory; this teleological flaw developed from popular interpretations of Darwin's writings that were steeped in the prejudices of the mid-1800s.

9. Ronald Hutton, personal communication, December 2002.

10. There is some overlap between the two movements; see Magliocco and Tannen, 1998.

11. This term was coined by Kirin Narayan, but first published by Lila Abu-Lughod (1991:137), to mean a person who for whatever reason has been raised in two cultures.

*Chapter 1*

1. Bendix, 1997:156ff., for a discussion of the development of this concept in Europe.
2. In this work, I capitalize *Pagan, Neo-Pagan* and *Witch* when they refer to modern religions; lower-case will be used for all other meanings.
3. I am indebted to Don Frew for many of the hypotheses I present here regarding the connections between Neoplatonism and Gardnerian Witchcraft.
4. These principles are summarized in Hutton, 1999:66–67.
5. For a full treatment of this, see Hutton, 1999:52–65.
6. See Chapman, 1992, for a history of this process.
7. For a thorough historical discussion, see Cocchiara, 1981, esp. 44–60.
8. See Dorson, 1968, esp. 1–43.
9. Dundes, 1969, makes clear that the cultural evolutionists were also operating on the basis of devolutionary premises: survivals are, after all, remnants of an earlier culture that survive in fragmentary form.
10. For a history of Spiritualism, see Moore, 1977. See also Isaacs, 1986:79–110, and Pimple, 1995: 75–89.
11. Leland of the American Folklore Society and Murray and Gardner of the British Folklore Society.
12. The German scholar Hans Moser first observed this phenomenon, which he called *Rücklauf*, literally "back-flow" (Moser, 1964).
13. For much of what follows I am indebted to Mathiesen, 1998:25–51.
14. For much of the following history I am indebted to Hutton, 1999:194–201.
15. The Dayak are an ethnic group that includes a number of different subgroups, including the Iban, Barito, Kayan-Kenyah-Modang, the Maloh, the Bidayuh, and the peoples of the Nualang Arc.
16. According to Hutton, this book was ghostwritten by Idries Shah but is based almost entirely on Gardner's own recollections, and can be considered quasi-autobiographical (Hutton, 1999:205).
17. According to my consultants, who are in touch with several members of Gardner's first coven, Yule was not a major Wiccan festival until 1957, but was celebrated at December's full moon in 1953, when the dates coincided.
18. Wiccan historican Philip Heselton (2000) has examined Dorothy Clutterbuck's diaries, finding many examples of poetry that took its inspiration from nature. Clutterbuck also seems to have been fascinated with fairies, a topic of interest to many Witches. Heselton argues that this is sufficient evidence to presume that Clutterbuck was indeed Pagan, and could have initiated Gardner into the New Forest Coven as he claimed. It is possible that in the future, new evidence will surface linking Clutterbuck to Gardner more substantially; until then, I do not find his evidence strong enough to concur with his conclusions.
19. Gardner possessed a diploma granting him a doctorate in philosophy from the MetaCollegiate Extension of the National Electronic Institute in Nevada, "for completion of course and published works," dated September 21, 1937. There is no evidence he ever pursued coursework in anthropology or folkloristics. Don Frew hypothesizes that he may have received the degree as a result of his publication and wide dissemination of *Keris and Other Malay Weapons* (1936) from some unknown official affiliated with the MetaCollegiate Extension. It is also possible he may have sent for the degree as a lark. Gardner never represented himself in writing as a Ph.D., but apparently did not correct those who addressed him as "doctor" (Frew, 2001); and according to Doreen Valiente, in *The Rebirth of Witchcraft* (1989:41–42), he told a journalist in 1951 that he had received a Ph.D. *honoris causa* from Singapore University. He told the same story to

Aleister Crowley at their first meeting; the record is preserved in Crowley's diary in London's Warburg Institute (Hutton, personal communication, 2001). However, when Valiente checked with the university in question, no record of a degree was found.

20. Many Pagans and Witches object to my use of the term *poaching* because it evokes the illegal hunting of game, often of endangered species killed as trophies. However, I use the term in reference to DeCerteau (1984) and Jenkins (1991) (see text for details). In their sense, I feel the term perfectly captures the spirit in which Neo-Pagans and Witches practice "textual poaching." My use of the term is not intended to excuse or romanticize the practice of illegal hunting.

*Chapter 2*

1. Adler (1986:14) points out that Paganism is "a religion without converts," that most Pagans do not convert in the strict sense, but come to feel that they have "always" been Pagan and that they have finally found others who feel as they do.

2. This is much higher than the percentage found by Orion, and may be unique to the San Francisco Bay Area Pagan community, with its high concentration of institutions of higher learning.

3. Allyn Wolfe, personal communication, 1996, 2002. Wolfe says he told the grocery stores, Laundromats, and other establishments where he posted the signs that he was a Syriac Christian, in order to allay any suspicions they might have had.

4. Http://home.earthlink.net/~jade-jaguar/path6.html

5. reweaving@renaissoft.com.

7. For example, thesis-title generators, post-modern jargon generators, and the like that circulate in occupational groups.

8. It is possible that other Witches came to North America shortly before the Bucklands, bringing their traditions with them; for example, central California's New Wiccan Church, a practice quite similar to Gardnerian Witchcraft, seems to have no links to the Bucklands, but may have evolved from practices brought by earlier immigrants from Britain. However, the Bucklands are the first documented Gardnerians to have brought the practice to North America.

9. Wicca has been extensively studied, perhaps more than any other Pagan tradition. See especially Adler, 1986,/997:118–19; Luhrmann, 1989; Berger, 1999.

10. While they share with Pagans the practice of magic, OTO ritual mixes Jewish and Christian liturgy with Egyptian elements, and can accomodate individuals who consider themselves Jewish, Christian, or Neo-Pagan. The preferred term is *Gnostic.*

11. It may, however, create political problems in areas where there is a high degree of intergroup conflict. Luhrmann (1989) also found that many of her London informants belonged to a number of different Neo-Pagan groups, without apparent conflicts. This pattern may be more frequent in high-density urban areas where a number of groups may flourish than where a single tradition dominates.

12. For an excellent ethnography of the Reclaiming collective and community, see Salomonsen (2002). The Reclaiming Collective disbanded in 1998 and has instead become a group of activist cells.

13. Diane Purkiss has criticized Starhawk's rituals from *The Spiral Dance* (1989) as solipsistic, offering little in the way of power and emphasizing women's nurturing and domestic qualities (1996:46–47). She cites Starhawk's spells for self-acceptance, safe space, and ridding oneself of anger as evidence of the fact that contemporary magic is nothing more than "psychic housecleaning" (Purkiss, 1996:47). Yet Purkiss's emphasis on the psychological details of two rituals led her to ignore the larger oppositional mes-

sage in Starhawk's works. She also fails to consider Starhawk's own distinctions between "power over," "power with," and "power from within," and the underlying assumption that working for social transformation is not possible if one is consumed by one's own personal problems.

14. Pagans frequently get lumped into the category of New Age religions, defined by Gordon Melton as a synthesis of Eastern religion and transpersonal psychology born of the 1960s counterculture (Melton, 1988:36–43; Hess, 1993:4). Scholars have differed in their understandings of the relationship between Neo-Paganism and the New Age movement. Luhrmann's British Witches saw themselves as part of the New Age (Luhrmann, 1989); yet Hess, in his examination of New Age beliefs, does not include Neo-Pagans as part of the movement. Hanegraaf, in what is surely the most exhaustive study of the New Age subculture, includes Neo-Pagans, but recognizes that they constitute a part of the movement unique unto itself (Hanegraaf, 1996). Regardless of how scholars have chosen to treat Neo-Paganism and the New Age, Pagans see themselves as quite distinct from it.

15. David Hess, in his study of the New Age movement, science, and parapsychology, describes New Agers as "predominantly middle-class," but points out that within that there is considerable diversity of ethnicity, class, education, and occupation (1993:5).

16. Some Pagans have remarked to me that they have a tendency to be overweight, and believe the joke reflects this. While percentages are impossible to determine, an impressionistic survey would tend to confirm this opinion. Why this is so remains unclear. One contributing factor might be the predominance of goddess images based on *zaftig* prehistoric figurines, such as the Venus of Willendorf. In a culture where extra weight is always negatively charged, these divine images become powerful positive messages for those with similar body types. Another factor could be Pagans' general rejection of media-diffused standards of beauty, and their greater acceptance of those whose physiques deviate from the ideal. Another informant commented that Pagan foodways contribute to an unhealthy diet: "junk food and plenty of it." Yet this is not ubiquitous; there are also Pagans whose lifestyles include healthy food choices (e.g., vegetarianism) and physical exercise. Finally, some have suggested that Pagans tend to value sedentary pastimes—reading, computers—over athletic pursuits, and that sedentarism can lead to weight gain. Without further study, however, all these hypotheses remain impressionistic and unsubstantiated, and beyond the scope of this study.

17. Christie Davies, in his study *Ethnic Humor around the World* (1990), has elaborated on this mechanism.

*Chapter 3*

1. I have shortened and simplified the circle casting here. This is not intended as a complete Gardnerian new moon ritual script, but only to give readers an impression of how sacred space was created in this instance.

2. See, for example, Bennett (1987), where elderly British women report instances of precognition and psychic communication with their loved ones as a normal part of their everyday patterns of nurturing; Virtanen (1989), a study of omens, precognition, and extrasensory perception in Finland, in which the author suggests the capacity to receive this kind of information may have evolved in humans as an "early warning" system long before the existence of technological means of communication; and Toelken (1995:47–58), in which the author demonstrates that interpretations of causality and determinations of rationality are culture-specific.

3. Some Witches would argue that the people one would like to turn into toads are in principle toads already; no additional action is necessary to effect a transformation.

4. This principle and the previous one were first synthesized in these terms by Sir James Frazer in *The Golden Bough* (1959).

5. Cf. the similar "Seven Hermetic Principles," outlined in Orion (1995:105–6). Pagans share a belief in these underlying principles regardless of training or geographic provenance.

6. Some dates are approximate because the exact moment of celestial events such as the equinoxes and solstices changes slightly each year.

7. Neo-Pagans in Australia and other parts of the southern hemisphere reverse the sabbats, celebrating the summer solstice in December and Samhain on May 1.

8. Academic calendars, alas, do not correspond to the Witchen year cycle.

9. A small number of Craft traditions, among them Reclaiming, associate bladed tools with air and east, and the wand with fire and south.

10. Twin serpents ring the caduceus, Hermes' staff, while in late Hellenistic Egypt, Hermes was associated with Anubis, the jackal deity who escorted the dead into the underworld.

11. Planetary hours are elastic, depending on the season. The process of determining which planet or deity rules each hour is based on the Roman system in which the first hour after sunrise represents the *prima hora*, or first hour of the day. This hour always belongs to the ruler of the day: thus the first hour of daylight on a Wednesday is sacred to Mercury; the first hour of a Thursday to Jupiter; and so on. Rulership of subsequent hours always follows a pattern called the Chaldean order, and is as follows: Saturn, Jupiter, Mars, the sun, Venus, Mercury, and the moon. The outer planets—Uranus, Neptune and Pluto—are not a part of the Chaldean order, having been discovered in recent centuries. Timing magic for success involves a series of calculations based on the time of sunrise, the day of the week, and the planet that most closely corresponds with the type of magic being performed.

12. This is essentially the same argument made by Berger's informants (1999:19).

13. The literature on European magic is vast and growing exponentially. The University of Pennsylvania Press's series Witchcraft and Magic in Europe, edited by Bengt Ankarloo and Stuart Clark, provides a learned overview on the role of magic in both elite and folk cultures, especially the volumes *Witchcraft and Magic in Europe: The Middle Ages* (2000), *Witchcraft and Magic in Europe: The Period of the Witch Trials* (2001), and *Witchcraft and Magic in Europe: The Eighteenth and Nineteenth Centuries* (2001). For a treatment of ritual magic, see Butler (1998) and Kieckhefer (1997). For the relationship between elite and folk magic in Britain, see Owen Davies (1999).

14. John Yohalem, personal communication, 1996.

15. See Weber (1922), and its explication in Berman (1991) and Spierenburg (1991:9–13).

### *Chapter 4*

Some material in this chapter appeared previously in Magliocco, 1996.

1. Judy Foster died in 2001. This task has since been taken over by other Reclaiming members.

2. "Set Sail" was written by Starhawk; music by Mara June Quicklightning.

3. For another description of this ritual, see Salomonsen (2002). Salomonson's description differs somewhat from mine, as she participated in an earlier, smaller, Spiral

Dance. The ritual performance has evolved over time since its inception in 1979 and varies considerably from one year to the next, although the basic outline remains the same. Spiral Dances are now performed at Samhain by a number of Reclaiming-derived groups all over North America.

4. Steven Posen, personal communication, 1993. The quotations in this chapter and the rest of the book are from interviews with my field consultants that took place between June 1993 and April 2002. The bulk of my fieldwork was conducted in Berkeley, California, from September 1995 to August 1997; I also did fieldwork in the Midwest during June 1993 and 1994, and in Atlanta, Georgia, in November 1995. I continue to visit my consultants in Berkeley on a regular basis, especially every February during Panthacon, a conference that combines academic papers with Neo-Pagan workshops and rituals; and we exchange frequent emails and telephone calls. Some comments were drawn from these later visits and exchanges and from the comments my consultants made on earlier drafts of my work.

5. Of all the holidays in the North American year cycle, Halloween is most commonly believed to be derived from an ancient Irish pagan holy day. Ronald Hutton, in *Stations of the Sun* (1996:360–70), concludes that Samhain indeed was a pagan festival observed in pastoral areas in the British Isles, and that magic and prognostications were associated with this day from an early time. The association of this period with dead souls, however, seems to have been a Christian phenomenon.

6. See Hutton (1996:134–38) for a discussion of the history of this calendar custom in Ireland.

7. Hutton (1996:179–81) discusses this origin myth for the holiday, and concludes that while it is possible that the Anglo-Saxons venerated a goddess named Eostar at this time of year, it is just as likely that *Eostar* was a descriptive term meaning "of openings or beginnings," a fitting description for the planting and sowing season, rather than the name of a specific goddess.

8. See Hutton (1996:218–43) for a fuller discussion of the origins of Beltane and May Day games, including the maypole and hobbyhorse. While the celebration of May Day may indeed be of pagan origins, there is little to link hobbyhorses and maypoles to a remote past.

9. See Salomonsen (2002:248–81) for an in-depth description of one Reclaiming Witch's initiation.

10. Craft initiations are described in *The Grimoire of Lady Sheba* (1971), Stewart Farrar's *What Witches Do* (1971), and Starhawk's *The Spiral Dance* (1989).

11. Copyright Susan Grace Falkenrath, 1981; used with permission.

*Chapter 5*

1. This interpretation was suggested by nineteenth-century folklorists, and has been adopted by the Neo-Pagan movement. For a full treatment of the maypole and its interpretations, see Hutton (1996:234–37).

2. Ironically, John Wesley, the founder of Methodism, had a number of ecstatic experiences himself, and founded the sect because of his belief that God can communicate directly with each individual through religious ecstasy. Somehow, though, these teachings were not communicated to Laurel by her pastor at a Methodist church in Southern California in the 1970s.

3. The Neo-Pagan otherworld, where, some say, reside the souls of those who have died and those who are yet to be born.

4. These characteristics are adapted from Evans (1979:33–48) and Sturm (2000). There is considerable overlap between the categories each author delineates.

5. See, for example, Behringer (1998); Bonomo (1959); and Ginzburg (1966, 1989), to cite just a few. These works suggest that in many parts of Europe, beliefs and practices involving ecstatic states, communication with the spirit world, and healing existed well into the late Middle Ages, during which they were interpreted by witch hunters as evidence of diabolical witchcraft.

6. For a thorough discussion of this lengthy historical process in England, see Hutton (1996).

7. Quote is from Erasmus, *The Praise of Folly* (1509), cited in Foucault (1965:xx).

8. Both Linda Dégh (1968:188) and Alessandro Falassi (1980:50–51) have noted how tale listeners readily identify with characters in folktales.

9. Farida Fox, interview by Holly Tannen, Mendocino, Calif., June 10, 1996.

10. Ibid.

*Chapter 6*

Parts of this chapter were previously published in an article co-written with Holly Tannen, entitled "The Real Old-Time Religion: Towards an Aesthetics of Neo-Pagan Song," (Magliocco and Tannen, 1978). I am indebted to Holly Tannen for her significant contributions to the analysis of "Heretic Heart," and for her collaboration on fieldwork associated with my study of Pagan songs.

1. For example, see Ellis (2000) for an account of how some Protestant charismatic Christians conceptualize witches and witchcraft as encompassing a broad range of activities, including folk magic and involvement in Neo-Paganism.

2. While there are African American, Asian, and Latina Witches and Neo-Pagans, they are in the minority; most African, Asian, and Hispanic Americans who want to explore their spiritual roots do so through other avenues; for example, African Americans and Latinos are often drawn to the practice of Lukumi/Santería, Yoruba, and other Afro-Caribbean religions.

3. Cf. Orion's broader sample, in which almost 40 percent completed college and another 28 percent had a postgraduate degree (Orion, 1995:67).

4. I use the term *myth* in William Bascom's sense, as a sacred story told as true about the origins of the cosmos and the human condition, but with some reservation, as the popular sense of the word is "something untrue." As I will argue below, Pagan myths, while historically false, contain a kind of metaphorical truth.

5. As both Cynthia Eller and Ronald Hutton point out, the core myths of American Paganism are very similar to those of American feminist spirituality; see Eller (2000:3–4) and Hutton (1999:340–45).

6. This figure is certainly incorrect, but Starhawk reproduces it from Gardner (1954:105), who probably got it from Gage (1972 [1893]:106–7).

7. See Mathiesen (1998:168). See also the discussion of Leland in Chapter 1.

8. See Gibbons (1998). The *Pomegranate* publishes academic articles of interest to Neo-Pagans. Gibbons's article also appears on the website of Covenant of the Goddess, a national networking organization for Witches: www.cog.org.

9. Lyrics by Charlie Murphy; from the album *Catch the Fire*, © Good Fairy Productions, 1981.

10. From the album *The Fäerie Shaman*, © Nemeton, 1981. Copyright Gwydion Pendderwen; used with permission.

11. Copyright 1982 by Catherine Madsen; used with permission.

*Chapter 7*

1. The coven also included members whose families had been in the United States for many generations and who identified predominantly as Americans of mixed northern European extraction.

2. Holly Tannen coined the ironic phrase in the title of this section to describe the obsession with things Celtic which permeates the movement. Marion Bowman (1996) has commented on the many images of Celts in British Paganism, and on how many Britons who are not of Celtic extraction nevertheless feel drawn to Celtic cultures.

3. For a very thorough treatment of Norse Pagan traditions, see Kaplan (1996). Kaplan points out that not all Norse Neo-Pagan traditions are racist; in fact, most Asatruars feel that a spiritual link to the Vikings is all that is necessary to be a member. The San Francisco Bay Area's Ring of Troth group has African American and Jewish members. However, some racist adherents remain in Asatru.

4. See Hutton (1996:81–94) for a discussion of the origins of the hobbyhorse. While hobbyhorses were popular entertainments in Tudor England, and remained so in some areas of Britain even after the Reformation, there is no written evidence of Padstow's hobbyhorse before about 1803. Interpretations of this custom as a pagan survival are a product of nineteenth- and early twentieth-century folkloristics, especially the works of E. C. Cawte, Roy Judge, and Violet Alford, who all relied heavily on the ideas of Lord Raglan and Sir James Frazer.

5. Wren Walker, *The Witches' Voice*, www.witchvox.com, accessed April 1, 2002.

6. Copyright Ruth Barrett, 1993; used with permission.

7. Early Christians worshipped in a circle, as the remains of early Roman churches demonstrate. The four elements (earth, air, fire, and water) and their corresponding directions (north, east, south, and west) are part of the tradition of Jewish magic in texts such as the *Key of Solomon*. Burning incense and herbs were used for purification from ancient Greek times.

8. For a discussion of this idea as it regards the tale of the walled-up wife, see Dundes (1995).

# Bibliography


Abrahams, Roger. 2003. "Identity." In *Eight Words for the Study of Expressive Culture*, ed. Burt Feintuch, 198–222. Urbana: University of Illinois Press.

Abu-Lughod, Lila. 1990. "The Romance of Resistance: Tracing Transformations of Power through Bedouin Women." In *Beyond the Second Sex: New Directions in the Anthropology of Gender*, ed. Peggy Reeves Sanday and Ruth G. Goodenough, 315–37. Philadelphia: University of Pennsylvania Press.

———. 1991. "Writing against Culture." In *Recapturing Anthropology*, ed. Richard G. Fox, 137–62. Santa Fe: School of American Research Press.

Adler, Margot. 1986 [1979]. *Drawing Down the Moon: Witches, Druids, Goddess-Worshippers, and Other Pagans in American Today*. Boston: Beacon Press.

———. 1997. *Heretic's Heart: A Journey through Spirit and Revolution*. Boston: Beacon Press.

Albanese, Catherine. 1990. *Nature Religion in America*. Chicago: University of Chicago Press.

Alford, Violet. 1968. "The Hobby Horse and Other Animal Masks." *Folklore* 79, 123–33.

Alighieri, Dante. 1964. *La divina commedia*. Ed. Ettore Mazzali. Milan: Nuova Accademica.

Anderson, Benedict. 1991 [1983]. *Imagined Communities: Reflections on the Origin and Spread of Nationalism*. London: Verso.

Ankarloo, Bengt, and Stuart Clark. 1999. *Witchcraft and Magic in Europe: The Twentieth Century*. Philadelphia: University of Pennsylvania Press.

Appadurai, Arjun. 1991. "Global Ethnoscapres: Notes and Queries for a Transnational Anthropology." In *Recapturing Anthropology: Working in the Present*, ed. Richard G. Fox, 191–210. Santa Fe: School of American Research Press.

Ashe, Geoffrey. 1974. *Do What You Will: A History of Anti-Morality*. New York: W. H. Allen and Unwin.

Babcock, Barbara, 1978. "Introduction." In *The Reversible World*, ed. Barbara Babcock, 13–38. Ithaca: Cornell University Press.

Bachofen, Johann Jakob. 1948 [1858]. *Das Mütterecht*. Basel: B. Scwabe.

Baker, James W. 1996. "White Witches: Historic Fact and Romantic Fantasy." In *Magical Religion and Modern Witchcraft*, ed. James R. Lewis, 171–91. Albany: State University of New York Press.

Bakhtin, Mikhail. 1968. *Rabelais and His World*. Trans. C. Emerson and M. Holquist, ed. M. Holquist. Cambridge: Cambridge University Press.

Bauman, Richard. 1984. *Verbal Art as Performance*. Prospect Heights, Ill.: Waveland Press.

Bay Laurel, Alicia. 1971. *Living on the Earth*. New York: Vintage Books.

Bay Laurel, Alicia, and Ramon Sender. 1973. *Being of the Sun*. New York: Harper and Row.
Behar, Ruth. 1996. *The Vulnerable Observer: Anthropology That Breaks Your Heart*. Boston: Beacon Press.
Behringer, Wolfgang. 1998. *Shaman of Oberstdorf*. Trans. H. C. Erik Midelfort Charlottesville: University of Virginia Press.
Bell, Catherine. 1997. *Ritual: Perspectives and Dimensions*. New York and Oxford: Oxford University Press.
Bell, Jessie Wicker. 2001 [1972]. *The Grimoire of Lady Sheba*. St. Paul, Minn.: Llewellyn.
Ben Amos, Dan. 1972. "Toward a Definition of Folklore in Context." In *Towards New Perspectives in Folklore*, ed. Americo Paredes and Richard Bauman, 3–15. Austin: University of Texas Press.
Bendix, Regina. 1988. "Folklorismus: the Challenge of a Concept." *International Folklore Review* 6:5–50.
———. 1997. *In Search of Authenticity: The Formation of Folklore Studies*. Madison: University of Wisconsin Press.
———. 2000. "The Pleasures of the Ear: Towards an Ethnography of Listening." *Cultural Analysis* 1:33–50.
Bendix, Regina, and Barbro Klein, eds. 1993. *Foreigners and Foreignness in Europe: Expressive Culture in Transcultural Encounters*. Special issue of *Journal of Folklore Research* 30, no. 1.
Bennett, Gillian. 1987. *Traditions of Belief: Women and the Supernatural*. Hammondsworth: Penguin Books.
Berger, Helen. 1999. *A Community of Witches*. Columbia: University of South Carolina Press.
Berman, Morris. 1984. *The Reenchantment of the World*. New York: Bantam Books.
Bonewits, P. E. Isaac. 1989 [1971]. *Real Magic*. New York: Samuel Weiser.
Bonomo, Giuseppe. 1959. *Caccia alle streghe*. Palermo: Palumbo.
Bourdieu, Pierre. 1991. *Language and Symbolic Power*. Cambridge: Polity Press.
Bourguignon, Erika. 1976. *Possession*. San Francisco: Chandler and Sharp.
Bowman, Marion. 1996. "Cardiac Celts: Images of Celts in Paganism." In *Paganism Today*, ed. Graham Harvey and Charlotte Hardman, 242–51. San Francisco: HarperCollins.
Bracelin, Jack L. 1960. *Gerald Gardner: Witch*. London: Octagon Press.
Brown, Michael. 1997. *The Channeling Zone: American Spirituality in an Anxious Age*. Cambridge, Mass.: Harvard University Press.
Bruner, Edward M. 1986. "Ethnography as Narrative." In *The Anthropology of Experience*, ed. Victor Turner and Edward M. Bruner, 139–55. Urbana: University of Illinois Press.
Buckland, Raymond. 1986 [1974]. *Buckland's Complete Book of Witchcraft*. St. Paul, Minn.: Llewellyn.
Butler, Elizabeth. 1998 [1949]. *Ritual Magic*. University Park: Pennsylvania State University Press.
Cantwell, Robert. 1993. *Ethnomimesis: Folklife and the Representation of Culture*. Chapel Hill: University of North Carolina Press.
Carpenter, Dennis. 1994. *Spiritual Experiences, Life Changes, and Ecological Viewpoints of Contemporary Pagans*. Ph.D. diss., Saybrook Institute.
Chapman, Malcolm. 1992. *The Celts: The Invention of a Myth*. New York: St. Martin's Press.
Clifford, James, and George E. Marcus, eds. 1986. *Writing Culture: The Poetics and Politics of Ethnography*. Berkeley: University of California Press.

Clifton, Chas. S. 1998. "The Significance of Aradia." In *Aradia, or the Gospel of the Witches*, ed. Charles G. Leland, 50–80. Trans. Mario Pazzaglini and Dina Pazzaglini. Blaine, Wash.: Phoenix Press.

Clulee, Nicholas H. 1988. *John Dee's Natural Philosophy: Between Science and Religion*. London: Routledge.

Cocchiara, Giuseppe. 1981. *The History of Folklore in Europe*. Trans. John McDaniel. Philadelphia: ISHI Press.

Cox, Harvey G. 1969. *The Feast of Fools: A theological Essay on Festivity and Fantasy*. Cambridge, Mass.: Harvard University Press.

Crowther, Patricia. 1974. *Witch Blood!* New York: House of Collectibles.

Danforth, Loring M. 1989. *Firewalking and Religious Healing*. Princeton, N.J.: Princeton University Press.

Davies, Christie. 1990. *Ethnic Humor around the World*. Bloomington: Indiana University Press.

Davies, Owen. 1999. *Witchcraft, Magic, and Culture, 1736–1951*. Manchester: Manchester University Press.

DeCerteau, Michel. 1984. *The Practice of Everyday Life*. Trans. Steven Randall. Berkeley: University of California Press.

Dégh, Linda. 1968. *Folktales and Society*. Bloomington: Indiana University Press.

———. 2001. *Legend and Belief: The Dialectics of a Genre*. Bloomington: Indiana University Press.

Dégh, Linda, and Andrew Vázsonyi. 1975. "The Hypothesis of Multi-Conduit Transmission in Folklore." In *Folklore: Performance and Communication*, ed. Dan Ben Amos and Kenneth S. Goldstein, 207–54. The Hague: Mouton.

DeMartino, Ernesto. 1961. *La terra del rimorso*. Milan: Il Saggiatore.

DeRobertis, Carolina. 1999. "Que Esté Benedicida: Blessed Be: Race, Magic, Community, and Life as a Latina Witch." *Reclaiming Quarterly* 75:4–58.

Devereaux, George. 1967. *From Anxiety to Method in the Behavioral Sciences*. The Hague: Mouton.

di Zerega, Gus. 2001. *Pagans and Christians: The Personal Spiritual Experience*. St. Paul, Minn.: Llewellyn.

Dorson, Richard M. 1968. *The British Folklorists: A History*. Chicago: University of Chicago Press.

———. 1969. "Folklore and Fakelore." In *American Folklore and the Historian*. Chicago: University of Chicago Press.

Dundes, Alan. 1969. "The Devolutionary Premise in Folklore Theory." *Journal of the Folklore Institute* 6:5–19.

———. 1981. "Many Hands Make Light Work, or Caught in the Act of Screwing in Light Bulbs." *Western Folklore* 40, no. 3:261–66.

———. 1995. "How Indic Parallels to the Ballad of the 'Walled-Up Wife' Reveal the Pitfalls of Parochial Nationalistic Folkloristics," *Journal of American Folklore* 108, no. 427:38–53.

Durkheim, Emile. 1947 [1912]. *The Elementary Forms of the Religious Life*. Trans. Joseph W. Swain. Glencoe, Ill.: Free Press.

Eller, Cynthia. 1995. *Living in the Lap of the Goddess: The Feminist Spirituality Movement in America*. Boston: Beacon Press.

———. 2000. *The Myth of Matriarchal Prehistory*. Boston: Beacon Press.

Ellis, Bill. 2000. *Raising the Devil: Satanism, New Religions, and the Media*. Lexington: University Press of Kentucky.

Engels, Friedrich. 1942. *The Origins of the Family, Private Property, and the State*. New York: International Publishers.

Evans, Hilary. 1989. *Alternate States of Consciousness*. Wellingborough, U.K.: Thorson's Publishing.
Evans-Pritchard, E. E. 1983. *Witchcraft, Oracles and Magic Among the Azande*. Abridged, with an introduction by Eva Gillies. Oxford: Oxford University Press.
Evans-Wentz, W. Y. 1966. *The Fairy Faith in Celtic Countries*. Oxford: Oxford University Press.
Fairgrove, Rowan. 1997. "What We Don't Know about the Ancient Celts." *Pomegranate* 2:3–21.
Falassi, Alessandro. 1980. *Folklore by the Fireside: Text and Context of the Tuscan Veglia*. Austin: University of Texas Press.
———, ed. 1987. *Time out of Time: Essays on the Festival*. Albuquerque: University of New Mexico Press.
Farrar, Stewart. 1971. *What Witches Do*. St. Paul, Minn.: Llewellyn.
Farrar, Stewart, and Janet Farrar. 1981. *The Witches' Way*. St. Paul, Minn.: Llewellyn.
Favret-Saada, Jeanne. 1980. *Deadly Words: Witchcraft in the Bocage*. New York: Cambridge University Press.
Feld, Steven. 1992. *Sound and Sentiment: Birds, Weeping, Poetics, and Song in Kalui Expression*. Philadelphia: University of Pennsylvania Press.
Fischer, Michael M. J. 1986. "Ethnicity and the Post-Modern Arts of Memory." In *Writing Culture: The Poetics and Politics of Ethnography*, ed. James Clifford and George E. Marcus, 194–233. Berkeley: University of California Press.
Foucault, Michel. 1965. *Madness and Civilization: A History of Insanity in the Age of Reason*. Trans. Richard Howard. New York: Random House.
———. 1984. *The Foucault Reader*. Ed. Paul Rabinow. New York: Pantheon Books.
Frazer, Sir James. 1959 [1890]. *The New Golden Bough*. Ed. Theodore Gaster. New York: Criterion Books.
Frew, Donald H. 1998. "Methodological Flaws in Recent Studies of Historical and Modern Witchcraft." *Ethnologies* 20, no. 1:33–65.
———. 2001. Presentation at the Pantheacon, Ancient Ways, San Francisco, February 17.
———. 2002. "Gardnerian Wica [*sic*] as Theurgic Ascent." Paper presented at the first and second Pagani Soteria symposia, Pagani Soteria, Richmond, CA June 29 and July 27.
Gage, Matilda Joslyn. 1972 [1893]. *Woman, Church, and State*. New York: Arno Press.
Gardner, Gerald B. 1954. *Witchcraft Today*. London: Rider and Company.
———. 1959. *The Meaning of Witchcraft*. London: Rider and Company.
Gaster, Theodore H. 1961 [1950]. *Thepsis: Ritual, Myth and Drama in the Ancient Near East*. Garden City, N.Y.: Doubleday.
Geertz, Clifford. 1998. "Religion, Meaning, Power, Identity." Lecture presented at the Getty Center, Los Angeles, California, May 4.
Gennep, Arnold van. 1960 [1909]. *The Rites of Passage*. Trans. M. Vizedom and G. Caffe. Chicago: University of Chicago Press.
Gibbons, Jenny. 1998. "Recent Developments in the Study of the Great European Witch Hunt." *Pomegranate* 5:2–16.
Ginzburg, Carlo. 1966. *I benandanti*. Turin: Einaudi.
———. 1989. *Storia notturna: Una decifrazione del sabba*. Turin: Einaudi.
Glassie, Henry. 1975. *All Silver and No Brass*. Bloomington: Indiana University Press.
Goffman, Erving. 1959. *The Presentation of Self in Everyday Life*. New York: Anchor Books.
———. 1974. *Frame Analysis: An Essay on the Organization of Experience*. New York: Harper and Row.

Goodman, Felicitas. 1988. *How about Demons? Possession and Exorcism in the Modern World.* Bloomington: Indiana University Press.
Gramsci, Antonio. 1992. *Prison Notebooks.* Translated by Joseph A. Buttigieg. New York: Columbia University Press.
Greenhill, Pauline. 1993. "The Folk Process in the Revival: 'Barrett's Privateers' and 'Barratt's Privateers.' " In *Transforming Tradition: Folk Music Revivals Examined*, ed. Neil Rosenberg, 137–59. Urbana: University of Illinois Press.
Griffin, Edward M. 1998. "The Melting Pot, Vegetable Soup, and the Martini Cocktail: Competing Explanations of U.S. Cultural Pluralism." *Midwest Quarterly* 39, no. 2:133–52.
Grimassi, Raven. 1995. *The Ways of the Strega.* St. Paul, Minn.: Llewellyn.
———. 1999. *Hereditary Witchcraft.* St. Paul, Minn.: Llewellyn.
———. 2000. *Italian Witchcraft.* St. Paul, Minn.: Llewellyn.
Grimes, Ronald L. 1990. *Ritual Criticism: Case Studies in Its Practice, Essays on Its Theory.* Columbia: University of South Carolina Press.
Grindal, Bruce. 1983. "Into the Heart of Sisala Experience." *Journal of Anthropological Research* 39:60–80.
Halliday, W. R. 1922. Review of Margaret Murray, *The Witch Cult of Western Europe. Folklore* 33:224–30.
Handler, Richard, and Joycelyn Linnekin. 1984. "Tradition: Genuine or Spurious." *Journal of American Folklore* 97:273–90.
Hanegraaf, Wouter J. 1996. *New Age Religion and Western Culture.* Albany: State University of New York Press.
Hartman, P. A. 1976. "Social Dimensions of Occult Participation: The Gnostica Study." *British Journal of Sociology* 27, no. 2:169–83.
Hebdige, Dick. 1979. *Subculture: The Meaning of Style.* London: Routledge.
Herzfeld, Michael. 1982. *Ours Once More: Folklore, Ideology, and the Making of Modern Greece.* Austin: University of Texas Press.
Heselton, Philip. 2000. *Wiccan Roots: Gerard Gardner and the Modern Witchcraft Revival.* Chieveley, U.K.: Capall Bann Publishing.
Hess, David. 1993. *Science and the New Age.* Madison: University of Wisconsin Press.
Hobsbawm, Eric, and Terence Ranger, eds. 1983. *The Invention of Tradition.* Cambridge: Cambridge University Press.
Hufford, David J. 1982. *The Terror That Comes in the Night: An Experience-Centered Study of Supernatural Assault Traditions.* Philadelphia: University of Pennsylvania Press.
———. 1995. "Beings without Bodies: An Experience-Centered Theory of the Belief in Spirits." In *Out of the Ordinary: Folklore and the Supernatural*, ed. Barbara Walker, 11–45. Logan: Utah State University Press.
Hutton, Ronald. 1996. *The Stations of the Sun: A History of the Ritual Year in Britain.* Oxford: Oxford University Press.
———. 1999. *The Triumph of the Moon: A History of Modern Pagan Witchcraft.* Oxford: Oxford University Press.
Isaacs, Ernest. 1986. "The Fox Sisters and American Spiritualism." In *The Occult in America: New Historical Perspectives*, ed. Howard Kerr and Charles L. Crow, 79–110. Urbana: University of Illinois Press.
Jenkins, Henry. 1993. *Textual Poachers: Television Fans and Participatory Culture.* New York: Routledge.
Jones, Leslie. 1994. "The Emergence of the Druid as Celtic Shaman." In *The Marketing of Tradition: Perspectives on Folklore, Tourism, and the Heritage Industry*, ed. Terri Brewer, 13–42. Enfield Lock, U.K.: Hisarlik Press.
Jones, Produce, and Nigel Pennick. 1995. *A History of Pagan Europe.* London: Routledge.

Jorgensen, D. L., and L. Jorgensen. 1982. "Social Meaning of the Occult." *The Sociological Quarterly* 23:373–89.

Kapchan, Deborah. 2002. "Possessed by Culture / Possessing culture: Giving Flesh to Voice." Position paper, University of Pennsylvania Department of Anthropology Conference, Spring 2002.

Kaplan, Jeffrey. 1996. "The Reconstruction of the Asatru and Odinist Traditions." In *Magical Religions and Modern Withcraft*, ed. James R. Lewis, 193–236. Albany: State University of New York Press.

Kelly, Aidan. 1991. *Crafting the Art of Magic, Book I: A History of Modern Witchcraft, 1939–1964*. St. Paul, Minn.: Llewellyn.

Kieckhefer, Richard. 1997. *Forbidden Rites*. University Park: Pennsylvania State University Press.

Kirkpatrick, R. G., R. Rainey, and K. Rubi. 1984. "Pagan Renaissance and Wiccan Witchcraft in Industrial Society: A Study of Parapsychology and the Sociology of Enchantment." *Iron Mountain: a Journal of Magical Religion* (Summer 1984):31–38.

Kirshenblatt-Gimblett, Barbara. 1996. "Afterlives." *Performance Ritual*, publication of New York University, (Summer 1996).

Lafferty, Anne. 1998. "How We Braid Our Lives Together with Our Ancestors." *Ethnologies* 20, no. 1:129–50.

Lee, Raymond. 1987. "Amulets and Anthropology: A Paranormal Encounter with Malay Magic." *Anthropology and Humanism Quarterly* 12, nos. 2–3:69–74.

Lefkowitz, Mary. 1999. *Not out of Africa: How Afrocentrism Became an Excuse to Teach Myth as History*. 2nd ed. New York: Basic Books.

LeGuin, Ursula K. 1985 [1979]. *The Language of the Night: Essays on Fantasy and Science Fiction*. New York: Berkeley Books.

Leland, Charles. 1892. *Etruscan Roman Remains*. London: T. F. Unwin.

———. 1896. *Legends of Florence*. New York: Macmillan.

———. 1990 [1890]. *Aradia; or The Gospel of the Witches*. Custer, Wash.: Phoenix Publishing.

Levi, Eliphas. 1845. *Paris dansante, ou les filles d'Hérodiade*. Paris: Paul Dupont.

Lex, Barbara. 1979. "The Neurobiology of Ritual Trance." In *The Spectrum of Ritual: A Biogenetic Structural Analysis*, ed. Eugene G. D'Aquili, C. D. Laughlin, J. McManus, et al., 117–51. New York: Columbia University Press.

Limon, José. 1994. *Dancing with the Devil*. Austin: University of Texas Press.

Lipsitz, George. 1994. *Dangerous Crossroads: Popular Music, Postmodernism, and the Poetics of Place*. New York: Verso.

Lloyd, Timothy C. 1995."Folklore, Foodways, and the Supernatural." *Out of the Ordinary: Folklore and the Supernatural*, ed. Barbara Walker, 59–71. Logan: Utah State University Press.

Lombardi-Satriani, Luigi. 1974. "Folklore as Culture of Contestation." *Journal of the Folklore Institute* 11:99–121.

Louÿs, Pierre. 1926. *Collected Works of Pierre Louys*. New York: Liveright Publishing.

Ludeke, Joan. 1989. "Wicca as a Revitalization Movement among Post-Industrial, Urban American Women." Ph.D. diss., Iliff School of Theology.

Luhrmann, Tanya M. 1989. *Persuasions of the Witches' Craft: Ritual Magic in Contemporary England*. Cambridge, Mass.: Harvard University Press.

Lyotard, Jean Francois. 1984. *The Postmodern Condition: A Report on Knowledge*. Minneapolis: University of Minnesota Press.

MacRitchie, David. 1890. *Testimony of Tradition*. London: Kegan Paul.

Magliocco, Sabina. 1993. *The Two Madonnas: The Politics of Festival in a Sardinian Community*. New York: Peter Lang.

———. 1996. "Ritual Is My Chosen Art Form: The Creation of Ritual as Folk Art among Contemporary Pagans." In *Magical Religions and Modern Witchcraft*, ed. James R. Lewis, 93–120. Albany: State University of New York Press.

———. 2001. *Neo-Pagan Sacred Art and Altars: Making Things Whole.* Jackson: University Press of Mississippi.

———. 2004. "Imagining the *Strega*: Folklore Reclamation and the Construction of Italian American Witchcraft." *Italian American Review* (forthcoming).

Magliocco, Sabina, and Holly Tannen. 1998. "The Real Old-Time Religion: Towards an Aesthetics of Neo-Pagan Song." *Ethnologies* 20, no. 1:175–201.

Mathiesen, Robert. 1998. "Charles G. Leland and the Witches of Italy: The Origin of Aradia." In *Aradia; or The Gospel of the Witches*, by Charles G. Leland, trans. Mario Pazzaglini and Dina Pazzaglini. Blaine, Wash.: Phoenix Publishing.

McClenon, James. 1994. *Wondrous Events: Foundations of Religious Belief.* Philadelphia: University of Pennsylvania Press.

Melton, J. Gordon, ed. 1988. *The Encyclopedia of American Religions and Religious Creeds.* Detroit: Gale Research Company.

Michelet, Jules. 1966 [1838]. *La Sorcière.* Paris: Garnier Flammarion.

Moore, R. Laurence. 1977. *In Search of White Crows: Spiritualism, Parapsychology, and American Culture.* Oxford: Oxford University Press.

Morgan, Prys. 1983. "From a Death to a View: The Hunt for the Welsh Past in the Romantic Period." In *The Invention of Tradition*, ed. Eric Hobsbawm and Terence Ranger, 43–100. London: Verso.

Moser, Hans. 1964. "Der Folklorismus als Forschungsproblem der Volkskunde." *Hessiche Blätter für Volkskunde* 55:9–57.

Motz, Marilyn. 1998. "The Practice of Belief." *Journal of American Folklore* 111, no. 441:339–55.

Murray, Margaret. 1921. *The Witch Cult in Western Europe.* Oxford: Clarendon Press.

———. 1933. *The God of the Witches.* Oxford: Oxford University Press.

Newberg, Andrew, and Eugene D'Aquili. 2001. *Why God Won't Go Away: Brain Science and the Biology of Belief.* New York: Ballantine Books.

NightMare, M. Macha (Aline O'Brien). 2001. *Witchcraft and the Web: Weaving Pagan Traditions Online.* Toronto, Ont.: ECW Press.

Noyes, Dorothy. 2003. "Group." In *Eight Words for the Study of Expressive Culture*, ed. Burt Feintuch, 7–41. Urbana: University of Illinois Press.

Orion, Loretta. 1995. *Never Again the Burning Times: Paganism Revived.* Prospect, Ill.: Waveland Press.

Pike, Sarah. 1996. "Rationalizing the Margins: A Review of Legitimation and Ethnographic Practice in Scholarly Research on Neo-Paganism." In *Magical Religions and Modern Witchcraft*, ed. James R. Lewis, 353–72. Albany: State University of New York Press.

———. 2001. *Earthly Bodies, Magical Selves: Contemporary Pagans and the Search for Community.* Berkeley: University of California Press.

Pimple, Kenneth. 1995. "Ghosts, Spirits, and Scholars: The Origins of Modern Spiritualism." In *Out of the Ordinary: Folklore and the Supernatural*, ed. Barbara Walker, 75–89. Logan: Utah State University Press.

Propp, Vladimir. 1968. *The Morphology of the Folktale.* Trans. Laurence Scott. Austin: University of Texas Press.

———. 1977. *Le radici storiche dei conti di magia.* Trans. Salvatore Arcella. Rome: Newton Compton.

Purkiss, Diana. 1996. *The Witch in History: Early Modern and Twentieth Century Representations.* London: Routledge.

Radner, Joan Newlon, and Susan Lanser. 1993. "Strategies of Coding in Women's Culture." In *Feminist Messages: Coding in Women's Folklore*, ed. Joan Newlon Radner, 1–29. Urbana: University of Illinois Press.

Reif, Jennifer. 1999. *Mysteries of Demeter*. York Beach Me.: Samuel Weiser.

Rogers, Nicholas. 2002. *Halloween: From Pagan Ritual to Party Night*. Oxford: Oxford University Press.

Rosaldo, Renato. 1989. "Introduction: Grief and a Headhunter's Rage." In *Culture and Truth*, 1–21. Boston: Beacon Press.

Rose, Elliott. 1962. *A Razor for a Goat*. Toronto: University of Toronto Press.

Salomonsen, Jone. 1999. "Methods of Compassion or Pretension? Anthropological Fieldwork in Modern Magical Communities." *Pomegranate* 8:4–13.

———. 2002. *Enchanted Feminism: The Reclaiming Witches of San Francisco*. London: Routledge.

Santino, Jack. 1995. *All Around the Year: Holidays and Celebrations in American Life*. Urbana and Chicago: University of Illinois Press.

———. 1996. *New Old-Fashioned Ways: Holidays and Popular Culture*. Knoxville: University of Tennessee Press.

Scott, James C. 1990. *Domination and the Arts of Resistance*. New Haven, Conn.: Yale University Press.

Simpson, Jacqueline. 1994. "Margaret Murray: Who Believed Her, and Why?" *Folklore* 105:89–96.

Smith, Robert J. 1975. *The Art of the Festival*. Lawrence: University of Kansas Publications in Anthropology, no. 6.

Sollors, Werner. 1989. "The Invention of Ethnicity." Introduction to *The Invention of Ethnicity*, ed. Werner Sollors, ix-xx. Oxford: Oxford University Press.

Spierenburg, Pieter. 1991. *The Broken Spell: A Cultural and Anthropological History of Preindustrial Europe*. New Brunswick, N.J.: Rutgers University Press.

Starhawk (Miriam Simos). 1988 [1982]. *Dreaming the Dark*. Boston: Beacon Press.

———. 1989 [1979]. *The Spiral Dance*. San Francisco: HarperCollins.

———. 1990 [1987]. *Truth or Dare: Encounters with Power, Authority, and Mystery*. San Francisco: HarperCollins.

Starhawk, and Anne Hill. 1998. *Circle Round: Raising Children in Goddess Traditions*. New York: Bantam Books.

Starhawk, and M. Macha NightMare. 1997. *The Pagan Book of Living and Dying*. San Francisco: HarperCollins.

Starhawk, and Hilary Valentine. 2000. *The Twelve Wild Swans: Rituals, Excercises, and Magical Training in the Reclaiming Tradition*. San Francisco: HarperCollins.

Stephen, Michele. 1989. "Self, the Sacred Other, and Autonomous Imagination." In *The Religious Imagination in New Guinea*, ed. Gilbert Herdt and Michele Stephen, 41–64. New Brunswick, N.J.: Rutgers University Press.

———. 1995. *A'aisa's Gifts: A Study in Magic and the Self*. Berkeley: University of California Press.

Stoller, Paul. 1987. *In Sorcery's Shadow: A Memoir of Apprenticeship among the Songhay of Niger*. Chicago: University of Chicago Press.

Storms, Godfrid. 1975 [1948]. *Anglo-Saxon Magic*. New York: Folcroft Library Editions.

Sturm, Brian W. 2000. "The 'Storylistening' Trance Experience." *Journal of American Folklore* 113, no. 449:287–304.

Tambiah, Stanley J. 1990. *Magic, Science, Religion, and the Scope of Rationality*. Cambridge: Cambridge University Press.

Tannen, Holly. 1985. *Between the Worlds*. Gold Leaf Records.

Tart, Charles T. 1972. "Scientific Foundations for the Study of Altered States of Consciousness." *Journal of Transpersonal Psychology* 18:93–124.
Thomas, Dylan. 1957. *Collected Poems of Dylan Thomas*. New York: New Directions.
Todorov, Tzvetan. 1993. *On Human Diversity: Nationalism, Racism, and Exoticism in French Thought*. Cambridge, Mass.: Harvard University Press.
Toelken, Barre. 1995. "The Moccasin Telegraph and Other Improbabilities." In *Out of the Ordinary: Folklore and the Supernatural*, ed. Barbara Walker, 46–58. Logan: Utah State University Press.
Towers, Eric. 1986. *Dashwood: The Man and the Myth*. New York: Crucible Press.
Turner, Edith. 1994. "A Visible Spirit from Zambia." In *Being Changed: The Anthropology of Extraordinary Experience*, ed. David E. Young and Jean-Guy Goulet, 71–95. Peterborough, Ont.: Broadview Press.
Turner, Victor. 1968. *The Ritual Process*. Ithaca, N.Y.: Cornell University Press.
Turner, Victor, and Edith Turner. 1982. *Image and Pilgrimage in Christian Culture*. New York: Columbia University Press.
Tyler, Stephen. 1986. "Post-Modern Ethnography: From Document of the Occult to Occult Document." In *Writing Culture*, ed. James Clifford, 122–40. Berkeley: University of California Press.
Valiente, Doreen. 1989. *The Rebirth of Witchcraft*. Custer, Wash.: Phoenix Publishing.
Virtanen, Leea. 1989. *That Must Have Been ESP!* Bloomington: Indiana University Press.
Wagner, Roy. 1981. *The Invention of Culture*. Chicago: University of Chicago Press.
Wallace, Anthony F. C. 1970. "Revitalization Movements." In Wallace, *Culture and Personality*. New York: Random House.
Walls, R. T. 1972. *Neoplatonism*. London: Gerald Duckworth and Company.
Weber, Max. 1922. *Gesammelte Aufsätze zur Religionssoziologie*. Tübingen: Mohr.
Weinstein, Marion. 1991. *Positive Magic*. Blaine, Wash.: Phoenix Publishing.
Young, David E., and Jean-Guy Goulet, eds. 1994. *Being Changed: The Anthropology of Extraordinary Experience*. Peterborough, Ont.: Broadview Press.
Zweig, Michael. 2000. *The Working Class Majority: America's Best Kept Secret*. Ithaca, N.Y.: Cornell University Press.

# Index

# Acknowledgments

This work would not have been possible without the generous support of many individuals and institutions. I gratefully acknowledge the support of the John Simon Guggenheim Memorial Foundation. I thank the National Endowment for the Humanities, whose fellowship support made this project possible. I also received generous support from the University of California, Berkeley, and California State University, Northridge. I am especially grateful to Alan Dundes, who in the role of my "fairy godfather" made possible my two-year sojourn at UC Berkeley, supported me in all my academic endeavors, and never stopped believing in me even though he thought my research was a bit eccentric. At California State University, Northridge, I am thankful for the continued support of the Department of Anthropology and the College of Social and Behavioral Sciences. Antonio Gilman, who was chair at the time, made it possible for me to take a year's research leave with the support of an NEH grant during 2001–2. Scott Pérez of Research and Sponsored Projects helped with budgeting and financial matters. Felicia Cousin and the entire staff of Inter-Library Loan at the Oviatt Library were patient and efficient with my frequent (and frequently arcane) requests. Benedicte Gilman was able to obtain a copy of a rare book from the Bibliothèque National de Paris, which I could not have gotten except with her generous assistance. Elizabeth Adams, Larae Brown and Carianne Swanson were invaluable in the technical aspects of preparing the final manuscript.

To my colleagues and fellow researchers on the Neo-Pagan movement, I owe a tremendous debt. Sarah Pike and Jone Salomonsen were my frequent companions in the field, as well as at academic conferences. We observed some of the same events and had some of the same consultants; we shared many insights with each other through both formal and informal exchanges. My work is intended to complement theirs, and greatly benefits from their having published before me. Loretta Orion was an inspiration to me, both in her focus on the creative aspects of Neo-Pagan culture and in her own impeccable aesthetics as an artist and gardener. I am grateful for her comments on several early versions, particularly of Chapters 2 and 3. Renee Rothman and I had a series of stimulating conversations that sparked new insights into a number of topics related to movement, the body, trance states, healing, and cultural borrowing. Roger

Abrahams supported this project from beginning to end in ways seen and unseen; I am profoundly beholden to him. Kirin Narayan, herself an exceptional writer, sustained me as I struggled to find the right voice; Izaly Zemtsovsky and Alma Kunanbay attended several rituals with me, encouraged me, and shared with me their great enthusiasm. To all of them, I am profoundly grateful.

Thanks to the good work of Peter Agree, my editor at the University of Pennsylvania Press, I was blessed with two extraordinary readers who immediately understood my aims and the scope of my work. I am especially grateful to Regina Bendix for her valuable criticisms on the Introduction and Chapters 2, 6, and 7, and to Ronald Hutton for his generous comments and corrections on Chapter 1. I feel fortunate to have both as friends as well as colleagues: Regina, whose friendship goes back to our graduate school days, and Ronald, with whom a friendship has developed from this collaboration.

My deepest thanks, as always, are reserved for the people who so generously gave of their time, resources, and lives: my field consultants. Without them this work never could have been, and my debt to them is too great to ever fully repay. During the course of this project, I spoke with over a hundred individuals; for the sake of space, I can mention only a few of them here. To Holly Tannen, who introduced me to the San Francisco Bay Area community, allowed me to perform music with her at festivals and coffeehouses, performed with me at academic conferences, and delighted me with her wicked sense of humor, I am especially obliged; this project would never have gotten off the ground without her. Together with M. Macha NightMare and Vibra Willow, she instructed me in some of the salient points of Reclaiming Witchcraft. Don Frew and Anna Korn were my guides and collaborators on many phases of this project. Studying Gardnerian Witchcraft with them was essentially equivalent to attending Wiccan graduate school; if I know anything about traditional Craft, it is because of their rigor, thoroughness, and patience. Both read through manuscript drafts, made copious suggestions, marked corrections painstakingly and precisely, and provided hospitality and support; without their help, this book would have been both less accurate and less interesting. I am also indebted to Laurel Olson Mendes, Gus di Zerega, Francesca De Grandis, Rowan Fairgrove, Russell Williams, Karen and Roy Tate, Sam and Tara Webster, and all the members of Coven Trismegiston in its various iterations, including Charles Bucklin, D. J. Hamouris, Katya Madrid, Paula Mangelen, Nancy McKinney, Melissa Oringer, Michael Shannon, and Tim Wallace. Two dear friends, Brian Williams and Tim Maroney, died before they could see this project bear fruit; as Reclaiming Witches say, "What is remembered lives."

Finally, special thanks to my parents, Bruno and Marisetta Magliocco, who read and commented on parts of the manuscript; to my partner, Susan E. Parker, a source of tremendous intellectual companionship, comfort, and joy; and to Merlin, Pinky, and Idgie Amelia, my familiar companions through the various stages of this project.

CPSIA information can be obtained
at www.ICGtesting.com
Printed in the USA
BVHW03s1639081018
R9197600001B/R91976PG528932BVX2B/2/P

9 780812 218794